AF736378

A. H. M. Ershad Uddin

The Regulation of Islamic Financial Institutions (IFIs) and Ethical Oversight in South Asia

An Islamic Law Perspective

palgrave
macmillan

A. H. M. Ershad Uddin
Department of Islamic Law, Faculty of Theology
Kocaeli University
İzmit, Türkiye

ISSN 2662-5121 ISSN 2662-513X (electronic)
Palgrave Studies in Islamic Banking, Finance, and Economics
ISBN 978-3-032-09827-6 ISBN 978-3-032-09828-3 (eBook)
https://doi.org/10.1007/978-3-032-09828-3

© The Editor(s) (if applicable) and The Author(s), under exclusive license to Springer Nature Switzerland AG 2025

This work is subject to copyright. All rights are solely and exclusively licensed by the Publisher, whether the whole or part of the material is concerned, specifically the rights of translation, reprinting, reuse of illustrations, recitation, broadcasting, reproduction on microfilms or in any other physical way, and transmission or information storage and retrieval, electronic adaptation, computer software, or by similar or dissimilar methodology now known or hereafter developed.
The use of general descriptive names, registered names, trademarks, service marks, etc. in this publication does not imply, even in the absence of a specific statement, that such names are exempt from the relevant protective laws and regulations and therefore free for general use.
The publisher, the authors and the editors are safe to assume that the advice and information in this book are believed to be true and accurate at the date of publication. Neither the publisher nor the authors or the editors give a warranty, expressed or implied, with respect to the material contained herein or for any errors or omissions that may have been made. The publisher remains neutral with regard to jurisdictional claims in published maps and institutional affiliations.

This Palgrave Macmillan imprint is published by the registered company Springer Nature Switzerland AG.
The registered company address is: Gewerbestrasse 11, 6330 Cham, Switzerland

If disposing of this product, please recycle the paper.

Acknowledgments I wish to express my deepest gratitude to my late father, Sheikh Mahmudul Hasan, and my mother, Kamrun Nesa, whose unwavering guidance and inspiration formed the foundation of my academic journey. I am profoundly indebted to my family, especially my wife, Ummel Khair Fatima, for her constant encouragement and support, and to my children, Zimam, Erdogan, and Saalem, who patiently endured my long hours of work and many absences.

I am also sincerely grateful to those scholars and mentors whose insights and encouragement have shaped this work: Prof. Dr. Abdullah Kahraman (Marmara University), Prof. Dr. Servet Bayindir (Istanbul Sabahattin Zaim University), and my uncle, Prof. Dr. Mohammed Nurul Alam (Yorkville University, Canada). Their intellectual generosity and personal support have been invaluable.

Introduction

Islamic Financial Regulation and Ethical Oversight in South Asia: From the Perspective of Islamic Law, Islamic finance is examined as both an ethical framework and a Sharīʿah-based economic system. Unlike my earlier doctoral research, which focused on corporate Sharīʿah compliance in Bangladesh, this book adopts a macro-regional lens to explore how Islamic legal and ethical frameworks influence financial institutions and regulatory regimes in South Asia.

This study is rooted in Islamic jurisprudence (fiqh) and draws from foundational sources and methodologies. It explores how principles such as justice (ʿadl), public welfare (maṣlaḥah), and accountability (ḥisbah) shape financial regulations. It presents Islamic finance not only as a legal system, but also as a framework for ethical governance in postcolonial South Asian societies characterized by economic disparity and pluralistic legal frameworks.

This book differs from my doctoral dissertation, titled *Bangladeş'teki İslam Bankacılık Uygulamasının Fıkhî Açıdan İncelenmesi* (2020) (*An Islamic Legal Analysis of Islamic Banking Practices in Bangladesh*). It avoids duplicating micro-level analyses of banking contracts and offers a regional and conceptual re-evaluation of Islamic finance through ethical and jurisprudential dimensions. While much of the existing literature on Islamic finance is shaped by paradigms emerging from the Gulf and Middle Eastern contexts, several scholars have argued that these regulatory practices tend to emphasize formal compliance over ethical intentionality.[1] In contrast, this book centers on the South Asian experience through a jurisprudential and ethical lens, exploring local adaptations rooted in maqāṣid al-sharīʿah and ḥisbah-oriented governance. Unlike the compliance-heavy frameworks prevalent in AAOIFI-guided institutions and the legally formalist approaches common in Gulf-based models, this study foregrounds ethical intentionality (niyyah), maqāṣid-oriented governance, and the institutional rehabilitation of classical principles, such as ḥisbah.

Moreover, this work departs from conventional doctrinal analyses by integrating regional legal pluralism, historical postcolonial legacies, and local socio-religious dynamics, offering a grounded alternative to the export-driven and decontextualized frameworks often imposed on the South Asian Islamic finance sector. In this respect, *Islamic Financial Regulation and Ethical Oversight in South Asia: From the Perspective of Islamic Law, it* offers not only a geographic shift but also a conceptual reorientation—one that privileges ethical authenticity over procedural mimicry and emphasizes endogenous regulatory development over external transplantation. To concretize this ethical and regional focus, the book introduces the *South Asian Ethical Finance Compliance (SAEFC) model*, a context-sensitive framework designed to bridge the persistent gap between Sharīʿah compliance and ethical intentionality in South Asian Islamic finance. Drawing from classical Islamic concepts, such as *ḥisbah*, and aligning them with contemporary governance needs, the SAEFC Model proposes a structured, ethically rooted oversight mechanism attuned to regional realities. This framework is elaborated in Chap. 3, and functions as a unifying thread throughout the book's evaluation of institutions, contracts, and regulatory practices.

A notable absence of academic research characterizes this book. South Asia has a large global Muslim population and a widespread Islamic finance industry growth across Pakistan, Bangladesh, India, Afghanistan, and the Maldives. However, this region lacks an academic book that examines the development of regional Islamic finance through the lens

[1] Mehmet Asutay, "A Political Economy Approach to Islamic Economics: Systemic Understanding for an Alternative Economic System", *Kyoto Bulletin of Islamic Area Studies* 1/2 (2007), 3–18; Irfan Ahmed et al., "Practices of Islamic Banking in the Light of Islamic Ethics: A Critical Review", *International Journal of Economics, Management and Accounting* 25/3 (November 30, 2017), 465–490; Mahmoud A. El-Gamal, *Islamic Finance: Law, Economics, and Practice* (Cambridge University Press, 2006).

of ethical-legal Islamic theories and regulatory principles. Most current research practices. The Middle Eastern Islamic financial systems follow secular economic approaches without considering South Asian Islamic practices based on Sharīʿah governance. The author devotes extensive analysis to South Asia's understanding of Islamic finance by examining its relationship with the Sharīʿah standards from an ethical perspective. The author organized the book to display his broader conceptual endeavors. The text contains three interconnected parts that build upon the central theme of Islamic financial regulations.

Chapter 1 establishes a theoretical framework by presenting Islamic finance as a legal-ethical system based on Sharīʿah's objectives (maqāṣid al-sharīʿah). This section of the book examines the ethical principles of justice alongside restrictions on public welfare and exploitative practices based on Qurʾānic revelation, prophetic tradition, and traditional Islamic jurisprudence (*fiqh al-muʿāmalāt*). Chapter 2 introduces fundamental Islamic finance contracts for illustration purposes only and shows how Sharīʿah moral principles found their place in financial contractual models. The primary concern is whether Islamic finance adheres to its conventional ethical principles as it incorporates inter-social equity with risk management procedures.

Chapter 2 conducts a regional and historical investigation that evaluates different South Asian countries' strategies for establishing Islamic finance institutions. This chapter analyzes the development of Islamic finance through detailed evaluations of Pakistan and Bangladesh, as well as analyses of India, Afghanistan, and other nations, examining the regulatory systems, Shari'ah board procedures, and public understanding that have defined this financial growth path. This chapter examines economic data while documenting how Islamic ethical and legal matters found solutions in postcolonial legal structures, secular governance, and pluralistic communities. Studying regional characteristics and common Islamic normative goals helps to explain the growth of Islamic finance in South Asia.

Chapter 3 elaborates on ḥisbah as a classical Islamic institution that maintains market morality and justice enforcement through public oversight and accountability systems. This chapter demonstrates how Ḥisbah maintained an ethical market order through commercial regulations and prevented fraud during the Prophet Muhammad, caliphates and medieval Muslim social groups in India. The book employs a qualitative, interpretive methodology, combining Islamic legal theory, comparative fiqh, and institutional analysis. It draws from classical texts, contemporary scholarship, and regulatory reports from bodies such as AAOIFI and IFSB.

Methodology

The primary sources for this study include the Qur'ān, major ḥadīth collections, and a wide range of classical texts of Islamic jurisprudence that have shaped Islamic thought on governance, public welfare, and market ethics. Rather than specifying individual works, the book engages deeply with foundational Islamic legal literature across various schools of law. These classical materials are further supported by contemporary regulatory documents, fatwā collections, academic monographs, and peer-reviewed journal articles that contextualize the development of Islamic finance in South Asia.

Rather than revisiting the doctrinal and contract-specific analyses conducted in my PhD dissertation, this book adopts a broader, macro-level perspective that integrates ethical theory, legal institutionalism, and region-specific regulatory developments. By focusing on systemic and normative frameworks, the study aims to bridge the gap between Sharīʿah principles and the operational realities of Islamic financial governance in South Asia.

To achieve this, the book employs qualitative interpretive methodologies, drawing upon Islamic legal/law theory, classical jurisprudence, and contemporary approaches to regulatory analysis and comparative law. It combines normative evaluations of Islamic finance principles with empirical observations on how these principles are applied in practice within South Asian financial institutions.

The research includes intra- and inter-madhhab comparisons, examining Ḥanafī, Mālikī, Shāfiʿī, Ḥanbalī, and Jaʿfarī perspectives on financial regulation and ethical norms, and how local institutions interpret Islamic rulings (aḥkām) in diverse legal environments.

Chapters 2 and 3 include evaluations of policy frameworks and regulatory systems in countries like Pakistan, Bangladesh, India, and the Maldives. The analysis investigates Sharīʿah-compliant banking, ḥisbah oversight mechanisms, and ethical accountability across modern institutions.

This study selects authorities and *fatwa*-issuing bodies according to their regulatory influence, legal authority, and regional significance. This research puts its primary focuses on reports and standards produced by four major Islamic financial institutions: the Accounting and Auditing Organization for Islamic Financial Institutions (AAOIFI), the Islamic Financial Services Board (IFSB), the State Bank of Pakistan (SBP), and Malaysia's Shari'ah Advisory Council (SAC). These institutions were chosen because they hold vital authority over Islamic finance regulations and actively work to establish ethical and legal standards for compliant financial practices. When several interpretations or policy positions emerged, the selection favored approaches that presented clear maqāṣid-based reasoning, in addition to achieving compatibility across all South Asian jurisdictions.

The interdisciplinary approach thoroughly reviews Islamic finance, which connects law to ethics and practical rules that benefit Islamic jurisprudent research and socioeconomic investigations.

While grounded in rich theoretical and documentary sources, this book does not include empirical fieldwork (e.g., interviews, surveys). It prioritizes conceptual and normative inquiry. Future research may extend this work through empirical validation and institutional case studies.

In addition to drawing upon classical Islamic legal sources and regulatory documents from institutions such as AAOIFI and IFSB, this book situates its argument within broader academic discourse on Islamic finance. It engages with the normative critiques advanced by Mahmoud El-Gamal (2006),[2] the jurisprudential insights of Mufti Taqi Usmani (2002),[3] and incorporates perspectives from recent peer-reviewed scholarship. Key contributions, such as Iqbal and Mirakhor's An Introduction to Islamic Finance: Theory and Practice (2011), Asutay's (2013) work on the Islamic moral economy paradigm, and numerous other analyses of Sharīʿah governance, serve as essential reference points. Relevant articles from journals such as *the Review of Islamic Economics*, *ISRA International Journal of Islamic Finance*, and the *Journal of Islamic Accounting and Business Research* have also informed the analysis, particularly in the critique of form-over-substance practices and the evolving discourse on maqāṣid-driven reform. By anchoring the study to both classical juristic thought and contemporary academic literature, this book aims to offer a balanced and theoretically robust account of Islamic finance in the South Asian context.

This study proposes that Islamic finance in South Asia should be evaluated as a unified ethical-legal system, integrating jurisprudential doctrines with institutional practices. It offers a fresh scholarly perspective for regulators, academics, and professionals working at the intersection of Islamic law, finance, and governance.

[2] Mahmoud A. El-Gamal, *Islamic Finance: Law, Economics, and Practice* (Cambridge University Press, 2006).

[3] Mufti Muhammad Taqi Usmani, *An Introduction to Islamic Finance* (Pakistan: Maktaba ma'ariful qur'an, 2002).

Contents

CHAPTER 1

Legal Ethics in Islamic Finance

This chapter lays the theoretical groundwork for this book by framing Islamic finance as a legal-ethical system rooted in Sharīʿah objectives and classical jurisprudential principles.

1.1 Framing Islamic Finance as a Legal-Ethical System

Commercial operations in Islamic finance utilize the Sharīʿah (Islamic law) principles to establish a value-oriented financial system that integrates ethical commitments with legal structures. Islamic finance functions as a distinct economic system grounded in moral values derived from Islamic jurisprudence and religious teaching.[1] Organizations in Islamic finance follow both legal and ethical frameworks, prioritizing Sharīʿah compliance and evaluating economic behavior through the lens of maqāṣid al-sharīʿah (the higher objectives of Islamic law). This contrasts with conventional finance, where secular law controls operations and achieves profit goals. The maqāṣid al-sharīʿah functioned as an overarching goal aimed at enhancing social justice

[1] Usman Hayat—Adeel Malik, *Islamic Finance: Ethics, Concepts, Practice* (Place of publication not identified: CFA Institute Research Foundation, 2014).

© The Author(s), under exclusive license to Springer Nature Switzerland AG 2025

A. H. M. E. Uddin, *The Regulation of Islamic Financial Institutions (IFIs) and Ethical Oversight in South Asia*, Palgrave Studies in Islamic Banking, Finance, and Economics,
https://doi.org/10.1007/978-3-032-09828-3_1

and promoting human welfare.[2] Under this framework, economic objectives uphold five essential values: religion (dīn), life (nafs), intellect (ʿaql), lineage (nasl), and property (māl). These objectives form the foundation of legal rule and guide ethical and economic governance. By implementing Sharīʿah principles in financial practice, Islamic finance aims to balance both individual and societal interests within the framework of maqāṣid.[3]

The core characteristic of Islamic finance involves incorporating ethical requirements such as *ʿadl* (justice), equity, and *maṣlaḥah* (public interest) into financial regulatory systems. Islam aims to identify justice with transparency, while forbidding destructive or exploitative practices in financial transactions.[4] Islamic teachings command believers to be just and benevolent in their transactions because Allah ordered *ʿadālah* (justice), *iḥsān* (benevolence) and *khilāfah* (the trusteeship of humans as stewards). According to Islamic beliefs, the moral ideas of responsibility and non-oppression form the foundation of financial ethics.[5]

The conceptual relationship among maqāṣid, ethics, ḥisbah, and governance is illustrated in Fig. 1.1. This figure visualizes how Maqāṣid al-Sharīʿah functions as the central normative anchor within Islamic legal theory. This figure visualizes the theoretical structure underlying Islamic finance as a legal-ethical system. At the center lies Maqāṣid al-Sharīʿah, which functions as the central normative anchor guiding moral and legal reasoning within Islamic jurisprudence. From this foundation, ethics emerged as a derivative sphere, emphasizing core values such as intentionality (niyyah), justice (ʿadl), and harm reduction (rafʿ al-ḍarar).

Ḥisbah serves as the operational mechanism that applies these ethical principles within real-world market contexts, acting as an oversight institution to ensure fairness and public accountability. Governance, including Sharīʿah boards and institutional auditing structures, formalizes and institutionalizes Ethics and Ḥisbah into enforceable regulatory practices.

[2] Necmeddin Güney, "Maqāsid Al-Sharīʿa in Islamic Finance: A Critical Analysis of Modern Discourses," *Religions* 15/1 (2024), 114.

[3] Salah Alhammadi et al., "Analysing Islamic Banking Ethical Performance from *Maqāṣid al-Sharīʿah* Perspective: Evidence from Indonesia," *Journal of Sustainable Finance & Investment* 12/4 (2022), 1171–1193.

[4] Mehmet Asutay, "Islamic Moral Economy as the Foundation of Islamic Finance," *Islamic Finance in Europe* (Edward Elgar, 2013), 55–68.

[5] Zulfahmi Alwi et al., "An Assessment on Islamic Banking Ethics through Some Salient Points in the Prophetic Tradition," *Heliyon* 7/5 (2021).

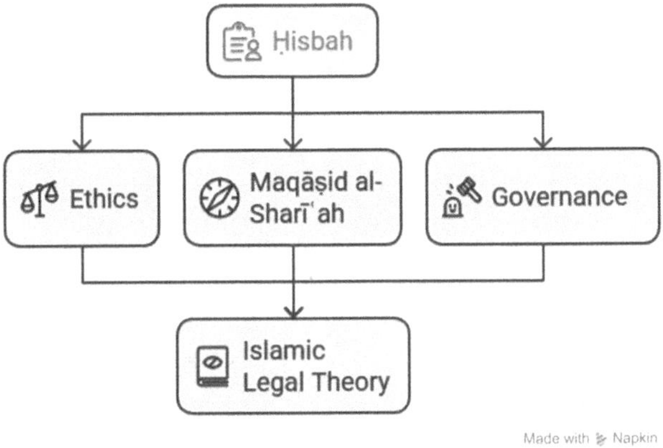

Fig. 1.1 Conceptual flowchart of Maqāṣid, Ethics, Ḥisbah, and Governance in Islamic Legal Theory

Together, these interconnected components reinforce a model of Islamic Legal Theory that integrates normative objectives with practical enforcement, illustrating how Sharīʿah-based finance aspires to harmonize moral intent with institutional integrity.

Knowledge of Islamic finance's ethical foundations remains vital because it helps define its original aspects and operational difficulties within the current financial structures throughout South Asia. This chapter creates foundations that bestow legal validity and moral substance on jurisprudence.

Figure 1.2 demonstrates Islamic finance methods based on maqāṣid al-sharīʿah, which produce legitimate contract specifications and prohibit ribā gharar and maysir. Modern financial practice operates by applying fiqh al-muʿāmalāt, as interpreted by Sunni and Jaʿfarī schools, to these principles.

The main differences between Islamic and conventional finance are summarized in Table 1.1, which highlights contrasts in risk-sharing, ethical oversight, and underlying philosophies. This table outlines the key conceptual and operational distinctions between conventional and Islamic finance. It contrasts with their underlying philosophies, treatment of interest (ribā), approach to risk sharing, stance on speculation (maysir), ethical governance structures, and moral underpinnings. The comparison illustrates how Islamic finance integrates legal prohibitions with ethical obligations rooted in Sharīʿah and maqāṣid al-sharīʿah, offering a value-driven alternative to the secular profit-centric model of conventional finance.

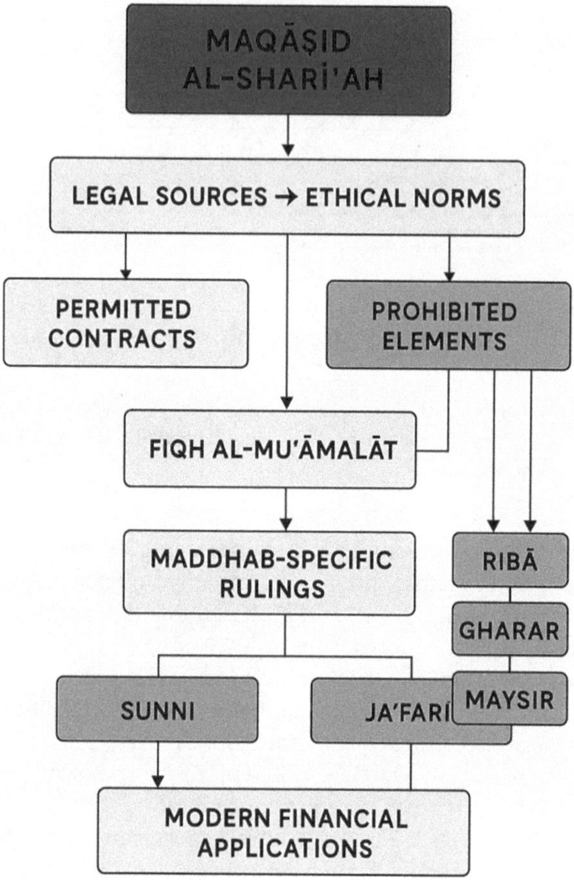

Fig. 1.2 Ethical architecture of Islamic finance. *Source* Author's own elaboration

1.1.1 The Role of Maqāṣid al-Sharīʿah in Economic Governance

Implementing Islamic finance ethics creates more stringent rules than conventional financial systems. The principles that combine honesty with risk-sharing and charity underlie Islamic financial expectations, because they forbid all forms of deception and fraud and safeguard honest practices in money management. Islamic commercial jurisprudence maintains a relationship separate from state law as its distinctive element. The rules

Table 1.1 Key differences between conventional finance and Islamic finance (Ethical perspective)

Feature	*Conventional finance*	*Islamic finance*
Underlying philosophy	Profit maximization	Ethical and social justice-based objectives
Interest (Ribā)	Permissible and foundational	Strictly prohibited
Risk sharing	Lender avoids risk	Risk is shared between parties
Speculation (Maysir)	Often tolerated or unregulated	Prohibited
Ethical oversight	Limited or optional (CSR-based)	Mandatory through Sharīʿah boards and governance
Moral framework	Secular regulatory compliance	Legal-ethical dual framework (Sharīʿah + maqāṣid)
Transparency requirement	Depending on local regulations	Ethical imperatives from the Qur'an and the Sunnah

Source Author's own elaboration

and standards of commercial activities derived from the Qur'an and Sunnah (prophetic teachings) define the jurisdiction of *Fiqh al-mu'amalat*- the branch of Islamic jurisprudence that governs commercial, contractual, and financial transactions, ensuring they adhere to principles of justice, transparency, and mutual consent by Sharīʿah.[6] The entire system of laws developed by Sharīʿah historically served the Muslim world by implementing ethical standards and legal practices. The separation between religious and ethical principles and commercial laws prevails in present-day secular countries, where finance lives without moral commitment. Islamic finance aims to reconcile Sharīʿah principles with the secular legal frameworks in financial operations.[7] The system comprises two independent legal frameworks in which institutions and banks adhere to national legal requirements alongside Sharīʿah-based frameworks.[8] Such

[6] Ameen Ahmed Abdullah Qasem Al-Nahari et al., "Common Conceptual Flaws in Realizing Maqāṣid Al-Sharīʿah Vis-à-Vis Islamic Finance," *ISRA International Journal of Islamic Finance* 14/2 (April 22, 2022), 190–205.

[7] Pejman Abedifar, "Formalism versus Purposivism in Islamic Jurisprudence: The Case of Islamic Finance Law," *Religions* 14/4 (April 2023), 465.

[8] Daing Maruak Sadek et al., "The Practices of Corporate Governance and Shariah Governance in Islamic Financial Institutions," *Ethics, Governance and Risk Management in Organizations*, ed. Intan Marzita Saidon—Roshima Said (Singapore: Springer, 2020), 131–147.

parallel operations generate tension that critically evaluates mainstream financial ethics. The principles of Islamic finance unite legal compliance with moral values, because Sharīʿah teaches that their connections are harmonious. An analyst distinguishes between ethical frameworks by stating that Islamic finances exceed rule-based implementation to integrate ethical processes directly into its operational structure. By contrast, conventional ethics and legal frameworks can be distinguished from one another. Islamic finance aligns with the legal and ethical requirements to achieve Sharīʿah's three normative societal goals: fairness, transparency, and financial welfare.[9]

Islamic Finance establishes itself through its features as an alternative financial system and comprehensive moral economy that represents Sharīʿah ethics. The financial system follows the goals of Maqāṣid al-Sharīʿah regarding both wealth preservation in society and social justice, because it bans exploitative methods that support fair deals.[10] All financial transactions within Islamic finance emphasize both ethical considerations and public benefits to defend Islamic principles of justice and public welfare. The subsequent sections demonstrate that Islamic finance encompasses prohibitions, including bans on interest and contractual mechanisms that distribute risk equally among parties. The marketplace execution of Islamic finance represents a dual perspective that seeks to unify ethical excellence and legal validity. To build on this foundation, the following section examines the key legal sources and concepts of fiqh al-muʿāmalāt.

1.2 Key Legal Sources and Concepts in Fiqh al-Muʿāmalāt

Islamic commercial law derives its ethical and legal authority from the Qurʾān and Sunnah.[11] These foundational sources establish the core values of justice (ʿadl),[12] transparency, mutual consent, and the prohibition of

[9] Muhammad Nouman et al., "Nexus between Higher Ethical Objectives (Maqasid Al Shari'ah) and Participatory Finance," *Qualitative Research in Financial Markets* 13/2 (2021), 226–251.

[10] Faris Kader, *Human Wellbeing and the Moral Economy: An Islamic Model* (Qatar: Hamad Bin Khalifa University, Ph.D., 2018).

[11] Luqman Zakariyah, "Harmonising Legality with Morality in Islamic Banking and Finance: A Quest for Maqāṣid al-Sharīʿah Paradigm," *Intellectual Discourse* 23 (2015).

[12] *Ṣaḥīḥ Muslim*, Book 1 (Faith), Hadith 102.

harm or exploitation.[13] In the South Asian context, these values are reflected in both the theoretical framing of Islamic finance and its practical application through local regulatory bodies and the Sharīʿah boards. This section provides a brief introduction to these sources and concepts as they relate to the ethical integrity of Islamic financial practices in the region.

1.2.1 *Qurʾānic Foundations of Economic Justice*

The Qurʾān provides the ethical framework for financial justice, with direct commands prohibiting ribā (interest),[14] enjoining fair trade,[15] and encouraging charity and documentation[16] in contractual agreements. These injunctions shape the legal consciousness of Islamic financial systems in Pakistan, Bangladesh, and India. Key verses—such as those that command the writing of debt contracts (2:282) and prohibit unjust enrichment (2:275–279)—form the moral rationale for ethical oversight mechanisms. In South Asian Islamic finance, these verses are not merely symbolic; they also influence banking policies, consumer protection standards, and the ethical review of products. As such, Qurʾānic injunctions are operationalized through both national banking legislation and the Sharīʿah supervisory board protocols.

1.2.2 *Prophetic Sunnah and Market Ethics*

Prophet Muhammad's guidance institutionalizes the market ethics.[17] His condemnation of deceitful sales, excessive speculation (gharar), and gambling-like transactions (maysir) remains central to Sharīʿah-based commercial practice.[18] His establishment of the role of muḥtasib—a market regulator responsible for overseeing fairness and transparency—is the basis of institutional

[13] *"The truthful, trustworthy merchant is with the Prophets and saints."*

[14] al-Baqarah 2/275.

[15] an-Nisa 4/29.

[16] al-Baqarah 2/282.

[17] Waeibrorheem Waemustafa—Sukri Suriani, "Theory of Gharar and Its Interpretation of Risk and Uncertainty from the Perspectives of Authentic Hadith and the Holy Quran: Review of Literatures," *International Journal of Economic Perspectives* 10/1 (2016), 1–27.

[18] Sulaymān ibn al-Ash'ath Abū Dāwūd, *Sunan Abī Dāwūd* (Beirut: al-Maktabah al-'Aṣrīyah, 2001). Kitāb al-Buyūʿ, (No. 3372); Abū ʿAbdillāh Muḥammad b. Ismāʿīl Bukhārī, *Ṣaḥīḥ Al-Bukhārī* (Dār Ṭawq al-Najāh, 1422).Kitāb al-Buyūʿ, (No.2147); Abū Dāwūd, *Kitāb Al-Buyūʿ*.(No. 3503).

ḥisbah,[19] which is revisited in Chap. 3 in the context of Sharīʿah governance in South Asia. South Asian regulatory bodies have drawn inspiration from these prophetic practices, particularly when establishing ethical standards for contracts, auditing procedures, and risk-sharing mechanisms. These principles are used to critique and refine product development in Islamic banks.

1.2.3 Overview of Major Islamic Financial Products

Islamic finance in South Asia typically operates through a set of widely recognized contracts such as ***murābaḥah*** (cost-plus sale),[20] ***mushārakah*** (partnership),[21] ***muḍārabah*** (trust-based investment),[22] ***ijārah*** (leasing),[23] ***salam***, and ***istisnā***ʿ.[24] These contracts are not explained in detail here, as their structures and juristic origins are thoroughly covered in standard references (e.g., Usmani 2002; El-Gamal 2006).[25] Instead, this book

[19] Taqī al-Dīn ʿAbd al-Salām Ibn Taymīyah, *Al-ḤisbahFī al-Islām Aw Waẓīfat al-Ḥukūmah al-Islāmīyah al-Muʾallif* (Beirut: Dār al-Kutub al-ʿIlmīyah, no date), 28; Abū Dāwūd, *Kitāb Al-Buyū*ʿ.(No.3451). Abū al-Ḥusayn Muslim ibn al-Ḥajjāj Muslim, *Ṣaḥīḥ Muslim* (Cairo: Maṭbaʿat ʿĪsá al-Bābī al-Ḥalabī wa-Shurakāh, 1374). Kitāb al-Īmān, (No. 102).

[20] Necmeddin Guney, "Murābaḥah Financing Revisited: The Contemporary Debate on Its Use in Islamic Banks," *Intellectual Discourse* 23 (2015).

[21] Edib Smolo—M. Kabir Hassan, "The Potentials of Mushārakah Mutanāqisah for Islamic Housing Finance," *International Journal of Islamic and Middle Eastern Finance and Management* 4/3 (January 1, 2011), 237–258.

[22] Muhlis Selman Sağlam—Taha Eğri, "Mudarebe Finansmanının Katılım Bankalarında Uygulanmasının Ahlaki Risk Yönünden Değerlendirilmesi: Türkiye Örneği," *Uluslararası İslam Ekonomisi ve Finansı Araştırmaları Dergisi* 6/2 (July 31, 2020), 197–226.

[23] Ahmet Akman, "İslam Borçlar Hukukunda Beklenmeyen Hal," *Sakarya Üniversitesi Hukuk Fakültesi Dergisi* 12/1 (July 23, 2024), 234–252.

[24] Muhammad Zahid Siddique—Muhammad Abubakar Siddique, "Reconciling the Irreconcilable (Talfeeq): The Case of Currency Salam," *International Journal of Finance & Economics* 28/1 (2023), 562–574.

[25] These contracts are only briefly summarized here, as they are examined in detail in the author's previous doctoral dissertation and audited in the compliance context in Chap. 3. Nurten Zeliha Şahin, "İslâmî Finans İlkeleri Çerçevesinde Akıllı Sözleşmeler -İcâre Temelli Azalan Müşâreke Sözleşmesi Özelinde-," *BEÜ İlahiyat Fakültesi Dergisi* 11/2 (December 16, 2024), 371–401; Ömer Çanakçı—Mustafa Yurttadur, "İslami Finans Perspektifinden Kitle Fonlamasının Araştırılması ve Model Önerileri," *Erzurum Teknik Üniversitesi Sosyal Bilimler Enstitüsü Dergisi* 21 (January 31, 2025), 34–49; Ahm Ershad Uddin, *Bangladeş'teki İslam Bankacılık Uygulamasının Fıkhî Açıdan* (Istanbul: Marmara University, Ph.D., 2020); İbrahim Ülker, "Ebüssuûd Efendi ve Şânizâde'nin Sakk Kayıtları Işığında İslam ve Osmanlı Hukukunda

emphasizes how these instruments are ethically interpreted, operationalized, or challenged in different South Asian contexts. For example, murābaḥah is heavily used in Bangladesh for asset-based lending, whereas mushārakah features more prominently in Pakistan's SME finance. These dynamics are explored in depth in Chaps. 2 and 3.

1.3 Prohibited Elements in Islamic Finance

Islamic finance operates on the foundational prohibition of three key unethical elements: ribā (usury or interest),[26] gharar (excessive uncertainty), and maysir (speculative risk or gambling). These prohibitions, rooted in the Qur'ān and Sunnah, reflect Sharīʿah's broader moral objectives: ensuring economic justice, protecting vulnerable parties, and directing capital toward productive, risk-sharing ventures.

The ban on ribā reflects the Qur'ān's condemnation of exploitative lending practices and demand for fair exchange.[27] In South Asia, this led to the replacement of interest-based loans with asset-backed modes such as *murābaḥah* and *ijārah*. Regulatory agencies and Sharīʿah boards across Pakistan and Bangladesh enforce these norms by auditing financial products for interest-bearing features and ensuring alignment with non-debt-based profit models.

Gharar, or contractual uncertainty, is avoided in Islamic finance.[28] This is interpreted by South Asian regulators as a call for full transparency,

İcâre (Kira)," *Necmettin Erbakan Üniversitesi Hukuk Fakültesi Dergisi* 6/2 (December 29, 2023), 730–755; Ismail Mohamed—Mariyam Fasaaha et al., "The Application of Service Ijarah in Islamic Finance," *International Journal of Management and Applied Research* 11/1 (2024), 80–106; Anjum Siddiqui, "Financial Contracts, Risk and Performance of Islamic Banking," ed. M. Mansoor Khan—M. Ishaq Bhatti, *Managerial Finance* 34/10 (January 1, 2008), 680–694.

[26] Abdulaziz Bayındır, *Ticaret Ve Faiz* (Istanbul: Süleymaniye Vakfi Yayınları, 2016).

[27] S. M. Hasanuzzaman, *Nabil A. Saleh, Unlawful Gain and Legitimate Profit in Islamic Law: Riba, Gharar and Islamic Banking* (SSRN Scholarly Paper, 1991), Social Science Research Network, papers.ssrn.com.

[28] Mohd Shahid Mohd Noh et al., "A Review on Gharar Dimension in Modern Islamic Finance Transactions," *Journal of Islamic Accounting and Business Research* (2024);Ian Alfian et al., "Unraveling Gharar Practices: A Literature Study on Islamic Economic Transactions in the Global," *Proceeding International Conference on Economic and Social Sciences* 2 (December 15, 2024), 707–715;Nafis Alam et al., "Prohibition of Riba and Gharar in Islamic Banking," *Islamic Finance: A Practical Perspective*, ed. Nafis Alam et al. (Cham: Springer International Publishing, 2017), 35–53.

documentation, and disclosure in contracts. This is why speculative instruments such as derivatives or ambiguous insurance contracts are often replaced with takāful models or structures backed by real assets.

Maysir, the third prohibition,[29] forbids zero-sum contracts driven by chance or gambling.[30] In financial practice, this translates into a ban on lottery-like schemes, games of chance, or high-risk speculative derivatives.[31] Instead, Islamic institutions across South Asia have developed investment tools tied to tangible economic activity and risk-sharing principles.

Together, these prohibitions form the ethical guardrails of Islamic finance, and directly shape product design, regulatory vetting, and public trust in Sharīʿah-compliant services. Their practical enforcement is further explored in country-specific analyses and Sharīʿah governance frameworks in Chaps. 2 and 3.

1.4 Structures, Jurisdictions, and Legal Diversity in Islamic Finance

In South Asia, Islamic finance functions within a mosaic of jurisprudential traditions. The coexistence of Ḥanafī, Shāfiʿī, Mālikī, Ḥanbalī, and Jaʿfarī schools enabled the selective adaptation of rulings to meet contemporary challenges.[32] For example, Indian Islamic finance relies on cooperative and informal models drawn from multiple schools, whereas Pakistan's Council of Islamic Ideology employs inter-madhhab principles to guide national policy. Rather than engaging in exhaustive comparative studies, this book emphasizes how South Asian institutions utilize this legal diversity to

[29] Quran 5/90-91).

[30] Rajesh K. Aggarwal—Tarik Yousef, "Islamic Banks and Investment Financing," *Journal of Money, Credit and Banking* 32/1 (2000), 93–120.

[31] Asep Ridwan Lubis et al., "Practical Implications Of The Prohibition Of Gambling In Islamic Economic Principles," *MIMBAR PENDIDIKAN* 8/2 (September 1, 2023), 117–128. Saadiah Mohamad—Ali Tabatabaei, *Islamic Hedging: Gambling or Risk Management?* (SSRN Scholarly Paper, August 27, 2008); Dewi Maliha—Mahdalina Nanda Alhusna, "The Meaning of Al-Maysir from the Perspective of Middle Eastern Mufasirs and Its Contex: English," *An-Nur International Journal of The Quran & Hadith* 2/2 (November 30, 2024), 11–23.

[32] Jonathan Ercanbrack, "The Standardization of Islamic Financial Law: Lawmaking in Modern Financial Markets," *The American Journal of Comparative Law* 67/4 (December 31, 2019), 825–860.

maintain ethical authenticity while navigating regulatory dualities. Chaps. 2 and 3 further examine how pluralism shapes Sharīʿah compliance and ethical governance frameworks.

1.4.1 *Overview of the Four Sunni Schools and Jaʿfarī Shīʿī Perspective*

All segments within Islamic jurisprudence prohibit business involvement in activities, such as interest, gambling, and transactions involving uncertainty. Each Islamic legal school agrees on the rules prohibiting business contracts with interest, uncertainty, or gambling, but might adopt slight variations in their practical applications. According to Ḥanafī religious scholars, commodities sold through *salam* (advance payment sale) must remain accessible continuously from the contract date until delivery; otherwise, the salam contract becomes void.[33] The jurists established this condition to prevent delivery failures and reduce gharar. The Shāfiʿī,[34] along with Mālikī and Ḥanbalī jurisprudence, did not enforce this requirement, as any anticipation of commodity availability at the time of delivery would validate the *salam* contract. Modern scholars find it practical to follow the broader interpretation of salam, which waives for the strict Hanafi requirements by allowing trade on seasonally produced commodities by assuming their availability (which illustrates why flexibility in the Shari'a position benefits present-day conditions).[35] Ḥanafī[36] and Ḥanbalī[37] fiqh required delivery in *salam* to occur at least one month after the deal to distinguish it from immediate sales. However, Shāfiʿī jurists accepted any specific future date as valid according to their interpretation of the Prophet's instructions.[38] Modern Islamic finance endorses the Shāfiʿī

[33] ʻAlāʼ al-Dīn Kāsānī Abū Bakr ibn Masʻūd, *Badāʼiʻ Al-Ṣanāʼiʻ Fī Tartīb al-Sharāʼiʻ* (Beirut: Dār al-Kutub al-ʻIlmīyah, 1328). Muḥammad Amīn Ibn ʻĀbidīn, *Ḥāshiyat Radd Al-Muḥtār, ʻalá al-Durr al-Mukhtār* (Egypt: Muṣṭafá al-Bābī al-Ḥalabī, 1386).

[34] Muḥyī al-Dīn Yaḥyá ibn Sharaf Nawawī, *Rawḍat Al-Ṭālibīn Wa-ʻumdat al-Muftīn* (Amman: al-Maktab al-Islāmī, 1991).

[35] Usmani, *An Introduction to Islamic Finance.* "AAOIFI Shariah Standard" (Manama: Accounting and Auditing Organization For Islamic Institutions, 2022).

[36] Kāsānī, *Badāʼiʻ Al-Ṣanāʼiʻ Fī Tartīb al-Sharāʼiʻ.*

[37] Abū Muḥammad ʻAbd Allāh Ibn Qudāmah, *Al-Mughnī* (Cairo: Maktabat al-Qāhirah, 1403).

[38] Abū Zakariyyāʼ Muḥyī al-Dīn Yaḥyā ibn Sharaf al-Nawawī, *Al-Majmūʻ Sharḥ al-Muhadhdhab* (Cairo: Muṣṭafá al-Bābī al-Ḥalabī, 1347).

stance by allowing a minimum time gap, as such rules align with Qur'anic and prophetic teachings without restricting contractual architecture.[39]

The schools disagreed on matters concerning contract combinations and legal tactics. According to the Ḥanafī scholar tradition, they accepted a broader scope of contract mixing, provided that particular conditions were met, combined with legal techniques (*Ḥiyiāl*) to obtain lawful objectives.[40] Some Ḥanafī experts recognized trade deals that circumvented banned practices by demonstrating their validity through persuasive arguments that were acceptable.[41] Ibn Taymiyyah[42] and Ibn al-Qayyim[43] of the Ḥanbalī school maintained strict positions on form and intent matching in legal matters by denouncing *bay' al-'īnah* (a sale and buy-back transaction used to simulate a cash loan) alongside other interference attempts to avoid riba.[44] Shafi'ī jurists from the classical era accepted *bay' al-'īnah*, but only under the condition that it remained separated into two distinct sales events, as it satisfied all required formalities. According to Hanbali's bay' al-'īnah, granted as a tool to avoid riba, was utterly unacceptable,[45] while Shafi'is considered it morally distasteful.[46] Malaysian laws endorse *bay' al-'īnah* in Islamic banking because of the Shāfi'ī fiqh background.[47] However, most Middle Eastern scholar groups influenced by Maliki fiqh

[39] Frank Vogel—Samuel Hayes, *Islamic Law and Finance: Religion, Risk and Return* (Kluwer Law International, 1998).

[40] Kāsānī, *Badā'i' Al-Ṣanā'i' Fī Tartīb al-Sharā'i'*. Muḥammad ibn Aḥmad Sarakhsī, *Al-Mabsūṭ* (Cairo: Maṭba'at al-Sa'ādah, no date).

[41] Kamāl al-Dīn Ibn Humām, *Sharḥ Fatḥ Al-Qadīr* (Egypt: Maktabat al-Bābī al-Ḥalabī, 1389).Muhammad Tahir Mansoori, "Is 'Islamic Banking' Islamic? Analysis of Current Debate on Sharī'ah Legitimacy of Islamic Banking and Finance," *Islamic Studies* 50/3/4 (2011), 383–411.

[42] Aḥmad Ibn Taymīyah, *Majmū' Al-Fatāwá* (Riyad: Majma' al-Malik Fahd li-Ṭibā'at al-Muṣḥaf, 2004), 29/432–439.

[43] Shams al-Dīn Ibn Qayyim al-Jawzīyah, *I'lām Al-Muwaqqi'īn 'an Rabb al-'ālamīn* (Beirut: Dār al-Kutub al-'Ilmīyah, 1991).

[44] al-Jawzīyah, *I'lām Al-Muwaqqi'īn 'an Rabb al-'ālamīn*, 3/148.

[45] Ibn Qudāmah, *Al-Mughnī*.

[46] al-Nawawī, *Al-Majmū' Sharḥ al-Muhadhdhab*.

[47] "Guidelines on Shariah Governance Framework for Islamic Financial Institutions," 2010.

reject this method,[48] opting instead for tawarruq and actual sale-based loans.[49] Each Islamic school's formal doctrine of financial transactions differs because it governs how partnerships affect debt sales, and permits the use of specific forward contracts and agency arrangements.

Jaʿfarī (Shīʿī) jurisprudence implements independent rules for interpretation.[50] Under Jaʿfarī jurisprudence, temporary marriage also exists, known as *mutʿaʾ*. The practice bases its authority on the religious interpretations of the Quranic verses and Hadith. The rule of temporary marriage depends most heavily on Surah An-Nisa (4:24) as the main reference verse. The Jaʿfarī scholar bases their approval of *mutʿa* on family traditions, which they claim justify this practice and support their interpretation of the verse Surah An-Nisa (4:24).[51] Apart from the prohibition of *mutʿa* within Sunni jurisprudence, religious authorities base their disapproval on the principle of abrogation and the associated social hazards.[52] The schools demonstrate their scriptural interpretation approach and legal systems through conflicting interpretations. Historically, the Jaʿfarī School has supported the possibility of charging interest to non-Muslims outside Dār al-Islām; however, this controversial stance has not been employed in current times, but it highlights the range of views within this school of thought. Islamic banking institutions in modern Iran use Jaʿfarī Fiqh principles for their profit-sharing financing model, which follows Sunni trade-based contracts.[53] Some variations arise in executing financial contracts through alternative methods of validating specific insurance products along with guarantee fees.[54] All schools of thought within Islamic law share common principles about broad concepts in finance, which enable the creation of products that meet the requirements of every school when structured appropriately.[55]

[48] *AAOIFI Shariah Standard No 30.*

[49] "Resolution No. 179 (19/5): On Organized Tawarruq" (Jeddah: OIC, 2009).

[50] Ashmita Mitra—Amulya Baid, "Muta Marriage: A Contractual Form of Live-in Relationship," *LexForti Legal Journal* 1 (2020 2019), 67.

[51] Abī Jaʻfar Muḥammad ibn al-Ḥasan al-Ṭūsī, *Al-Nihāyah Fī Mujarrad al-Fiqh Wa-al-Fatāwá* (Beirut: Dār al-Kitāb al-ʻArabī, 1980), 490.

[52] Ibn Qudāmah, *Al-Mughnī.*

[53] S. Husain Ashraf—Alizadeh Giashi Ali, "Islamic Banking in Iran-Progress and Challenges," *Arabian Journal of Business and Management Review* 12 (2011), 31–44.

[54] Mohammad Hashim Kamali, "Islamic Commercial Law: An Analysis of Futures," *American Journal of Islamic Social Sciences* 13, no. 2 (1996): 197–224.

[55] El-Gamal, *Islamic Finance*, 2006.

1.4.2 Comparative Legal Reasoning and Contemporary Ijtihād

Contemporary Shari'ah scholars employ different opinions to perform *takhayyur* (preference) based on their personal preferences.[56] Modern jurist practitioners of ijtihād have developed innovative legal approaches to resolve contemporary financial instruments that previous Islamic books have not specifically addressed.[57] Their approach falls under the principle of *takhayyur* as it allows them to draw upon positions other than the traditional historical interpretations of a single madhhab. Understanding the same Shari'ah texts leads Muslim jurists to discover several valid approaches through which to find solutions. Modern-day Shari'ah scholars are free to issue fatwas by selecting valid interpretations that do not contravene existing Shari'ah principles, regardless of their affiliation with classical schools.

A practical methodology enables Malaysian regulators to select rulings from various schools, such as the Mālikī and Ḥanafī schools, while developing solutions compatible with contemporary circumstances. This process is recognized in the fiqh al-muqaran, or comparative fiqh, within the modern judiciary. The directive states that it can function provided that the opinion is based on sound Sharīʿah criteria derived from the Quran and Sunnah, as well as analogical reasoning. The ability to flexibly innovate products through ijtihād led to the creation of innovations, such as takāful insurance, ṣukūk bonds, and hedging instruments, as none of these had strict parallels in classical jurisprudence.[58] The cornerstone legal maxim of Islamic financial law states that transactions default to being permissible according to this condition: "al-aṣl fī al-muʿāmalāt al-ibāḥah" (the default principle in transactions is permissibility."[59] Unless specifically prohibited, all financial transactions are permissible under the Shari'ah principles,

[56] Mohammad Hashim Kamali, *Shariah and the Halal Industry* (Oxford University Press, 2021), 191.

[57] Shaheen Whyte, "Are Fatwas Dispensable? Examining the Contemporary Relevance and Authority of Fatwas in Australia," *Oxford Journal of Law and Religion* 11/2–3 (2022), 314–342.

[58] Habib Ahmed, "Islamic Law and Finance: Concepts and Principles," *Product Development in Islamic Banks* (Edinburgh University Press, 2011), 17–52.

[59] Zayn al-Dīn ibn Ibrāhīm Ibn Nujaym, *Al'ashbāhu Wālnnaẓā'ir* (Beirut: Dār al-Kutub al-'Ilmīyah, 1999), 60.

which offer suitable prospects for economic innovation.[60] This phrase serves contemporary scholars by helping them develop Shari' ah-compliant financial products. The default status of new economic structures becomes ḥalāl because they can function without ribā, gharar, and maysir and do not contravene explicit Sharīʿah texts. Islamic banks created home financing through mushārakah mutanāqiṣah (diminishing partnership)[61] while implementing Ṣukūk al-Ijārah[62] for liquidity management, although these specific arrangements were not conventional practices in the past. They established approval by maintaining compliance with the Sharīʿah rules throughout every component of the deal. Qiyās and istiḥsān, as tools of ijtihād, enable Islamic scholars to generalize traditional rulings to modern situations, allowing them to authorize configurations when they serve the maṣlaḥah (public welfare).[63]

1.4.3 *Application to Modern Financial Contracts and Standardization Bodies*

Islamic law encompasses various legal schools that both advance and restrict the development of modern Islamic finances. Islamic finance has developed its financial tools through various interpretational approaches offered by multiple legal schools. Foreign transactions and mixed-confession religious areas are characterized by prominent regulatory uncertainties stemming from the coexistence of numerous legal schools within Islamic law.[64] One solution to resolving religious pluralism emerges in the case of Pakistan, as the nation demonstrates how it addresses this issue.[65] Pakistani officials and jurists select principles from several Islamic branches to fill the voids in

[60] Usmani, *An Introduction to Islamic Finance*, 13–17.

[61] Marjan Muhammad, *Islamic Financial System Principles & Operations*, ed. Mezbah Uddin Ahmed (Kuala Lumpur: International Shariah Research Academy for Islamic Finance, 2016), 225–234.

[62] *AAOIFI Shariah Standard no 17 Ijārah. AAOIFI Shariah Standard no 18 Ṣukūk.*

[63] Al-Sarakhsī, *Uṣūl al-Sarakhsī*, vol. 2/Al-Shāṭibī, *al-Muwāfaqāt*, vol. 4/ISRA Compendium (2016): Applications of qiyās in modern Islamic derivatives and credit risk/ AAOIFI, Standard No. 21.

[64] Kilian Bälz, "Islamic Law as Governing Law under the Rome Convention: The Case of Arbitration," *Yearbook of Islamic and Middle Eastern Law* 5 (1998): 37–51.

[65] Wael B. Hallaq, *An Introduction to Islamic Law* (Cambridge: Cambridge University Press, 2009), 143–150.

traditional Ḥanafī financial law regarding modern commercial agreements.[66] The Council of Islamic Ideology, in collaboration with the Shari'aht Appellate Bench, plays a crucial role in determining the methods to be adopted.[67] Cooperative insurance practices in Pakistan implement Mālikī and Shāfiʿī behavioral patterns for donor-driven insurance pooling, for which orthodox Ḥanafī jurisprudence is not fully supported.[68] For instance, Pakistan's Council of Islamic Ideology has issued detailed opinions on banking structures and the elimination of interest, supporting maqāṣid-oriented reforms while navigating fiqh diversity. Similarly, the Islamic Fiqh Academy of India has addressed contractual clarity, digital finance, and mutual cooperative banking through fatwa sessions and national seminars, which have influenced regional Islamic finance discourses.[69]

In Bangladesh, the Bangladesh Bank established a dedicated Islamic Banking Wing that issues detailed guidelines to ensure the soundness and Sharīʿah compliance of financial institutions.[70] Meanwhile, the Shari'ah Supervisory Committee of Islami Bank Bangladesh Limited (IBBL) regularly publishes annual reports that evaluate product structures, fatwa applications, and maqāṣid alignment in product design. These institutional actors play a crucial role in balancing classical *fiqh* with regulatory pragmatism, particularly in managing Islamic finance within a dual banking system that must coexist with interest-based frameworks.[71] The inter-madhhab

[66] Imran Ahsan Khan Nyazee, *Islamic Jurisprudence* (2019), 153–159.

[67] Chawla, Muhammad Iqbal, and Ahmad Riaz-ul-Huda. "Islamization in Pakistan: An overview." *Journal of the Research Society of Pakistan* 52.1 (2015). Holz, Sarah. *Governance of Islam in Pakistan: An Institutional Study of the Council of Islamic Ideology*. Liverpool University Press, 2022.

[68] Usmani, Muhammad Taqi, *An Introduction to Islamic Finance* (Karachi: Maktaba Ma'ariful Qur'an, 2002), 113–120.

[69] "Practical Islamic Laws," https://Imamsadiq.Ac/Imam *Sadiq Academy* (Accessed July 30, 2025).

[70] M. K. Alam—Ahm Ershad Uddın, "Legal and Regulatory Frameworks For Sharī'a Governance Practices in the Islamic Banking Industry of Bangladesh," *Mizanü'l-Hak: İslami İlimler Dergisi* 17 (December 30, 2023), 663–688.

[71] While Pakistan, India, and Bangladesh have well-established regulatory bodies and *fiqh* councils shaping Islamic finance discourse, other South Asian jurisdictions such as Afghanistan, the Maldives, and Sri Lanka are developing distinct frameworks of Islamic financial governance. Chapter 2 will explore these cases, providing a country-specific comparative analysis of regulatory evolution, institutional models, and legal adaptations in diverse socio-political environments.

principle demonstrates active support for the maqāṣid al-Sharī'ah principles while also preserving traditional Sharī'ah principles through contemporary ijtihād.[72] The Malaysian legal system operates within a pluralistic framework that governs its structure.[73] Through inter-madhhab reasoning, the Central Shari'ah Advisory Council (SAC) created fresh, contemporary interpretations of law as needed.[74] The Special Conditions of the SAC enable debt trading, thereby facilitating secondary market ṣukūk transactions.[75]

Malaysia follows the normative debt transfer principles of the Shāfi'ī Fiqh in financial matters. At the same time, its Shari'ah Advisory Council finds additional interpretation methods from Shāfi'ī fiqh and alternative approaches to fulfilling development objectives. Islamic law functions as an extensive system of communal benefits that meets economic criteria today through its approach.[76] Organizations led by AAOIFI generate standards that employ cautious restrictions throughout their framework. The methodological framework of AAOIFI leads to the development of merged standards that create unified opinions rather than allowing the diversification of interpretations.[77] The standardization process, which is based on this methodology, limits local institutions from making independent operational changes. The process is justified by economic globalization requirements, which lead to standardized principles that improve legal transparency alongside market confidence but decrease local adaptability capabilities. The OIC Fiqh Academy demonstrates that institutions can foster shared views instead of enforcing single regulations through the collaborative ijtihād process. The OIC Fiqh Academy unifies doctrinal policy decisions for law-making through scholarly meetings that gain

[72] Al-Shāṭibī, Ibrāhīm ibn Mūsā, *al-Muwāfaqāt fī Uṣūl al-Sharī'ah*, ed. Dār Ibn 'Affān, 4 vols. (Riyadh: Dār Ibn 'Affān, 1997), vol. 2, 355–367.

[73] Miskam, Surianom, and Muhammad Amrullah Nasrul. "Shariah governance in Islamic finance: the effects of the Islamic financial services act 2013." *Proceedings of World Conference on Integration of Knowledge*. 2013.

[74] Shariah Advisory Council (SAC), *Resolutions of the Shariah Advisory Council of Bank Negara Malaysia*, (Kuala Lumpur: Bank Negara Malaysia, 2010), Resolutions 1, 18, 22.

[75] ISRA (International Shariah Research Academy), *Islamic Financial System: Principles and Operations* (Kuala Lumpur: ISRA, 2016), 225–234.

[76] Mohammad Hashim Kamali, *Principles of Islamic Jurisprudence*, 3rd ed. (Cambridge: Islamic Texts Society, 2003), 372–386.

[77] Mahmoud A. El-Gamal, *Islamic Finance: Law, Economics, and Practice* (Cambridge: Cambridge University Press, 2006), 119–122.

legitimate religious authority from all four Sunni schools.[78] The OIC Fiqh Academy and similar Fiqh councils facilitate cross-border expansion of Islamic finance through ijtihad endorsement, which combines multiple perspectives to generate financially viable solutions recognized by various jurisdictions.

A collective ban on organized *tawarruq* showed that diverse perspectives between forum members do not hinder their ability to address modern challenges. People must understand that school-level harmonization initiatives do not aim to eliminate the differences between schools of thought. The complete theological principles of fiqh remain preserved, while regulators and institutions make deliberate moves to maintain organizational unity. This doctrine of uṣūl al-fiqh illustrates the proper approach to managing diverse theological perspectives, as the unity of action becomes essential for preserving doctrinal diversity.[79] Various Muslim legal schools have maintained connections with religious resources that inform local policy decisions. The Shāfiʿī School provides step-by-step procedures to create specific contractual terms. The Mālikī school bases its customary rulings on particular situations. In contrast, Ḥanbalī scholars employ substantial analysis to distinguish between form and intent, and Ḥanafī provides methods for organized analogical reasoning.[80] A combination of these principles persists in public policy creation, as lawmakers extract specific elements from various doctrines to develop realistic Shari'ah-based regulations that prioritize profitability. Islamic law has become stronger because of its interpretations, which seem to be in conflict. The diverse range of Islamic jurist opinions serves as a regulatory process, allowing concept-based adaptability through changes that address different situations. Various Islamic financial principles uphold traditional Islamic traditions and meet contemporary financial requirements through a maqāṣid-based rationale and Qur'ānic and Prophetic instructions.[81] Numerous religious laws in operation have led to the establishment of organizations such as AAOIFI and the OIC Fiqh Academy, which set standards for financial interpretation worldwide.

[78] Majmaʿ al-Fiqh al-Islāmī (OIC), *Majallat Majmaʿ al-Fiqh al-Islāmī* (Jeddah: Organization of Islamic Cooperation, 1985–present).

[79] Al-Shāṭibī, *al-Muwāfaqāt*, vol. 4, 400–407.

[80] Imran Ahsan Khan Nyazee, *Theories of Islamic Law* (Islamabad: Islamic Research Institute, 1994), 182–194.

[81] Kamali, *Principles of Islamic Jurisprudence*, 285–288.

This comparative legal reasoning across Islamic schools demonstrates the flexibility and adaptability of Sharīʿah-based frameworks, which enable context-sensitive financial innovation. However, diversity in legal reasoning also introduces complexities. These complexities affect how ethical principles are applied in practice, often leading to inconsistencies between the ideal Islamic finance models and their practical implementation. Consequently, the transition from legal theory to ethical outcomes reveals several challenges in aligning forms with substances.

The legal diversity explored above has enriched Islamic finance by enabling adaptive jurisprudential solutions in various contexts. However, this flexibility introduces new ethical challenges. As Islamic finance institutions navigate multiple interpretations and regulatory expectations, a growing tension emerges between formal Sharīʿah compliance and substantive ethical fulfillment. The following section examines how these tensions impact the credibility of Islamic finance and its alignment with the maqāṣid al-sharīʿah.

1.5 Relevance in Contemporary Financial Systems

The contemporary Islamic financial sector operates within a global economic framework that follows secular legislative structures alongside prevailing conventional trends. This creates convergence and tension between Islamic principles and secular, legal, and economic norms. Islamic financial institutions must strike a balance between competitiveness and integration, as they share similarities with conventional banks in their national financial regulatory framework. Institutions continually strive to maintain their distinct identities rooted in Sharīʿah principles. The interaction between different economic, legal, and ethical factors affects Islamic finance's legal standards, ethical dedication, and authenticity.

It should be noted that while this section critiques certain operational trends in Islamic finance, it does so in the context of scholarly debates on Sharīʿah fidelity and ethical practices. These observations align with prior literature that has identified tensions between Islamic ideals and the realities of modern financial structures.[82]

[82] See, El-Gamal, *Islamic Finance*, 2006; Asutay, "A Political Economy Approach to Islamic Economics."

1.6 Ethical Challenges in Contemporary Islamic Finance

Islamic finance faces several contemporary ethical challenges arising from global legal structures, market pressures, and the tension between Sharīʿah form and economic substance. As Islamic financial institutions expand into international markets, they increasingly adopt contractual and regulatory frameworks that mirror those of conventional finance, sparking debates over authenticity, ethical purpose, and compliance with maqāṣid. These challenges include structural convergence, reliance on secular courts, limited enforceability of Sharīʿah clauses, and the growing risk of Sharīʿah-washing. The following subsections examine these issues in depth, beginning with the legal and ethical tensions shaping the operation of Islamic finance in global financial systems.

1.6.1 Legal and Ethical Tensions in Global Finance

The operational procedures of Islamic banks essentially replicate conventional banking practices by adjusting only those components that contravene Sharīʿah guidelines. Financial products exhibit similar economic outcomes despite their legal and structural differences stemming from the convergence of banking systems.[83] Islamic banks transform established banking services, which include savings accounts and financing as well as trade finance, through Islamic contracts such as Murabaha for loans and Ijārah for leases, among others. Institutions follow international capital adequacy requirements based on the Basel Accords and accounting standards that combine IFRS standards and additional requirements of the AAOIFI. Real market convergence enables Islamic banks to provide conventional bank products that function similarly to their counterparts, even though they involve different contractual arrangements (for instance, a Murabaha home finance product produces economic effects equivalent to interest-based payments, but differs in its legal structure).

While the operational purpose is comparable between the Shari'ah and secular legal fields, these systems maintain distinct legal structures that become evident in non-religious domains. The problem persists regarding the legal ability to enforce Islamic contracts in external court systems. Choosing English or New York Law when establishing contract principles provides certainty for international deals. English courts have demonstrated an unwillingness to

[83] Marwan Izzeldin et al., "Efficiency Convergence in Islamic and Conventional Banks," *Journal of International Financial Markets, Institutions and Money* 70 (2021), 101279.

understand the essence of Shari'ah behind Islamic financial transactions in the landmark case of Shamil Bank of Bahrain. In the Beximco case (2004 EWCA Civ 1278), the English High Court was required to implement a Murabaha agreement that specified English law as the governing principle while remaining subject to Shari'ah principles from the Glorious Shari'ah.[84] The High Court ruled that Islamic law was not a viable source of conflict with English law; therefore, it was the only binding authority. Consequently, the Shari'ah compatibility of the contract became irrelevant for proper execution. The court's decision in this situation demonstrates that disputes regarding Islamic financial contracts receive standard treatment from English courts in the same manner as regular monetary agreements, while avoiding intervention in matters of religious compliance. The dispute highlights a struggle between Islamic financial institutions, which desire Sharīʻah-compliant contracts, and secular courts, which may finalize agreements from a purely secular perspective.[85] Contracts today are drafted to achieve Shari'ah compliance through their wording rather than being enforced through religious requirements, as this protects deals from being invalidated by courts. Some legal scholars advocate using a "doctrine of incorporation," which explicitly incorporates Shari'ah standards into contractual terms, such as "no interest shall be payable; any late fee shall go to charity," thereby enabling English courts to enforce them. Many Islamic finance agreements establish arbitration in Muslim jurisdictions or under customized rules that examine Shari'ah compliance.

Some Muslim-majority countries have started changing their legislation to support Islamic banking operations. The Central Bank Act and Islamic Financial Services Act of Malaysia ensure that Shari'ah rulings by the National Shari'ah Advisory Council remain mandatory for civil courts to handle Islamic finance disputes. The Malaysian court system refers to all Shari'ah compliance matters to the SAC to determine the outcomes that satisfy Islamic legal standards.[86] In 2022, the Supreme Court of Pakistan declared

[84] Court of Appeal of England and Wales. (2004). *Shamil Bank of Bahrain EC v Beximco Pharmaceuticals Ltd and Others* (2004) EWCA Civ 19; (2004) 1 WLR 1784.

[85] Alam, M. K.—Ershad Uddın, Ahm. "Legal and Regulatory Frameworks For Sharī'a Governance Practices in the Islamic Banking Industry of Bangladesh". Mizanü'l-Hak: İslami İlimler Dergisi 17 (Aralık 2023), 663–688; El-Gamal, Mahmoud A. *Islamic finance: Law, economics, and practice.* Cambridge University Press, 2006.

[86] NF Abu Kamar et al., "The Role of Shariah Advisory Council (SAC) of Bank Negara Malaysia on Islamic Finance Disputes: Legal Analysis" (UiTM International Conference on Law & Society, Kuala Lumpur: UiTM, 2021).

that eliminating interest rates would be necessary to establish Islamic banking as the dominant banking method in the country.[87] Making this effort successful in a complex modern economy remains difficult throughout the ongoing process. Britain implements a facilitative approach by modifying tax rules and allowing companies to issue Shari'ah-compliant products.

However, it leaves institutional boards to handle Islamic matters rather than intervening in court. An internal struggle exists within Islamic financial institutions, as they strive to balance embracing standard legal structures with relying on rating agencies for global operations. However, their domestic Shari'ah supervisory boards ensure contract and operational compliance with Islamic law.[88] Utilizing such mechanisms produces innovative solutions for sovereign sukuk issuance, which involves English as the governing law, arbitration clauses, and statements about Shari'ah principles, accompanied by the Shari'ah fatwas as a supportive exhibit. Despite maintaining its distinct identity, Islamic finance can match secular standards through familiar legal instruments, while satisfying regulatory standards. Core differentiation occurs because motivation and particular constraints are directly derived from Islamic law. Technical adherence to ethical finance principles in Islamic finance raises scholarly resistance concerning its fidelity to ethical aims and purpose in society.

1.6.2 Ethical versus Legal Compliance

Islamic finance faces several contemporary ethical challenges arising from global legal structures, market pressures, and the tension between Sharīʿah form and economic substance. As Islamic financial institutions expand into international markets, they increasingly adopt contractual and regulatory frameworks that mirror those of conventional finance, sparking debates over authenticity, ethical purpose, and compliance with maqāṣid. These challenges include structural convergence, reliance on secular courts, limited enforceability of Sharīʿah clauses, and the growing risk of Sharīʿah-washing. The following subsections examine these issues in

[87] Rafiullah Sheikh et al., "Federal Shariat Court's Judgment on Ribā-Free Economy of Pakistan: Challenges in Implementation and the Way Forward," *Islamic Banking and Finance Review* 11/1 (September 25, 2024), 47–79.

[88] Jonathan Ercanbrack, *The Transformation of Islamic Law in Global Financial Markets* (Cambridge: Cambridge University Press, 2015).

depth, beginning with the legal and ethical tensions shaping the operation of Islamic finance in global financial systems.

1.6.2.1 The Risk-Sharing Gap

A fundamental ongoing discussion examines how Islamic finance balances legal compliance with Sharīʿah's ethical objectives. According to critics, Islamic finance has failed to meet the expectations that its promoters promised it would be an ethically guided, risk-sharing, community-oriented system.[89] Islamic economics literature first described financial entities that would support socioeconomic growth and minimize disparities while reflecting the Islamic values of societal equality. According to theoretical frameworks, Islamic finance requires institutions to practice sharing risks through mudarabah and musharakah while refraining from excessive debt and investing in society's beneficial projects.[90] This heavy reliance on murābaḥah—accounting for over 80% of assets in some banks—has led some scholars to question whether Islamic finance continues to fulfill its original ethical promise of risk-sharing and equitable justice (Warde, 2000).[91] Most Islamic bank financing operates as debt-based transactions, as the murābaḥah and ijārah modes dominate their investment portfolios despite the theoretical concept of profit-and-loss sharing.[92] An examination of Islamic bank assets revealed that 80% of their business is conducted through fixed-income instruments, despite operating with a small portion utilizing real profit-sharing methods.[93] Mark-up financing is popular because financial institutions find it less risky and easier to promote than PLS partnerships.

[89] M. Kabir Hassan, *Ethical Principles of Islamic Financial Institutions* (SSRN Scholarly Paper, 2013), Social Science Research Network, papers.ssrn.com.

[90] Zakariya Mustapha et al., "Legal and Sharīʿah Non-Compliance Risks in Nigerian Islamic Finance Industry: A Review of the Literature," *International Journal of Law and Management* 63/2 (November 12, 2020), 275–299.

[91] Ibrahim Warde, *Islamic Finance in the Global Economy* (Edinburgh: Edinburgh University Press, 2000).

[92] Zaheer Anwer et al., "Sharīʿah-Compliant Central Banking Practices: Lessons from Muslim Countries' Experience," *ISRA International Journal of Islamic Finance* 12/1 (March 18, 2020), 7–26. Irfan Ahmed et al., "Practices of Islamic Banking in the Light of Islamic Ethics: A Critical Review," *International Journal of Economics, Management and Accounting* 25/3 (2017), 465–490.

[93] Feisal Khan, "How 'Islamic' Is Islamic Banking?," *Journal of Economic Behavior & Organization* 76/3 (December 1, 2010), 805–820.

1.6.2.2 The Compliance Illusion

Using Arabic terminology, questions have emerged regarding whether Islamic finance creates a new paradigm or functions identical to conventional banking. The debate surrounding Sharīʿah-compliant versus Sharīʿah-based operations has led to the creation of this terminology in Islamic finance.[94] The Sharīʿah-compliant sector contains operations that implement the clear rulings of Sharīʿah (contracts that adhere to halal requirements).[95] However, Sharīʿah-based finance goes beyond technicalities to foster Sharīʿah values, including risk sharing, economic benefits, and justice principles.[96] Critics argue that while many contemporary finance practices meet technical Sharīʿah requirements, they may not fully align with broader Sharīʿah-based ethical objectives such as justice, social benefit, and equity (Asutay, 2007; Iqbal & Mirakhor, 2011).[97] Does the profit-sharing credit card offered by an Islamic bank, which donates late fees to charity under Shari'ah law and has payment rates similar to interest, solve debt-related problems associated with traditional cards? Some scholars (e.g., Abdelrahman, 2019; El-Gamal, 2006) have raised concerns that certain Islamic bond-structuring arrangements closely resemble conventional bonds, particularly when they offer fixed returns and repurchase guarantees despite being labeled as ṣukūk.[98] The industry has implemented structural modifications to sukuk to improve their asset linkages, yet this core dilemma persists: commercial systems must coexist with true Islamic economic principles.[99]

[94] Ryan Calder, "Sharīʿah-Compliant or Sharīʿah-Based? The Changing Ethical Discourse of Islamic Finance," *Arab Law Quarterly* 35/1/2 (2021), 50–73.

[95] Sami Uddin et al., "Legal Foundations For Sharīʿah-Compliant Islamic Banking in Pakistan: Challenges and Way Forward," *Majallah-e-Talim o Tahqiq* 6/4 (December 31, 2024).

[96] Ahmad A. Alkhamees, *A Critique of Creative Shari'ah Compliance in the Islamic Finance Industry* (Martinus Nijhoff Publishers, 2017).

[97] Zamir Iqbal—Abbas Mirakhor, *An Introduction to Islamic Finance: Theory and Practice* (Wiley, 2011); Asutay, "A Political Economy Approach to Islamic Economics."

[98] Abdelrahman Yousri Abdelrahman, "Sukuk: A Critique of Experience, and Their Possible Role in Muslim Countries Development," *International Journal of Islamic Economics and Finance Studies*, (2019); El-Gamal, *Islamic Finance*.

[99] Ahm Ershad Uddın—Ayhan Hira, "Bangladeş'te Kira Sertifikası (Sukuk) Uygulamasının İslam Hukuku Açısından Analizi," *Kafkas Üniversitesi İlahiyat Fakültesi Dergisi* 10/20 (July 28, 2023), 577–601.

1.6.2.3 Form versus Substance: The Ethical Shortfall in Islamic Finance

The tendency to prioritize formal and substantive ethical integrity in the Islamic finance discourse is a common concern. Although contracts such as murābahah, ijārah, and bayʿ al-ʿīnah fit the structural parameters of Sharīʿah, they frequently lack ethical essence (rūḥ al-sharīʿah) based on the maqāṣid al-sharīʿah construct, that is, justice, rationality, and equitable allocation.

According to practical analysis, the widespread use of debt-like instruments to emulate traditional interest-based financing systems has drawn criticism. For example, murābaḥah is often structured in a way that avoids genuine risk-sharing and effectively transforms the entire matter into a de facto loan. The same criticism may also be made of sukūk al-ijārah and tawarruq, which, while being formally Sharīʿah compliant, frequently disguises economic relationships under the guise of legal allegories.

A disagreement between permissibility (ḥilliyyah) and ethical ends (maqṣad) has been called by critics "Sharīʿah-washing," where observed conformity to the norms of Sharīʿah cloaks the absence of moral gravity. Compliance is essential but insufficient. In keeping with the burgeoning maturation of Islamic finance, it has become increasingly evident that contracts must be reviewed not only in terms of their form but also in terms of their function, effect, and moral purpose.

These challenges vary across regions. For example, these problems are exacerbated in South Asia by dual legal regimes, institutional barriers, and a disparity in Sharīʿah understanding between practitioners and consumers. Consequently, ethical critiques are not just theoretical; they are also applicable to product design, governance, and legitimacy.

1.6.3 Sharīʿah-Washing and the Formalism Critique

Some critics have started using the term "*Sharīʿah-washing*" as a financial relationship analogy to "*green-washing*," which happens in environmental finance. The practice involves declaring financial products Islamic when they do not adhere to Islamic principles in their actual substance. A narrow approach that seeks a simple fatwa by meeting bare requirements may cause people to disregard the wider ethical aspects of transactions. An Islamic bank can secure an Islamic identity by funding short-term murabah investments, which provide liquidity for luxury item purchases.

However, these transactions failed to serve fundamental Islamic societal purposes.[100] Institutes of Islamic finance occasionally neglect essential Islamic poverty relief tools such as zero-interest benevolent loans[101] and zakāt service integration because they do not generate adequate profit margins.[102] Many Islamic banks exploit Islamic branding to gain Muslim clients while having little genuine dedication to Islamic economic values. Analysis of Islamic bank *Maqāṣid* performance includes checking how these institutions promote well-being and achieve social justice, while ensuring fair access. Research demonstrates advancement, yet Islamic financial institutions remain below their optimal best practice standards. Research reveals that Islamic banks have enhanced their social and ethical reporting from 2008 to 2016; however, their attainment of the *Maqāṣid* industry standards remains insufficient.[103]

A comparative ethical assessment of Sharīʿah-compliant financial instruments, including murābaḥah, ṣukūk, and Islamic credit cards, is provided in Table 1.2. This table presents three real-world Islamic finance case studies: Murābaḥah for luxury cars, fixed-return ṣukūk, and Islamic credit cards, evaluating their Sharīʿah compliance and ethical concerns. While each product technically meets legal requirements, the table interrogates its alignment with the higher objectives of Islamic law (maqāṣid al-sharīʿah), particularly in areas such as risk-sharing, social welfare, and economic justice. Discussion prompts encourage critical reflection on whether these instruments genuinely fulfill Islamic ethical principles or risk replicating conventional financial logic under Islamic labels.

[100] Calder, "Sharīʿah-Compliant or Sharīʿah-Based?," 55.

[101] Ahm Ershad Uddın, "Through Islamic Banks' Zakat House (IBZH): Investment of Zakah Funds in Microfinance to Remove Poverty in Bangladesh: A New Model," *Uluslararası İslam Ekonomisi ve Finansı Araştırmaları Dergisi* 2/1 (March 1, 2016), 1–25.

[102] Ahm Ershad Uddın—Hüseyin Okur, "Empowering Communities: Redefining Zakat Distribution in Bangladesh Post-Covid-19," *Kocatepe İslami İlimler Dergisi* 6/2 (December 15, 2023), 419–438.

[103] Arman Mergaliyev et al., "Higher Ethical Objective (Maqasid al-Shari'ah) Augmented Framework for Islamic Banks: Assessing Ethical Performance and Exploring Its Determinants," *Journal of Business Ethics* 170/4 (2021), 797–834.

Table 1.2 Comparative ethical assessment of Sharīʿah-compliant financial instruments

No	*Case study*	*Category*	*Details*
1	Murābaḥah for luxury car	Scenario	A leading Islamic bank advertises a Sharīʿah-compliant murābaḥah financing scheme for high-end luxury cars. The bank purchases the car, adds profit, and resells it with deferred payments over 5 years
1	Murābaḥah for luxury car	Sharīʿah compliance	✓ Avoids ribā (interest) ✓ Asset-based structure ✓ Approved by the Sharīʿah board
1	Murābaḥah for luxury car	Ethical concerns	✕ Is a luxury item aligned with maqāṣid (public welfare)? ✕ Replicates conventional loans in structure ✕ Weak on social justice/need-based financing
1	Murābaḥah for luxury car	Discussion prompt	Does this deal fulfill the form of Sharīʿah while neglecting its ethical purpose? Can such a product reflect Islamic finance's maqāṣid-based identity?
2	Sukuk with guaranteed repurchase	Scenario	An Islamic bank issues ṣukūk that offer a fixed annual return and guarantee full principal repayment through a repurchase agreement
2	Sukuk with guaranteed repurchase	Sharīʿah compliance	✓ No explicit interest stated ✓ Backed by tangible assets ✓ Approved by internal Sharīʿah board
2	Sukuk with guaranteed repurchase	Ethical concerns	✕ Guarantees on returns and principal mimic conventional bonds ✕ Little risk-sharing involved ✕ The structure may violate the spirit of Islamic economic justice
2	Sukuk with guaranteed repurchase	Discussion prompt	Does guaranteeing returns compromise the risk-sharing principle in Islamic finance? Should ṣukūk replicate conventional bond effects under Islamic names?
3	Islamic credit cards	Scenario	An Islamic bank offers a 'profit-based' credit card that charges late fees to charity. However, delayed payments still incur additional charges
3	Islamic credit cards	Sharīʿah compliance	✓ No interest charged explicitly ✓ Late fees directed to charity ✓ Endorsed by the Sharīʿah board
3	Islamic credit cards	Ethical concerns	✕ Pricing and fee structure resemble conventional interest-based cards

(continued)

Table 1.2 (continued)

No	*Case study*	*Category*	*Details*
			✕ Lacks encouragement for responsible spending ✕ Questionable alignment with maqāṣid principles like fairness and transparency
3	Islamic credit cards	Discussion prompt	Does this credit card structure genuinely serve Islamic ethics, or is it a form of Sharīʿah-washing? Can such instruments reduce the financial burden while remaining profitable?

Source Author's elaboration

1.7 Reform Responses and Ethical Innovation in Islamic Finance

People in the Islamic finance industry actively confront these criticisms. A new trend toward value-based intermediation (VBI) and the integration of ESG principles into Islamic banking has emerged, creating business models that embody ethical values.

1.7.1 Responses and Institutional Innovation

People in the Islamic finance industry actively confront these criticisms. A new trend toward value-based intermediation (VBI) and the integration of ESG principles in Islamic banking has emerged, creating business models that embody moral values. Countries, including Malaysia, Indonesia, and Pakistan, have established value-based intermediation guidelines to motivate Islamic banks to tackle financial inclusion goals while implementing green finance solutions related to the maqāṣid aims of environmental and life protection.[104] More creative profit-and-loss sharing products, including

[104] Zuraida Rastam Shahrom—Sherin Kunhibava, "Malaysia's Sustainable Banking Regulatory Framework: Value-Based Intermediation and Climate Change Principle-Based Taxonomy," *Green Finance Instruments, FinTech, and Investment Strategies: Sustainable Portfolio Management in the Post-COVID Era*, ed. Nader Naifar—Ahmed Elsayed (Cham: Springer International Publishing, 2023), 125–166. Aisyah Syahidah Shafruddin—Shahida Shahimi, "Strategy and Challenges of Value-Based Intermediation Implementation: The Case of BIMB," *Qualitative Research in Financial Markets* 17/1 (May 16, 2024), 153–168. Muhammad Musa, "Integration between ESG Goals and Value-Based Intermediation

venture capital funds and crowdfunding platforms, operate as modern implementations of mushārakah and muḍārabah principles.[105] The concept of "Sharīʿah-based" in product development encompasses micro-sukuk that support charitable endowments and educational projects, extending beyond basic compliance requirements to serve social purposes.[106] Islamic banks comply with the same economic system while meeting performance requirements and financial expectations, similar to those of conventional banks. Islamic financial institutions operate under competitive profitability requirements while managing customers, who typically prefer fixed-return investments, resulting in the dominance of debt-like products. Islamic banks maintain regulatory approval, because their profit-sharing modes present risks that regulators want to decrease. The resulting circumstances sometimes lead Islamic finance to adopt restricted operational models.

The industry meets Sharīʿah legal requirements at Islamic financial institutions; however, doubts persist regarding their adherence to complete ethical principles and genuine Islamic economic justice standards. Scholars' sense of moral inadequacy prompts them to question whether legal compliance indicates proper ethical conduct in Islamic finance. The tension between appearance and reality gives rise to the term "Sharīʿah-washing," which symbolizes these contrasting discrepancies in contemporary Islamic finance operations.

1.7.2 Secular versus Islamic Ethical Paradigms

Islamic finance compares with wider ethical financial practices known as ESG (Environmental, Social, and Governance) investing. Islamic financial systems operate within ethical boundaries by rejecting businesses that can lead to societal damage.[107] This component prevents financiers from funding pork production, alcohol manufacturing, and gambling. The philosophy of secular ethical finance permits interest, while its focus

Approach within the Paradigm of Islamic Finance," *Islamic Banking and Finance Review* 10/2 (December 28, 2023), 31–54.

[105] Norliana Hamber—Mohamed Haneef, *Waqf-Based Social Micro Venture Fund: A Proposal for the Malay-Muslim Community in Singapore* (SSRN Scholarly Paper, October 23, 2017), Social Science Research Network, papers.ssrn.com.

[106] Uddın, "Through Islamic Banks' Zakat House (IBZH)."

[107] Beebee Salma Sairally, "Integrating Environmental, Social and Governance (ESG) Factors in Islamic Finance: Towards the Realisation of Maqāṣid al-Sharīʿah," *ISRA International Journal of Islamic Finance* 7/2 (December 15, 2015), 145–154.

centers on other critical matters such as climate change and labor rights. However, tensions arise when Islamic finance fund sectors like fossil fuels or unsustainable resource extraction, which, while permissible under Sharīʿah, conflict with global ESG metrics. For instance, several GCC-based Islamic financial institutions financed unacceptable oil infrastructure projects under ESG screening. Conversely, ethical investment funds often invest in interest-based green bonds, which Islamic investors must avoid, despite their environmental benefits. Islamic funds adopt ESG screening methods, whereas ethical funds view Islamic finance as a partner to support responsible investment practices.[108]

The ethical foundation of Islamic finance and the ESG framework create practical conflicts due to variations in their operational methodologies. A typical real-world example illustrates the different paths between ESG and Islamic finance principles. Islamic financial institutions within the Gulf, such as Al Rajhi Bank and Dubai Islamic Bank, use Sharīʿah-compliant murābaḥah and ijārah contracts to finance oil development and infrastructure. These investments have clear Islamic legal backing since they prevent both the ribā and the trade of prohibited goods. Investments create social and environmental dilemmas, primarily when judged according to maqāṣid-based criteria, including ecological care and principles of public well-being. European and U.S. ESG-aligned investment funds that run ESG-aware funds and purchase Climate Awareness Bonds from the European Investment Bank match the sustainability criteria but retain their interest-based nature, invalidating them according to Islamic law. Islamic finance upholds formal Sharīʿah standards, whereas ESG finance relies on performance-based ethical standards, particularly assessments related to climate change and workplace welfare. An optimal integration demands that Islamic finance enhances its environmental ethics through istiḥsān or maṣlaḥah mursalah and permits ESG frameworks to recognize religious-exclusive criteria, thereby forming an all-encompassing ethical financial system worldwide.[109]

[108] Hazik Mohamed, "Integrating Shariah Principles with ESG for Sustainable Finance: A Comprehensive Framework," *World Scientific Annual Review of Islamic Finance* 02 (January 2024), 2450002.

[109] For real-world parallels, see: Qatar Islamic Bank (2020). *Annual Report* [https://www.qib.com.qa/en]; European Investment Bank (2023). *Green and Sustainability Bonds* [https://www.eib.org]; BlackRock (2023). *ESG Aware iShares Fund Details* [https://www.blackrock.com].

Table 1.3 presents a structured comparison of Sharīʿah compliance and ESG principles, demonstrating areas of convergence and ethical tension. This table provides a side-by-side comparison of Islamic Sharīʿah-compliant finance and the globally recognized Environmental, Social, and Governance (ESG) framework. It highlights key areas of convergence, such as ethical investment, social responsibility, and risk avoidance, while also noting the differences in foundational sources, enforcement mechanisms, and religious grounding. This comparison underscores the potential for dialogue and integration between Islamic financial ethics and modern sustainable finance discourse.

The lending processes of conventional ethical banks enable them to support responsible projects with interest, but Islamic banking institutions are prohibited from participating in this practice. An Islamic bank supports the financing of a halal-certified business, even though it involves fossil

Table 1.3 Sharīʿah compliance versus ESG principles in practice

Aspect	*Islamic finance example*	*ESG finance example*
Project	Financing of upstream oil development in the Gulf	Investment in European Investment Bank (EIB) Green Bonds
Institution	Qatar Islamic Bank (QIB), Al Rajhi Bank (via syndicated Sharīʿah-compliant funding)	BlackRock ESG Mutual Funds; EIB's Climate Awareness Bonds
Compliance	Compliant with Sharīʿah (oil is not haram; no ribā)	ESG-compliant (climate positive, green-rated)
Ethical tension	Project contributes to long-term carbon emissions, challenging *istiḥsān* and *maṣlaḥah*	Fund earns interest income, violating Islamic prohibition on ribā
Social impact	Supports national revenue and jobs but harms ecological maqāṣid	Environmentally responsible, but inaccessible to Muslim investors
Broader implication	Lack of climate screening in Islamic finance weakens ethical positioning	ESG ethics overlook religious finance values like Sharīʿah compliance
Ribā	Prohibited	Permissible
Ethical screening	Based on Sharīʿah categories	Based on sustainability metrics
Charity obligations	Zakāt/Waqf integral	Voluntary CSR frameworks

Source Author's elaboration

fuel production, because Islam permits it. However, green ethical funds remain away from such investments. A perfect outcome will occur when Islamic finance unites its distinctive operational principles of risk-sharing and asset-backing with the global finance reform debate, alongside inclusive learning from conventional ethical approaches to transparency standards and measurement methods.

A major criticism of modern Islamic finance is its growing preference for strict legal formality, which undermines the ethical and economic substance and social objectives envisioned by Islamic law. Several regulatory bodies and scholars support the restoration of maqāṣid al-Sharīʿah, the higher objective of Islamic law, within financial operations.[110] The renewal movement relies on the proper implementation of risk-sharing principles rather than their symbolic presence alone. Financial instruments require a structured design that bases their essential function on profit- and loss-sharing, as equity and partnership are fundamental Islamic economic values. Muḍārabah and mushārakah instruments should not be used to transfer total financial risk to one party while the financier secures almost certain profits.[111] Specific Islamic contracts may follow Sharīʿah's legal requirements, but such use damages the core risk-sharing principle that their original purpose is intended to create. Promoting the value of ʿAdl (justice) demands proactive action regarding prices, contractual terms, and customer interaction. Islamic financial institutions must implement ethical pricing and transparent operations in combination with non-exploitative practices to effectively implement the substantive value of justice in their operations.[112] Islamic finance mandates avoiding the use of multiple contracts within short periods in order to create a facility that imitates interest-bearing loans through alternative arrangements. Strategies that may satisfy official legal requirements represent possible violations of the essential understanding of prohibitions involving riba (usury), gharar (excessive uncertainty), and maysir (speculation).[113]

[110] M. Umer Chapra, *The Future of Economics: An Islamic Perspective* (Kube Publishing Ltd, 2016).

[111] Mahmoud A. El-Gamal, *Islamic Finance: Law, Economics, and Practice* (Cambridge University Press, 2006).

[112] Usmani, *An Introduction to Islamic Finance.*

[113] Hans Visser, *Islamic Finance: Principles and Practice, Third Edition* (Edward Elgar Publishing, 2019).

Standard-setting bodies at the forefront voiced their agreement on this matter. The Accounting and Auditing Organization for Islamic Financial Institutions (AAOIFI) and Islamic Financial Services Board (IFSB) have officially warned about formal contracts that lack fundamental objectives derived from Sharīʿah.[114] Several standards published by these institutions show that Islamic financial products must fulfill their contractual terms while avoiding any denials of Sharīʿah purposes, whether explicitly stated or implied.[115] AAOIFI Shari'ah Standard No. 29 warns financial institutions to avoid designing deferred payment sales that resemble interest-based conventional transactions while highlighting Islamic finance features.[116] These concerns have prompted national panel bodies of Shari'ah advisors to respond through established boards. Central Shari'ah boards operating in Malaysia, Pakistan, and Bahrain have prohibited certain agreements that they consider deceptively engineered and include questionable methods, such as ʿīnah (buy-back) and tawarruq arrangements. Current measures show increasing acceptance within institutional frameworks that formal compliance standards should replace ethical authenticity in Islamic finance.[117] The substance-based method now appears in the newly developed banking solutions. Several Islamic banks now combine their credit cards with debt management consultations and debt payment mechanisms linked to zakat and waqf funds, making it difficult for borrowers to default on payments.[118]

This strategic shift within Islamic finance represents a conceptual departure from mere conventional replication, as it aims to fulfill both the ethical and social goals and developmental objectives of the Sharīʿah. Islamic finance regains its status as a moral financial model by integrating maqāṣid-based criteria across its design and management process, including delivery systems.

[114] Htay, S., & Salman, S. (2015). Theoretical Concepts of Good Governance Practices for Waqf (Islamic Endowment) Institutions. International Conference on Management, Leadership & Governance, (), 111–117.

[115] "STANDARDS," *Islamic Financial Services Board* (Accessed April 6, 2025).

[116] "Accounting and Auditing Organization for Islamic Financial Institutions" (Accessed April 6, 2025).

[117] "Shariah Resolutions in Islamic Finance" (Accessed April 6, 2025).

[118] Patria Yunita, "Developing A Modern Zakat Management Model Digital Technology 4.0 Version," *AZKA International Journal of Zakat & Social Finance*, (March 30, 2021), 139–156.

1.7.3 Community-Based Critiques and Reform Recommendations

Part of the Muslim community has directed critical evaluation in Islamic banking because Muslims, and particularly Islamist organizations, believe that it fails to deliver an authentic substitute for traditional banking frameworks.

A significant point of debate lies in how Islamic banks circumvent riba-related interests by charging fees through markup systems that produce comparable or higher financing expenses than conventional banks. The financial experience of customers at Islamic banks has gained approval from users owing to its relative advantage over traditional banking. According to the research findings, the economic outcomes experienced by consumers at Islamic banks that follow Shari'ah principles show little distinction from those of conventional banks.[119]

In many Muslim societies, segments of the religious community continue to express concern that Islamic banks, despite their formal adherence to Sharīʿah principles, remain subject to secular legal and regulatory frameworks that do not fully reflect the aspirations of Islamic economic justice. These individuals observe that the broader financial architecture, often rooted in Western legal and economic models, constrains the operations of Islamic banks, particularly in areas such as governance, dispute resolution, risk sharing, and social impact. As a result, suspicions arise regarding the true distinctiveness of Islamic banking practices, with questions about whether Sharīʿah-compliant structures can fully deliver the ethical and redistributive aims of Islamic law while operating within systems that prioritize profitability, market stability, and consumer protection from a secular perspective. This tension underscores the necessity for ongoing reform and innovation to align Islamic financial institutions more closely with the values and objectives inherent in maqāṣid al-Sharīʿah.

A substantial proportion of religious members in Muslim nations doubt that Islamic banks respect Islamic economic justice principles because they operate within secular legal systems that conflict with their laws. Members of this group observe how Western financial structures, grounded in legal and economic models, influence Islamic banking practices by limiting their operations in areas such as organizational governance, dispute resolution systems, risk-sharing, and social outcomes. People have begun to question the true depth of Islamic banking practices because their

[119] "Islamic Banking, American Regulation | Richmond Fed" (Accessed April 6, 2025).

operations under financial systems are still dominated by secular standards that emphasize profit generation, market stability, and consumer protection. The need for continuous improvement through innovation is vital to enable Islamic financial institutions to align fully with their maqāṣid al-Sharīʿah, the foundational principles of Islamic law.

In response to these challenges, some Muslims advocate for a re-evaluation of the current Islamic banking framework. Several activists recommend establishing cooperative and credit union financial institutions under local community control, as these institutions align better with Islamic values related to communal responsibility and mutual interdependence. The recommendation includes integrating social finance with Islamic finance through obligatory almsgiving, comments, and microfinance instruments to financially benefit both wealthy and underprivileged populations. Research has investigated combination models of the zakāt and waqf principles to develop Islamic microfinance approaches to address poverty in its different forms.[120] The Islamic finance sector has begun to recognize the criticisms leveled against it. Through its strategic objectives, the Islamic Development Bank (IsDB) incorporates approaches that promote sustainability and inclusiveness to address poverty and resilience concerns. IsDB's strategic approach focuses on sustainable economic growth and human capital development, demonstrating its commitment to comprehensive social and financial objectives.[121]

Islamic banking experiences substantial tensions because its religious and ethical standards conflict with those established by modern regulatory systems. Islamic banks interact with secular financial frameworks for consumer protection and risk management when operating in existing regulatory systems. Oversight bodies express concern about marketwide interest-free lending, as it may impact profitability and financial stability. Under these regulatory requirements, Islamic banks face boundaries when implementing merciful banking practices. Certain jurisdictions require Islamic banks to participate in conventional deposit insurance systems and central bank facilities that operate through interest-based mechanisms. Initiatives to create Shari'ah-compliant deposit insurance systems are ongoing, but operational hurdles remain in reconciling them with existing

[120] Khalifa Mohamed Ali, *Working Papers*, "Integrating Zakah, Awqaf and Islamic Microfinance for Poverty Alleviation: Three Models Of Islamic Micro Finance," *Working Papers*, (January 19, 2014). Uddın, "Through Islamic Banks' Zakat House (IBZH)."

[121] "IsDB Just Transition Conceptual Framework & Action Plan 2023–2025," 2022.

regulatory structures. Ongoing negotiations with regulatory compliance and Islamic ethical standards requirements exist, because these regulatory frictions demand innovative solutions to keep both types mutually aligned. The development of financial instruments at Islamic financial institutions requires engineers to create solutions that satisfy regulatory standards and Shari'ah principles through dialogue with regulators. Islamic finance maintains its significance in the present age because it combines religious principles with the modern necessities of financial systems. The Islamic financial industry has experienced rapid growth, with a projected $6.7 trillion in assets by 2027 as it expands its operations across 80 countries. The massive growth of Shari'ah-compliant systems worldwide confirms that Islamic financial principles are practical in international markets.[122]

Experts continue to research Islamic finance in order to determine its ethical role and distinctiveness. The buildings used by Islamic and conventional finance systems share similarities; however, distinct core values establish differences in operational frameworks. The goal of Islamic finance promotion should be to build maximum distinctiveness toward establishing a finance system that combines unbiased approaches and fundamental Islamic values. The genuine implementation of Islamic finance depends on the effective execution of the developed ethical principles. Riba avoidance ensures equal treatment in contracts, while gharar avoidance facilitates clear client disclosures to prevent speculative bubbles. Islamic financial resources should promote shared profits by funding small and medium-sized enterprises (SMEs) and social programs rather than focusing on high-end consumer products and government debts. Islamic financing is crucial in Turkey as it offers long-term financing to SMEs, thereby supporting the nation's economic stability.[123]

The global financial world can benefit from Islamic finance, as it provides ethical guidance through concepts that extend their influence throughout multiple regions. The industry can achieve its full potential by avoiding simple Shari'ah compliance and developing innovative Shari' ah-based solutions that fulfill societal financial requirements. The fundamental structures of Islamic finance are already well-developed thanks to

[122] Chloe Domat, "Islamic Finance: Just For Muslim-Majority Nations?," *Global Finance Magazine* (August 1, 2024). Shaima Hasan—Shereen Mohamed, "Navigating Uncertainty: Global Islamic Finance Assets Expected to Exceed 6.7 Trillion by 2027," Financial Market Analyst, *LSEG* (February 26, 2024).

[123] "Turkey's SMEs Prosper Through Islamic Financing," *World Bank* (2016).

their rich legal history and strong scholarly direction, backed by an expanding set of standards, as explained in this chapter. Existing foundations must be utilized appropriately to keep Islamic finance within lawful (halal) parameters while achieving the noble aims (maqāṣid) that justify ethical financing for everyone.

The Islamic finance model offers Muslim societies ethical financial transaction methods while establishing a powerful, universal approach to economic systems that promote social justice in the face of global inequalities.

1.8 Conclusion

The fundamental structures of Islamic finance are already well-developed, thanks to their rich legal history and strong scholarly direction, backed by an expanding set of standards, as explained throughout this chapter. The existing foundations must be utilized appropriately to keep Islamic finance within lawful (halal) parameters while achieving the noble aims (maqāṣid) that justify ethical financing for everyone.

Islamic finance constructs its regulatory framework based on maqāṣid al-sharīʿah, enabling the creation of financial structures that prioritize moral values including justice, transparency, and public benefit. This chapter found that Islamic finance seeks to operate as a legal and ethical system, rather than functioning exclusively through technical or business principles, by analyzing ancient jurisprudential foundations and present-day contract revisions. We need to examine these notions objectively in specific social and economic situations. The subsequent chapter explores practical insights into the implementation and interpretation of legal and ethical foundations in South Asian nations, including Pakistan, Bangladesh, India, Afghanistan, Sri Lanka, and the Maldives. Islamic finance principles experience the development, support, and constraints of diverse regulatory factors, political mandates, and local community standards. This chapter lays the theoretical foundation for understanding Islamic finance as a legal and ethical system rooted in the Sharīʿah. The theoretical framework and jurisprudential building blocks of Islamic finance, as presented in this chapter, are applied to real-world market implementations within regional legal structures in Chap. 2. The comparative analysis examines the patterns and practical adaptations that ethical finance must adopt to thrive in pluralistic postcolonial societies. The chapter uses these findings to introduce an analysis in Chap. 3, examining how the ḥisbah doctrine has managed ethical market oversight in the past and how it could be adapted for modern Islamic financial oversight.

This chapter established the legal and ethical parameters of Islamic finance, emphasizing its fundamental values, contract underpinnings, and the importance of justice, transparency, and maqāṣid-based practices. However, although ethics are not self-contained, they are shaped, contested, or influenced by regional history, political structures, and institutional realities. The subsequent chapter will discuss how these lessons have been applied in diverse environments in South Asia, where Islamic law interacts with secular governments, postcolonial history, and pluralism.

CHAPTER 2

Regional Development of Islamic Finance in South Asia

This chapter lays the theoretical groundwork for the book by framing Islamic finance as a legal-ethical system grounded in Sharīʿah objectives (maqāṣid al-sharīʿah) and classical jurisprudential principles (uṣūl al-fiqh). Having established this ethical and doctrinal foundation, the next chapter shifts focus to the historical development and regional adaptation of Islamic finance across South Asia, beginning with its early manifestations through Muslim trade networks and Sufi institutions.

2.1 Early Islamic Banking Practices in South Asia

2.1.1 Role of Muslim Merchants and Sufi Saints

Early Muslim businesspeople and Sufi saints played pivotal roles in spreading Islamic economic ideas across South Asia by implementing ethical and moral business standards. Their contributions are arranged into multiple essential sections. Muslim businesspeople sought to follow Islamic teachings by offering fair compensation and distributing wealth equally while prioritizing justice at the center of their commercial activities.[1] Sajid and

[1] Rodney Wilson, "Islamic Finance: Principles and Practice By Hans Visser," *Journal of Islamic Studies* 22/1 (January 1, 2011), 143–146.

© The Author(s), under exclusive license to Springer Nature Switzerland AG 2025

A. H. M. E. Uddin, *The Regulation of Islamic Financial Institutions (IFIs) and Ethical Oversight in South Asia*, Palgrave Studies in Islamic Banking, Finance, and Economics,
https://doi.org/10.1007/978-3-032-09828-3_2

Puthenpeedikayil (2015) explain the fundamental concepts of Islamic economics that restrict financial charges and advocate a market-based approach to advance prosperity and social fairness.[2] Sufi saints from the Chishtī order demonstrated a social justice approach that served as the foundation of Islamic economic principles, while they applied spiritual knowledge to their business operations.[3] Sufis incorporated Islamic principles into everyday life by collaborating with locals, promoting sustainable business practices, and distributing charity, known as Zakat.[4] The essential involvement of businesspeople and Sufis cannot hide the barriers they face when implementing Islamic economic principles because of regional customs and conflicting interpretations of Islamic teachings, which sometimes lead to real-life disagreements. The ethical principles developed by Muslim merchants and saints created a framework for Muslim leaders to implement Islamic financial principles in the Mughal era.

The Mughal dynasty, established during the formal empires, was built upon previous foundations by merging Islamic values with their trading systems, public policies, and welfare initiatives.

2.1.2 Economic Ethics and Social Welfare Under the Mughals

Social welfare was the foundational principle of the Mughal Empire because of its essential role in establishing Islamic financial standards. People primarily reached their goals by establishing a waqf with other Shari'ah-compliant practices. Islamic principles integrated by rulers into taxation, trade regulation, and public financing were established within the region's economic framework, enabling economic development and creating a benevolent atmosphere. Waqf established itself as a core Islamic funding tool for the Mughal society to finance social projects. Islamic tradition requires donors to provide assets or properties to charitable organizations, such as mosques and public works, because helping the needy is an Islamic

[2] Sajid Puthenpeedikayil, "Notions of Free Market and Social Welfare in Islamic Economics," *Journal of Modern Accounting and Auditing* 11/9 (September 28, 2015), 476–486.

[3] Sakir Hossain Laskar, "Islam and Sufism in South Asia: Dynamics of the Chishtī Sufi Order," *Islamic Studies* 61/3 (September 30, 2022), 331–343.

[4] Nandini Chatterjee, "The Mughals and the Sufis: Islam and the Political Imagination in India, 1500–1750 By Muzaffar Alam," *Journal of Islamic Studies* 34/3 (September 1, 2023), 423–426.

duty.[5] Through absolute support, the Mughal state preserved waqf operations to achieve its purpose of helping the community.[6] Through this support, the Mughal Empire displayed its dedication to public welfare because Islam required it to follow the Islamic obligation to aid needy people. Zakat and other Mughal rulers followed Islamic taxation doctrines to distribute wealth through Zakat, which supported charitable projects.[7]

The Mughal rule employed Islamic financial standards to organize social welfare programmes through Zakat, Waqf, and Riba restrictions, aiming to diminish poverty and promote economic welfare. During that period, Akbar, along with other Mughal emperors, prioritized Zakat because it was an Islamic requirement that enabled the distribution of funds to support the poor and community development initiatives.[8] Through charitable endowments, Waqf has expanded significantly across the Islamic world, providing sustained funding sources for education, healthcare, and infrastructure development to enhance social welfare.[9]

The broader ethical values of welfare received financial support through legal frameworks that respected Islamic religious law, enabling the development of systematic financial systems based on Shari'ah principles.

2.1.3 *Shari'ah-Compliant Trade and Finance Instruments*

Islamic finance principles guided the Mughals in establishing riba-free, interest-free loan programs, which enabled underprivileged individuals to access financial capital while stimulating economic development beyond traditional interest rates. Through Qard-e-Hassan, they provided benevolent loans that

[5] Beebee Salma Sairally, "Editorial," *ISRA International Journal of Islamic Finance* 16/S1 (May 6, 2024), 1–3.

[6] Minlib Dallh, "Accumulate but Distribute: Islamic Emphasis on the Establishment of Waqf (Pious Endowment): Research Article," *Religion and Development* 2/1 (September 20, 2023), 21–40.

[7] Ahmed Imran Hunjra et al., "The Role of Islamic Social Finance in Poverty Eradication," *Islamic Finance in the Modern Era* (London: Routledge, 2024), 26–39.

[8] Michael Calabria, "Mughal Munificence: Care and Concern for the Poor in Islamic Hindustan from Tuladan to the Taj," *Poverty and Wealth in Judaism, Christianity, and Islam*, ed. Nathan R. Kollar—Muhammad Shafiq (New York: Palgrave Macmillan US, 2016), 31–53.

[9] Ali Akbar Tajmazinani—Zahra Mahdavi Mazinani, "Foundations of Social Policy and Welfare in Islam," *Social Policy in the Islamic World*, ed. Ali Akbar Tajmazinani, International Series on Public Policy (Cham: Springer International Publishing, 2021), 15–35.

embodied shared Islamic values of charity.[10] Islamic teachings, as outlined in the Quran, influenced Mughal policies to promote equal wealth distribution among the different social classes. The rulers implemented these social welfare measures based on divine duty while strengthening their Islamic rulership and devotion to Islamic teachings, according to Gulzar (2022).[11]

Shari'ah-based trade regulations served to protect ethical business standards and prevent unfair business deals. Large-scale funding for infrastructure projects through modern Islamic financial instruments, such as Islamic bonds and insurance, allows the integration of waqf while maintaining Islamic ethical principles.[12] The method successfully included more people in the financial systems and empowered local communities through sustainable practices.[13] The advancement of Islamic financial laws by the Mughal Empire encountered operational hurdles when managing waqfs or charitable trusts, as transparency remains a present-day challenge in contemporary Islamic finance.[14] Before British colonial dominance introduced Western financial principles, South Asia had its own organic system of Islamic economic norms.

The following section explores how colonial influence transformed regional financial institutions and disrupted the Islamic models.

2.2 Influence of the Colonial Period on Financial Systems

2.2.1 Suppression of Islamic Financial Norms Under British Rule

South Asia underwent a significant financial transformation during the British colonial period, which impacted traditional Islamic banking practices. Colonial laws established Western banking practices that violated the

[10] Syed M. Imran Haider Naqvi et al., "Riba Free Loan in Islamic Finance: Key to Social Development and Welfare," *European Online Journal of Natural and Social Sciences* 5/2 (June 26, 2016), 559–567.

[11] Sadia Gulzar, "The Quranic Concept of Economic Welfare," *ĪQĀN* 4/2 (July 30, 2022), 85–95.

[12] Nur Izzatul Afrina Azham, "Islamic Finance for Social Good: Exploring the Synergy Between Sukuk and Waqf," *SSRN Electronic Journal*, (2024).

[13] Toru Miura, "Strategy for Religious Endowment: A Comparative Study of the Waqf," *Endowment Studies* 7/1 (November 17, 2023), 5–21.

[14] Beebee Salma Sairally, "Editorial," *ISRA International Journal of Islamic Finance* 16/S1 (2024), 1–3.

fundamental principles of Islamic financing as they were based on interest rates and profit-making operations. The administration of Islamic financial systems faced suppression due to new regulations that targeted waqf administrations. During British colonial rule, South Asia was introduced to conventional banking systems that utilized interest or riba- and risk-sharing mechanisms as their primary business operations. Islamic financial principles ban interest-based transactions. However, this banking system operates contrary to their viewpoint, as Islamic finance accepts risk sharing only in profit-and-loss arrangements.

A profound change emerged from colonial laws, which altered how waqf was operated by subjecting it to direct control by colonial officials.[15] The British administration assumed control of waqf management, thereby reducing the autonomy of Islamic regional authorities and altering the established local support mechanisms. Under colonial oversight, the change in control authority resulted in a diminished ability of the waqf to benefit the community through the loss of funds that were diverted to non-charitable purposes and mismanaged by colonial officials. Yilmaz (2018) reported that colonial administrators, along with misusing waqf funds, channeled these funds to noncharitable purposes through mismanagement.[16]

Traditional financial instruments aligned with Islamic principles, such as benevolent loans through qard al-hasan, profit-sharing through mudharabah, and endowment through waqf, became less central to conventional banking and gradually gained dominance in Malaysia. The financial sector underwent this change, which caused Islamic finance operations to decrease drastically when people started using conventional banks. Traditional Islamic financial norms are separate from the practices introduced by newly developed banking institutions. The conventional banking system presented Muslims with a challenge because they wanted to follow Shari'ah principles, but did not have many acceptable alternatives. South Asian Muslims worked towards the revival of Islamic finance at the end of colonial times by harmonizing it with emerging state systems and global capitalist frameworks.

[15] Muhammad Zubair Abbasi, *Sharīʿa Under the English Legal System in British India: Awqāf (Endowments) in the Making of Anglo-Muhammadan Law* (University of Oxford, 2013).

[16] ISA YILMAZ, *Essays in Islamic Moral Economy: Developmentalist Promises, the Delusion of Financialisation and Methodological Dilemma* (Durham University, Doctoral, 2018).

2.2.2 *Post-Colonial Responses and Legal Adaptation*

Muslim legal scholars and community leaders have implemented sophisticated discussions to safeguard specific aspects of Islamic law through the dynamic relationship between European administrators and traditional Islamic practices.[17] The emergence of Islamic banking systems following the end of colonial rule sought to bring back Islamic financial principles.[18]

The effects of colonialism have not diminished Islamic financial practices since they have adapted to current circumstances without abandoning core principles. Islamic finance continues to adapt because Western legal systems have not diminished their strong foundation, as shown by ongoing developments in the field.[19]

South Asian economic growth has expanded significantly due to the implementation of Islamic economic concepts, which have promoted social welfare, justice, and equality. Combining these financial concepts creates a system focused on shared risks, moral investments, and altruistic behavior, which fights against poverty while stabilizing the economy. The principles of Islamic banking, which incorporate transaction processes that share profits and losses without involving the riba, lead investors to experience equitable risk distributions.[20] Islamic banks, established as financial institutions, provide underserved individuals with easy access to financial resources, stimulating economic growth and entrepreneurial activities.[21] Islam teaches about sustainable development through its teachings and the importance of zakat and charitable donations.[22] Implementing Islamic-based programs leads to enhanced socioeconomic

[17] Walid Hegazy, "Contemporary Islamic Finance: From Socioeconomic Idealism to Pure Legalism," *Chicago Journal of International Law* 7/2 (January 1, 2007), 581–603.

[18] abdul Ghafar Ismail—Noraziah Che Arshad, "TrackingtThe Pre-and Post Colonial Banking: The Quest for Islamic Banking" (Persidangan Kebangsaan K0-V Malaysia Innovasi Dan Pertumbuhan Ekonomi, Malaysia, 2010), 173–184.

[19] Wang Yongbao, "The Impact of Colonialism and Nationalism on the Marginalization of Islamic Law in the Muslim World," *Malaysian Journal of Syariah and Law* 12/2 (August 21, 2024), 375–387.

[20] See, Wilson, "Islamic Finance."

[21] K. Bjorvatn, *Papers*, "Islamic Economics in Principle and Practice," *Forum for Development Studies* 2 (1998), 229–243.

[22] Muhammad Iqbal Fasa, "Islamizing The System of Economy: Solution Toward An Economical Welfare For The Islamic Landscape," *Yogyakarta State University* 2/1 (2017), 1–23.

outcomes, supplying rural areas with better healthcare and educational services.[23]

Askari et al. (2015) state that Islamic economics contradicts capitalist social standards by championing wealth distribution equality. Islamic economics reforms economic operations through stakeholder participation and participatory decision-making to establish an inclusive economic system.[24] Islamic financial principles provide guidelines for growth; however, the financialization process and market-distorting possibilities limit the effectiveness of social outcomes.

During the initial phase of operations in South Asia, Islamic banks employed two Shari'ah-compliant funding approaches and various deposit methods. The community received financial liquidity support from these revenue streams and achieved economic growth throughout the local area. Islamic banking institutions offer clients savings, current, and investment accounts, as well as various other deposit types. Balancing these financing deposits as liabilities appeared on the balance sheet, according to Alam et al. (2017).[25] The necessary Wadiah (safekeeping) and Mudharabah (profit-sharing) contracts serve financial purposes. Fund deposits in Wadiah arrangements remain untouched; therefore, no profit-sharing exists, yet Mudharabah involves profit-sharing agreements between depositors and banks. Rural interest-free lending societies have become prominent historical practices because of their focus on interest-free financing.[26] Different regions have varying interpretations of Shari'ah compliance, which leads to inconsistent product acceptability, as different areas apply different criteria.[27]

Islamic financial concepts spread widely throughout South Asian communities because of several enabling factors such as qard al-hasan and bay' al-salam. These Islamic finance concepts meet South Asian economic

[23] Bjorvatn, *Papers*, 238.

[24] Hossein Askari et al., *Introduction to Islamic Economics: Theory and Application* (John Wiley & Sons, 2015), 37.

[25] Nafis Alam et al., "Islamic Deposits in Practice," *Islamic Finance*, by Nafis Alam et al., 79–130 (Cham: Springer International Publishing, 2017), 90–93.

[26] Abdul Azim Islahi, "History of Islamic Banking and Finance," *Intellectual Discourse* 26/2 (2018), 403–429.

[27] J. M. Muslimin, "Early Islamic Banking Practices And Current Development: A Survey of Legal History And Service Innovation Nisbah: Jurnal Perbankan Syariah," (2019), 148–157.

requirements, especially for agricultural and small business funding, and resolve concerns regarding moral interest-based lending. According to Bay al-Salam, farmers can access funds ahead of harvest, enabling them to increase their agricultural output. According to a study by Manoori et al. (2018).[28] Qard al-Hasan, or benevolent loans, offers interest-free financing to small and medium enterprises (SMEs), which is crucial for economic growth and job creation in South Asia (Sa'ad & Pitchay, 2019).[29] Research evidence demonstrates the benefits of these concepts, but society does not understand them well. Most farmers and prospective borrowers demonstrate a limited comprehension of contracting operations for Islamic financial products. Islamic financial institutions must launch advanced promotional campaigns supported by educational initiatives to promote their financial products for wider marketplace adoption.

The financial system needs enabling laws to allow card al-hasan and bay' al-salam implementation, because supportive legislation helps these concepts take root effectively. These Islamic financial concepts show great potential; however, South Asian communities face two main implementation obstacles: outreach and regulatory hurdles.[30] To maximize the benefits of these financial solutions, South Asian communities must resolve these problems.

During the colonial period, Islamic financial traditions were disrupted and an institutional void developed alongside public doubt about local financial standards. The termination of colonial administration brought more than just political liberation, as it opened up possibilities for Islamic principles to interact across the legal, financial, and cultural domains. South Asian communities began their journey to recover religious principles and ethical standards, leading to the increased popularity of financial approaches under Islamic law. The period transitioned into new institutional innovation,

[28] Muhammad Tahir Manoori et al., "Feasibility of Bay Salam Finance: A Survey of the Opinions of Stakeholders," *Global Review of Islamic Economics and Business* 6/1 (December 25, 2018), 001.

[29] Auwal Adam Sa'ad—Anwar Bin Allah Pitchay, "Financing SMEs Through the Islamic Qard Al-Hasan: A Proposal of Islamic FinTech Interest-Free Lending for Government Initiatives," *Advances in Finance, Accounting, and Economics*, ed. Nader Naifar (IGI Global, 2020), 54–64.

[30] Badruddin Ibad, "Implementation of Salam and Istishna' Contracts in Islamic Financial Institutions," *Rangkiang: Journal of Islamic Economics and Business* 1/1 (December 28, 2023), 12–24.

merging Islamic principles with economic development requirements in modern times. These early revivalist efforts reinvigorated Islamic identity and reasserted ethical values into Muslim societies.

The following section analyzes how these movements evolved into concrete institutional developments during the postcolonial era.

2.3 Revival of Islamic Finance in the Post-Colonial Period

2.3.1 *Reassertion of Islamic Identity and Ethical Economic Values*

The revival of Islamic finance in the postcolonial period was a result of various interweaving patterns that displayed combined economic and cultural developments. The resurgence of Islamic finance occurred because Muslim communities reestablished their Islamic identity while establishing financial institutions and experienced an increasing demand for ethical financial products. In the post-colonial era, Muslim communities undergoing a cultural revival based on Islamic identity established an interest in connecting financial practices with Islamic principles.[31] Islamic finance established itself as a valid financial system because of this religious movement, which demonstrated Muslims' need to merge religious principles with economic methods.

2.3.2 *Role of Islamic Scholars and Reformist Thinkers*

Islamic scholars, along with intellectuals, led this postcolonial movement through their reinterpretation of Islamic economic principles, adapting them to current socioeconomic needs. Muhammad Nejatullah Siddiqi explained through his work that Shari'ah and fiqh are strong forces behind Islamic finance, which targets social justice above all else, including profit-seeking.[32] Islamic economic practices acquired the maqāṣid al-Shari'ah framework to direct their activities toward societal welfare. Profit and loss sharing have served as the core operational model for Islamic financial institutions, enabling them to function as alternative banking systems that

[31] Abdullah Ibneyy Shahid, *Emergence of Islamic Finance Organizations, 1948–2016* (USA: Cornell University, M.A., 2022).

[32] Muhammad Siddiqi, "Islamic Economics: Where From, Where To?," *Journal of King Abdulaziz University-Islamic Economics* 27/2 (2014), 59–68.

support moral economy principles. These establishments were recognized as modern economic instruments of "re-Islamicization" to support the developmental needs of post-colonial Muslim societies.[33] Muhammad Baqir al-Sadr developed a functional jurisprudence theory that helped Islamic finance adapt to modern needs through compliance with fundamental texts. The strategy developed an adaptable Islamic law system that synchronized financial operations with the modern aspirations of Muslim populations (Hamoudi 2008).[34]

Promoting Islamic finance recovery throughout South Asia depends on competent institutions, strategic infrastructure, innovative regulations, and factors other than ideologies.

2.3.3 Institutional Development and Financial Infrastructure

Islamic financial organizations laid the foundation for this financial revival through Shari'ah-compliant contracts, which cut transaction expenses and built user trust (Shahid, 2022). Moreover, institutions emerged to remedy the traditional financial system failures observed during the global financial crisis, as Benchea (2015) outlined.[35] After colonial rule, Islamic banking emerged as an official system in South Asia through sociopolitical shifts, economic requirements, and religious and financial system integration needs. The Mit Ghamr Savings Bank in Egypt presented an initial template for Islamic financial institutions that South Asia adapted.

The establishment of ethical banking institutions continued to develop Islamic banking and financial services as more organizations emerged to face common challenges. Regulatory backing combined with expanding product diversity creates excellent conditions for Islamic finance expansion, while addressing multiple financial requirements within Shari'ah-compliant standards. South Asian nations, especially Pakistan and Bangladesh, developed their strategies for Islamic banking systems between the 1970s and the

[33] Salah El-Sheikh, "Islamic Economics and Finance, Then and Now: A Fiqhä^{a}-Conomic Perspective on Its Doctrines and Debates," *International Journal of Economics, Management and Accounting* 19/1 (2011).

[34] Haider Hamoudi, "You Say You Want a Revolution: Interpretive Communities and the Origins of Islamic Finance," *Virginia Journal of International Law* 48 (January 1, 2008), 249.

[35] Laura-Ramona Benchea, "Islamic Economics and Finance—a Revival After the Recent Global Financial Crisis," *Ovidius University Annals* 17/2 (2015), 7–12.

1980s. After gaining independence from colonial powers, they searched for financial alternatives to conventional banking models. They sought financial practice reforms that followed the teachings of Islam after colonials weakened religious institutions through interest-based lending, zakat, and waqf deinstitutionalization.[36]

Under the administration of Zia-ul-Haq, Pakistan emerged as the first nation in South Asia to create Islamic banking through economic reforms that focused on Islamic guidelines in the late 1970s. In 1979, the Pakistani government initiated riba-free financial transaction policies and Islamic banking regulations for financial institutions. Between 1985 and 1985, Pakistan started transforming its entire banking system into interest-free operations through profit-and-loss-sharing models. As Chapra (2000) determined, this transition failed because of difficulties reconciling the existing international financial systems.[37]

Bangladesh began accepting Islamic banking in 1971, following its independence, for ideological and practical reasons. The first Islamic bank in Bangladesh, Islami Bank Bangladesh Limited (IBBL), opened its doors in 1983 following local investor participation and funding partnerships with Middle Eastern countries. IBBL provided services under Islamic Shari'ah laws by utilizing partnership-based mudarabah (partnership) and joint venture-based musharakah (joint venture) modes, which attracted customers seeking non-interest-based banking. The continuous growth of the IBBL triggered the opening of other Islamic banks in Bangladesh, which created a strong dual banking system. Since its inception in 1975, the Islamic Development Bank (IDB) has enhanced South Asian Islamic banking development through strategic knowledge exchange programs and financial help. IDB is a primary catalyst for creating Islamic banking systems across Pakistan and Bangladesh. The Organization of Islamic Cooperation (OIC) and related forums motivated South Asian nations to embrace Islamic finance to develop socioeconomic projects based on Islamic values (Iqbal & Molyneux, 2005).[38] This growth caused concern

[36] Muhammad N. Siddiqi, *Muslim Economic Thinking: A Survey of Contemporary Literature (Islamic Economic)* (Islamic Foundation, 2007).

[37] Ahmad Alharbi, "Development of the Islamic Banking System," *Journal of Islamic Banking and Finance* 3/1 (2015), 1–10; M. Umer Chapra, *The Future of Economics: An Islamic Perspective* (The Islamic Foundation, 2000).

[38] M. Iqbal—P. Molyneux, *Thirty Years of Islamic Banking: History, Performance and Prospects* (Palgrave Macmillan, 2005).

about how Islamic finance would preserve its moral and economic principles when it seemed to replicate capitalist systems.

2.3.4 *Profit-and-Loss Sharing and Moral Economy Model*

Problems with conventional financial systems have motivated researchers to implement Islamic finance through sharing methods that establish economic equality and social justice (Yilmaz, 2018). Islamic finance embodies the principles of a moral economy through its profit-and-loss sharing system, which draws support from people who disapprove of traditional capitalist economics. Islamic finance builds its distinctive worth in Muslim societies by combining ethical standards with equitable results in its operational framework.

The development of Islamic banking in South Asia faced major setbacks due to inadequate regulatory mechanisms that could not authorize Shari'ah-compliant financial operations. Programs to establish Shari'ah supervisory boards at financial institutions formed the basis of their first compliance assurance strategy. Authorities in Pakistan and Bangladesh have created progressive financial regulations. However, Islamic finance within conventional banking systems, as well as risk management and liquidity control, remains a significant obstacle according to Khan and Bhatti (2008).[39]

2.3.5 *Capitalist Convergence and Critical Ethical Reflections*

Critics argue that the growth of Islamic finance could create conditions that replicate capitalist systems, although it does not intentionally aim to do so. This critique presents an opportunity to consider Islamic finance as a catalyst for profound social transformation within Muslim communities. Conventional financial patterns pose a significant concern among critics, who argue that Islamic finance falls short of adequately addressing economic inequality and social unrest.[40] Scholarly discussion is needed to return Islamic finance to its true principles, as continuous ethical challenges threaten its social value. The intellectual works of Muhammad Nejatullah Siddiqi and Khurshid Ahmad significantly contributed to the

[39] Fadillah Mansor, "Developments in Islamic Banking: The Case of Pakistan—By M. Mansoor Khan and M. Ishaq Bhatti," *Asian Politics & Policy* 2/2 (April 2010), 301–303.

[40] Siddiqi, "Islamic Economics," 63.

development of Islamic banking theory in South Asia. These scholars have approached Islamic finance as a justice tool. They advocate profit-and-loss sharing, rejecting interest-based lending as exploitative and economically harmful. Through their intellectual efforts, these theorists have created an enriched theoretical base that supports the expansion and development of Islamic Banking. The re-emergence of Islamic finance throughout South Asia occurred through people's initiatives and intellectual discussions; however, its formal establishment required robust state intervention. Pakistan has become the leading nation in the region to integrate Islamic principles into its national financial framework. Pakistan has progressively shifted from spiritual ideals to organizational changes, becoming the leading champion of Islamic banking across South Asia.

South Asian country-specific developments tell different stories because historical, legal, and ethical elements have shaped distinct growth pathways.

2.4 Country Case Studies: Institutional Trajectories and Ethical Audits

2.4.1 Pakistan: Institutional Roots and Applied Ethics

The development of Islamic finance in South Asia took initial steps in Pakistan. The development of Islamic banking within Pakistan's regions remains closely tied to the country's religious foundations, local population demographics, and government support for Shari'ah-compliant financing.[41]

Pakistan's Islamic finance framework emerged from a series of judicial and regulatory efforts aimed at eliminating the ribā and building an alternative financial structure rooted in Sharīʿah. The establishment of the Islamic Ideology Council (IIC), constitutional amendments, and rulings from the Federal Shariat Court (FSC) laid the legal foundation. The State Bank of Pakistan (SBP) and the Securities and Exchange Commission of Pakistan (SECP) became key actors in shaping modern Islamic finance through regulatory frameworks, product guidelines, and Sharīʿah Governance Regulations.[42]

[41] Abu U. Ahmad—Kabir Hassan, "Regulation and Performance of Islamic Banking in Bangladesh," *Thunderbird International Business Review* 49/2 (2007), 251–277.

[42] "State Bank of Pakistan" (Accessed July 30, 2025).

State-supported Islamic financial institutions, such as Meezan Bank and Al Baraka Pakistan, have grown in this environment. Regulatory authorities maintain Sharīʿah boards that vet financial products and contracts based on classical principles, thus allowing a blend of traditional jurisprudence and modern financial instruments.

2.4.1.1 Islamization Policies and Financial Reforms (1977–1985)

When Pakistan gained independence in 1947, everything stemmed from the Muslim history that fought for their independent Islamic nation, free to practice their religious principles openly.[43] Pakistan's national religion is identified as Islam within the framework of the 1973 Constitution, as stated in Articles 1 and 2.[44] In 2024, Pakistan had a total population of 252 million individuals, ranking fifth worldwide in terms of population size.

The strong religious identity of Pakistan shaped the fundamental structures of both politics and economics in the country, which led to nationwide discussions on applying the Shari'ah law to policies. General Zia-ul-Haq implemented the most influential advancement of the Shari'ah law in 1977 during his military dictatorship. When General Zia-ul-Haq took over national leadership, he implemented an Islamization agenda, with financial reform as its core component. In the early 1980s, the banking sector began its mission to eliminate interest-based financial transactions from its operations. These initiatives created essential components for implementing Islamic finance as a structured component of Pakistan's national economic system.[45]

2.4.1.2 Establishment of Meezan Bank and State Bank Guidelines

In 2002, the State Bank of Pakistan developed a strategic framework to boost Islamic banking operations by issuing new guidelines. The institution is guided to assist conventional financial institutions in initiating Islamic banking divisions or separate subsidiaries. During this period,

[43] J. Henry Korson, "Endogamous Marriage in a Traditional Muslim Society: West Pakistan; a Study in Intergenerational Change," *Journal of Comparative Family Studies* 2/2 (1971), 145–155.

[44] The Constitution of Pakistan, 1973,

[45] Usmani, M. T. (2002). *An Introduction to Islamic Finance*. Idara Isha'at-e-Diniyat. Ahmed, H. (2011). "Maqasid al-Shariah and Islamic financial products: A framework for assessment." *Islamic Economic Studies*, 19(1), 1–29.

Meezan Bank opened its doors as Pakistan's initial standalone Islamic bank, thus launching an expansion phase for Shari'ah-compliant financial services.[46]

Subsequent years have brought about substantial changes to the financial industry. The Islamic banking market has been transformed by dedicated Islamic banks and operations managed by conventional institutions. Ghouse and Bhatti (2024) report that Islamic banking in Pakistan has demonstrated powerful resistance, despite pandemic difficulties and political uncertainties.[47]

Pakistan has a mix of conventional and Islamic banks as part of its assorted banking environment in March 2025. The list of six active Islamic financial institutions in Pakistan includes Meezan Bank and others, which operate as full-fledged Islamic banks. Moreover, 16 conventional banks operate Islamic banking branches, referred to as Islamic Banking Windows (IBWs), in addition to a fully functional Islamic banking sector. There are 16 conventional banks operating in Pakistan, all of which provide Islamic banking products. The financial sector of Pakistan contains traditional banking institutions alongside Islamic banking institutions, which total 22 institutions.[48]

2.4.1.3 Shari'ah Governance, SECP Regulations, and AAOIFI Standards

A high-quality Shari'ah governance system establishes the foundation of Islamic banking legitimacy and sustainability. The Pakistani framework for this system has undergone substantial development in the last two decades. The State Bank of Pakistan (SBP) has led Islamic financial institutions (IFIs) in regulation since 2015, forcing all Islamic banks to establish Shari' ah Boards staffed with qualified scholars to monitor compliance. Shari'ah boards maintain dual responsibilities to authorize products and monitor Islamic legal and ethical operational adherence.

The State Bank of Pakistan created extensive regulations on Shari'ah governance in 2018 before issuing new circulars to further develop the system. These cover everything, from the fit-and-proper criteria for Shari'ah scholars to internal and external audit obligations. According to

[46] "State Bank of Pakistan," *Islamic Banking* (Accessed April 21, 2025).

[47] Ghulam Ghouse—M. Ishaq Bhatti, "Strident Response of Islamic Banking Industry to Political, Financial, and Pandemic Events," *Islamic Finance in the Modern Era*, by Hussain Mohi-ud-Din Qadri—M. Ishaq Bhatti, 254–264 (London: Routledge, 2024), 254–264.

[48] "Islamic Banking."State Bank of Pakistan

Zafar and Sulaiman (2023),[49] externally audited Shari'ah standards constitute substantial development that boosts transparency while stopping conflicts of interest. By implementing this system, both Pakistani and global stakeholders experience a high level of assurance about the religious compliance of Shari'ah-compliant assets.

Pakistan's governance model includes AAOIFI guidelines as part of its alignment with international industry standards. Bahrain's founding institution AAOIFI endorses international Shari'ah standards for risk-sharing programs and the framework of *mudarabah* contracts, sukuk issuance rules, and ethical investment criteria testing.[50] Pakistan has selected parts of these standards to provide governance consistency with local-context flexibility. The study conducted by Wasim and Zafar (2023) identified dissimilarities between authority delegation and performance evaluation systems, emphasizing the need to achieve greater standardization.[51]

The Securities and Exchange Commission of Pakistan (SECP) issued SRO 1314(I)/2023 as Shari'ah Governance Regulations to support SBP's initiatives. All Shari'ah-compliant stocks, mutual funds, and corporate entities must follow the set regulations. Companies making Shari'ah compliance claims fulfil three requirements according to these guidelines.

A company participating in Islamic finance must eliminate core business operations that contain elements of prohibited activities, such as interest-based transactions and gambling, as well as industries involving pork products.

- Companies should use official strategies and income limits to screen for noncompliant activities.
- A Shari'ah Supervisory Board must exist and include two qualified scholars in its operational structure.
- The SECP must formally issue a Shari'ah compliance certificate to the organization.

[49] Muhammad Bilal Zafar—Ahmad Azam Sulaiman, "Islamic Banking in Pakistan: Emergence, Growth, and Prospects," *Advances in Finance, Accounting, and Economics*, ed. Abdul Rafay (IGI Global, 2020), 61–77.

[50] Sahibzada Muhammad Wasim Jan, "Shari'ah Governance of Islamic Banking Institutions in Pakistan: An Analytical Overview," *International Journal of Business and Administrative Studies* 6/6 (December 22, 2020), 286–299.

[51] Mustanir Hussain Wasim—Muhammad Bilal Zafar, "Shariah Governance Framework for Islamic Banking in Pakistan: A Critical Review and Comparison with AAOIFI," *Journal of Islamic Accounting and Business Research*, (2023).

These guidelines demonstrate Pakistan's dual objective of preserving Islamic authenticity and stimulating investor trust. However, implementation varies across institutions. Small financial institutions face challenges in achieving compliance standards and transparency, which the major players represented by the Meezan Bank and Dubai Islamic Bank Pakistan manage to achieve success. The independence of Shari'ah boards faces criticism because they bear the responsibility for payment and selection from institutions where they serve as oversight bodies. Several observers contend that central Shari'ah authorities, such as those present in Malaysia and Sudan, should establish standard interpretation methods and stop banks from seeking favorable rulings. The growing Islamic finance sector requires increased harmony among the SBP, SECP, and AAOIFI guidelines for stability purposes, risk management, and global market development.

2.4.1.4 *Risk Management, Financial Products, and Market Share*

Islamic banking in Pakistan employs ethical investment systems through risk-sharing practices because this approach differs from traditional interest-based banking models. The Shari'ah-compliant financing tools, including Murabaha (cost-plus sale), Ijarah (leasing), Musharakah (diminishing partnership), Istisna (manufacturing finance), Salam (forward sale), and Sukuk (Islamic bonds), provide Shari'ah-compliant investment options for a diverse investment strategy. Qard non-profit current accounts, Mudarabah profit-sharing savings, and term deposits operate in the deposit category to promote participatory banking across the system.

The risk management system in Islamic banking emphasizes operational control, credit analysis, and liquidity oversight. However, some researchers claim that this oversight is comparable to traditional banking measurements (Akram & Rahman, 2018).[52] Although social responsibility remains the core focus of this approach to investing, emphasis remains on practices that promote inclusive welfare management (Asad et al., 2018).[53]

Islamic banking institutions in Pakistan have demonstrated ongoing growth in their market share alongside an expansion of their network

[52] Hassan Akram—Khalil Ur Rahman, "Credit Risk Management: A Comparative Study of Islamic Banks and Conventional Banks in Pakistan," *ISRA International Journal of Islamic Finance* 10/2 (December 10, 2018), 185–205.

[53] Dr. Muzaffar Asad et al., "A Crital Review of Islamic and Conventional Banking in Digital Era: A Case of Pakistan," *International Journal of Engineering & Technology* 7/4.7 (September 27, 2018), 57–59.

systems. During March 2024, Islamic banks managed to control 20% of the country's total assets and secure 23% of the total deposits within the Pakistani banking sector while demonstrating consistent yearly growth. The sector advanced with increased funding from Shari'ah-compliant financial activities as net financing and investment activities expanded significantly.

Islamic financial institutions expanded their banking branch presence by 15.2% during this period, and conventional banks increased their Islamic banking window (IBW) offerings by 4.6% annually, as growing institutions and customers sought to utilize Islamic financial services.[54] The State Bank of Pakistan's Strategic Plan (2021–2025) outlines specific targets for the expansion of Islamic banking. The plan aims for assets to reach 30% of total assets, deposits to reach 30%, and the national branch network to reach 35% by 2025.[55]

2.4.1.5 Institutional Challenges: Profitability, Regulation, and Duality

Despite facing multiple institutional challenges, Pakistan's Islamic banking sector continues to maintain strong growth rates. Potential solutions are being addressed to Islamic finance's three main challenges: profitability issues, regulatory alignment problems, and the concurrent operation of multiple banking systems. This instills a sense of hope and optimism in the audience regarding the future of Islamic banking in Pakistan. Islamic banking institutions in Pakistan face unique profitability challenges, operating amid economic instability and rising inflation.

While large institutions, such as Meezan Bank, demonstrate robust profit margins through operational scale benefits and existing customer networks, smaller Islamic banks face cost inefficiencies due to their limited client reach and compliance requirements.[56] According to Junejo et al. (2023), increasing capital adequacy requirements and liquidity rules from the SBP lead to heightened profitability pressure.[57]

[54] State Bank of Pakistan. (2023). *Islamic Banking Bulletin.*

[55] "Pakistan's Islamic Finance Prospects Positive on Government Push" (Accessed April 21, 2025).

[56] Nafisa Awan et al., "X-Efficiency Analysis of Islamic Banks in Pakistan," *Contemporary Issues in Social Sciences and Management Practices* 4/4 (December 31, 2023), 340–354.

[57] Safiullah Junejo et al., "Unravelling the Drivers of Profitability in Pakistani Islamic Banking: An Investigation of Key Factors," *Jurnal Ekonomi Pembangunan: Kajian Masalah Ekonomi Dan Pembangunan*, (April 1, 2023), 161–171.

The business constraints on conventional hedging tools and interest-based income have led Pakistani Islamic banks to develop new revenue-generating approaches.

The regulatory structures between Islamic banking regulations and conventional laws create the second major obstacle for cross-examining the frameworks. Pakistan's dual banking structure requires Islamic institutions to comply with the Shari'ah requirements and all original SBP regulations intended for interest-based financial organizations. The dual nature of Islamic financial regulations leads to an assessment process in which products are occasionally evaluated using conventional risk models that can produce incorrect results and hinder innovative ideas. Liquidity management instruments that conform to the Shari'ah principles require further development, as they still present operational restrictions in short-term interbank market transactions (Bashir & Azeez, 2022; Kisman, 2020).[58]

Standardization is a crucial requirement that must be addressed urgently. While the SBP has made excellent progress in unifying Shari'ah governance, individual institutions have maintained distinct governance systems. The lack of standardization in Islamic banking creates uncertainty regarding its genuine Islamic nature. Standardization is vital for Islamic banking to ensure credibility and development.

Markets expect specific financial performance returns from Islamic banking institutions. Customers often compare Islamic banking services with conventional banking products in terms of profit and service, forcing Islamic banks to deliver returns that mimic interest by using Shari'ah-compatible investment methods. However, Ahmad and Zakariyah (2020) revealed that accusations of superficial ethical transformations have emerged through standard financial operations observed in Islamic banking, which fail to uphold their core moral values.[59]

The Federal Shari'ah Court (FSC) enforced the April 2022 changes, which introduced the dual effect of positive potential and heightened

[58] Zainul Kisman, "Risk Management: Comparative Study Between Islamic Banks and Conventional Banks," *Journal of Economics and Business* 3/1 (2020).

[59] Altaf Ahmad—Habeebullah Zakariyah, "A Comparative Performance Analysis of Islamic and Conventional Banking: A Case Study of Pakistan," *The Importance of New Technologies and Entrepreneurship in Business Development: In The Context of Economic Diversity in Developing Countries*, ed. Bahaaeddin Alareeni et al., Lecture Notes in Networks and Systems (Cham: Springer International Publishing, 2021), 1772–1809.

demanding conditions. The decision requires all Pakistani banking institutions to establish interest-free banking operations by December 2027, with substantial support from religious experts and reform leaders. Such implementation requires substantial barrier breakthroughs. The State Bank of Pakistan highlights its concerns about the significant financial needs needed to build capacity, update laws, and introduce new products into the market. Pakistan struggles between its doctrine of interest-free finance and its dependency on loans from the Asian Infrastructure Investment Bank (AIIB) through interest-bearing agreements. Pakistan relies on traditional and climate-focused borrowing activities to bridge its financial gaps. It is working towards acquiring $2-3 billion in the following years for its climate resilience. Pakistan was the first Muslim nation to declare modern bank interest arrangements unlawful through an official declaration.[60]

The future success of Islamic banking in Pakistan depends heavily on overcoming fundamental issues, despite current achievements in growth, public trust, and institutional development. To lead the Islamic finance sector internationally, the country requires standardized policies and innovative liquidity solutions backed by clear regulatory frameworks and a genuine commitment to ethical principles.

Bangladesh established its Islamic finance system through cultural pluralism rather than Pakistan's state-directed approach to Islamization. The evolution of Islamic finance in Bangladesh occurred through the development of Bengali Muslim culture, which merged religious doctrine with language, expression, and visual arts, alongside communal traditions. The following section analyses how Islamic banking adopted its structure by combining religious morals with social support systems and communal financial services.

Table 2.1 presents a targeted set of policy tools designed to enhance the governance infrastructure of Islamic finance in Pakistan. It addresses key areas, such as Sharīʿah board effectiveness, regulatory integration, transparency mechanisms, and institutional coordination. This table provides practical recommendations for regulators, financial institutions, and academic bodies to reinforce ethical and legal compliance across sectors.

Ethical Implications in Practice: While Pakistan's formal Sharīʿah governance appears rigorous, real-world tensions often arise between compliance

[60] Shahbaz Rana, "Govt Announces End to Riba in Five Years," *The Express Tribune* (November 9, 2022).

Table 2.1 Policy Toolkit-Strengthening Islamic finance governance in Pakistan

Policy action	*Lead actor(s)*	*Timeline*
Expand Shari'ah Supervisory Boards to include independent ethics scholars	SECP + Meezan Bank + SBP	Within 1–2 years
Institutionalize *Maqāṣid Performance Ratings* in annual reports	Pakistan Banking Association + SBP	Medium-term (2–3 yrs)
Digitize fatwa repositories and connect them to Islamic product portfolios	Ministry of IT + SBP Shari'ah Boards	1 year
Formalize the inter-madhhab legal harmonization committee	Council of Islamic Ideology	Immediate rollout
Create Ḥisbah-inspired regulatory offices within major Islamic banks	Internal Compliance Divisions	Within 2 years

Source Author's own

and profitability. For instance, ***murābaḥah*** (cost-plus financing) remains the dominant product despite ethical concerns over its resemblance to conventional interest-based loans.[61] Though formally compliant, the excessive markup practices in some institutions risk undermining the maqāṣid al-sharīʿah's aim of fairness and social welfare. In 2022, the SBP had to issue guidance to discourage banks from inflating profit rates disguised as administrative charges.[62]

In addition, ethical dilemmas emerge when liquidity constraints compel institutions to park funds in Sharīʿah-compliant treasury instruments that functionally resemble bonds. These examples show how institutional pressure and market realities test Islamic finance's ethical aspirations. Moreover, cases of "Sharīʿah arbitrage" have been reported, in which banks switch between interpretations to justify questionable practices.[63] Such actions raise questions about the integrity of the compliance process and the independence of the Sharīʿah boards. A more maqāṣid-oriented audit structure and ongoing ethics training for practitioners could help reduce this form-over-substance dilemma.

[61] Hasan Zubair, *Islamic Banking and Finance* (London: Routledge India, 2022); Sami Uddin et al., "Legal Foundations for Shariah-Compliant Islamic Banking in Pakistan: Challenges and the Way Forward (پاکستان میں اسلامی بینکاری کی قانونی بنیادیں: درپیش چیلنجز اور لائحہ عمل)," *Majallah-Yi Talim o Tahqiq* 6/4 (2024), 1–18.

[62] "State Bank of Pakistan."

[63] Maria Bhatti et al., "Need for Reform in AAOIFI Standards on Murabaha Financing: Evidence from Islamic Banks in Pakistan," *Quality & Quantity* 59/1 (2025), 59–78.

2.4.2 Bangladesh: Institutional Infrastructure and Legal Complexities

Islamic finance in Bangladesh is largely private-sector led, with key players such as the Islami Bank Bangladesh Limited (IBBL), Al-Arafah Islami Bank, and Social Islami Bank. These institutions operate under the oversight of Bangladesh Bank, which does not maintain centralized Sharīʿah authority but allows independent Sharīʿah boards within each bank. Bangladesh has also experimented with dual-window systems that enable conventional banks to offer Sharīʿah-compliant services.

Despite the strong market penetration, critics note that some institutions treat Sharīʿah compliance as a formality. The absence of a unified Sharīʿah supervisory board has led to inconsistencies in rulings and lenient interpretations of core prohibitions, such as ribā and gharar.

2.4.2.1 Historical Evolution of Bengali Muslim Identity

A distinct Bengali Muslim identity began to form after Arabs and Persians conducted business in the delta region, and Sufi shaykhs wandered through the area during the 11th through 13th centuries[64]. Shāh Jalāl of Sylhet established a devotional Islamic tradition that united Quranic moral teachings with local village customs through mosque and khānqāh centers that functioned as religious and community institutions for cultivation, farming, dispute resolution, and charity work.[65] Over time, this syncretic form of agricultural Islam merged Islamic monotheistic beliefs and zakat practices with traditional village celebrations, thus creating a distinctive Muslim culture in Bengal that distinguished itself from elite North Indian *ashraf* communities.[66]

During the Bengal Sultanate (c. 1342–1576), Muslims established their royal authority, while Bengali cultural products flourished in parallel with Persian artistic traditions (Alam, 2003, pp. 67–92). Dhaka transformed into a textile trade hub ruled by Mughal subahs (16th-18th

[64] Richard Maxwell Eaton, *The Rise of Islam and the Bengal Frontier, 1204–1760* (University of California Press, 1993), 1–4.

[65] A. B. M. Habibullah, *The Foundation Of Muslim Rule In India* (Calcutta: University of Calcutta, 1945), 45–53.

[66] Rafiuddin Ahmed, *The Bengal Muslims: 1871–1906; a Quest for Identity* (Oxford University Press, 1981), 20–34.

century). Simultaneously, their bilingual elites worked to build a Shari'ah administration with local artistic elements.[67]

The Hindu bhadralok groups obtained preferences through British colonial policies from 1757 to 1947, which worsened Muslim marginalization, according to Chatterjee.[68] The rural reformer Ḥājī Shāriʿatullāh (c. 1820–1860), alongside other Faraizi members, defended peasant rights against landlord exactions while purging all un-Islamic religious rituals from their cultural practices.[69]

Communal tensions rose after the 1905 Partition of Bengal, yet Bengali Muslims united their religious faith with the preservation of their native languages. The political push by West Pakistan to enforce the use of Urdu led Bangla-speaking Muslims to start the Language Movement of 1952, and they declared that preserving their religious heritage required the protection of Bangla.[70]

During the 1971 Liberation War, Bengali Muslims, together with non-Muslims, combined political grievances with cultural grievances to defend their linguistic heritage and economic rights from West Pakistani dominance.[71] According to Riaz, the post-independence constitutions united secular Bengali nationalism with Islamic values to show the plurality of Bengali Muslim identity, which incorporates elements from both faith and heritage.[72]

2.4.2.2 Cultural–Political Mobilization and Pluralistic Islamic Identity

Throughout the years, Bangladeshi protesters have developed a tradition that combines verses written in Bangla alongside traditional rituals and

[67] Catherine B. Asher—Cynthia Talbot, *India before Europe* (England: Cambridge University Press, 2006), 230–237.

[68] Partha Chatterjee, *Nationalist Thought and the Colonial World: A Derivative Discourse* (Zed Books, 1986), 43–49; Sucharita Sen, *Theorizing a Bengali Nation: Abul Hashim and the United Bengal Movement, 1937–1947* (London: Routledge India, 2024).

[69] Dilip Kumar Chattopadhyay, "The Ferazee and Wahabi Movements of Bengal," *Social Scientist* 6/2 (1977), 42–51.

[70] S.M. Shamsul Alam, "Language as Political Articulation: East Bengal in 1952," *Journal of Contemporary Asia* 21/4 (January 1, 1991), 469–487.

[71] Rounaq Jahan, *Pakistan: Failure in National Integration* (USA: Columbia University Press, 1972), 125–162.

[72] Peter Fowler, "Ali Riaz. Bangladesh: A Political History since Independence," *Asian Affairs* 48/1 (January 2, 2017), 159–161. Abdul Wohab, *Secularism and Islam in Bangladesh: 50 Years After Independence* (London: Routledge, 2023).

calls for justice from the Qur'ān. Although Ziaur Rahman (1977) and H.M. Ershad (1988) added Absolute Trust in Almighty Allah and made Islam the state religion in the Constitution, activists continued to transition seamlessly between mosque sermons and the streets, where they performed Kazi Nazrul's poetry.[73]

In 2011, the Fifteenth Amendment adopted an official doctrine of hybrid practice by reinforcing secularism and upholding Islam as the state religion.[74] in. modern life, Hindus and Christians attend Sufi festivals alongside Muslims, and television broadcasts Islamic Qur'ānic recitation competitions and Tagore musical performances, as noted by Lewis.[75]

The Islamic finance sector employs an approach similar to its operations. According to Bangladesh Bank regulations, every Islamic bank is required to maintain a Shari'ah Supervisory Committee.[76] However, their marketing materials and microfinance handbooks were created in Bangla by coupling fiqh principles with rural village proverbs (nītimālā). Islam Bank Bangladesh Limited positions itself through its annual reports as an "inclusive pious institution" by funding Pohela Boishakh fairs and applying prophetic trade instructions to support both local savers and Gulf investors. Bengali Muslims who relied on syncretic tools to defy colonial powers and dictatorships now use these instruments to support dual banking systems that unite Islamic compliance with Bengali cultural values.

2.4.2.3 The Historical Development of Islamic Finance in Bangladesh

Scholars and policy writers have documented three distinct phases of Islamic finance development in Bangladesh as part of their research. The chronological development of Islamic finance in Bangladesh began with pioneering institutions from 1983 to 1990, followed by regulatory consolidation from 1991 to 2008, and then evolved into a dual-system expansion, which started in 2009 and continues.[77]

[73] Fowler, "Ali Riaz. Bangladesh."

[74] Ali Riaz, *Lived Islam and Islamism in Bangladesh:* (Dhaka: Prothoma Prokashan, 2017).

[75] David Lewis, *Bangladesh: Politics, Economy and Civil Society* (Cambridge University Press, 2011), 209–214.

[76] Alam—Uddın, "Legal and Regulatory Frameworks For Sharī'a Governance Practices in the Islamic Banking Industry of Bangladesh."

[77] Uddin, *Bangladeş'teki İslam Bankacılık Uygulamasının Fıkhî Açıdan.*

Pioneer institution, 1983–1990. Analysts from an Islamic Development Bank Ministry of Finance feasibility mission judged in 1982 that an interest-free bank could succeed by implementing financing through mudarabah and musharakah contracts, and deposits through mudarabah contracts.[78] The Islamic Development Bank and Bangladesh Ministry of Finance made their recommendations in 1982, which led to the creation of Islami Bank Bangladesh Limited (IBBL) in March 1983 for South Asian services.[79] Uddin (2020) evaluated early balance sheet data from IBBL, demonstrating that its asset base grew at 26% annually throughout the first seven years, while state-owned banks showed half that growth.[80]

In 1999, the Bangladesh Bank issued its first Islamic Banking Guidelines as conventional lenders opened "Islamic banking windows" throughout the decade. Uddin (2020) found that the guidelines established by the Bangladesh Bank created profit-and-loss sharing arrangements and post-transaction profit-sharing reserves, which reduced the liquidity risk spread to traditional financial institutions.[81]

Dual-system expansion, 2009-present. In 2009, the Central Shari'ah Board for Islamic Banks of Bangladesh (CSBIB) emerged as a significant upgrade through its standardization of fatāwā procedures while beginning the certification of Shari'ah scholars.[82] Between 2010 and 2020, Bangladesh Bank introduced two guidelines that required every Islamic banking institution to form a five-member Shari'ah Supervisory Committee for quarterly document reporting and the translation of retail financial documentation into Bangla to expand financial access.[83] As a result, the Islamic segment's market share rose from 8.5% of the total banking assets in 2000 to 25% by March 2024. The research performed by Uddin (2024) established that Bangladesh-based Shari'ah-governed banks maintain lower non-performing-loan ratios than conventional banks, despite accounting for asset diversification and economic fluctuations. Through proper governance mechanisms and

[78] Kabir Hassan—Mervyn Lewis, *Handbook of Islamic Banking* (Edward Elgar Publishing, 2009), 292–295.

[79] Habib Ahmed—Mohammad Umar Chapra, *Occasional Papers*, "Corporate Governance in Islamic Financial Institution (Occasional Paper)," *Occasional Papers*, (2002), 118.

[80] Uddin, *Bangladeş'teki İslam Bankacılık Uygulamasının Fıkhî Açıdan.*

[81] Uddin, *Bangladeş'teki İslam Bankacılık Uygulamasının Fıkhî Açıdan.*

[82] Uddin, *Bangladeş'teki İslam Bankacılık Uygulamasının Fıkhî Açıdan.*

[83] Alam—Uddın, "Legal and Regulatory Frameworks For Sharī'a Governance Practices in the Islamic Banking Industry of Bangladesh."

an independent Shari'ah board, Bangladesh has become a premier example of South Asian Islamic finance advancement, establishing a dual banking system with over 25% of total banking assets.[84]

2.4.2.4 Bangladesh's Dual Banking System

In the early 2010s, Bangladesh established a dual banking infrastructure that officially united conventional banking institutions with dedicated Islamic banks and specialized Shari'ah banking operations under unified regulatory oversight. Bangladesh Bank Operates Islamic Banking Operations (rev., 2020) and serves as the core legal framework for the sector, requiring the use of equivalent prudential regulations for Islamic and conventional financial institutions, except when Shari'ah principles restrict their application (Bangladesh Bank, 2020, § 1.2). All Islamic financial entities, including standalone banks or windows, must establish a five-member Shari'ah Supervisory Committee, submit quarterly compliance reports, and maintain separate information and communication technology (ICT) systems and risk-management limits.[85] Section 2 of the Banking Companies (Amendment) Act 2013, which outlines the legal validity of Shari'ah-based contracts, assumes their inclusion in Bangladesh Bank's authorized list.[86]

The Islamic financial sector consists of 10 standalone Islamic banks, 19 Islamic windows, and 31 conventional banks in Bangladesh, as of December 2024. The inter-sector connections within the Bangladesh Bank structure are strong, as Islamic banks deposit their surplus funds into Islamic bond funds and access daily liquidity from conventional financial institutions through commodity murābaḥah transactions. Traditional banks utilize their windows to collect informal rural savings.[87]

[84] Ahm Ershad Uddın, "Bangladeş'teki İslami Bankalarin Vedîa ve Fon Toplama Faaliyetleri: İslam Hukuku Perspektifinden Bir İnceleme," *Akademik Platform İslami Araştırmalar Dergisi* 8/2 (August 30, 2024), 203–227.

[85] A. H. M. Ershad Uddin, "Development of Islamic Insurance (Takaful) in Bangladesh: Legal Barriers and Challenges," *Trabzon İlahiyat Dergisi* 10/2 (2023), 7–30.

[86] Uddin, *Bangladeş'teki İslam Bankacılık Uygulamasının Fıkhî Açıdan.*

[87] Uddin, *Bangladeş'teki İslam Bankacılık Uygulamasının Fıkhî Açıdan.* Alam—Uddın, "Legal and Regulatory Frameworks For Sharī'a Governance Practices in the Islamic Banking Industry of Bangladesh."

These data indicate that Shari'ah governance improves institutional stability. Islamic banks exhibited a 3.2% non-performing loan ratio from 2010 to 2021, while conventional banks maintained a 7.8% ratio according to panel data results that control for macroeconomic factors. The study of the IMF dual system findings supports the COVID-19 data on banks' high liquidity levels. The model gains policymakers' favor by ensuring standardized supervisory regulations and faithful product design, which attracts more Muslims who abstain from using interest-based products.[88] The Bangladeshi template serves as a benchmark standard in the State Bank of Pakistan's Strategic Plan 2019 and the Central Bank of Nigeria's Islamic Finance Roadmap 2021, to advance the dual-system approach.

2.4.2.5 *Shari'ah Governance and Oversight Mechanisms*

The three-tier Shari'ah governance framework polices Bangladesh's Islamic finance sector. At the institutional level, each Islamic bank or window needs to appoint a five-member Shari'ah Supervisory Committee (SSC), empowered to vet products ex-ante and audit compliance; Bangladesh Bank's *Guidelines for Islamic Banking Operations* (2020) stipulate that SSC members may not simultaneously serve on the bank's audit or risk committees, a safeguard designed to curb conflicts of interest.[89] At the industry level, the Central Shari'ah Board for Islamic Banks of Bangladesh (CSBIB)—a not-for-profit body registered in 20—issues sector-wide fatāwā, organizes scholar certification, and, since 2018, conducts peer reviews of SSC, and the CSBIB review score significantly with low Shari'ah noncompliance income in member banks.[90] Finally, Bangladesh Bank exercises macro-oversight through its Islamic Banking Cell, which performs on-site Shari'ah inspections and can impose fines for repeated noncompliance. In 2022, the central bank levied penalties on three institutions for misbooking murābaḥah receivables as trading income (Islamic Financial Services Board).[91]

[88] Hasanul Banna et al., "Islamic Banking Stability amidst the COVID-19 Pandemic: The Role of Digital Financial Inclusion," *International Journal of Islamic and Middle Eastern Finance and Management* 15/2 (August 18, 2021), 310–330.

[89] "Guideline for Islamic Banking" (Accessed July 30, 2025).

[90] Uddin, *Bangladeş'teki İslam Bankacılık Uygulamasının Fıkhî Açıdan*; Alam—Uddın, "Legal and Regulatory Frameworks For Sharī'a Governance Practices in the Islamic Banking Industry of Bangladesh."

[91] *Islamic Financial Services Industry Stability Report 2024* (Malaysia: Islamic Financial Services Board, 2024), 104.

A survey of 112 SSC members found that 63% held concurrent directorships in the same banks they supervise, raising concerns about independence.[92] Capacity constraints are also acute: fewer than 40 scholars in the country possess *fiqh* credentials and formal banking qualifications. Therefore, Bangladesh Bank's 2021 circular introduced an external Shari'ah audit requirement and a mandatory 30-hour annual CPD program for SSC members—measures aligned with AAOIFI Governance Standard No. 9–and designed to align the system with IFSB 10 best practices. Early evidence suggests an improvement: noncompliance income across Islamic banks fell from 0.76% of the total revenue in 2020 to 0.41% in 2023.[93]

2.4.2.6 Risk Management and Ethical Financial Practices

Islamic banking in Bangladesh stands out because oversight institutions combine ethical and economic objectives with strict banking regulations. These institutions collaborate through three layers of Shari'ah structure, including SSCs at the bank level, the industry-wide CSBIB, and the Islamic banking inspection cell at the Bangladesh Bank. From 2010 to 2021, the average delinquency ratio for Islamic banks was 3.2%, while that of conventional institutions was 7.8%.[94]

Mudarabah and musharakah financing risks are reduced through profit-equalization systems, investment-risk reserves, and enhanced collateral requirements (Bangladesh Bank, 2020). Shari'ah-compliant Commodity Murābaḥah is employed by banks as a repo-style transaction to access liquidity from the central bank and Islamic Bond Fund window.[95] Stress testing under Sharīʿah-breach scenarios, together with contract execution

[92] Md Kausar Alam, "A Proposed Centralized Shariah Governance Framework for Islamic Banks in Bangladesh," *Journal of Islamic Accounting and Business Research* 13/2 (December 17, 2021), 364–389.

[93] *Islamic Financial Services Industry Stability Report 2024*, 105.

[94] Dedy Mainata et al., "Mapping Global Trends and Future Opportunities in Islamic Banking Windows: A 15-Year Bibliometric Perspective (2008–2023)," *Journal of Islamic Accounting and Business Research* ahead-of-print/ahead-of-print (February 19, 2025). Mohsin Ali et al., "Credit Risk in Dual Banking Systems: Does Competition Matter? Empirical Evidence," *International Journal of Emerging Markets* 18/4 (May 24, 2021), 822–844.

[95] Sadia Sardar—Muhammad Farooq Iqbal, "Risk Management in Islamic Banking System: An Overview of Current Modules," *Journal of Religious and Social Studies* 3/1 Jan–Jun (June 30, 2023), 11–26.

audits performed by SSCs, form the core system for managing operational and market risks. The protection of public confidence is ensured through legal requirements for straightforward Sharīʿah-compliant reports, while the Bangladesh Bank retains the authority to penalize banks for incorrect murābaḥah income reporting.[96] BB promotes advanced AI systems for fast risk detection that display missing documentation records in current operations.

The charitable endowments of Islami Bank Bangladesh support events such as Pohela Boishakh fairs and zakāt clinics, as the institution promotes itself through its message of becoming an "inclusive pious institution uniting Bengali cultural values with Sharīʿah requirements."[97] Banks must implement a negative-sector screening process by SSC audit procedures, as mandated by the Bangladesh Bank.[98]

The Banking Companies Act of 1991 still lacks a binding Sharīʿah Governance Framework. Fewer than forty scholars with fiqh and finance expertise serve as SSC members on bank boards, leading to decreased independence. Banks must implement more equity-based contracts and green and social sukuk to avoid maintaining excessive debt-type murābaḥah financing activities.

These institutional dynamics raise key ethical considerations for the future of Islamic finance in Bangladesh. Bangladesh's Islamic banks face recurring ethical scrutiny of how they interpret *muḍārabah* and *wakālah* contracts. For example, several *fatwās* issued by internal Sharīʿah boards permit ambiguous forms of income guarantees in profit-sharing investments, contradicting the principle of risk-sharing central to Islamic finance.[99] Moreover, periodic media investigations have revealed cases in which Sharīʿah boards allegedly failed to challenge questionable

[96] Alam—Uddın, "Legal and Regulatory Frameworks For Sharī'a Governance Practices in the Islamic Banking Industry of Bangladesh."

[97] Wan Ahmad Wan Omar—Hafizah Abdul Rahim, "Perception of Non-Muslims towards Islamic Banking Revisited: SEM Approach," *Mediterranean Journal of Social Sciences*, (December 25, 2015).

[98] Nurul Rofiqoh Lubis et al., "Relevansi Strategi Manajemen Risiko Pembiayaan Dalam Konteks Perbankan Syariah," *El-Mal: Jurnal Kajian Ekonomi & Bisnis Islam* 5/4 (February 9, 2024).

[99] M. Kabir Hassan et al., "Case Studies of Shariah Governance Practices in Bangladesh: HBKU-QFC Roundtable on Islamic Finance," *The Edinburgh Companion to Shari'ah Governance in Islamic Finance*, ed. Syed Nazim Ali et al. (Edinburgh University Press, 2020).

transactions due to board member affiliations or financial incentives.[100] The lack of external auditing for Sharīʿah compliance and insufficient training among bank employees further weakens ethical integrity. Additionally, emerging fintech–Islamic finance hybrids, such as mobile-based crowdfunding or digital *zakāt* platforms—often operate without clear ethical oversight, risking consumer exploitation under the guise of innovation. Therefore, both legacy institutions and fintech ventures in Bangladesh must commit to transparency, disclosure, and *maqāṣid*-aligned governance reforms to ensure the legal and moral authenticity of their practices.

2.4.2.7 Discussion

Most South Asians view Bangladesh's Islamic finance sector as a notable achievement, as Shari'ah-compliant bank assets comprise 25% of the country's total bank assets. However, Islamic banks maintained NPLs at 3.2% compared with traditional banks at 7.8% during 2010–2021. The current analysis reveals that Bangladesh's institutional development exceeds legal infrastructure standards and that statistical data conceal inner organizational challenges.

The sector applies marketing approaches through reports that combine ethical Islamic principles with the Bengali cultural standards. The organization combines local village wisdom with Islamic moral principles to recruit depositors who practice Bengali traditions and have Muslim beliefs. Using a multicultural strategy to attract more customers undermines the legal boundaries defining religious integration. The author explores how informal Muslim charitable contributions would become established requirements for zakāt payments. This section calls for a detailed evaluation of how commercial interests affect pure Islamic doctrine while gaining strength.

The Islamic financial oversight at Bangladesh Bank through its Shari'ah Supervisory Committees (SSCs), Central Shari'ah Board for Islamic Banks of Bangladesh (CSBIB), and Islamic Banking Cell has reduced Sharīʿah non-compliant income from 0.76% to 0.41% in the timeframe between 2020 and 2023. However, these two vulnerabilities persisted. Under the Banking Companies Act 1991 provisions, Shari'ah contracts exist, but

[100] Muhammad Ayub et al., "Revisiting the Paradigm of Sharīʿah Governance of Islamic Financial Institutions," *Journal of Islamic Accounting and Business Research* 15/8 (2024), 1245–1265.

without compulsory Shari'ah governance rules, so the CSBIB guidelines become voluntary. Members of the SSC who serve dual roles as board directors maintain authority over sixty-three percent of the committees. The number of qualified scholars specialized in banking and fiqh who participate remains below forty or a lower figure. The introduction of Shari'ah audits alongside annual mandatory CPD for thirty hours in the 2021 circular advanced the scenario. However, executive control of auditors remains an issue because legal enforcement is absent.

Islamic banks access Bangladesh Bank's Islamic Bond Fund to obtain liquidity that supports their commodity murābaḥah operations with conventional market participants. Such financial practices lead to market integration through increased debt instruments compared to equity modes. Asset groups continue to utilize deals that are primarily based on murābaḥah transactions. Actual mushārakah partnerships and ṣukūk structures exist only at a minimal level, thus creating inconsistency with Islamic finance distribution methods. The analysis of product data and in-depth examination enable readers to confirm whether Islamic finance exceeds minimum standards.

Regional industry standards define proficient management methods for profit-equalization reserves, investment-risk reserves, and stress testing of the Shari'ah breaches. The central bank penalized banking institutions for improper profit handling from murābaḥah trading, but smaller banking units avoided detection. The sector uses a moral-economic storyline, which contradicts its limited understanding of social and environmental risk monitoring.

The low number of dual-qualified scholars nationwide amounts to less than 40 individuals, prompting worries about potential group thinking within the community and continuous scholarly shopping between SSCs. A national daftar al-fatāwā should create a scholar registry to publish SSC opinions and scholarly rules to prevent banking participation after prior bank approvals. The chapter should identify the necessary capacity-building measures, such as doctoral studies in fiqh and finance programs.

Commercial banks in Bangladesh operate under a voluntary compliance framework. Pakistan's financial standards come from AAOIFI, which is issued by regulators, while India does not allow religious entities to affect its framework. The strategy could become stronger by examining financial operations throughout Bangladesh and creating peer-review systems for Sri Lanka and other emerging financial sectors.

Quick equity-based financing methods, digital micro-takāful prototypes, and green/social ṣukūk programs reduce Islamic financial institutions' need for murābaḥah practices. Islamic banks should implement financial measures that incorporate maqāṣid principles and capital ratios to effectively track essential operational activities. Bangladesh Bank should establish a stipend payment system to substitute bank-funded SSC member payments and external auditor distributions to end client-related affiliations.

Bangladesh's financial regulatory picture demonstrates how inclusive Muslim practices share a mutually beneficial relationship with Islamic financial regulation. Bangladesh's success as an ethical finance model depends on establishing an enforceable law-based Shari'ah compliance that integrates ethical investment structures.

Bangladesh's successful Islamic finance institutions exhibit three key features of institutional maturity but lack sufficient legal mechanisms that may have strengthened their overall framework. India's approach differs from Bangladesh's since its Islamic finance sector encounters obstacles due to rigid legal framework restrictions. The transformation from institutional expansion to regulatory restrictions between Pakistan and India has led to an investigation of how South Asian laws and politics control the development of ethical finance (Table 2.2).

This table outlines strategic approaches to ensure that Sharīʿah-compliant banking in South Asia aligns not only with formal legal requirements, but also with the higher ethical objectives of Islamic law (maqāṣid

Table 2.2 Policy Toolkit: Align Shari'ah-compliant banking with maqāṣid al-sharīʿah through institutional mechanisms

Policy action	*Lead actor(s)*	*Timeline*
Establish a *Maqāṣid-Based Ethical Finance Index* (MEFI)	Bangladesh Bank + Islamic Research Institutions	Within 2 years
Create a Central Fatwā Repository linked to bank products	Islamic Foundation Bangladesh + Shari'ah Boards	Within 1 year
Pilot an urban *ḤisbahOffice* in Dhaka financial district	Ministry of Finance + Local Municipality	Within 3 years
Add "Ethical Audit Certification" to bank compliance checklists	Bangladesh Bank Shari'ah Wing + Auditors	Immediate rollout
Launch national public awareness on ethics in Islamic finance	Bangladesh Television + Islamic Banks	Ongoing

al-sharīʿah). It categorizes action points under key dimensions, such as financial inclusion, social justice, transparency, and equitable wealth distribution, offering a framework to move Islamic banking beyond technical compliance toward value-based impact.

2.4.3 India: Minority Ethics and Regulatory Constraints

India is the world's largest nation, with over 1.4 billion residents of diverse religious backgrounds and multiple languages spoken within its republican structure.[101] A total of 14% of Indian people identify as native Muslims, despite Islam retaining its position as the second largest religion in the country. India's main Muslim population centers reside in Uttar Pradesh, West Bengal, Kerala, Maharashtra, and Bihar.[102] The Indian Constitution establishes India as a secular nation by combining complex state programmes with elements of religious heritage.[103] Even though Muslim citizens enjoy complete religious freedom according to the Constitution, central laws and post-colonial banking rules have prevented the implementation of Islamic finance. Under the Indian legal system, Muslims, Hindus, and Christians maintain their private law systems while operating under their secular constitutional guidelines. Several financial laws, specifically the Banking Regulation Act of 1949, maintain standard banking regulations throughout national territory.[104] The Indian economic system upholds religious freedom through its fiscal standards but maintains independence from personal liberties, so Islam-oriented financial operations remain prohibited. Indian legal protections for religious rights, as stated in Articles 25–28, do not extend to Islamic banking as they operate outside official legal frameworks. Different state control systems and public

[101] Gilles Pison, "World population: 8 billion today, how many tomorrow?," *Population & Societies* 604/9 (October 19, 2022), 1–4; Nityanand Jain et al., "Global Population Surpasses Eight Billion: Are We Ready for the next Billion?," *AIMS Public Health* 10/4 (October 25, 2023), 849–866.

[102] Zainab Farhat, "Spatial Segregation and Muslims in India: A Review," *Journal of Muslim Minority Affairs* 43/1–2 (January 2, 2023), 60–69. Raphael Susewind, "Muslims in Indian Cities: Degrees of Segregation and the Elusive Ghetto," *Environment and Planning A* 49/6 (June 1, 2017), 1286–1307.

[103] Manish Telikicherla Chary, *India: Nation on the Move: An Overview of India's People, Culture, History, Economy, IT Industry, & More* (iUniverse, 2009).

[104] Neeru Gupta, "Interest-Free Banking in India Legal Challenges," *International Journal of Law Management & Humanities* 5 Issue 5 (2022), 1315.

opinions about religious finance practices make the development of Islamic financial institutions in the country challenging.

India restricts formal Islamic banking adoption through its secular constitution and unified banking laws, which, together, force Muslims to establish alternative grassroots financial solutions. This section investigates Muslim population activities in ethical finance, although regulatory barriers exist through cooperatives, fintech platforms, and community-led financial projects.

Operating outside formal banking systems, Indian Islamic finance initiatives often rely on grassroots credibility, rather than legal enforceability. This dynamic presents ethical strengths and vulnerabilities. Cooperative models such as the Al-Khair Cooperative Credit Society in Hyderabad demonstrate a strong commitment to justice and transparency, fostering genuine community empowerment.[105] However, the absence of oversight has led to unethical fundraising and financial mismanagement. In recent years, media investigations have reported failed ventures where the misrepresentation of Sharīʿah principles misled investors—highlighting the urgent need for ethical education and informal regulatory safeguards.[106]

Moreover, the scarcity of qualified Sharīʿah scholars and limited financial literacy among Indian Muslim communities pose ethical risks. To address these challenges, supporting informal networks with standardized training, ethics advisory partnerships, and community-based audit mechanisms could enhance trust and consistency without requiring formal legal changes.

2.4.3.1 Legal Framework and Institutional Barriers

Constitutional Constraints

The Indian Constitution defends religious freedom through Articles 25–28, without allowing any overlap between religious institutions and financial oversight.[107] The Indian Constitution enables Muslims to practice

[105] Wasiullah Shaik Mohammed Wasiullah Shaik Mohammed, "Interest-Free Microfinance in India:A Case Study of the Al-Khair Cooperative Credit Society," *Journal of King Abdulaziz University Islamic Economics* 31/1 (January 3, 2018), 47–66.

[106] Manu Abraham, "Shariah Compliance and Earnings Management in India: Insights on Reporting Transparency and Financial Stability," *Modern Finance* 2/1 (2024), 145–165.

[107] Omar Khalidi, "Hinduising India: Secularism in Practice," *Third World Quarterly* 29/8 (December 2008), 1545–1562.

their religion in personal matters yet does not allow them to apply Islamic financial principles through official systems. However, India has the largest Muslim population in the world.[108] The governments of Pakistan and Bangladesh specifically support Islamic finance, whereas India maintains a different regulatory stance. India's present approach to financial systems actively removes mainstream recognition of Islamic financial models.

Reserve Bank of India Policy

The Banking Regulation Act of 1949 did not establish provisions that validate essential Islamic banking principles, especially those related to profit-sharing methods and interest restrictions.[109] The Reserve Bank of India analyzed the possibility of an Islamic banking window, but the organization decided to establish formal regulatory changes. The RBI abandoned its interest-free banking initiative in 2017, because it achieved universal access and operational interest-free solutions.[110]

The RBI and the central government have evaluated the concept of interest-free banking multiple times. In 2006, a working group from the RBI estimated the possibility of interest-free investment bonds until it determined that current legal frameworks required better development. The committee rejected the initiative because of recognized issues. A Ministry of Finance committee formed after the 2008 global financial crisis chose financial reform methods with interest-free banking as their primary decision point.[111]

An Independent Departmental Group (IDG) reviewed the implementation of non-interest banking from legal, regulatory, and technical perspectives to trigger a deeper assessment. The IDG reports that Islamic financial products need to enter the Indian market through multi-stage implementation procedures. Several communities avoided traditional banking operations because they did not accept products based on interest

[108] Ramphul Ohlan, "Muslim Women in India: Status of Demographic, Socioeconomic and Health Inequalities," *Journal of Muslim Minority Affairs* 40/3 (2020), 429–440.

[109] Murtuza Bohra, "Is Indian Banking System Ready to Introduce Globally Acclaimed Concept of Indian Banking System?," (September 1, 2011), 1–10.

[110] *The Economic Times*, "Sharia Banking: RBI Proposes Islamic Window in Banks" (November 20, 2016).

[111] Taufeeque Ahmad Siddiqui et al., "A Study on Islamic Finance as an Approach for Financial Inclusion in India," *Accounting*, (January 1, 2021), 487–496.

rates, as the December 2015 Medium-term Path on Financial Inclusion Committee of the RBI noted. The 2016–17 RBI Annual Report showed that various population segments did not obtain financial services.[112] Laboratory research has studied bank procedures for interest-free product delivery using standard financial tools, including demand deposits with cost-plus financing and deferred payment systems. The proposed services will start operations after regulatory guidelines are approved under the current frameworks. At present, the government does not issue official positions on this matter.

Missed Opportunities for Formalization

The Sachar Committee Report of 2006 found that Muslims face severe restrictions in terms of educational opportunities, job opportunities, and financial resources. A substantial Muslim population and growing ethical finance interest exist in India, yet the nation has not established official Islamic finance alternatives. Multiple academic studies advocate for interest-free banking to resolve the identified gaps.[113] The process has stalled because of political disagreements and legal delays, despite substantial evidence of the need for Islamic banking. Since formal Islamic banking remains incomplete, the alternative market has developed informal cooperative and community lending platforms and ethical fintech solutions for Shari'ah-compliant financing.

Grassroots Responses and Informal Islamic Finance

Many Indian Muslims turn to unlicensed finance organizations to obtain Islamic religious loans through interest-free (qard al-ḥasan) operations and profit-sharing investments, known as muḍārabah. The Muslim communities of Kerala and Hyderabad operate implied ethical networks that enforce Sharīʿah laws by prioritizing social justice and public welfare.[114] These networks in Kerala and Hyderabad operate based on Islamic beliefs about the objectives of Shari'ah through the core principles of social

[112] Khurshid Ahmad, "Islamic Banking Can Tap Into New Sources of Finance" (Accessed April 19, 2025).

[113] Chishti, "Sachar Committee Report: A Review—Mainstream Weekly" (April 24, 2007).

[114] Farah Muneer—Foyasal Khan, "Qard-Al-Hassan As a Tool for Poverty Alleviation: A Case Study of the Fael Khair Waqf Program in Bangladesh," *Journal of Islamic Monetary Economics and Finance* 5/4 (December 27, 2019), 829–848.

justice ('adl) and public welfare (maṣlaḥah). Community trust operates as the main governance mechanism, enabling members to exhibit their ethics through open financial practices, risk-management principles, and inclusive access to services.[115]

Indian Islamic banking operations began to take shape in the 1980s, with Kerala-based institutions being among the first to apply interest-free models.[116] Through its bank policy stance, the Reserve Bank of India states that standard banking operations require a uniform approach and mirrors its opposition to interest-free banking systems, which prevents the integration of Islamic finance into traditional banking.[117]

2.4.3.2 Community Cooperatives and Islamic Ethical Workarounds

Mandatory laws restrict Islamic financial services from operating through non-banking financial companies (NBFCs) and cooperative societies, with an emphasis on areas with substantial Muslim populations, including Kerala and other states such as Maharashtra, Karnataka, Tamil Nadu, and West Bengal.[118] NBFCs and cooperative societies offer limited Islamic financial services, including ethical investment opportunities and interest-free microloans to Indian Muslims.[119] Supplementary banking operations constrain these financial institutions because regulatory principles and restricted market access govern their business activities.[120] India's informal Islamic finance sector includes three main operational areas.

[115] Faisal Fasih, *The International Conference on Emerging Economies—Prospects and Challenges (ICEE-2012), 12–13 January 2012*, "Inclusive Growth in India through Islamic Banking," *Procedia—Social and Behavioral Sciences* 37 (January 1, 2012), 97–110.

[116] Meenakshi Ramesh Kurpad, "Making a Case for Islamic Finance in India," *Law and Financial Markets Review* 10/1 (2016), 38–45.

[117] Amit K. Kashyap, *INDIAN BANKING: Contemporary Issues in Law and Challenges* (Allied Publishers, 2014).

[118] Huma Mahmood et al., "Prospects of Islamic Microfinance: A Study in India," *Journal of Administrative and Business Studies* 6/5 (October 20, 2020).

[119] Salaam Gateway, "India's 'Shariah-Compliant' NBFCs and Cooperative Credit Societies Held Back by Lack of Islamic Capital," *Salaam Gateway—Global Islamic Economy Gateway* (2017).

[120] Viral V. Acharya et al., *Macroeconomic and financial policy challenges of China and India*, "The Growth of a Shadow Banking System in Emerging Markets: Evidence from India," *Journal of International Money and Finance* 39 (December 1, 2013), 207–230.

In the absence of formal Islamic banking, Muslim communities in India have developed informal channels with Islamic underpinnings on which to build. They also consist of cooperative credit societies, chit funds as rotating savings groups, and qard ḥasan micro-loans. Although not formally Shari'ah-regulated, these are practical examples of Islamic ethics in financial practice, especially for the downtrodden.

1. Rotating Savings and Credit Associations (ROSCAs), such as informal "jamaats" operating in Hyderabad.
2. The second type of interest-free lending network develops through joint operations between local mosques and community members based on qard al-ḥasan principles and trust agreements.
3. Small cooperative organizations in India base their financial transactions on ijārah and murābaḥah contracts that follow cooperative law regulations.

The models feature delegation of moral responsibility, shared communal commitments, and the minimization of risks through localized operations, which separates them from traditional microfinance arrangements that use collateral.

The partnership between Dr. Shariq Nisar and TASIS resulted in the creation of Taqwaa Advising and Shari'ah Investment Solutions (TASIS), which provides Shari'ah consultancy and established the BSE TASIS Shari'ah 50 index through its collaboration with the Bombay Stock Exchange.[121] Despite the enormous structural obstacles, the initiatives demonstrated are local financial progress indicators.

Cooperative models and halal investments have emerged to resolve issues related to capital access, and moral and financial practices. Modern financial markets experience growing demand from Muslim investors looking for faith-based asset management solutions during their investment decisions.

2.4.3.3 Faith-Based Innovation in India's Informal Sector

Despite the official legislative barriers in the conventional banking sector, several Islamic financial models have emerged in India. The Bait-un-Nasr

[121] Syed Nazim Ali, *Edinburgh Companion to Shari'ah Governance in Islamic Finance* (Edinburgh University Press, 2020). Shariq Nisar, "Shrinking Space for Islamic Finance in India," *Economic and Political Weekly* 50/17 (2015), 23–25.

Cooperative Credit Society is an important example because it follows cooperative law by managing interest-free savings and financing.[122] Applying *fiqh al-mu'amalāt* ethical principles through these societies enables the provision of dignity-based microfinance to underserved Muslim communities.

Indian Islamic microfinance institutions employ murābaḥah sale and ijārah leasing agreements to support small businesses and provide an ethical financing solution that counters exploitative moneylending practices.[123] These initiatives demonstrate how Islamic finance is a robust ethical tool for empowering the economy while removing poverty from communities. These financial systems support Islamic beliefs that protect economic fairness while banning all forms of exploitation.

Women entrepreneurs in Maharashtra receive financing from the SAFI Microfinance Foundation through its small-scale qard al-ḥasan and mushārakah investments programs. This successful model shows that Islamic finance works as an ethical system to empower women.

2.4.3.4 Digital Shari'ah Compliance Trends

The increase in halal investment interest in India demonstrates a widespread phenomenon in which Muslim investors want to conduct their financial activities according to Islamic moral guidelines. Because India lacks licensed Islamic banks, many Muslim investors choose halal investment approaches to practice their faith while participating in financial market operations.

Halal Investment and Ethical Screening

According to Shari'ah law, all investments must meet three criteria to earn the halal label: avoiding exposure to riba interest, maysir gambling, and excessive gharar uncertainty. Several technological platforms screen stock portfolios so that investors can comply with Islamic ethical principles.

[122] Pupun Saepul Rohman et al., "A Review on Literature of Islamic Microfinance from 2010–2020: Lesson for Practitioners and Future Directions," *Heliyon* 7/12 (December 1, 2021). See, Mansha Rafiq—Khaliq Ahmad, "Financial Inclusion of the Deprived in India: Historical Perspectives," *Islamic Finance and Sustainable Development* (Routledge, 2025), 1–17.

[123] Dalal Aassouli et al., "Can UGITs Promote Liquidity Management and Sustainable Development?," *ISRA International Journal of Islamic Finance* 10/2 (October 11, 2018), 126–142.

These platforms block investment opportunities from alcohol manufacturers and operators in gambling, along with companies in the interest-based finance industry.

Prospective investors can leverage the services of these notable platforms for halal investing:

- Through *Islamicly*, users can access transparency regarding the Shari'ah compliance status of more than 30,000 globally screened stock assets, which helps Muslim investors make better investment choices.[124]
- *Zoya* provides complete Shari'ah compliance reports about worldwide stocks and has features for portfolio tracking, along with Zakat calculation capabilities.[125]
- *The HalalStock.in* website concentrates on the Indian marketplace by helping users discover stocks from Indian stock exchanges that meet Islamic religious requirements.[126]

These platforms enjoy rising popularity because they serve educated Muslim youth and middle-class professionals living in Mumbai, Bengaluru, and Delhi. Investors get simple protocols, educational resources, and professional advice about building halal investment accounts through their platforms.

Shari'ah-compliant indices, which assist investors; there exist Shari'ah-compliant indices that serve as a reference point:

- *S&P BSE 500 Shari'ah Index*: Represents all Shari'ah-compliant companies within the broad-based S&P BSE 500 index.
- *NIFTY 50 Shari'ah Index* is essential to identify Shari'ah-compliant investment opportunities by providing a list of halal stocks operating in India.[127]

[124] "Halal Stocks Finder and Screener | Shariah Advisor for Your Halal Investments-Islamicly" (Accessed April 20, 2025).

[125] "Zoya Blog," *Zoya Blog* (April 2, 2025).

[126] "Search Indian Ethical, Halal & Shariah Compliant Share IPO & Mutual Fund" (Accessed April 20, 2025).

[127] Harshit Singh, "List of Top Halal Stocks in India: Shariah-Compliant Shares on NSE (2025)—Blog by Tickertape," September 29, 2022.

These indices have defined criteria for checking adherence to Islamic principles, which include eliminating companies with higher debts and businesses earning profits from banned activities.

The growing number of ethical investments by Indian Muslims demonstrates the expanding ethical mindset in Indian culture. Individuals who utilize these platforms and indices can invest responsibly according to their ethical and religious principles. Ethical investing positively affects innovation and inclusiveness in corporate financial operations.

2.4.3.5 India's Potential Role in Global Islamic Finance

These limitations do not hinder India's strong potential to take advantage of Islamic financial practices. An opportunity exists to enlarge financial service access through Islamic banking because approximately 14% of the Indian population aligns with Muslim beliefs, whereas traditional banking violates religious principles.[128]

The risk-sharing components of Islamic finance, ethical investment practices, and asset-based trading methods harmonize smoothly with India's developmental targets toward sustainable and inclusive growth. The proposed systems will create favorable results for SMEs, agricultural businesses, and infrastructure development.[129]

As global Islamic finance approaches $6.7 trillion by 2027,[130] India would become an attractive destination for Muslim-majority capital investments in the Gulf and Southeast Asia.[131] India's participation in global Islamic finance markets positively affects commercial relations and diplomatic partnerships. The introduction of modern technology enables the

[128] Ch. Raja Kamal—V. Santhosh, "A Perspective on the Existence and Development of Islamic Banking in India," *Islamic Finance: New Trends in Law and Regulation*, ed. Nadia Mansour—Lorenzo Bujosa (Cham: Springer Nature Switzerland, 2024), 207–214.

[129] Anitha F. N. D'Souza—H. Sai Sundar, "Overcoming the Challenges of Establishing Islamic Banks in India: A Case Study of Al-Arafah Islamic Investment Bank," *Current Trends in Economics, Business and Sustainability*, ed. J. Aloysius Edward et al., Contributions to Environmental Sciences & Innovative Business Technology (Singapore: Springer Nature Singapore, 2023), 192–197.

[130] Shaima Hasan—Shereen Mohamed, "Navigating Uncertainty: Global Islamic Finance Assets Expected to Exceed 6.7 Trillion by 2027" (February 26, 2024).

[131] David Brewster—Kadira Pethiyagoda, "India and the Gulf States," *External Powers and the Gulf Monarchies* (Routledge, 2018). Md. Muddassir Quamar, "India and the Gulf: Regional Security and India's Multialignment Policy," *Asian Politics & Policy* 15/2 (2023), 274–294.

creation of Shari'ah-compliant service channels for transmission.[132] Digital platforms and AI-powered tools allow businesses to lower operational costs while reaching new markets, particularly those communities that lack adequate access.

Inclusion-based investment groups operate in Bengaluru, Pune, and Hyderabad to fulfill Islamic standards of stock screening. Muslim professionals form grassroots cooperative funds through which members participate in the ethical financing of real estate development, halal logistics, and startup investments following religious principles and community input. These models display Islamic mutuality principles and demonstrate how a new generation seeks to establish religious and ethical practices in financial investment.

Despite state institutional backing, the developments demonstrate how Indian Islamic finance operates as an ethical system based on faith values, the community's trust, and economic and social fairness principles. India provides a pedagogical example that demonstrates how limited environments enable Islamic ethical finance to grow through adaptive measures.

The approach to investments proves that Islamic finance in India serves the dual functions of providing financial services and enabling ethical standard preservation for each commercial deal. Investigating religious identity units with ethical discourse and pluralistic structures in Indian financial institutions reveals deeper insights.

2.4.3.6 Impact of the Waqf (Amendment) Act 2025 on Islamic Finance in India

On April 8, 2025, President Droupadi Murmu executed the Waqf (Amendment) bill to enable the federal government to control Muslim charitable trust (waqf) in properties worth billions of rupees.[133] The Hindu nationalist BJP government presents the Waqf (Amendment) Bill as an anti-corruption measure, yet this legislation demonstrates the broader trend of minority suppression that targets Muslims.

According to Islamic legal tradition, waqf describes giving either movable or immovable assets to charity while establishing permanent ownership rights of the gifted property. India possesses the world's biggest stock of

[132] Ashwini Shrivastava, "Indian Banks Should Exploit Untapped Potential in Islamic Banking: Experts" (2024).

[133] Aaratrika Bhaumik, "What Are the Key Changes Proposed in the New Waqf Bill? | Explained," *The Hindu* (April 2, 2025), sec. India.

waqf properties, positioning it as the third-largest landowner following Indian military forces and railway entities. The administration of such assets commenced under the 1954 Waqf Act, but Muslim-only State Waqf Boards received the authority to manage them. Officials attained more organizational independence through the Waqf Act of 1995, and their jurisdiction expanded beyond civil courts while independent Waqf Tribunals were established.[134]

Opposition toward the Waqf (Amendment) Bill 2025 has intensified because of resistance from Muslim civil society, secular parties, and Sikh leaders. Non-Muslims would gain access to leadership and membership positions through provisions in the 2025 Waqf (Amendment) bill. Furthermore, this bill demanded that Waqf Boards produce formal records of historical Waqf properties and submit all disputes to civil courts instead of Waqf Tribunals. The opposition claims that these modifications will lead to widespread theft of religious holdings, while permitting political control.

According to widespread assessment, judicial changes represent essential components of the BJP's Hindutva policy. Critics accept these events, forming a downward pattern of legal steps alongside administrative measures, which begins with the Babri Masjid demolition, followed by the Article 370 repeal in Jammu and Kashmir through the Citizenship Amendment Act (2019), before finishing with waqf record digitization that excludes Muslim ownership proposals as proof of an organized anti-Muslim government plan.[135]

The proposed amendments give district collectors power over land disputes, bringing changes to waqf properties that lack documentation while enabling changes in board membership that might alter the community-focused nature of waqf governance. Observers indicate that recent developments have damaged religious self-regulation principles while reducing state impartiality regarding Islamic endowment control.

This new law has unforeseen economic and social effects on the community. Such measures are likely to prevent faith-based investments while reducing community confidence in Islamic financial operations.[136] The

[134] Umair Pervez Khan, "Hindutva through Legislation: The Waqf Amendment Act in India | Opinion," *Daily Sabah* (April 15, 2025).

[135] Khan, "Hindutva through Legislation" (April 15, 2025).

[136] Feyaad Allie, "India's New Minority Politics," *Journal of Democracy* 36/2 (April 2025), 78–91.

availability of educational services and healthcare, along with social welfare programs funded through waqf, will probably decrease in areas with major Muslim populations. Because of these concerns, inclusive policy dialogue, transparent institutions, and constitutional safeguards must exist to protect the waqf's ethical development in India's pluralistic environment.

The loss of institutional independence directly damages public faith in Islamic charitable administration and the standing of religious, financial, and moral standards in India. Ethical finance represents financial structures operating according to Islamic principles of justice, risk-sharing, and social welfare delivery across legal jurisdictions. The markets emphasize collective duty, equitable lending practices, and moral innovation rather than exclusive revenue generation.

2.4.3.7 Discussion: Ethical Finance and the Indian Case

India's Islamic finance model follows an unprecedented path within the broader South Asian framework because Pakistan uses state intervention for Islamic finance development, and Bangladesh continues on a dual-tracked path. Muslim communities in India chose to develop religious banking practices through parallel paths while operating under laws that are not Islamic. A discussion follows to explore the theoretical implications of these changes in "ethical finance." Ethical finance operates as a financial system grounded in Islamic ethical values, including justice, risk-sharing, and social welfare, while adapting to varying legal frameworks across different contexts. These markets prioritize the principles of communal responsibility alongside inclusive finance and ethical innovation, rather than mere commercial profit. The development of ethical finance has been demonstrated in India, despite the country lacking a formal Islamic finance infrastructure.

Figure 2.1 presents a comparative visual analysis of the formal and informal Islamic finance ecosystems operating in India. It delineates key distinctions in terms of legal recognition, regulatory engagement, Sharīʿah compliance mechanisms, institutional setups, and community outreach. The figure highlights the resilience of informal networks despite formal prohibition and illustrates the dual-track development of Islamic financial practices within a secular legal framework.

Despite legal restrictions and political challenges, people continue to maintain moral and economic practices based on Islamic values through cooperative societies, fintech platforms, and waqf-based services. Informal financial systems operating within India's legal pluralism environment

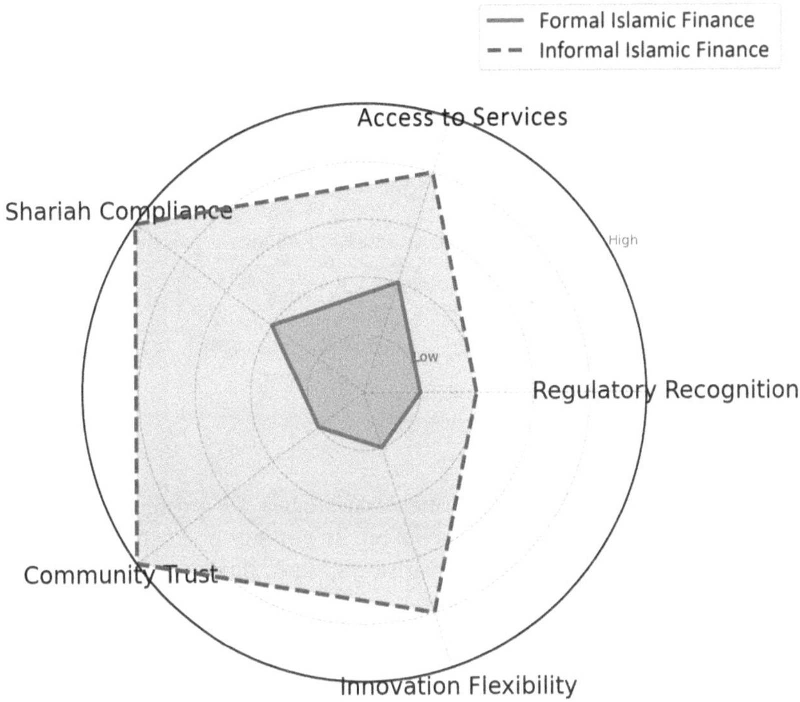

Fig. 2.1 Formal versus informal Islamic finance structures in India

demonstrate how community-based innovation facilitates the development of ethical financial operations. Rather than emerging from top-down Islamization policies, India's ethical finance organically grows from localized ethics, communal trust, and adaptive regulatory improvisation. The priority of these markets rests on community-oriented responsibility and inclusive financing methods while encouraging ethical innovation more than simply raising profits. India demonstrates that moral marketplaces develop naturally, even without formal Islamic financial institutions. These markets evolve independently of formal Islamization programs, drawing instead on localized ethics, social trust, and regulatory improvisation. This informal development model contrasts sharply with that of Afghanistan, where Islamic finance faces different structural and ideological challenges under a shifting political regime (Table 2.3).

Table 2.3 Policy toolkit: Advancing Islamic Ethical finance in India

Policy action	*Lead actor(s)*	*Timeline*
Establish a national fatwa council for cooperative Islamic finance	Muslim Personal Law Board + Legal NGOs	Medium-term
Recognize Islamic microfinance under the RBI's Non-Profit MFIs.	Reserve Bank of India + Parliament	Policy recommendation phase
Promote ESG-compliant waqf projects using Islamic finance tools	Ministry of Minority Affairs + Waqf Boards	Immediate pilot
Introduce Shari'ah-based fintech lending platforms.	Startups + Islamic Foundations	Within 1–2 years
Expand financial literacy on Shari'ah-compliant products.	Jamia Millia + Aligarh Muslim University	Continuous

Source Author's own

This table examines the actionable strategies for promoting Islamic ethical finance within the Indian context. It outlines policy recommendations, institutional development pathways, and community-based initiatives that are designed to overcome legal, regulatory, and societal barriers. The table highlights potential reforms through academic engagement, alternative finance models, and harmonization with broader ethical finance frameworks.

2.4.4 Afghanistan: Islamic Finance in a Fragile State

2.4.4.1 Political and Economic Overview

Geopolitical and Demographic Profile

Afghanistan occupies a landlocked territory that connects South and Central Asia, spanning 647,500 square kilometers.[137] The geographical region is dominated by mountainous highlands and narrow valleys, with only 12.13% of the total land area suitable for cultivation, which seriously

[137] Stuti Bhatnagar—Zahid and Shahab Ahmed, "Geopolitics of Landlocked States in South Asia: A Comparative Analysis of Afghanistan and Nepal," *Australian Journal of International Affairs* 75/1 (January 2, 2021), 60–79.

limits food production capabilities.[138] The population exceeding 40 million makes Afghanistan one of the most diverse nations in the region. Four main ethnic groups dominate the country: the largest group is the Pashtuns, followed by the Tajiks, Hazaras, and Uzbeks.[139] As stated by Julie Di Cristofaro et al (2013), both Dari and Pashto represent the main official languages spoken by 77 and 48% of the population, respectively.[140] Nationwide religious dominance belongs to Islam, as Sunni Muslims make up 85–90% of the population, while Shia Muslims form 10–15% of the total religious groups.[141]

The Taliban's Return to Power and Centralization under Shari'ah
The Taliban seized control of the nation in August 2021, thus causing profound modifications in political leadership frameworks and national institutional features. As the U.S. and NATO forces exited the country, the Taliban took control of Kabul and created the Islamic Emirate of Afghanistan under the leadership of Hibatullah Akhundzada.[142] Under Taliban rule, Afghanistan has adopted a centralized political system that draws from strict interpretations of Shari'ah law to base its governance model.[143] The government bureaucracy persists as an institution that is predominantly a Pashtun male establishment that dismisses all forms of ethnic and gender diversity.

[138] M. Najim Nasimi et al., "Climate and Water Resources Variation in Afghanistan and the Need for Urgent Adaptation Measures," *International Journal of Food Science and Agriculture* 4/1 (March 5, 2020), 49–64.

[139] Zabihullah Dashti, "Afghan External Migration Movements in the Historical Process," *Asya Studies* 6/20 (June 30, 2022), 301–314.

[140] Julie Di Cristofaro et al., "Afghan Hindu Kush: Where Eurasian Sub-Continent Gene Flows Converge," *PLOS ONE* 8/10 (October 18, 2013), e76748.

[141] Thomas J. Barfield, "Afghanistan: A Cultural and Political History, Second Edition," (2022), 14.

[142] Hassan Abbas, *The Return of the Taliban: Afghanistan after the Americans Left* (Yale University Press, 2023), 69–75.

[143] Emilia Justyna Powell—Joshua Paldino, "The Taliban, Afghan Constitutionalism and Modern Islamic Law States: Renegotiating the Balance of Religious and Secular Law," *Global Constitutionalism*, (March 18, 2025), 1–28.

Some Afghan groups acknowledge that the Taliban government reduced corruption in state civil services and gained a small degree of popular support. The Taliban enhanced its reputation through official dismissals of corrupt personnel, mandatory reporting requirements, and restrictions on bribery practices.[144] These measures differentiate the Taliban's administrative strategy because they stand apart from the corruption-tainted policies of the past U.S.-supported government.

Economic Collapse: Frozen Assets, Suspended Aid, and Inflation

Economic collapse ensued through asset-freeze practices, suspended aid, and inflation-driven staff losses. The suspension of international development aid forced Afghanistan into economic collapse by bringing down investments that funded approximately 75% of its national budget.[145] Da Afghanistan Bank (DAB) national central bank assets obtained more than $9 billion in financial freezes from the United States, limiting access to foreign reserves and blocking necessary liquidity management operations.[146] The public sector faced an impeded salary distribution, while health services and infrastructure work stopped dead. The prices of essential goods such as wheat, cooking oil, and fuel increased during the inflationary period because of increased import expenses resulting from currency devaluation and trade system interruptions.[147]

The Taliban's return to power worsened Afghanistan's fragility. Combined with institutional distrust and an underdeveloped financial infrastructure, it pushed most Afghans toward informal, cash-based trade. The economic downturn and banking liquidity reductions eliminated all previous progress toward financial inclusion, creating substantial threats to Afghanistan's weak economic framework.[148]

[144] Bako Kheladze—Nima Zahir, "Corruption Issues in Afghanistan: How Did Corruption Enable the Taliban to Gain Control in Afghanistan?," *Confluences Méditerranée* 129/2 (2024), 125–138.

[145] "Humanitarian Crisis in Afghanistan: Changing Global Dynamics and Pakistan's Policy Choices—Muhammad Fahim Khan, Asad Hassan, Aamer Raza, 2023" (2025).

[146] Saleha Mohsin, "US Freezes Afghan Central Bank's Assets of $9.5bn," *Al Jazeera* (Accessed April 21, 2025).

[147] "Afghanistan: People Suffer as Spending Capacity Shrinks, Prices Rise" (July 13, 2022).

[148] Hannah Duncan—Kate Clark, "Afghanistan's looming economic catastrophe: What next for the Taleban and the donors?," *Afghanistan Analysts Network—English* (September 6, 2021).

However, the newly established Taliban government used anti-corruption measures and expense reduction tactics to stop economic decline during the crisis.

Stabilization and the Recovery of the Afghan Currency

The initial economic crisis caused the Afghan (AFN) to recover significantly by 2023. The Afghan currency stabilized to the point where it gained more than 9% against U.S. dollars in 2023 while becoming one of the highest-performing currencies worldwide. The recovery of Afghan currency showed unexpected stability because of multiple concurrent circumstances. Through official currency controls, the Taliban restricted Hawala systems and banned foreign currencies from domestic trading activities. These interventions sought to improve the national monetary authority and assert financial flow regulation.[149]

International humanitarian funds arranged by the United Nations provide a central bank with approximately $40 million weekly emergency cash assistance.[150] According to UNDP (2022), such funds enabled the maintenance of essential public services while preventing the country from experiencing hyperinflation.[151] Economic stabilization does not necessarily signal a full economic recovery, yet it demonstrates that proper macroeconomic tools can function within isolated political systems with limited institutions.[152]

2.4.4.2 *Historical Background of Financial Services*

Early State-Controlled Banking Institutions

State-owned banks created Afghanistan's modern financial sector during the early twentieth century. The formal banking sector of Afghanistan began with Bank-e-Millie Afghan (BMA), which was established in 1933,

[149] *Afghanistan Development Update: Uncertainty After Fleeting Stability* (The World Bank, 2023), 11–15.

[150] "US Senator Claims Cash Shipments Still Flowing into Afghanistan despite Foreign Aid Freeze | Ariana News," February 9, 2025.

[151] "UNDP Core Funding: Powering Sustainable Development Where It Matters Most," *UNDP* (Accessed April 21, 2025).

[152] "DAB and Chamber of Commerce Unite to Stabilize Afghan Currency—Bakhtar News Agency" (Accessed April 21, 2025).

marking a centralized, state-directed method of economic administration.[153] The banking industry functioned as a branch of state direction because private and international stakeholders were minimally involved in this era. Financial sector operations primarily focus on serving state governments, state-run businesses, and urban high-income classes. The lack of independent institutions and diversified regulations prevented the sector from evolving as needed by changing economic requirements.

During most of the twentieth century, Afghanistan maintained a stagnant financial infrastructure because of its limited banking presence and the small number of banks. Artificial political turmoil, followed by war and successive regime changes, especially from the 1979 Soviet invasion until the 1990s civil war, significantly damaged the sector.[154] The wildfires of upheaval disintegrated the financial system to the point that it lost its connections with global and regional economic movements.

Post-2001 Liberalization: Emergence of Private Banks and Financial Innovations

Afghanistan's financial sector underwent significant liberalization after the U.S.-led intervention in 2001 and the subsequent installation of a new internationally backed government. The passage of the 2003 Banking Law provided the legal framework for establishing private commercial banks, leading to the entry of multiple domestic and foreign banking institutions.[155] These included Azizi Bank, Afghanistan International Bank (AIB), and the Islamic Bank of Afghanistan.[156] The central bank, the Da Afghanistan Bank (DAB), assumed a regulatory role under the 2004 DAB Law, overseeing monetary policy, licensing, and supervision.

[153] Khatera Naseri—Ashurov Sharofiddin, "Exploring the Challenges of the Historical Development of Islamic Banking System in Afghanistan Using Document Analysis," *Journal of Islamic Finance* 9/2 (December 30, 2020), 13–25.

[154] Nazif M. Shahrani, "War, Factionalism, and the State in Afghanistan," *American Anthropologist* 104/3 (2002), 715–722.

[155] Willemijn Verkoren—Bertine Kamphuis, "State Building in a Rentier State: How Development Policies Fail to Promote Democracy in Afghanistan," *Development and Change* 44/3 (2013), 501–526.

[156] Ibrahim Erem Şahin—Humayun Humta, "Micro Finance in Afghanistan Banking System: A Case Study of First Micro Finance Bank in Afghanistan:" *Asian Journal of Management, Entrepreneurship and Social Science* 3/01 (2023), 92–135.

The post-2001 era also saw the introduction of financial technologies and microfinance initiatives aimed at enhancing financial inclusion. Mobile banking and electronic payment systems have begun to emerge, especially in urban centers, offering services such as digital transfers and mobile wallets.[157] Microfinance institutions, often supported by donor agencies, targeted underserved populations with small-scale credit and savings products.[158] However, while these developments signified progress, they were limited in scope and reach, restricted mainly to secure, urbanized areas.

Continued Reliance on Informal Financial Systems

The financial sector in Afghanistan continues to face fundamental difficulties that persist despite recent innovations and reforms. A substantial segment of the population remains outside formal financial services because they cannot access banking facilities, according to a World Bank report (2020). This segment comprises almost 85% of the population who lack banking access, do not possess the required literacy skills, and still do not trust traditional banking institutions.[159] The banking system in Afghanistan is expected to expand at an increased rate until 2025, despite starting from a low base.[160] The statistics reveal that formal sector expansion has been extremely slow during almost twenty years of development assistance programs.

Instead, the informal financial system, most notably the Hawala network, remains the dominant mode of financial intermediation.[161] Hawala's traditional money transfer system functions through trust-based social networks to provide better and faster financial services than banks, especially in

[157] Musawer Hakimi et al., "Digital Transformation of Afghanistan Banking: Exploring E-Banking Trends and Impacts," *KEUNIS* 12/1 (January 21, 2024), 90.

[158] Osman Kurter—İmam Ali Husseini, "Evaluation of Strategic Management Issues Related to The Microfinance Industry and Small and Medium Enterprises in Afghanistan," *Uluslararası Finansal Ekonomi ve Bankacılık Uygulamaları Dergisi* 2/2 (2021), 34–67.

[159] Amin Stanikzai, "Impacts of the Afghan Frozen Assets on The Trade And Banking of Afghanistan," *International Journal of Humanities and Social Science* 8/2 (April 18, 2023), 8–15.

[160] Hashmatullah Ateed—Atiq Ur Rehman, "Determinants of Bank Choice in Afghanistan," *Journal of Islamic Finance* 9/1 (June 4, 2020), 061–075.

[161] Haroun Rahimi, "How to Create Better Hawala Regulations: A Case Study of Hawala Regulations in Afghanistan," *Crime, Law and Social Change* 76/2 (September 1, 2021), 131–148.

remote areas.[162] The Hawala system successfully meets basic economic needs. However, it operates without formal regulation, limiting the state's ability to enforce monetary control and transparency.[163]

A combination of elements drives the public to maintain its reliance on informal financial systems. Trust in national institutions continues to deteriorate rapidly, primarily due to institutional corruption, regulatory shortcomings, and the 2010 Kabul Bank scandal, a major political scandal.[164] The financial collapse led to severe erosion of trust in banking institutions, as thieves stole nearly $1 billion, highlighting weak oversight and governance practices.[165] The religious principles followed by Afghans create a barrier against interest-based (riba) banking since its practice violates Islamic doctrine, discouraging the use of conventional financial products.

2.4.4.3 Development of Islamic Banking: Between Necessity and Symbolism

According to reports, the dual banking system, which involves conventional and Islamic windows at the Bank-e-Millie Afghan and Afghan United Bank, fits the international banking models used by Muslim countries.[166] The adoption of Islamic banking in Afghanistan stemmed primarily from political needs and the need to affirm national identity rather than respond to broad-based public demand.[167]

When choosing services, Afghan customers value secure services and personal trust from financial institutions more than official Islamic finance compliance. Many Afghans from rural areas have selected informal financial networks such as Hawala because they combine high trust with swift

[162] Bilal Moin, "Taming the Untamable: Rethinking, Regulating, and Revamping Hawala," *Journal of Academics Stand Against Poverty* 5/1 (June 1, 2024), 20–43.

[163] Haroun Rahimi, "Hawala as Credit: Recognizing How Hawala Supports the Business Climate in Afghanistan," *Journal of Money Laundering Control* 23/1 (January 20, 2020), 224–244.

[164] See Abdul Qadeer Fitrat, *The Tragedy of Kabul Bank* (Page Publishing Inc., 2022).

[165] Matt Waldman, "System Failure: The Underlying Causes of US Policy-Making Errors in Afghanistan," *International Affairs* 89/4 (July 2013), 825–843.

[166] Sameer Ahmad Mastoor, *Proceedings of International Academic Conferences*, "Islamic Banking System in Afghanistan," *Proceedings of International Academic Conferences*, (June 2014).

[167] Fayaz Gul Mazloum Yar, "The Necessity and Importance of Research and Its Role in Afghan Society," *COMPETITIVE: Journal of Education* 3/4 (2024), 257–270.

services and community support. However, they do not comply with formal Sharīʿah guidelines. A conflict exists within Afghanistan's Islamic finance model because its local structure shows signs of divergence from the essential requirements of Islamic regulation.[168]

The adoption of Islamic finance established religious authenticity for national governing institutions.[169] However, the implementation of this system remains minimal because people lack confidence in official organizations and continue to favor operations through informal relationships.

However, Islamic banks' financial services, including their windows in Afghanistan, include a variety of Shari'ah-compliant products such as Qard (interest-free loans), Mudarabah (profit-sharing savings), Murabaha (cost-plus sales), Ijarah (leasing), and Baiʿ Salam (forward sales).[170]

The products demonstrate a commitment to deliver ethical services and practices that foster risk-sharing relationships and promote inclusive financial access. These financial instruments raise important questions regarding their validity in terms of genuine implementation according to Muslim principles.

The prevalent use of Murabaha financing creates suspicions that Islamic banks fail to pursue profit-and-loss sharing features and welfare-based benefits. The general public's knowledge of these products remains minimal. Most Afghans fail to understand how Islamic financial rules differ from standard banking principles, resulting in a failure to achieve ethical objectives.[171]

[168] Lutfullah Safi, "Review of Afghanistan's Development Pattern from 2001 to 2021: A Relative Lack of Sustainability, Inclusiveness, and Prosperity," *Journal of Social and Economic Development* 26/1 (2024), 333–352.

[169] Muhammad Syarif Hidayatullah et al., "Reconceptualization of Ideal Islamic Bankers in The Sharia Framework (An Effort to Create a Sharia Compliance Ecosystem)," *Afkaruna: Indonesian Interdisciplinary Journal of Islamic Studies* 20/1 (June 30, 2024), 107–127.

[170] Najeebullah Aman, "Islamic Banking Deposits and Finance Products in Afghanistan," *Nangarhar University Social Science Journal* 1/01 (November 24, 2024), 28–31; Buerhan Saiti et al., "Financing Agricultural Activities in Afghanistan: A Proposed Salam-Based Crowdfunding Structure," *ISRA International Journal of Islamic Finance* 10/1 (June 19, 2018), 52–61.

[171] Ziarmal Abdullah et al., "The Influence of Awareness, Knowledge, and Religiosity towards Public Perception of Islamic Banking Usage in Southwestern Afghanistan," *El Barka: Journal of Islamic Economics and Business* 7/1 (June 14, 2024), 1–26.

People in Afghanistan currently face a societal gap between those who understand Islamic banking systems and those who do not. The modern and educated population of cities can utilize Islamic banking products effectively, yet residents of rural areas, often more devout, tend to stick to their traditional practices by opting for hawala transactions and dealing exclusively in cash. Islamic financial products in Afghanistan serve more as idealistic schemes than as operational, ethical, and economic frameworks.

Unlike Pakistan's state-led Islamization and Bangladesh's dual-track expansion, Afghanistan's Islamic finance remains fragmented, symbolically established, and institutionally fragile. Pakistan's financial system underwent a state-sanctioned Islamic transformation through the development of a legal framework and regulatory systems, despite Bangladesh's successful community-based Islamic financial expansion facing certain administrative restrictions. Afghanistan presents a situation where Islamic finance objectives coexist with the informal hawala system, resulting in a weak yet ethically grounded financial structure. Socio-political conditions shape how ethical finance evolves into its final forms throughout South Asia.

Applied Ethical Reflection

Afghanistan's fragmented legal and financial environment poses major ethical challenges for Islamic finance implementation. The reliance on informal trust-based systems like hawala, though socially embedded and trusted, operates without transparent Sharīʿah audits or regulatory scrutiny, blurring the ethical boundaries between Islamic and illicit finance. Additionally, the symbolic adoption of Islamic finance by government institutions often prioritizes legitimacy over genuine compliance with the maqāṣid al-sharīʿah.[172] While products like murābaḥah and qarḍ are offered under Sharīʿah labels, many lack the institutional depth to ensure true risk-sharing or social justice outcomes.[173] Furthermore, insufficient training for Sharīʿah board members and the absence of independent oversight bodies create space for interpretive leniency and ethical inconsistency.

[172] Mustafa Disli et al., "Faithful Finance: Unlocking Banking Islamization in Afghanistan," *Economies* 11/7 (2023), 189.

[173] Dulce M. Redín et al., "Exploring the Ethical Dimension of Hawala," *Journal of Business Ethics* 124/2 (2014), 327–337.

Given Afghanistan's unique post-conflict context, embedding Islamic finance within broader social trust frameworks is both a strength and a vulnerability. Future reforms must balance traditional legitimacy with ethical education, robust governance, and accessible rural outreach if Islamic finance is to serve as more than a symbolic tool.

2.4.4.4 Hawala and the Islamic Financial Ethos: Cultural Embeddedness or Legal Anomaly

The Hawala exhibits operational efficiencies that surpass those of traditional banking methods. Afghanistan's financial dealings have remained predominantly hawala-based since 2001, despite attempts at formalization in the international sector. Hawala transactions control 80–90% of all financial activities.[174]

This enduring presence prompts fundamental inquiries about Hawala's integrated position in Afghan culture, moral standing, and prospective function in the country's developing Islamic financial sector.

Hawala's control persists because it maintains operational features that exceed traditional banking methods in efficiency. Speed and Efficiency Transfers through Hawala are completed in less than 24 hours, which allows money to be transferred freely between international borders without waiting for the bureaucracy of the bank system.

Ordinary Afghans can benefit from Hawaladars' lower service costs because their commission fees are less expensive than traditional bank fees. Personal honor, family connections, and reputation are trustworthy foundations for financial transactions throughout Afghanistan's tribal system because formal legal agreements are less dependable. Geographical Reach Hawala reaches the most isolated locations, providing services to communities lacking conventional banking services in city centers.[175]

Security Hawala offers safe and decentralized financial transfer methods in situations where conflict-driven insecurity prevails throughout the region. Hawala exists beyond financial service boundaries since it is a social

[174] Haroun Rahimi, "Hawala as Credit: Recognizing How Hawala Supports the Business Climate in Afghanistan," *Journal of Money Laundering Control* 23/1 (January 20, 2020), 224–244.

[175] Jonathan G. Ercanbrack, "Hawala in Criminal Court: The Role of Law and Commercial Culture in Informal Financial Exchange," *Crime, Law and Social Change* 82/3 (October 1, 2024), 659–683.

construction that combines economic activities, familial bonds, and religious principles into an adaptable system.[176]

Is Hawala Sharīʿah-Compliant? A Divided Debate could arise, but the Islamic legitimacy of hawala leads scholars to different conclusions about its compatibility with Sharīʿah rules. Islamic scholars endorse the hawala system because they see its core elements trace their origins to the debt transfer tradition, ḥawālah, which all major schools, including Ḥanafī, Mālikī, Shāfiʿī, and Ḥanbalī, fully acknowledge.

The Islamic Fiqh Academy defined the principles required for hawala transactions in its 1988 statement to the Organization of Islamic Cooperation.

- Absence of riba (interest),
- The lawful purpose of the transaction,
- Friends or business counterparts must share complete information while actively agreeing to hawala transactions.

Hawala, as an ideal process, demonstrates Islamic principles of trustworthiness through amānah and honesty through ṣidq while supporting community welfare through maṣlaḥah. It provides financial solutions that follow Islamic ethical objectives (maqāṣid al-sharīʿah).

Critical Concerns and Ethical Ambiguities

According to its critics, contemporary operational activities in Hawala respond differently to the classical Sharīʿah framework. There are also documentation deficiencies, which means that companies run into enforceability issues without written contracts and formal audits that violate Islamic evidentiary security standards (bayyinah).[177] Concealed riba and unfair practices in which the application of vázia remains prohibited even when financial transactions involve exchange rate manipulations and hidden commissions due to unethical practices that may violate Muslim law.

[176] Khurram Sharif et al., "Analyzing Informal Value Transfer Networks through the Lens of Social Exchanges," *Society and Business Review* 17/3 (December 23, 2021), 394–420.

[177] Haroun Rahimi, "How to Create Better Hawala Regulations: A Case Study of Hawala Regulations in Afghanistan," *Crime, Law and Social Change* 76/2 (September 1, 2021), 131–148.

Illicit Financing Risks could include Hawala's anonymous nature, which exposes it to illegal earnings that violate Islam's absolute prohibition against *ḥarām rizq*. In theoretical terms, hawala remains compliant with Islamic law, but actual usage has ethical issues that require careful assessment.

2.4.4.5 Regulatory Framework and Role of DAB: Fragile Authority, Ethical Dilemmas

The regulatory framework that supports Islamic banking is highly vulnerable, creating a strange crossroads for Islamic banking institutions. Ethical finance models establish trust in post-conflict economies by implementing fairness, risk distribution, and community benefit principles.[178] Strong independent regulatory structures protect Islamic banking from becoming merely symbolic through political abuse and monopoly control by specific privileged entities.

The Afghan regulatory model exists at a point where ethical ideals intersect with political instrumentalism because it attempts to determine if Islamic finance will be used for genuine economic reform or remain a symbol of religion and politics. However, the banking evolution in Afghanistan through establishing Major Bank Da Afghanistan (DAB), its supervision system for Sharīʿah compliance. Before 2000, the financial sector of Afghanistan maintained limited strength and intense foreign commercial dominance after the Indians took control following capitalist instability. The Afghan National Bank (Bank-e-Millie Afghan) became the first national financial institution in 1933. However, DAB emerged as the regulatory body in 1939 to oversee currency production and banking operations. The arrest of the Taliban rule in 2001 led to banking sector development in Afghanistan through reformed banking laws that attracted private and foreign banks to establish operations.

The Sharīʿah supervision system of DAB functioned as a regulatory body for Islamic financial operations, yet the bank did not establish an independent Sharīʿah governance system. Islamic banking in Afghanistan mainly functions as a conventional bank's Islamic window operations instead of running its independent Islamic banking system.[179] DAB

[178] Ismail Cebeci, "Product Development in Islamic Banks By Habib Ahmed," *Journal of Islamic Studies* 24/1 (January 1, 2013), 122–124.

[179] Hezbullah Naseh—Bouhedda Ghalia, "The Impact of Legislative Environment on the Development of Islamic Banking: A Comparative Study between Malaysia and Afghanistan," *AL-HIKMAH: INTERNATIONAL JOURNAL OF ISLAMIC STUDIES AND HUMAN SCIENCES* 7/4 (December 12, 2024), 31–54.

made critical contributions to establishing financial regulations based on Sharīʿah principles, yet its system became limited because it did not have clear laws to govern Islamic finance operations. DAB obtained favorable outcomes in Sharīʿah reference unification through its efforts to produce standardized Shari'ah rules for different Islamic banking operations and distribute some unification achievements. Nevertheless, substantial challenges remain. A unified legal authority to oversee Islamic banking does not exist in any national capacity across banks, nor does the required specialized legal code for handling Islamic banking matters.[180]

The country's weak financial infrastructure, together with political instability and insufficient qualified experts and scholars of Sharīʿah, prevents the complete unification of Sharīʿah. The Afghan Central Bank played a stabilizing role in the financial sector, yet major structural flaws and efforts in Islamic banking supervision continue to exist. The Islamic finance sector in Afghanistan remains in a transitional stage because there are no complete Islamic banking regulations, alongside a lack of complete institutional partitions between conventional and Islamic financial systems.

The establishment of Sharīʿah supervisory mechanisms by Da Afghanistan Bank (DAB) after 2008 has not been sufficient to establish a unified national Sharīʿah Supervisory Board that would provide standardization for Islamic banking operations. The current structure of Islamic banking windows in conventional banks worldwide depends on independent Sharīʿah advisory committees that cause differences between product frameworks and interpretations of fatwā. Afghanistan has not implemented the complete set of international AAOIFI IFSB standards for Sharīʿah regulation, which causes its regulatory oversight to be fragmented. The Islamic finance sector of Afghanistan faces the danger of reduced public trust due to the absence of a unified Sharīʿah supervision of its activities.

Afghanistan's Islamic finance sector embodies a paradox: while grounded in ethical aspirations and religious symbolism, its reliance on informal mechanisms like hawala highlights the absence of a robust institutional framework. True transformation requires reconciling cultural

[180] Zaif Ullah Athari et al., "History of the Afghan Central Bank, Its Sharīʿah Supervision System and Its Effect on Unifying the Sharīʿah Reference: تاريخ البنك المركزي الأفغاني ونظام الرقابة الشرعية فيه وأثره في توحيد المرجعية الشرعية," *International Journal of Fiqh and Usul Al-Fiqh Studies* 8/2 (July 31, 2024), 38–54.

practices with formal regulatory reform. Without strengthening regulatory credibility and public trust, Islamic finance in Afghanistan risks remaining more symbolic than operational.

2.4.4.6 Discussion: Afghanistan and Islamic Ethical Finance

Islamic financial operations in Taliban-controlled Afghanistan represent a sound system that attempts ethical market construction based on Islamic principles. Islamic finance in Pakistan evolved through an Islamization process led by the state. However, India developed its ethical finance systems despite legal obstacles. In contrast, Afghanistan has developed its Islamic finance structure within institutional weakness, political isolation, and economic ruin. The financial model in Afghanistan bases its traditional practices directly on Islamic ethical principles that include justice (*ʿadl*), risk-sharing (*mushārakah*), prohibition of exploitation (*iḥtirām al-ḥuqūq*), along with social welfare (*maṣlaḥah*).

Islamic finance initiatives receive religious backing from the Taliban because they actively pursue Sharīʿah implementation throughout governance structures, which includes finance sector operations. The foundations of the actual organizational framework are weak, but they performed very well in reducing corruption, which is a good sign of development. The operations of Islamic banks in Afghanistan are subject to limited regulatory oversight from the Da Afghanistan Bank (DAB) because the institution does not maintain an independent Sharīʿah supervisory body. The nation demonstrates Islamic financial principles embracing Sharīʿah strictness, but its financial transactions depend mainly on fragmented hawala and cash dealings. A mismatch between Afghanistan's ethically oriented aspirations and its underdeveloped institutional framework makes its Islamic financial sector ethical in theory and unstable in practice.

The Afghan financial sector demonstrates a distinct model originating from survival needs instead of state-driven development or purposeful strategic transformation like Pakistan and India. According to research in Afghanistan, Islamic financial ethics have proven to flourish and endure instability. The preservation of Islamic finance systems in Afghanistan leads to instability in the financial regulatory authority and systematic breakdown while restricting financial inclusivity. Islamic finance in Afghanistan exists as a vulnerable moral market that tries to live by Islamic values, even though it faces political instability, inadequate infrastructure, and widespread distrust from the public.

The developing ethical market of Afghanistan requires a detailed analysis of translating ethical intentions into resilient institutions, which becomes more essential during our study of regional Islamic finance in South Asia.

The future direction of Islamic finance in Afghanistan remains unclear. Stabilization initiatives, paired with religious acceptability, may encourage the development of an ethical Islamic financial sector over time, alongside international capacity-building support. Islamic finance has limited prospects for substantial change, as institutional reforms essential for its practical development are not being implemented. This leaves hawala networks, which have cultural strengths in trust systems, running the financial sector. The nation faces a crucial decision: whether to establish ethical institutional norms or retain informal survival techniques.

2.4.5 Sri Lanka: Emerging Islamic Finance Under a Pluralistic Legal System

2.4.5.1 Historical Overview of Muslims and Financial Practices in Sri Lanka

The island republic of Sri Lanka exists in a crucial Indian Ocean location, serving as a marine commercial center alongside a cultural nexus. The location of the land attracted Arab traders in the 7th century CE, which led to the establishment of Muslim settlements. The first Muslim settlements, comprising Moors, Malays, and Indian Muslims, contributed substantially to trade, finance, and commercial enterprises throughout Sri Lanka.[181] The current Muslim population accounts for 9.7% of Sri Lanka's total population. It holds most of its members in the Eastern Province (Batticaloa, Ampara) and Western Province (Colombo, Gampaha), as well as parts of the Central and Southern regions (Kandy, Galle). Most Sri Lankan Muslims adhere to the Shāfiʿī school of Sunni jurisprudence.[182]

The development of Islamic financial consciousness happened as an organized movement only in the final years of the twentieth century.

[181] Mohamed Arkam Mohamed Razzak—Fatmir Shehu, "Exploring the History of Islamic Revivalism in Modern Sri Lanka," *Journal of Islam in Asia (E-ISSN 2289–8077)* 21/1 (June 28, 2024), 206–229.

[182] Ahamed Sarjoon Razick et al., *Buddhist and Muslim Interaction in the Post-War of Sri Lanka* (Malaysia: Universiti Kebangsaan Malaysia Press, 2021).

Shari'ah-compliant finance started receiving early discussion through the Islamic Service Society during the 1980s before organized activities began in the 1990s. The foundation for institutional development was built through initial dialogues between Sri Lankan scholars Ismail Deen Marikar and Uthman Qasim and international expert Mufti Taqi Usmani. Fazal Saleem participated in these sessions alongside them. The establishment of Amana Investments in 1997 rose to become Amana Bank by 2005, marking the regulated start of Islamic financing in Sri Lanka.[183] The establishment of Islamic finance in Sri Lanka emerged from its mission to deliver moral, financial solutions free of interest-based systems that support Islamic principles of justice, risk-sharing, and financial access for all.

2.4.5.2 Legal Environment and Islamic Finance Regulation

Sri Lanka functions under three distinct legal systems: English common law, Roman-Dutch law, and personal laws based on religious traditions.[184] The country regulates its law through secular legislation but displays tolerance towards Islamic financial systems. The Central Bank of Sri Lanka (CBSL) obtained authorization to start Shari'ah-compliant banking operations from Section 86 under the Banking Act No. 30 of 1988, which underwent amendments in 2005.[185]

The Sale of Goods Ordinance No. 11 of 1896 includes bayʿ al-istisnāʿ (manufacturing contracts) and bayʿ al-wasf (sales by description) along with other Islamic modes of finance that commercial statutes allow. Current legislation incorporates new options for creative product designs.[186] The main weakness in dispute resolution systems continues to present itself. The present settlement of Islamic finance disputes

[183] S. M. Nafees—M. T. Habeebullah, *Enhancement of Islamic Banking Industry: A Sri Lankan Perspective* (Sri Lanka: South Eastern University of Sri Lanka, 2016).

[184] Dinesha Samararatne, "Judicial Borrowing and Creeping Influences: Indian Jurisprudence in Sri Lankan Public Law," *Indian Law Review* 2/3 (September 2, 2018), 205–223.

[185] S. M. M. Nafees et al., "Problems and Prospects of Islamic Banking: A Case Analysis of Sri Lanka," *Sri Lankan Journal of Arabic & Islamic Studies (SLJAIS)* 1/2 (2018), 57–70.

[186] Hayathu Mohamed Ahamed Hilmy et al., "Legal Aspects of Shariah Governance Practices in Sri Lankan Islamic Financial Institutions: A Literature Review," *Journal of Enterprise and Development (JED)* 4/1 (June 1, 2022), 99–113; Althaf Marsoof, "Chapter 7: Challenges in Achieving Public Health Objectives through Product Labelling Regulation: Reflections on Sri Lankan Trademark and Constitutional Law," 2016.

progresses through civil courts implementing standard law methodologies, though these approaches might fail to support Shari'ah objectives (maqāṣid al-sharīʿah). Islamic contracts lose their credibility because this legal uncertainty is an industry-wide issue. The general support from the CBSL exists, yet the lack of a specific Islamic finance legal framework remains a barrier to sector expansion and standardization advancement.[187]

2.4.5.3 Development of Islamic Banking Institutions

The initiation of Amana Bank as Sri Lanka's main Islamic commercial banking outlet transformed the process of establishing Islamic finance institutions at a critical moment. Since obtaining its license in 2011, Amana Bank has enabled customers to access a complete range of Islamic financial products, which incorporate murābaḥah (cost-plus sales), mushārakah (equity partnership), ijārah (leasing), wakālah (agency), and qard al-ḥasan (benevolent loans). Amana Bank serves its customers from retail to SME segments through products including deposit accounts, personal financing, trade financing services, and real estate deals.[188]

The entry of Amana Bank has been accompanied by the establishment of eight Islamic divisions within conventional banks. The self-directed financial units within these banks maintain their compliance systems; however, they face obstacles to large-scale expansion due to internal organizational and structural constraints. The market for Shari'ah-compliant financial services includes Islamic windows operated by non-bank financial institutions and investment firms. However, they do not have regulatory licensing from CBSL as Islamic banks.[189]

[187] S. Issath Nimsith et al., "Study on Marketing Strategy for Islamic Banking Industry in Sri Lanka" (6th International Symposium of FIA-2019, Sri Lanka: South Eastern University of Sri Lanka, 2019), 239–253.

[188] Abi Huraira Rifas et al., "Involvement of Micro, Small and Medium Entrepreneurs (MSMEs) in Takaful in Sri Lanka: An Extension of Theory of Planned Behaviour," *Journal of Islamic Marketing* 14/11 (February 3, 2023), 2715–2740; M. H. M. Abdullah—Rusni Hassan, "Evaluation on the Practice of Ijarah for Vehicle Financing and Its Regulation in Islamic Financial Institutions in Sri Lanka," *Islamic Sustainable Finance, Law and Innovation: Opportunities and Challenges*, ed. Nadia Mansour—Lorenzo Mateo Bujosa Vadell (Cham: Springer Nature Switzerland, 2023), 335–343.

[189] M. N. M. Minaz et al., "The Enhancement of Fintech on Islamic Banking and Financial Sector in Sri Lanka: A Literature Review" (11th International Symposium—2023, South Eastern University of Sri Lanka, 2023).

The market penetration rate stays below its proposed levels. The presence of Islamic finance institutions in Mauritius constitutes less than one percent of the total banking assets in the country. Islamic banking institutions have struggled to grow because of strict institutional constraints, limited public knowledge, and insufficient funding capabilities. The symbolic appearance of Islamic banking facilities serves to satisfy the long-desired community's need for financial products that adhere to ethical Islamic principles.

2.4.5.4 Shari'ah Governance Framework

Sri Lanka fails to maintain a single national organization that provides Shari'ah governance for finance. Malaysia operates through its Shari'ah Advisory Council, and Pakistan through Shari'ah Boards under SBP and SECP. Bank institutions develop Shari'ah Supervisory Boards (SSBs) for both product screening and operational oversight as part of their Shari'ah compliance process. Amana Bank has strengthened its credibility by appointing international scholar Mufti Imran Ashraf Usmani to its SSB.[190]

Most Shari'ah Supervisory Boards adopt guidelines from AAOIFI (Accounting and Auditing Organization for Islamic Financial Institutions); however, their compliance standards remain different between institutions. Traditional internal audit systems control most current operations without providing transparency and standardized procedures.[191] A unified Supreme Shari'ah interpretation oversight system does not exist to provide uniform bank guidance. Shari'ah audits in financial institutions remain voluntary under current legal frameworks since neither standardization, central supervisory bodies, nor fatwa repositories exist.

Sri Lanka needs to create a national Shari'ah governance structure that includes regulatory oversight and qualified personnel to ensure that banks follow ethical compliance guidelines through systematic audits, transparency requirements, and conflict-of-interest safeguards. This will ensure the long-term excellence and growth of the Islamic financial sector.

[190] Hilmy et al., "Legal Aspects of Shariah Governance Practices in Sri Lankan Islamic Financial Institutions."

[191] "Shariah Governance Structure of Islamic Financial Institutions in Sri Lanka," *International Journal of Management and Applied Research* 6/4 (2019), 245–258.

2.4.5.5 Market Penetration and Challenges

The market penetration of Islamic finance in Sri Lanka stands at a restricted level, even as institutional advancements have been made slowly. The proportion of Shari'ah-compliant financial services remains relatively low within national banking operations for 2024. The country maintains Amana Bank as its Islamic commercial financial institution, although conventional banks operate Java-based Islamic banking services. The institutions operate within restrictive parameters since their primary customer base includes members of the Muslim minority, which restricts business growth opportunities.[192]

Factors linked to one another create obstacles to expanding and normalizing Islamic finance activities in the Sri Lankan financial sector. A fundamental obstacle stands in the way of Islamic finance's growth because people in every segment of the population, including Muslims themselves, know very few fundamental aspects of Islamic finance. The scarcity of understanding in the Muslim population regarding financial structures like mushārakah, mudarabah, and ijārah results in low demand for equity-based financing products. Muslim finance primarily consists of debt mechanisms directed toward cost-plus sales structures known as murābaḥah, despite these financial instruments lacking legal or ethical distinction from conventional financing.[193]

Specific industrial expansion encounters barriers through mandatory regulations. Modern laws prevent institutions from utilizing Shari'ah-compliant liquidity instruments like ṣukūk (Islamic bonds) and Islamic repo agreements, which are necessary for capital market integration and liquidity management.[194] Resolving disputes in Islamic finance requires courts to interpret legal cases through civil justice, although these courts have minimal expertise in Shari'ah principles. The failure of judgments to match ethical principles and legal terms within Islamic finance results in decreased investor confidence.

[192] "Our Model—Amāna Bank PLC, Sri Lanka" (Accessed April 30, 2025).

[193] Subaideen Issath Nimsith et al., "Factors Influencing Demand for Islamic Bank Products in Sri Lanka," *Journal of Enterprise and Development (JED)* 6/1 (2024), 160–171; Mohamad Sabri B. Zakaria et al., "Evaluating Murābaḥah Financing in Sri Lanka: Practitioner Perception," *Sprin Journal of Arts, Humanities and Social Sciences* 2/05 (May 20, 2023), 72–86.

[194] "IFN—Vidullanka Pioneers Sri Lanka's First Listed Sukuk Issuance," *Islamic Finance News* (April 22, 2025).

A severe shortage of skilled professionals exists within Islamic law, Islamic finance, and regulatory affairs in this sector. A lack of skilled professionals who understand Shari'ah-compliant finance hinders product development, management, and Shari'ah audit processes, resulting in poor institutional innovation and consistency. Several obstacles have combined to create a situation where Asian people view Islamic finance in Sri Lanka as a minority religious system instead of an effective, ethical financial intermediary.

Sri Lanka needs to launch nationwide education campaigns and develop more Islamic finance training programs and legal frameworks to endorse dispute mediation systems and financial product developments under Shari'ah principles. Developing Islamic finance as a competitive financial solution for the nation requires well-coordinated initiatives between various stakeholders.

2.4.5.6 Opportunities and Future Outlook

Although still modest in scale, Sri Lanka's Islamic finance sector holds considerable potential for ethical and inclusive financial growth. The most promising Islamic insurance system expansion is Takaful. Amana Takaful leads the market in creating micro-insurance products that help low-income Muslim households practice risk-sharing while improving social welfare standards. Establishing Sukuk (Islamic bonds) legislation would enable Sri Lanka to attract Gulf and Southeast Asian investors to build infrastructure by issuing these bonds. The proper regulatory backing for Sukuk services will strengthen Sri Lanka's presence in ethical global finance while creating new financing channels for public institutions.[195]

The investment market for halal mutual funds and Shari'ah-compliant equity products has recently demonstrated a growing interest. Islamic bonds serve ethical investors, Muslim and non-Muslim, because they enable investor transparency and maintain asset value and social accountability standards.[196] Financially literate urban populations in Colombo and Kandy create favorable market conditions for such products. Southeastern University focuses on developing qualified personnel through its Islamic

[195] Aamer Yaqub, "Sri Lanka to See First Listed Sukuk Issuance by Local Firm," *The Halal Times* (blog), April 2, 2025.

[196] Achmad Firdaus—Kamilah Kamilah, "Sustainable Financing for Green Businesses from the Perspective of Islamic Finance," *Advances in Business and Management* (Nova Science Publishers, 2024), 1–36.

finance education programs while responding to the shortage of qualified professionals.[197]

The widespread adoption of digital innovation has been detected as a main development sector.[198] Fintech platforms enable the extension of mobile-based services that comply with Shari'ah law through digital wallets, microfinance solutions, and automated compliance systems. These technological solutions enhance availability in distant geographic areas through compliance with Islamic law.[199]

The geographic advantage and trade relationships between the Gulf and Southeast Asian economies make Sri Lanka suitable for establishing itself as a regional center for Islamic financial transactions across borders.[200] To achieve these opportunities, the country needs tax reforms alongside detailed Shari'ah dispute resolution procedures, and new liquidity tools must be developed. Strategic policy backing and institutional growth will transform Sri Lanka from a secondary market into a dynamic moral marketplace in the international Islamic finance system.

2.4.5.7 Discussion: Sri Lanka's Hybrid Moral Market Model

Sri Lanka showcases an exceptional moral and financial system that unites constitutional secular leadership with religion-based ethical funding practices. Islamic finance in Sri Lanka operates through an organic development process that combines grassroots community activism with proportional regulation and essential market demands rather than the centralized Islamization approach used by Pakistan or the culturally diverse model of Bangladesh.

The grassroots development of Islamic finance enables the system to adapt to a set of legal systems while remaining independent from politics and fostering new products within existing boundaries. Without unified

[197] "Faculty of Islamic Studies and Arabic Language (FIA) | SEUSL" (Accessed April 30, 2025).

[198] Staff Reporter, "Alipay + Goes Live in Sri Lanka with 14 E-Wallets Enabled for Payment | Asian Banking & Finance" (March 26, 2025).

[199] Hayathu Mohamed Ahamed Hilmy—I. Saujan, "Customer Satisfaction on Digital Banking Services: Evidence from Islamic Financial Institutions in Sri Lanka," *Journal of Islamic Economic Law* 8/1 (2025).

[200] Mohamed Ismail Mohamed Riyath—Khaled Hussainey, "Co-Movement and Information Transmission between Conventional and Islamic Equities in Sri Lanka," *Review of Accounting and Finance* ahead-of-print/ahead-of-print (March 4, 2025).

Shari'ah leadership and uniform product guidelines, the local Islamic finance industry faces difficulties maintaining qualitative standards and ensuring market trust.[201]

The discourse surrounding the moral economy continues to retain its relevant legitimacy. Amana Bank is an ethical service provider with financial capacity because it dedicates itself to maintaining justice and fostering trust and inclusion for its customers. The statistical numerical output demonstrates substantial philosophical and moral value within Sri Lanka's social and financial systems.[202]

A strengthened Islamic finance model requires that Sri Lanka accept these three measures:

1. Standardization: via a national Shari'ah council and audit regime.
2. The law must be reformed by implementing dispute resolution solutions that apply Shari'ah principles and taxation systems that achieve parity.
3. The market will benefit from three innovations that combine Islamic microfinance with digital waqf platforms and green sukuk.

The Islamic finance sector in Sri Lanka plans to establish a separate moral, financial space within the existing system without pursuing its dominance over the entire financial sector. The model serves as a guideline for plural societies to implement ethical finance solutions while upholding legal secularism and religious diversity.

However, a national Shari'ah Supervisory Board must be established in Sri Lanka for reasons beyond regulatory convenience that become vital strategic needs. Such an institutional board would resolve diverse interpretation methods while raising market reliability through standardization, allowing domestic financial operations to match AAOIFI and IFSB specifications. A national Shari'ah Supervisory Board obtained from the Central Bank functions while serving as an education center that trains qualified scholars to maintain operational quality according to Shari'ah principles. Islamic finance in Sri Lanka faces stagnation due to a divided

[201] Hilmy et al., "Legal Aspects of Shariah Governance Practices in Sri Lankan Islamic Financial Institutions," 109.

[202] Aamer Yaqub, "Amana Bank Sri Lanka Named Best Islamic Bank in South Asia," *The Halal Times* (blog), August 29, 2024; "IFN—The Association of Alternate Financial Institutions of Sri Lanka," *Islamic Finance News* (October 3, 2024).

sector structure that hinders its development into an ethical financial system available to the entire population.

Sri Lanka's Islamic financial institutions often rely on outsourced Sharīʿah consultancy firms, which raises concerns about standardized accountability. The commercial success of Amana Bank has encouraged growth, but critics warn of a growing disconnect between Sharīʿah compliance and social justice goals.[203] For example, lease-to-own contracts (*ijārah muntahiyah bi-tamlīk*) have been structured in ways that shift disproportionate burdens to clients in low-income housing schemes.[204] This creates tension between profitability and *maqāṣid*-based equity, especially in a context where Muslims remain a demographic minority. To reinforce ethical credibility, Sri Lanka's regulators could consider standardizing Sharīʿah qualifications, mandating local audit mechanisms, and fostering dialogue between consumer protection bodies and Islamic finance institutions.

Sri Lanka, which stands between South and Southeast Asia, displays a split Islamic finance system that operates in a fragmented legal setting but demonstrates Islamic finance's compatibility with plural legal systems. The following analysis explores the Islamic finance development of the Maldives, a neighboring country with a Muslim majority, through a state-driven approach. Different socio-political and religious contexts across the South Asian region determine how Islamic finance institutions develop.

2.4.6 The Maldives: Ethical Finance in a Small-Island Islamic Economy

2.4.6.1 Historical and Religious Foundations

The Maldives officially adopted Islam in 1153 CE by converting the Buddhist Maldivian king Dhovemi into Sunni Islam after North African traveler Abul Barakat al-Barbari inspired him. Some historians contend that his role in spreading Islam was a critical religious and legal transition for the

[203] Shaista Arshad et al., "Outsourcing the Islamic Way: A Look into the Challenges Faced by Financial Institutions," *Journal of Islamic Economics Banking and Finance* 11/2 (2015), 51–63.

[204] Mohamed Haniffa Mohamed Nairoos, "The Contribution of Amana Bank in the Islamic Financial Industry in Sri Lanka," *Cognizance Journal of Multidisciplinary Studies* 3/6 (2023), 231–253.

Maldives' national development.[205] From its adoption, Islam has evolved into an individual spiritual practice and an organization that controls nationwide legal principles, educational programs, and political institutions.

The 2008 Maldivian Constitution's state religion position of Islam (Article 9(d)) requires Muslim faith from everyone seeking citizenship. According to Article 10, public authorities must safeguard Islamic principles, while Islamic legal sources become the country's dominant legal foundation.[206] The Maldives stands apart from other South Asian states through its unique constitutional setup since it employs Islam as a single exclusive legal foundation rather than just one among various legal-religious influences.[207]

The theocratic nature of the Maldives directs its public finance operations as well as its ethical governance practices. Islamic moral principles that include interest bans, alms donations, and risk-sharing structures have traditionally shaped local economic practices between fishing communities and trading networks.[208] Islamic finance made its official entry during the 21st century because of foreign investments that received technical assistance from Islamic financial organizations, including the Islamic Development Bank (IDB).

The Maldives entered Islamic banking later than Pakistan and Bangladesh. However, its unified religious environment and constitutional priority in Islamic law may create solid conditions for Islamic ethical finance development. The Maldives is a nation with a faith-congruent economic landscape because shared social values synchronize with financial and ethical principles and accommodate Shari'ah-compliant institutions for building trustworthy relations with the public.[209]

205 Meirison Meirison et al., "The Role of Islamic Da'wah and the Implementation of Sharia on the Existence of Muslims in the Maldives Islands Past and Present," *Jurnal Ilmiah Islam Futura* 24/1 (February 1, 2024), 85–101.

206 Mohamed Ibrahim—Ahmad Hidayat Buang, "Maldivian Legal System: Islamic Influence and Legal Reform," *Jurnal Syariah* 26/1 (May 22, 2018), 71–98.

207 Boris Wille, "The Appropriation of Islam in the Maldives," *Oxford Research Encyclopedia of Asian History*, 2022.

208 Aishath Muneeza, "Enhancing Zakat Framework of Maldives: A Hundred Muslim Country," *International Conference of Zakat*, (February 18, 2019).

209 Jiayu Cui—Tao Li, "Religion, Power, and National Identity: The Dual Role of Islam in the History and Modernization of the Maldives," *Religions* 16/2 (February 2025), 201.

Religious harmony among Maldivian citizens generates positive outcomes for widespread acceptance of Islamic finance due to the collective cultural affection for Islamic moral traditions.[210] The Maldives requires a smooth integration of international economic markets with its religious heritage to establish its Islamic identity. The country now serves as a suitable setting to develop and test maqāṣid al-sharīʿah-oriented development approaches, particularly in sustainable tourism alongside climate resilience financing methods.[211]

2.4.6.2 Economic Profile and Sectoral Composition

The Maldives' economy has three defining characteristics: miniature size, modest sectoral diversity, and intense sensitivity to outside disruptions. Tourism is the nation's fundamental economic driver, generating 28% of GDP and more than 60% of foreign exchange earnings.[212]

The success of high-end tourism as an economic model has boosted national income, yet it has made the country depend more on outside finance and development support. The financial situation creates an exclusive space through which Islamic finance can replace ethical investments alongside resource acquisition and inclusive growth strategies.

The macroeconomic issues of the Maldives have the potential for meaningful transformation through Islamic financial approaches. Risk-sharing with asset-backed transactions in Islamic finance creates a solid foundation for infrastructure development and sustainable tourism and fisheries infrastructure expansion.[213] Secondly, Islamic financial instruments, including sukuk (Islamic bonds) and wakālah-based investment contracts, should respond to ethically motivated capital investments

[210] Aishath Shakeela—David Weaver, "'Managed Evils' of Hedonistic Tourism in the Maldives: Islamic Social Representations and Their Mediation of Local Social Exchange," *Annals of Tourism Research* 71 (July 1, 2018), 13–24.

[211] Mariyam Rafaa Abdul Latheef, "Does Community-Based Tourism Contribute to Halal Tourism from a Maqasid Al-Shariah Perspective? A Case Study of Maldives: Adakah Pelancongan Berasaskan Komuniti Menyumbang Kepada Pelancongan Halal Menurut Perspektif Maqasid Al-Shariah? Kajian Kes Di Maldives," *Journal of Muwafaqat* 7/1 (April 30, 2024), 39–66.

[212] Tk Jayaraman, Keshmeer Makun, "Tourism and Economic Growth Nexus in Maldives: Asymmetric Analysis and Role of ICT," *International Journal of Business and Society* 23/2 (August 8, 2022), 1086–1105.

[213] Aishath Muneeza et al., "Need to Pioneer Islamic Tourism in Tourist Resorts in Maldives," *Journal of Islamic Marketing* 11/4 (July 25, 2019), 895–916.

from Gulf and Southeast Asian markets, primarily through sovereign or green sukuk issuance.[214] The Islamic microfinance model utilizes qard al-ḥasan and mushārakah tools to provide financial support, including women SMEs and fishers who lack access to conventional credit markets.[215]

The launch of Islamic finance initiatives to protect coral reefs, sustainable solar-powered tourism amenities, and halal eco-tourism schemes align perfectly with the maqāṣid al-sharīʿah framework of public good and environmental stewardship. By implementing adequate strategies, the Maldives would become an Islamic sustainable development blueprint for all small island developing states (SIDS).

2.4.6.3 Emergence and Growth of Islamic Finance

The Maldives initiated its Islamic finance structure when the Maldives Islamic Bank (MIB) launched in 2011 to set a key development point for their financial system.[216] MIB started as a partnership between the Government of the Maldives and the Islamic Development Bank (IDB). However, the IDB exercises a controlling stake while extending policy and technical assistance to MIB. MIB started operations to provide ethical and Shari'ah-compliant financial services to the Maldivian people while aligning with national religious values and constitutional standards.[217]

MIB is the first and exclusive complete Islamic commercial bank established in the country.[218] MIB operates through a complete product range that includes cost-plus financing through murābaḥah and ijārāh leasing alongside muḍārabah profit-sharing accounts. The bank has

[214] "Developing Regional Healthcare Facilities in Maldives through Mudharabah Perpetual Sukuk," *International Journal of Management and Applied Research* 6/2 (2019), 81–96.

[215] Aishath Muneeza, "Short-Term Sharīʿah-Compliant Islamic Liquidity Management Instruments to Sustain Islamic Banking: The Case of Maldives," *Journal of Islamic Accounting and Business Research* 11/2 (January 20, 2020), 428–439.

[216] See Muneeza et al., "Need to Pioneer Islamic Tourism in Tourist Resorts in Maldives." "Home | Maldives Islamic Bank" (Accessed May 1, 2025).

[217] "Islamic Finance in South Asian Association for Regional Cooperation (SAARC) Countries," *Islamic Finance in Eurasia* (Edward Elgar Publishing, 2024), 45–79.

[218] Ubais Parayil Iqbal et al., "Integrating Trust with Extended UTAUT Model: A Study on Islamic Banking Customers' m-Banking Adoption in the Maldives," *Journal of Islamic Marketing* 14/7 (June 3, 2022), 1836–1858.

shown consistent progress while its locations have spread across multiple atolls and the central city of Malé.[219] Since 2021, the bank has launched a digital transformation of its operations, particularly through new mobile banking platforms and online Islamically compliant financing instruments.[220]

HDFC Amna emerged as an Islamic window of the Housing Development Finance Corporation to deliver Shari'ah-compliant housing finance solutions. The Bank of Maldives operated its Islamic banking services through a specific window while acting as the country's largest conventional bank, thus advancing dual banking structures in the Maldives' financial industry.[221] The delivery of Islamic window services reaches only a fraction of the total customer base in conventional banking operations.

The Maldives Monetary Authority (MMA) provides regulatory oversight as the country's central bank and financial regulator. The Financial Institutions Act (2011) grants the MMA the power to authorize Islamic financial institutions and conduct compliance oversight on Islamic banking principles while issuing development-related guidelines for the sector. Each Islamic institution that MMA licenses must fulfill a requirement for establishing an internal Shari'ah Supervisory Board responsible for examining product validity and operational adherence to Islamic principles.[222]

2.4.6.4 Shari'ah Governance and Institutional Framework

The Islamic financial sector of the Maldives operates without a unified Shari'ah supervisory board like those in Pakistan or Bangladesh. Every Islamic financial institution sets up its own Shari'ah Supervisory Board (SSB) as an internal body that guarantees its financial offerings follow Islamic legal principles. Each institution within the decentralized structure maintains substantial independence in interpreting Shari'ah standards, developing varying product designs and rulings.

[219] Aishath Muneeza, "Establishment of Islamic Capital Market in Jurisdictions with Limited Islamic Financial Services: Case Study of Maldives," *International Journal of Law and Management* 60/2 (March 12, 2018), 373–385.

[220] Iqbal et al., "Integrating Trust with Extended UTAUT Model," 1843–1847.

[221] Aishath Imthisal Ahmed—Ismail Nizam, "The Determinants of Customer Patronage in the Case of Islamic Finance Products in the Maldives," *International Journal of Accounting & Business Management* 7/1 (2019), 1–32.

[222] "Maldives Monetary Authority" (Accessed May 1, 2025).

Maldives Islamic Bank (MIB) is the country's sole Islamic bank, and its structured SSB consists of qualified scholarship board members from distinguished global institutions. This team of scholars executes duties related to financial product review and issues permanent opinions about operational aspects while performing Shari'ah audits for the bank's operations. MIB's SSB functions as a consultative body regarding Islamic commercial jurisprudence in-company training, product design, and strategic planning processes.[223]

The Maldives Monetary Authority (MMA) is the central financial regulatory entity that directs Islamic financial operations through the Financial Institutions Act (2011). MMA demands both functioning Sharīʿah Supervisory Boards from institutions and compliance reporting,[224] but the authority does not operate an extensive national Sharīʿah governance system or issue its fatāwā. A lack of centralized Shari'ah guidance produces diverse regulatory practices by institutions interpreting Islamic finance contracts using different Shari'ah doctrines. Besides this, local Shari'ah scholars lack standardized training, certification programs remain absent, and the number of scholars is minimal; only three scholars' profiles exist on their websites; thus, institutions depend on imported Shari'ah oversight experts.[225] The need for domestic Shari'ah governance infrastructure has led policymakers to discuss development and practice standardization that follows international guidelines from both AAOIFI and IFSB.

2.4.6.5 Challenges and Opportunities

Islamic financial penetration in the Maldives remains limited but stable. MIB dominates the sector, offering a range of Shari'ah-compliant products including murābaḥah (cost-plus financing), ijārah (leasing), muḍārabah (profit-sharing investments), and wakālah (agency contracts). Islamic banking assets remain below 12% of total financial assets in the country, reflecting the small market size and the dominance of conventional banks.

[223] Rabsha Waheed—Baharom Abdul Hamid, "Overcoming Implementation Challenges for Shariah Governance in the Maldives," *International Journal of Islamic Economics and Finance Research* 1 (October 11, 2023), 63–77.

[224] See "Maldives Monetary Authority."

[225] Mohamed Shujau et al., "Islamic Capital Market in Maldives: A Reform-Oriented Analysis," *IIUM Law Journal* 30/S2 (November 12, 2022), 359–384.

Nonetheless, innovation continues.[226] In 2023, digital banking services expanded through mobile applications offering simplified Islamic financing tools aimed at younger and unbanked populations, signaling a turn toward fintech solutions.

Despite its foundational religious alignment with Islamic finance, the Maldives faces several structural challenges. The small population, limited number of qualified Shari'ah scholars, lack of domestic sukuk issuance, and restricted awareness of Islamic financial instruments hinder growth. The absence of Islamic insurance (takāful) and dedicated microfinance schemes further narrows consumer options.

However, significant opportunities exist. The country's religious homogeneity and public trust in Islamic principles make it a fertile ground for faith-based finance. The tourism sector presents an untapped area for Shari'ah-compliant investment, particularly in eco-tourism and real estate. Moreover, international collaboration with bodies such as the Islamic Corporation for the Development of the Private Sector (ICD) and adherence to AAOIFI standards could help overcome regulatory and capacity limitations.

2.4.6.6 Discussion

The unique aspects of Islamic finance in the Maldives unite religiously sanctioned operations with economic insecurities while developing new financial institutions. As a small island developing state and a Muslim nation with a religious obligation to preserve Islamic values, the Maldives demonstrates compatibility with Islamic economics through Islamic economic principles. The Maldivian experience shows that implementing Shari'ah-compliant finance in restrictive environmental conditions demonstrates both positive opportunities and negative consequences.

From the perspective of ethical foundations vs structural constraints, the Maldives establishes all requirements for Islamic finance to thrive at its basic moral level. The Constitution and public demographics establish Islam as the official religion throughout the territory, where all people belong to the Muslim faith. The profile of the Maldives stands opposite to India regarding legal secularism barriers to Islamic banking, as well as Sri Lanka, which requires Muslim minority accommodations for Islamic finance in a Buddhist state. The Maldives experiences natural religious

[226] Ahmed Riza, "Islamic Banking and Financing Industry of Maldives: Snapshot of Today," *Corporatemaldives.Com* (blog), July 2, 2020.

acceptance of financial ethics based on faith due to its lack of ideological resistance against Islamic principles.

The state-religion alignment does not necessarily result in prosperous or numerous Islamic finance products. The Islamic finance sector of the Maldives largely depends on murābaḥah-based transactions while excluding many ijārah and muḍārabah options. The capital market of this jurisdiction remains underdeveloped as both ṣukūk issuance and takāful provider activities are inactive. The Islamic financial sector in Pakistan expands while Bangladesh provides its citizens with dual banking opportunities featuring diverse Islamic financial products.

The main obstacle for the Maldivian system stems from an incomplete sharing framework for Shari'ah governance. The separate Shari'ah Supervisory Boards appointed by Islamic financial institutions across different organizations lead to divided oversight and random interpretation of Islamic law. Conditions not unlike those found in Bangladesh were detected before CSBIB established itself as the Central Shari'ah Board for Islamic Banks. The State Bank and SECP of Pakistan implemented their centralized model, which shows potential for system reform.

Sri Lanka serves as a lesson for Islamic finance in the region. Islamic banking starts worldwide operations as the country's Muslim population represents 9.7% of the total population while permitting both Amana Bank and conventional banks' Islamic banking windows through specific legislative authorization. The Central Bank of Sri Lanka (CBSL) has established clear regulations, yet its program operates without specific Shari'ah authority oversight. Sri Lanka shows similar characteristics to the Maldives because it lacks a national Shari'ah board, yet its pluralistic legal framework demonstrates surprising regulatory flexibility, which the Maldives has not established officially.

The Maldivian financial model demonstrates how the requirements to adhere to Shari'ah law clash with progress toward achieving the maqāṣid substantial goals. Islamic finance has gained legal approval and social acceptance, but it needs to realize its ethical potential. Islamic insurance, social finance (qard al-ḥasan), and equity-based instruments are absent from the financial framework, which needs a proactive rather than reactive design.

The existence of Islamic finance as an official marker of identity, rather than a practical economic system, aligns with observations about Afghanistan. Unlike the Maldives, Afghanistan's political and infrastructural issues are confronted by financial, strategic, and legal-formal restrictions on its growth paths.

Despite the marginalization of Muslim minorities in Sri Lanka, there exists a practical legal framework that supports Islamic finance development. The listing of Amana Bank and its sukuk initiatives, along with regulatory accommodative measures, demonstrates that minority-led financial systems can innovate in a supportive legal environment. The governing framework of the Maldives can benefit by adopting Sri Lanka's enabling legal system and Pakistan's streamlined regulatory system.

Both the Maldives and Afghanistan have made tentative efforts to develop Islamic finance within complex political and institutional environments. The Maldives Monetary Authority has allowed Islamic windows and supports a limited regulatory framework. Afghanistan, under various regimes, attempted to establish Islamic banking law and institutions such as the Islamic Bank of Afghanistan.[227]

In both countries, legal uncertainty and political volatility affect ethical consistency. Afghanistan's Islamic banks have struggled to maintain public confidence, especially after changes in government led to disruptions in regulatory continuity. In the Maldives, Islamic windows sometimes operate without adequate internal auditing or Sharīʿah governance, which risks reputational and ethical slippage.[228] The limited number of qualified Sharīʿah scholars and the absence of unified training programs further restrict institutional maturity.

Encouraging cross-border partnerships for ethics training, regional standardization initiatives, and remote supervision tools (e.g., AI-aided Sharīʿah audit checklists) could support long-term development.

2.4.7 *Discussion: Rethinking Islamic Finance Through South Asian and Gulf Integration*

South Asia's Islamic finance environment presents regulatory distinctions combined with variable market accessibility and institutional plan differences. Pakistan and Bangladesh maintain dual-track systems, while India excludes Islamic finance. The Maldives, Afghanistan, and Sri Lanka show signs of developing this financial approach. South Asia demonstrates a hidden strength through its substantial socio-economic connections

[227] Mohammad Salim Salim, "Establishment of Islamic Banking System in Afghanistan: Factors Have Led to the Late Establishment of Islamic Banking," *HIKMATUNA: Journal for Integrative Islamic Studies* 6/2 (January 25, 2021), 90–102.

[228] "Maldives Monetary Authority" (Accessed July 30, 2025).

to the GCC countries, which are leading Islamic finance institutions internationally.

The proposed regional vision transcends basic comparison by adopting three foundational initiatives that link South Asian nations and Gulf states through Islamic finance based on migrant labor, while uniting them through both new platforms. This proposal establishes a complete transformation of Islamic finance through the ethical alignment of remittances and development activities for mutual regional advantages.

2.4.7.1 Labor Markets as Financial Gateways: The Gulf–South Asia Nexus

The GCC states have accepted approximately 20 million South Asian workers from India, Pakistan, Bangladesh, and an increasing number of workers from Sri Lanka and the Maldives. Foreign laborers in the GCC send their home nations billion-dollar sums yearly through official banking channels and unofficial systems. According to World Bank data, South Asia received over $170 billion in remittances in 2022, originating from GCC countries (World Bank, 2023).

The money transfers between countries are independent of Islamic financial institutions. These remittances are processed primarily through traditional banking and hawala systems, which fail to provide the chance to invest ethically or develop the system. South Asian and Gulf countries should direct these flows through Shari'ah-compliant platforms to build an ethical remittance-finance circuit that will suit senders' values and directly enhance poverty reduction, job market growth, and sustainable infrastructure development in home countries.

2.4.7.2 Toward a Transregional Islamic Finance Institution: A Mini-IDB for South Asia

This proposal entails founding the South Asia-Gulf Islamic Development Bank (SAG-IDB) to serve as an institution for South Asian migrants alongside their families by using ethical reinvestment and microfinance as core activities. This "mini-IDB" would:

- The institution will establish its headquarters in the Gulf through Bahrain, Doha, or Dubai as potential locations.
- The bank should operate licensed subordinate divisions throughout South Asian metropolitan areas.

- The institution should provide migrant workers with three main investment options: remittance savings accounts, Hajj funds, Islamic pension plans, and mortgage finance services.
- The institution should invest through qard al-ḥasan, mushārakah, and wakālah structures to fund enterprises in workers' home villages.
- The organization will introduce cross-border sukuk to obtain halal investment from Gulf-based diaspora members.

Such a bank would serve two functions: providing developmental financing and collaborating with Islamic principles for economic justice and Muslim transnational economic solidarity.

2.4.7.3 Sharīʿah Governance as Diplomacy: A Multilateral Council of ʿUlamāʾ

A distinctive element of this vision brings forward the recommendation of establishing a Transregional Sharīʿah Governance Council comprising leading scholars across the South Asian countries and the GCC. This council would:

All Islamic financial products should be harmonized across different jurisdictions. The migrant finance system needs to achieve uniformity in its fatwā production. The council should bring together scholars to explore ijtihād-based innovation in digital Zakat, blockchain waqf, and ethical climate finance.

When acting as an advisory council, it would function both technically and serve as a forum where intra-Muslim legal pluralism exists, maintaining different jurisprudential traditions (Ḥanafī, Shāfiʿī, Mālikī) from both regions. However, it would also be beneficial to achieve jurisprudential harmony whenever possible.

As South Asia continues to develop its Islamic finance ecosystem, the region must move beyond the passive adoption of Gulf-centric regulatory models and instead foster a more autonomous and context-sensitive jurisprudential framework. One promising approach is the formation of collaborative South Asian fiqh councils or regional Sharīʿah advisory platforms that bring together scholars from Pakistan, Bangladesh, India, and other neighboring countries. Such bodies could facilitate harmonization of legal interpretations through mutual ijtihād, promote the localization of maqāṣid-based principles, and issue regionally adapted standards that reflect both shared ethical commitments and socio-economic realities.

Rather than depending on standards developed for different economic environments, this intra-regional jurisprudential collaboration would enhance legitimacy, responsiveness, and cross-border regulatory coherence within South Asia's pluralistic legal landscape.

2.4.7.4 Strategic Integration: Beyond Fragmentation to Collective Power

The development of the Islamic finance industry in South Asian countries has occurred independently of one another throughout history.

- The penetration levels in Pakistan and Bangladesh persist, as both countries face conflicting internal challenges.
- Afghanistan and the Maldives deliver religious binding principles, although their market size remains limited.
- Sri Lanka and India face political and legal marginalization.
- Institutions can convert their weaknesses into strengths through collaboration on design initiatives. The SAG-IDB could serve as a:
- Liquidity stabilizer for fragile states like Afghanistan, a catalyst for financial inclusion among minorities in India and Sri Lanka, and an innovation hub for digital finance in the Maldives.
- Policy harmonizer for dualistic systems in Pakistan and Bangladesh.

Such a framework would foster the development of Islamic finance across the region, aligning with ethical finance guided by maqāṣid al-sharīʿah principles, much like the Asian Development Bank (ADB) operates in Asia and the African Export-Import Bank (Afreximbank) works in Africa.

People tend to treat South Asia and Gulf Islamic finance territories as separate domains. Multiple institutional partnerships are necessary to address the connections between these regions through labor networks, faith systems, and financial channels. A comprehensive Islamic finance platform, focusing on remittance services and migrant solutions, as well as microfinance lending and legal research development, will create an innovative era of interregional ethical finance that addresses underbanked communities and builds Islamic finance into a sustainable tool for social development and unity.

As institutions establish this vision, South Asia will transition from being a fragmented peripheral area in Islamic finance to a central driver for the creation of its next development front.

As illustrated in the present case, Islamic finance in South Asia develops at the intersection of Sharīʿah principles, postcolonial governance, and regional diversity. However, the question remains: Who holds these systems accountable for their ethics? Chap. 3 answers by tracking the heritage and contemporary changes in ḥisbah-Islam's historical platform of judicial and market monitoring and outlines its revival within a contemporary institutional structure to chart South Asia's ethically coherent financial future (Table 2.4).

This table outlines the strategic landscape of Islamic finance across key South Asian countries, focusing on institutional presence, regulatory support, Sharīʿah compliance mechanisms, and the role of government and civil society. It facilitates a comparative understanding of the maturity, scope, and structural features of Islamic finance in various contexts, including Pakistan, Bangladesh, India, Sri Lanka, the Maldives, and Afghanistan.

Figure 2.2 visualizes the historical trajectory of Islamic finance institutions in South Asia, tracing significant milestones such as the establishment of pioneering banks, regulatory reforms, the creation of Sharīʿah boards, and important policy shifts. This chronological mapping provides insight into the evolution, national differences, and regional patterns in the Islamic financial landscape.

Table 2.4 Strategic overview of Islamic finance in South Asia

Country	*Regulatory structure*	*Legal status*	*Governance*	*Market depth*
Pakistan	Centralized via SBP	Constitutionally Islamic	Centralized	>20%
Bangladesh	Moderate (CSBIB + BB)	Dual (Secular + Islamic)	Semi-centralized	~25%
Afghanistan	Fragmented (IEA & DAB)	Theocratic (Taliban-era)	Fragmented	5–6%
India	None (RBI blocks entry)	Secular, exclusionary	None	Informal
Sri Lanka	Limited via CBSL	Secular, accommodative	Decentralized	Low
Maldives	Moderate via MMA	Constitutionally Islamic	Decentralized	<10%

Source From different websites

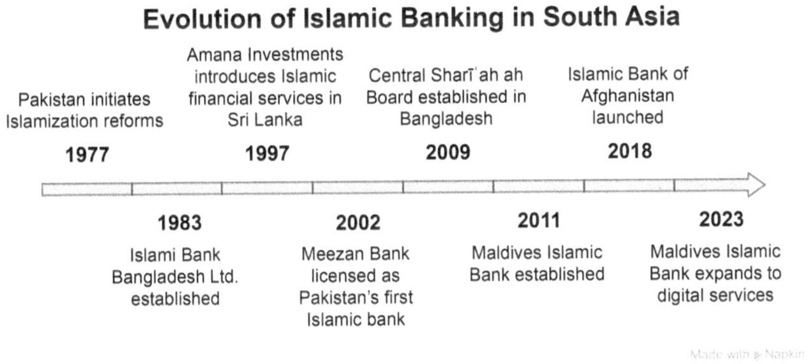

Fig. 2.2 Timeline of Islamic finance development in South Asia

Key Policy Takeaways:

- South Asian countries should collaborate to create a regional Sharīʿah governance framework, reducing reliance on externally produced standards.
- Regulators and Sharīʿah boards must invest in context-sensitive applications of Islamic legal principles, rooted in local maqāṣid and jurisprudential diversity.
- Institutions should prioritize translation and localization of AAOIFI standards to increase accessibility, transparency, and legal integration.
- A South Asian Ethical Finance Council (SAEFC) could facilitate cross-border regulatory harmonization, ethical compliance, and collective policy development.

CHAPTER 3

Ethical Oversight in Islamic Finance: Institutions and Standards

Building on the regional and historical analyses of Islamic finance institutions across South Asia presented in Chap. 2, this chapter shifts focus from national trajectories to the normative and institutional mechanisms that uphold ethical integrity within Islamic financial systems. While the previous chapter examined how legal, cultural, and regulatory factors have shaped the development of Islamic finance across various jurisdictions, this chapter explores the foundational role of ḥisbah, a classical institution of Islamic public oversight, and its relevance to modern Sharīʿah auditing, ethical governance, and market accountability. This transition from descriptive institutional mapping to normative governance analysis enables a deeper understanding of how Islamic finance can preserve its moral distinctiveness amid contemporary regulatory pressures.

3.1 Introduction: Three Axes of Ethical Oversight

Although institutional expansion is evident, the practical implementation of ethical priorities remains a perennial challenge in South Asian Islamic finance. Although the use of Sharīʿah-compliant instruments has increased dramatically, many institutions fall short of the Islamic moral standards they are required to maintain. This chapter responds to concerns regarding ethical inconsistency, fragmented regulation, and overemphasis on procedural

© The Author(s), under exclusive license to Springer Nature Switzerland AG 2025
A. H. M. E. Uddin, *The Regulation of Islamic Financial Institutions (IFIs) and Ethical Oversight in South Asia*, Palgrave Studies in Islamic Banking, Finance, and Economics,
https://doi.org/10.1007/978-3-032-09828-3_3

formality by proposing a framework based on classical Islamic oversight theories. The chapter, therefore, presents a framework comprising three axes of ethical oversight: normative foundations, institutional reforms, and integration with regional standards, thereby fostering effective oversight.

Axis I outlines the original jurisprudential roots of ḥisbah, the classical Islamic institution responsible for regulating trade and protecting public interest. Based on a study of Qur'anic teachings, the Prophet's behavior, and historical examples on the Indian continent, this axis illustrates how ḥisbah served as a moral enforcement device in ensuring justice in economic transactions.

Axis II examines the evolution of conventional ḥisbah concepts into contemporary Sharīʿah management practices, encompassing the establishment of supervisory boards, audit procedures, and internal control systems. This part of the paper analyzes to what extent institutional reforms have maintained or undermined the essence of ḥisbah ethical principles in modern finance.

Axis III examines how AAOIFI standards have impacted the institutional landscape in South Asia. It examines how countries such as Pakistan, Bangladesh, and the Maldives have implemented these standards, highlighting the gaps between global rules and local ethical requirements. This axis highlights that attempts to harmonize international guidelines with local contexts do not quite meet the mark in developing robust ethical governance structures.

Introducing ḥisbah as an element of history and a present-day principle, this chapter calls for restructuring Islamic finance oversight, distancing itself from the individualistic nature of compliance measures to adopt a merged or unified, justice-based outlook. While incorporating normative objectives and established structures, this three-step process provides South Asian Islamic finance systems with a systematic direction toward ethical governance.

3.2 Axis I: Normative Origin—Reclaiming the Jurisprudential Foundations of Ḥisbah

3.2.1 Conceptual Foundations of Ḥisbah: From Classical Definition to Contemporary Relevance

While this section explores the classical foundations of ḥisbah, its primary aim is to trace how these normative principles have evolved into operational frameworks for ethical financial oversight in modern South Asia.

Ḥisbah, in classical Islamic jurisprudence, refers to the institutional mechanism by which public morality, market fairness,[1] and lawful conduct are upheld.[2] It is grounded in the Qur'anic imperative of *al-amr bi-l-ma'rūf wa-n-nahy 'an al-munkar* (commanding good and forbidding wrong) and derived from the root *ḥ-s-b*, meaning to account, regulate, or assess.[3] Classical jurists such as al-Māwardī (*al-Aḥkām al-Sulṭāniyyah*) and Ibn Taymiyyah (*al-Ḥisbah fī al-Islām*) described the role of the *muḥtasib* as a public official tasked with ensuring justice in marketplaces,[4] including oversight of contracts, weights and measures, and pricing.

In this book, *ḥisbah* is not treated merely as a historical function but as a conceptual framework for ethical regulation in contemporary Islamic finance. It offers a holistic model of governance where legal enforcement and moral accountability converge—unlike secular systems, which separate compliance from ethics.

Modern parallels to *ḥisbah* can be found in Sharīʿah Supervisory Boards (SSBs), internal Sharīʿah compliance departments, and Sharīʿah auditors. However, these structures often emphasize legal conformity over ethical substance. Reviving the ethical core of *ḥisbah* requires moving beyond procedural checks toward a more integrated model that embodies moral intentionality, public welfare (*maṣlaḥah*), and institutional integrity.

The following sections trace how *ḥisbah* evolved and was transformed under various historical and regional contexts, with special emphasis on its reinterpretation and institutional application in South Asian Islamic finance systems.

3.2.2 Qur'anic Mandate for Ethical Oversight

The Qur'an provides foundational directives that undergird the institution of *ḥisbah* and ethical regulation. *Surah Āl 'Imrān* (3:110) affirms the duty of

[1] Sami Hamarneh, "Origin and Functions of the ḤisbahSystem in Islam and Its Impact on the Health Professions," *Sudhoffs Archiv Für Geschichte Der Medizin Und Der Naturwissenschaften* 48/2 (1964), 157–173.

[2] Ahmad Ghabin, *Ḥisba, Arts and Craft in Islam* (Deutschland: Otto Harrassowitz Verlag, 2009), 26.

[3] Muḥammad ibn Mukarram Abū al-Faḍl Jamāl al-Dīn Ibn Manẓūr, (Beirut: Dār Ṣādir, 1414), "Lisān Al-ʿArab," 1/310–316.

[4] Abu Hamid Muhammad ibn Muhammad al-Ghazali, *Ihya Ulum Al-Din* (Cairo: Islamic Publication, 1418), 2/306, 312.

the Muslim ummah to enjoin what is right and forbid what is wrong, while *Surah al-Mā'idah* (5:78–79) warns against the communal consequences of moral neglect. These obligations are not limited to ritual life but extend to commercial integrity, social fairness, and public accountability.

Financial behavior is also addressed explicitly. *Surah al-Baqarah* (2:275–279) forbids *ribā* (usury), while *Surah al-Nisā'* (4:29) prohibits unjust enrichment. These verses reinforce the Qur'anic ethic of fairness, transparency, and mutual consent in trade. Other references—such as 3:114, 4:114, and 11:116—underscore the imperative of collective oversight in ensuring a just society.

Rather than catalog every verse, it is more fruitful to extract a governing ethos: the Qur'an calls not only for legal compliance but for ethical excellence in all economic affairs. In today's context, this translates into regulatory structures that are rooted in trust (*amānah*), social welfare (*maṣlaḥah*), and ethical accountability. Institutions guided by the *ḥisbah* spirit must move beyond procedural formality to realize the Qur'an's deeper commitment to justice and equity in finance.

3.2.3 Prophetic Practice and the Evolution of Institutional Ḥisbah

The Prophet Muhammad ﷺ laid the foundational model of ḥisbah through both his personal conduct and structured governance.[5] His marketplace interventions—prohibiting deceptive sales, inspecting weights and measures, and appointing market supervisors like Saʿīd ibn Saʿīd ibn al-ʿĀṣ[6]—demonstrate the earliest applications of public financial ethics.

Beyond structural steps, the Prophet's teachings emphasized internalized accountability through *taqwā* (God-consciousness)[7] and *muraqabah* (divine

[5] Abū ʿĪsā Muḥammad ibn ʿĪsā as-Sulamī aḍ-Ḍarīr Tirmidhī, *Sunan Al-Tirmidhī* (Beirut: Dār al-Gharb al-Islāmī, 1996); Tirmidhī,"Kitab al-Birr wa al-Silah", 1987; Muslim, "Kitāb al-Īmān", 55; Abū Dāwūd, *Kitāb Al-Buyū'*, "Bāb fī al-Nuṣḥ wa al-Ḥifẓ", 4918.

[6] Abū ʿAbd Allāh Muḥammad Ibn Saʿd, *Al-Ṭabaqāt al-Kubrā* (Beirut: Dār Ṣādir, 1998), 5/7; Yūsuf b. ʿAbd Allāh İbn ʿAbd al-Barr, *Al-Istī'āb Fī Ma'rifat al-Aṣḥāb* (Beirut: Dār al-Jīl, 1992), 1/185.

[7] Muslim, "Kitāb al-Īmān" 102; Abū Dāwūd, *Kitāb Al-Buyū' 3452*; Tirmidhī, "Kitāb al-Buyūʿ" 1315; Bukhārī, "Kitāb Al-Buyūʿ" 2123; Muslim, "Kitāb Al-Buyūʿ" 1516.

vigilance). As recorded in the famous ḥadīth of Jibrīl: "Iḥsān is to worship Allah as if you see Him ... ",[8] these spiritual principles embed ethical mindfulness at the heart of public and financial dealings. The Prophet inspected both business locations and examined the conduct of public employees. A well-known occurrence showed his use of Ibn al-Lutbiyyah from the tribe of al-Azd as the new tax collector for alms. Upon his return, the man said, *"This is for you, and this was gifted to me."* The Prophet responded: *"Why doesn't he stay at his father's or mother's house to see if gifts would be given to him there? By Allah, whoever we appoint over a task and conceals anything, it will be brought forth on the Day of Judgment."*[9] This ḥadīth illustrates the Prophet's firm stance on conflict of interest and public trust, rendering ḥisbah an ethical expectation and an administrative necessity.

The Prophet's example also affirmed:

- *Anti-Corruption Measures*: His rebuke of public officers who accepted gifts ("Why does not he sit in his father's house to see if he'd be gifted?") underscores integrity and fiduciary responsibility.
- *Consumer Protection*: His prohibition on buying goods from caravan traders before market entry was a safeguard against insider dealing.
- *Women's Role*: The case of Samrah bint Nuhayk, a woman enforcer of ḥisbah, confirms gender inclusivity in regulatory roles.[10]
- *Institutionalization and Terminology*: While the term *muḥtasib* emerged during Umayyad-Abbasid administrations, the Prophet's actions prefigured its functions.[11] This ethical-administrative synergy—combining ethical spirit with regulatory structure—is the blueprint for today's Sharīʿah compliance frameworks.

Islamic finance must go beyond formal audits to embody these Prophetic ethics. Reclaiming ḥisbah as a living, ethical tradition can invigorate regulatory models and restore trust in Sharīʿah governance.

[8] Muslim, "Kitāb al-Īmān", 8.

[9] Bukhārī, "Kitāb al-Aḥkām", 7174; Muslim, "Kitāb al-Imārah", 1832.

[10] Ibn ʿAbd al-Barr, *Al-Istīʿāb Fī Maʿrifat al-Aṣḥāb*, 4/1863.

[11] ʿAlī Muḥammad Ṣallābī, *Al-Dawlah al-Umawiyyah (The Umayyad State)* (Beirut: Dār al-Maʿrifah, 2000), 1/315.

3.2.4 Conditions, Authority, and Jurisdiction of the Muḥtasib

In classical Islamic governance, the muḥtasib was not merely a market inspector but a state-appointed moral agent entrusted with the responsibility of *amr bi–l-ma'rūf wa–n-nahy 'an al-munkar* (commanding right and forbidding wrong). Jurists such as al-Māwardī and al-Shayzarī emphasized that this role demanded profound knowledge of Islamic jurisprudence (*fiqh*), sincerity in devotion, and impeccable moral character. The muḥtasib's authority extended beyond the market to include public ethics, urban regulation, hygiene, and even professional standards, operating within the ethical boundaries of Sharī'ah.

Al-Shayzarī, in his *Nihāyat al-Rutba fī Ṭalab al-Ḥisba*, outlines the ideal qualifications: jurisprudential competence, sincere devotion to Allah, and absolute integrity. The muḥtasib's actions should mirror prophetic conduct, with conformity to Islamic principles in worship and social behavior.[12] According to al-Māwardī, this position was not only administrative but also spiritual, serving to protect economic integrity and communal harmony. The muḥtasib's jurisdiction included enforcing standards in weights and measures, ensuring fair pricing, preventing fraud, maintaining public decency, and addressing grievances within the market. Juristic consensus affirmed the need for adult maturity (*bulūgh*), religious uprightness (*'adālah*), courage, and discernment in identifying manifest wrongdoing.[13] Later elaborations complemented these formal expectations—such as those by Ibn Farḥūn and Bassam—that added specific responsibilities like resisting bribery, avoiding unethical enrichment, and setting exemplary standards for subordinates.[14]

Islamic legal tradition also recognized a dual model of authority: the official muḥtasib, appointed and salaried by the ruler through *Bayt al-Māl*, and voluntary enforcers (*mutatawwi'ūn*) who acted without formal designation.[15] Al-Māwardī distinguished the two by noting that while both

[12] 'Abd al-Raḥmān ibn Naṣr Shayzarī, *Nihāyat Al-Rutba Fī Ṭalab al-Ḥisba* (Cairo: Lajnat al-Ta'līf wa-al-Tarjamah wa-al-Nashr, 1946), 6–9.

[13] Abū al-Ḥasan 'Alī ibn Muḥammad ibn Ḥabīb al-Māwardī, *Al-Rutbah Fī Ṭilib al-Ḥisbah* (Beirut: Dār al-Risālah al-'Ālamīyah, 2002), 55.

[14] See, Muḥammad ibn Aḥmad Ibn Bassām, *Nihāyat Al-Rutbah Fī Ṭalab al-Ḥisbah*(Beirut: Dār al-Kutub al-'Ilmīyah, 2003); Ibrāhīm ibn 'Alī ibn Muḥammad Ibn Farḥūn, *Tabṣirat Al-Ḥukkām Fī Uṣūl al-Aqḍiyah Wa-Manāhij al-Aḥkām* (Cairo: Maktabat al-Kullīyāt al-Azharīyah, 1986).

[15] Mehdi Berriah, "A Lack of Resources in the Bayt Al-Māl: A Sine Qua Non Condition for the Imposition of a Tax?," *Islamic Law Blog* (blog), September 30, 2021; Mohamad El-

worked toward moral order, the muḥtasib bore legal responsibility and punitive authority. His duties included addressing commercial malpractice, public disorder, and moral violations, all while maintaining impartiality and accountability.[16]

Practically, the muḥtasib was expected to ensure market cleanliness, monitor religious observance, protect vulnerable groups, enforce appropriate dress codes, and uphold urban order. He was to remain independent and impartial, avoiding personal entanglements and ensuring that justice was served equitably, without favoring the wealthy or influential.

Historical sources extend the muḥtasib's role well beyond economic oversight. *Kashf al-Ẓunūn* states that the essential function of *ḥisbah* is to manage social relationships with justice and mutual satisfaction in every transaction.[17] Ibn ʿAbdūn of Andalusia warned against allowing unqualified individuals to practice medicine due to risks to human life.[18] Kamāl al-Dīn Ibn Abī Jarāda recounts how the muḥtasib of Tarsus helped organize youth and merchants for wartime patrols and civic defense.[19]

In Mamlūk-era Egypt, Mustafa Kashif Kurd inspected merchant transactions and required trade documentation. He was supported by jurists like Shaykh Ibn al-Rifʿa, who praised his scientific precision in performing audits.[20] Meanwhile, under Umayyad rule, policing was divided: *al-shurṭa*

Merheb—Mehdi Berriah (eds.), *Professional Mobility in Islamic Societies (700–1750)* (Brill, 2021); Adnan Zulfiqar, *Collective Duties (Farḍ Kifāya) In Islamic Law: The Moral Community, State Authority And Ethical Speculation In The Premodern Period* (Pennsylvania: University of Pennsylvania, Doctorate, 2018).

[16] Abū al-Ḥasan ʿAlī ibn Muḥammad al-Māwardī, *Al-Aḥkām al-Sulṭānīyah* (Cairo: Dār al-ḥadīth, 1409), 260; Ibrāhīm Salmān al-karūyu—ʿAbd al-Tawwāb Sharaf al-Dīn, *Al-Marjiʿ Fī al-Ḥaḍārah al-ʿArabīyah al-Islāmīyah* (Kuwait: Dhāt al-Salāsil lil-Ṭibāʿah wa-al-Nashr, 1984), 93; Abū al-Ṭayyib Muḥammad Ṣiddīq Khān, *Abjad Al-ʿUlūm Alwshy Almrqwm Fī Bayān Aḥwāl al-ʿUlūm* (Dār Ibn Ḥazm, 2002), 2/36.

[17] Muṣṭafá ibn ʿAbdullāh Ḥājjī Khalīfah, *Kashf Al-Ẓunūn ʿan Asāmī al-Kutub Wa-al-Funūn* (Tehran: Dār al-Nashr al-Islāmīyah, 1943), 1/15.

[18] Amīn Tawfīq al-Ṭībī, *Dirāsāt Fī Tārīkh Ṣiqillīyah Al-Islāmīyah* (Iqraʾ lil-Ṭibāʿah wa-al-Tarjamah, 1990), 132.

[19] Kamāl al-Dīn Ibn al-ʿAdīm ʿUmar ibn Aḥmad Ibn Abī Jarādah, *Bughyah Aṭ-Ṭalab Fī Tārīkh Ḥalab* (Damascus: Dār al-Fikr, 2000), 1/188.

[20] ʿAbd al-Raḥmān ibn Ḥasan al-Jabartī, *Tārīkh ʿAjāʾib Al-Āthār Fī al-Tarājim Wa-al-Akhbār* (Beirut: Dār al-Jīl, 1997), 3/565.

al-kubrā handled elite oversight, while *al-shurṭa al-ṣughrā*[21] dealt with public discipline and routine enforcement.[22]

A telling example from *Siyāsatnāmeh* by Niẓām al-Mulk illustrates the reach of ḥisbah authority. During the Seljuk reign, a drunken military commander, ʿAlī ibn Nushtekin, ignored Sultan Maḥmūd ibn Malikshāh's warning and entered the marketplace. The muḥtasib, undeterred by ʿAlī's rank, arrested him and administered a punishment of forty lashes—demonstrating that even elite figures were not above the moral and legal authority of the ḥisbah system.[23]

These examples reflect how classical jurisprudence positioned the muḥtasib as a figure symbolizing both moral accountability and legal authority, tasked with safeguarding public ethics, market integrity, and communal justice within the framework of Sharīʿah.

3.2.5 Development Under the Caliphs and Classical Jurists

This section traces the institutional evolution of *ḥisbah* throughout Islamic history, demonstrating how its practical implementation shaped the ethical regulation of both economic and social life. Understanding these models is essential for revitalizing *ḥisbah* within modern Islamic finance.

As Muslim societies urbanized, the role of the *muḥtasib* evolved into a formalized institution tasked with maintaining market integrity and public morality.[24] Appointed by judges or rulers, the *muḥtasib* supervised pricing, prevented fraud, and enforced ethical norms—laying the groundwork for a system of oversight that integrated legal enforcement with moral accountability. The *muḥtasib* was responsible for overseeing market transactions, inspecting social behavior, monitoring women's appearance,

[21] 'Abd al-Raḥmān Ibn Khaldūn, *Muqaddimah Ibn Khaldūn* (Egypt: Dār Nahḍat, 1377), 277.

[22] Muḥammad Ḥusayn Maḥāsinah, *Binā' Al-Dawlah al-'Arabīyah al-Islāmīyah: Al-Nuẓum Wa-al-Ḥaḍārah* (Amman, 1999), 129; Zayn al-Dīn ibn 'Abd al-Qādir al-Ḥanafī al-Rāzī, *Mukhtār Al-Ṣiḥāḥ* (Beirut: al-Maktabah al-'Aṣrīyah, 1999), 1/141.

[23] al-Ḥasan ibn 'Alī ibn Isḥāq al-Ṭūsī Niẓām al-Mulk, *Siyāsat Nāmah* (Qatar: Dār al-Thaqāfah, 1407), 80–82.

[24] 'Abd al-Raḥmān Ibn Khaldūn, *Dīwān Al-Mubtada' Wa-al-Khabar Fī Tārīkh al-'Arab Wa-al-Barbar Wa-Man 'āṣarahum* (Beirut: Dār al-Fikr, 1981), 1/225.

ensuring humane treatment of animals, and maintaining environmental hygiene. In Islamic governance, ethical values were deeply embedded in state administration.[25]

This increasing institutional complexity prompted jurists to codify *ḥisbah* in legal manuals blending spiritual purpose with procedural detail. Key works include al-Māwardī's *al-Aḥkām al-Sulṭāniyyah*, al-Ghazālī's *Iḥyā'*, and Ibn Taymiyyah's *Risālat al-Ḥisbah*. These texts emphasized justice, fair trade, and moral stewardship—principles still relevant for Sharī'ah governance today. Other foundational treatises include: *Aḥkām al-Sūq* by Yaḥyā ibn 'Umar al-Andalusī (d. 289 AH),[26] The chapter on *ḥisbah*in al-Ghazālī's *Iḥyā' 'Ulūm al-Dīn*,[27] *al-Aḥkām al-Sulṭāniyyah* by al-Māwardī (d. 450 AH),[28] *Fi Ādāb al-Ḥisbah*by al-Saqṭī al-Mālikī (d. 500 AH),[29] *Risālah fī al-Qaḍā' wa al-Ḥisbah*by Ibn 'Abdūn al-Tujībī (d. 541 AH),[30] *Nihāyat al-Rutbah* by al-Shayzarī (d. 589 AH)[31] and *Ma'ālim al-Qurbah* by Ibn al-Ukhuwwah (d. 729 AH),[32] *Risālat al-Ḥisbahfī al-Islām* by Ibn Taymiyyah (d. 728 AH),[33] and *al-Ṭuruq al-Ḥukmiyyah* by Ibn al-Qayyim (d. 751 AH)[34] and encyclopedic works such as *Nihāyat al-Arab*

[25] al-Māwardī, *Al-Aḥkām al-Sulṭānīyah*, 211; 'Abd al-Mun'im Mājid, *Tārīkh Al-Ḥaḍārah al-Islāmīyah Fī al-'uṣūr al-Wusṭá* (Cairo: Maktabat al-Anjlū al-Miṣrīyah, 2010), 57.

[26] Yaḥyá ibn 'Umar al-Andalusī, *Aḥkām Al-Sūq* (Beirut: Dār Ibn Ḥazm, 2011).

[27] Abū Ḥāmid Muḥammad ibn Muḥammad al-Ghazālī, *Iḥyā' 'Ulūm Al-Dīn* (Beirut: Dār al-Ma'rifah, 1998).

[28] Abū al-Ḥasan 'Alī ibn Muḥammad ibn Ḥabīb al-Māwardī, *Al-Aḥkām al-Sulṭāniyyah Wa al-Wilāyāt al-Dīniyyah* (Beirut: Dār al-Fikr, 1990).

[29] Abū 'Abd Allāh Muḥammad ibn Muḥammad al-Saqṭī, *Fi Ādāb Al-Ḥisbah* (Beirut: Mu'assasat Dār al-Fikr al-Ḥadīth, 1991).

[30] Muḥammad ibn Aḥmad ibn 'Abdūn al-Tujībī, *Risālah Fī Al-Qaḍā' Wa al-Ḥisbah* (Beirut: Dār Ibn Ḥazm, 2009).

[31] 'Abd al-Raḥmān ibn Naṣr ibn 'Abd Allāh al-Shayzarī, *Nihāyat Al-Rutbah Fī Ṭalab al-Ḥisbah* (Cairo: Maṭba'at Lajnat al-Ta'līf wa al-Tarjamah wa al-Nashr, 1946).

[32] Ḍiyā' al-Dīn Muḥammad ibn Aḥmad ibn Abī Zayd Ibn al-Ukhuwwah, *Ma'ālim Al-Qurbah Fī Aḥkām al-Ḥisbah* (Cairo: The General Egyptian Book Organization, 1408).

[33] Taqī al-Dīn Aḥmad ibn 'Abd al-Ḥalīm ibn 'Abd al-Salām Ibn Taymiyyah, *Al-ḤisbahFī al-Islām* (Cairo: Dār al-Sha'b, 1976).

[34] Muḥammad ibn Abī Bakr Ibn al-Qayyim al-Jawziyya, *Al-Ṭuruq al-Ḥukmiyyah Fī al-Siyāsah al-Shar'iyyah* (Beirut: Dār Ibn Ḥazm, 2003).

by al-Nuwayrī[35] and *Ṣubḥ al-Aʿshā* by al-Qalqashandī.[36] These works articulated both the duties and ethical limitations of the *muḥtasib*, framing the institution as a moral backbone of Islamic governance.

The Rāshidūn Caliphs personally exemplified ethical oversight. Caliph Abū Bakr (11–13 AH), formerly a merchant, accepted a public stipend to focus entirely on governance.[37] ʿUmar ibn al-Khaṭṭāb (13–23 AH), also a former merchant, regularly patrolled markets, directly addressing pricing abuse and poor labor conditions.[38] He famously appointed al-Shifāʾ bint ʿAbdullāh as a market inspector,[39] an early example of women in public regulatory roles.[40]

Caliph ʿUthmān ibn ʿAffān (23–35 AH) introduced a second *muʾadhdhin* in the marketplace to enforce prayer-time discipline.[41] Caliph ʿAlī ibn Abī Ṭālib (35–40 AH) actively patrolled markets and emphasized fairness: "Take what is yours and give what is due; modest profits today lead to sustainable gains tomorrow."[42]

Under the Umayyads, *ḥisbah* was institutionalized. Dedicated officials (*ʿāmil ʿala al-sūq*) were appointed,[43] and infrastructure like *khāns*[44] (traveler inns)[45] was built to support traders. Caliph ʿUmar ibn ʿAbd al-ʿAzīz

[35] Shihāb al-Dīn Aḥmad ibn ʿAbd al-Wahhāb al-Nuwayrī, "Nihāyat Al-Arab Fī Funūn al-Adab" (Beirut: Daru'l-Kutubi'l-İlmiyye, 2004).

[36] Shihāb al-Dīn Abū al-ʿAbbās Aḥmad al-Qalqashandī, *Ṣubḥ Al-Aʿshā Fī Ṣināʿat al-Inshāʾ* (Beirut: Daru'l-Kutubi'l-İlmiyye, 1987).

[37] Muḥammad Ibn Saʿd, *Ṭabaqāt Al-Kubrā* (Cairo: Maktabat al-Khānjī, 2001), 3/137–140.

[38] Jalāl al-Dīn al-Suyūṭī, *Tārīkh Al-Khulafāʾ* (Beirut: Dār al-Kutub al-ʿIlmiyyah, 2004), 137.

[39] Aḥmad ibn ʿAlī Ibn Ḥajar al-ʿAsqalānī, *Al-Iṣābah Fī Tamyīz al-Ṣaḥābah* (Beirut: Dār al-Kutub al-ʿIlmiyyah, 1995), 4/358.

[40] al-Māwardī, *Al-Aḥkām al-Sulṭāniyyah Wa al-Wilāyāt al-Dīniyyah*, 206–208.

[41] al-Māwardī, *Al-Aḥkām al-Sulṭāniyyah Wa al-Wilāyāt al-Dīniyyah*, 206–210.

[42] Bāqir Sharīf al-Qurashī, *The Life of Ali Ibn Abi Talib* (Qum: Ansariyan Publications, 1999).

[43] ʿAlī ibn al-Ḥasan al-Dimashqī al-Shāfiʿī Ibn ʿAsākir, *Tārīkh Madīnat Dimashq* (Beirut: Dār al-Fikr, 1995), 23/201–203.

[44] M. A. Shaban, *Islamic History: A New Interpretation* (Cambridge: Cambridge University Press, 1971), 1/148.

[45] Ibn Saʿd, *Ṭabaqāt Al-Kubrā*, 5/119–125; Yaʿqūb ibn Ibrāhīm ibn Ḥabīb Abū Yūsuf, *Kitāb Al-Kharāj* (Beirut: Dār al-Maʿrifa, 1979), 115–116.

banned commercial stall rent, promoting egalitarian access to market space, a precedent for modern anti-exploitation policies.[46]

During the Abbasid period, caliphs such as al-Manṣūr (136–158 AH) reviewed daily market reports, demonstrating an executive commitment to economic ethics. The *muḥtasib* shared responsibility for maintaining order, ensuring that pricing data and commercial conduct aligned with Islamic values.[47]

The Ottoman Empire further institutionalized *ḥisbah* through trade guilds, market courts, and state-appointed *muḥtasibs*. Bayezid II's *qānūnnāme* codified pricing regulations and consumer protection laws, showing how legal instruments served Sharīʿah goals.[48] The *shaykh al-miḥna*, assigned to each trade, worked with the *muḥtasib* to ensure ethical and technical standards among artisans.[49]

Ottoman *ḥisbah* authority covered three main domains:[50]

- *Market Regulation*: Monitoring weights, prices, and fair trade.
- *Public Morality*: Enforcing dress codes, prayer observance, and gender norms.
- *Urban Management*: Overseeing sanitation, infrastructure, and public utility efficiency.[51]

[46] A. A. K. M. H. Al-Shaiji, *Critical Study and Edition of Al-Turuq al-Ḥukmiyya Fī al-Siyāsa al-Sharʿiyya* (Wales: University of Wales Trinity Saint David, PhD, 2001), 123–140.

[47] Abū Bakr Aḥmad ibn ʻAlī Khaṭīb al-Baghdādī, *Tārīkh Baghdād* (Baghdad, 1966), 1/285; Naji al-Hasan, *Al-ḤisbahFī al-Islām* (Riyadh: Dār al-Sumayʿī, 2005), 71–75; Hamilton Alexander Rosskeen Gibb, *Studies on the Civilization of Islam* (Princeton: Princeton University Press, 1982), 109–110; Muḥammad Rawwās Qalʿajī, *Al-ḤisbahFī al-Fiqh al-Islāmī* (Damascus: Dār al-Nafāʾis, 1983), 44–58.

[48] Suraiya Faroqhi, *Subjects of the Sultan: Culture and Daily Life in the Ottoman Empire* (London: I.B. Tauris, 2005), 98–100; Carter Vaughn Findley, *Turkey, Islam, Nationalism, and Modernity: A History, 1789–2007* (New Haven: Yale University Press, 2010), 248–253.

[49] Haim Gerber, *The Social Origins of the Modern Middle East* (Routledge, 1987), 69–72; Halil Inalcik—Donald Quataert, *An Economic and Social History of the Ottoman Empire* (Cambridge: Cambridge University Press, 1997), 1/313–318.

[50] Boğaç A Ergene, *Local Court, Provincial Society and Justice in the Ottoman Empire* (Brill, 2003), 49–52.

[51] Zeynep Çelik, *The Remaking of Istanbul: Portrait of an Ottoman City in the Nineteenth Century* (Berkeley: University of California Press, 1993), 43–44; Timur Kuran, *The Long Divergence: How Islamic Law Held Back the Middle East* (New Jersey: Princeton University Press, 2011), 130–132.

Ibn Taymiyyah emphasized that *ḥisbah*, like other administrative systems, aims to command good and prevent harm. Sultan Mehmed the Conqueror's legal reforms formalized public governance, empowering *muḥtasibs* to enforce morality alongside judges and viziers. Grand viziers delegated ethical oversight to trusted officials, creating an integrated moral-administrative framework.[52]

The Ottoman Sultan personally appointed each *muḥtasib*, considering their legal expertise, (*qānūn*)[53] reputation, and ability to act decisively. Secret market inspections and price audits were common.[54] The grand vizier oversaw food supplies, while city officials ensured pricing integrity and consumer rights.

Bayezid II's *qānūnnāme* (1502–1507 CE/908–913 AH) established over 100 laws regulating market activity, including punishments[55] and procedures. Each city adapted these laws locally, creating a comprehensive ethical infrastructure.[56]

[52] Ibn Taymiyyah, *Al-ḤisbahFī al-Islām*, 9–15; Abdulaziz Sachedina, *Islamic Ethics Fundamental Aspects of Human Conduct* (Oxford: Oxford University Press, 2022), 101–102.

[53] Colin Imber, *Ebu's-Su'ud: The Islamic Legal Tradition* (Edinburgh: Edinburgh University Press, 1997), 45–47; Uriel Heyd, *Studies in Old Ottoman Criminal Law* (Oxford: Clarendon Press, 1973), 11–13.

[54] Haim Gerber, *State, Society, and Law in Islam: Ottoman Law in Comparative Perspective* (New York: SUNY Press, 1994), 106–110; Faroqhi, *Subjects of the Sultan: Culture and Daily Life in the Ottoman Empire*, 90–91; Halil İnalcık, *The Ottoman Empire: The Classical Age 1300–1600* (Phoenix Press, 2000), 101–102; İsmail Hakkı Uzunçarşılı, *Osmanlı Devleti Teşkilâtından Kapukulu Ocakları* (Ankara: Türk Tarih Kurumu, 1988), 1/157–160; Linda T. Darling, "Revenue-Raising and Legitimacy: Tax Collection and Finance Administration in the Ottoman Empire, 1560–1660" (Brill, 1966), 68–71; Jane Hathaway, *The Arab Lands under Ottoman Rule 1516–1800* (Routledge, 2008), 108–110; Karen Barkey, *Bandits and Bureaucrats: The Ottoman Route to State Centralization* (Cornell University Press, 1994), 115–118; Fariba Zarinebaf, *Crime and Punishment in Istanbul: 1700–1800* (California: University of California Press, 2010), 25–27; Inalcik—Quataert, *An Economic and Social History of the Ottoman Empire*, 1/301–303.

[55] Ahmet Akgündüz, *Osmanlı kanunnâmeleri ve hukukî tahlilleri* (İstanbul: FEY Vakfi, 1990), 597–642.

[56] Fatma Gül Karagöz, *The Evolution of Kânûnnâme Writing in the 16th and 17th Century-Ottoman Empire: A Comparison of Kânûn-i'Osmânî of Bayezid II and of Kânûnnâme-i Cedîd* (Ankara: Bilkent Universitesi, Master's Thesis, 2010), 90–149; Mübahat S. Kütükoğlu, *Osmanlılarda narh müessesesi ve 1640 tarihli narh defteri* (İstanbul: Enderun Kitabevi, 1983), 24–30; Şevket Pamuk, *A Monetary History of the Ottoman Empire* (Cambridge: Cambridge University Press, 2000), 80–82.

Though modern Turkey is officially secular, its legal system still reflects tensions between procedural governance and ethical expectations. Reviving the spirit of *ḥisbah*, not just its form, could help Islamic finance institutions today blend regulatory authority with ethical intentionality.[57]

The historical evolution of ḥisbah reveals enduring ethical principles that remain relevant for contemporary Islamic finance. First, community involvement was central to effective oversight, as demonstrated by the participatory models of the Rāshidūn and Ottoman periods, where both state officials and citizens shared a commitment to market justice. Second, gender inclusion was not absent from the classical implementation of ḥisbah; figures such as al-Shifāʾ bint ʿAbdullāh and Samrah bint Nuhayk exemplify the presence of women in supervisory and enforcement roles—highlighting a precedent for modern gender-inclusive regulatory practices. Third, Islamic governance consistently integrated ethics with enforcement; legal procedures were grounded in moral objectives, not separated from them. This historical fusion of legal structure and ethical intentionality offers a powerful model for modern audits and Sharīʿah compliance systems, which must go beyond formal legality to embody the spirit and purpose of Islamic law.

3.2.6 The Institution of Ḥisbahin the Indian Subcontinent

3.2.6.1 Practices Under Delhi Sultanate, Mughal Padshāhs, and Localized Muḥtasibs

Understanding the historical development of ḥisbah in the Indian subcontinent is essential to appreciating how Islamic ethical oversight systems adapted across time and pluralistic contexts. Unlike the centralized models observed in Arab regions, South Asia's ḥisbah mechanisms evolved under diverse sociopolitical conditions marked by religious heterogeneity, decentralization, and successive imperial regimes. This regional variation offers critical insights into how Islamic governance principles—particularly public morality, market ethics, and legal pluralism—were localized and transformed. For modern Islamic finance, especially in post-colonial states such as Pakistan, the legacy of South Asian ḥisbah underscores the

[57] Jenny White, *Muslim Nationalism and the New Turks* (New Jersey: Princeton University Press, 2013), 22–25; M. Hakan Yavuz, *Islamic Political Identity in Turkey* (Oxford: Oxford University Press, 2005), 17–19.

enduring challenge of balancing Sharīʿah-based ethical oversight with complex governance realities. Studying these historical precedents enriches contemporary efforts to formulate ethics-based regulatory structures that are both contextually grounded and normatively consistent.

Despite the changing regimes, the ḥisbah institution in the Indian subcontinent, which corresponds to the present-day South Asian geography, demonstrated remarkable resilience. Under the Delhi Sultanate, the Tughlaq dynasty (1320–1413 CE) strengthened the ḥisbah institution by appointing muḥtasibs to oversee markets and public morals. This system was meticulously documented by ʿUmar b. Muḥammad al-Sunāmī, in his specialized handbook Nisāb al-Iḥtisāb in the 8th century AH (14th century CE), provides crucial insights into the muḥtasib's responsibilities during this era.[58] In his written manual, Al-Sunāmī thoroughly explains the duties of public officials, known as muḥtasibs, who were responsible for enforcing the law and upholding public safety. According to the manual, the muḥtasib needed to follow Quranic principles combined with Sunnah and demanded strict avoidance of religious innovations, which included any act of worshiping beings besides Allah, followed by the use of talismans and magic, and association with gambling, wine, or narcotics alongside other banned materials. Islamic public ethics, within his framework, demonstrated two classifications of human behavior: maʿrūf (commendable and permissible) and munkar (forbidden and objectionable).[59]

Al-Sunāmī's binary classification of maʿrūf (commendable) and munkar (forbidden) offers an early template for contemporary compliance mechanisms such as ethical screening criteria, Sharīʿah audit checklists, and supervisory benchmarks used in modern Islamic finance.

Under the Mughal padshāhs' rule, the muḥtasib served as the spiritual authority; however, decentralization occurred gradually over time. The

[58] Vladislav V. Gruzdev, "Public Administration of the Sultanate of Delhi in the 13th—15th Centuries-Historical and Legal Review," *Vestnik of Kostroma State University* 30/1 (June 28, 2024), 201–205; Abdul Azim Islahi, "Works on Market Supervision and Shar'iyah Governance (al-Hisbah Wa al-Siyasah al-Shar'iyah) by the Sixteenth Century Scholars," *Quarterly Journal of the Pakistan Historical Cociety* 54/3 (2008), 7–20; Robert Gleave, "The Near and Middle East—M. Izzi Dien: The Theory and Practice of Market Law in Medieval Islam: A Study of Kitāb Nisāb al-Iḥtisāb of 'Umar b. Muḥammad al-Sunāmī," *Bulletin of the School of Oriental and African Studies* 62/1 (January 1999), 128–129.

[59] Hamza Ateş, "A Pioneering Institution for Ombudsman: Hisbah," *Ombudsman Akademik* 6 (2017), 21–48; Safir Akhtar, "The Institution of Ḥisbahand Demand for Its Revival," *Policy Perspectives* 6/1 (2009), 89–104.

muḥtasib maintained his official position, particularly in principal cities and regional headquarters, where he oversaw marketplaces, set prices, and monitored weight standards and public religious practices. The political developments, combined with the empire's heterogeneous social composition, led to a decline in the institution's authority and stability.[60] Alam (1997) notes that the decline of central authority and the rise of regional governance provide crucial context for understanding the conditions that led to the diminished role of officials such as the muḥtasib. He offers essential background on the political and administrative transformations that weakened such institutions.[61]

3.2.6.2 Negotiating Sharīʿah Oversight in Pluralistic Empires

Under the Mughal rule in the Indian subcontinent, ḥisbah transformed because the Mughals governed an extensive area that encompassed Muslim, Hindu, Sikh, and numerous other communities. The Islamic governance system in this period coexisted with other traditional religious and community rules throughout various regions. Muḥtasibs maintained exclusive adherence to Islamic ethical laws in Muslim territories, yet needed to find viable solutions for executing justice and maintaining public security across diverse communities.[62] Although Richard Eaton (2020) does not directly address the transformation of the ḥisbah institution, his analysis suggests that between 1530 and 1622, the Mughal administrative system, particularly under Akbar and Jahangir, favored pragmatic political arrangements over strict adherence to ḥisbah manuals advocating Islamic law and reforms, such as those proposed by al-Sunāmī.[63] The officials permitted the coexistence of practices that orthodox Islamic jurisprudence would deem unacceptable, as they recognized the need for social unity and political stability. In jurisdictions governed by Islamic law, the muḥtasib retained all essential parts of their authority and their significant influence.

[60] Irfan Habib, *The Agrarian System of Mughal India, 1556–1707* (New York: Oxford University Press, 1999), 210; Satish Chandra, *Medieval India: From Sultanat to the Mughals Part—II* (New Delhi: Har-Anand Publications, 2005), 374.

[61] Muzaffar Alam, *The Crisis of Empire in Mughal North India: Awadh and the Punjab 1707–1748* (Delhi: Oxford University Press, 1997), 117.

[62] André Wink, "11 Religion and Politics in the Mughal Empire of India," *Volume 1 Empires and Gods: The Role of Religions in Imperial History*, ed. Jörg Rüpke et al. (De Gruyter, 2024), 321–350.

[63] Richard Eton, *India in the Persianate Age, 1000–1765*, 2020.

This pragmatic blending of Islamic oversight with pluralistic governance highlights a historically grounded model of regulatory flexibility. Rather than enforcing uniform Sharīʿah norms across all subjects, Mughal-era administrators adapted ethical enforcement to match demographic and political realities. This adaptive approach resonates with today's ongoing debates in Islamic finance ethics—especially regarding localized Sharīʿah standards, context-specific ḥisbah models, and the tension between universal norms and regional implementations in multi-religious societies.

3.2.7 Decline and Transformation Under Colonial Pressures

The late Mughal period witnessed the decline of the ḥisbah institution, as political incompetence and moral degeneration led to a weakening of public Islamic ethical enforcement. The British colonial governance period (1170–1367 AH/1757–1947 CE) accelerated the deterioration of the ḥisbah establishment. Under colonial administration, British authorities implemented a codified legal system that eliminated traditional Islamic institutions, rendering the muḥtasib's role in its classical form unfeasible.[64] The colonial government established exclusive secular and bureaucratic systems of governance, which stripped public administration of Islamic moral regulations. Due to these changes, all components of the Islamic legal order underwent marginalization or dissolution. The governance system based on Islamic principles underwent centuries of change, which severed the historical connection between religion and government functions.

Following the end of British colonial rule in 1947, the Indian subcontinent was partitioned into two independent states, India and Pakistan, with Bangladesh as part of Pakistan. Pakistan, a newly established independent Muslim nation, declared its aspiration to base its governance on Islamic teachings. However, since 1947, Pakistan has been grappling with the challenge of reconciling Islamic management principles with modern state development paradigms, a struggle that continues to this day.[65] The Objectives Resolution (March 12, 1949) formed the basis of a Pakistani

[64] Ateş, "A Pioneering Institution for Ombudsman," 25; Abdul Azim Islahi, *History of Islamic Economic Thought: Contributions of Muslim Scholars to Economic Thought and Analysis* (Cheltenham (GB): Edward Elgar Publishing, 2014).

[65] C. H. Philips—Mary Doreen Wainwright (eds.), *The Partition of India: Policies and Perspectives 1935–1947* (London: Routledge, 2025), 275; R. J. Moore, "Jinnah and the Pakistan Demand," *Modern Asian Studies* 17/4 (1983), 529–561.

Islamic order when it was passed through the Constituent Assembly to guide future constitutional development. Political instability lasted nine years until Pakistan established its first Constitution on March 23, 1956, by incorporating the Objectives Resolution as its opening statement. The country's Islamic orientation was interrupted after martial law was imposed on October 8, 1958, resulting in the cancellation of the constitution.[66]

Military ruler Muhammad Ayub Khan presented a new constitution on March 1, 1962, which weakened the Islamic elements present in the state. The country adopted the Republic of Pakistan, marginalizing its Islamic legal foundations.[67] The regime was pressured by public demands to merge Islamic principles into the system through the Basic Democracies. The new form of governance restricted public voting rights and mass participation levels in national decision-making processes. President Ayub Khan utilized the system for his reelection bid in 1964, but public activism compelled him to resign. General Yahya Khan established another martial law on March 28, 1969, through his military authority. The government conducted general elections in December 1970; however, East Pakistan separated from the nation due to political errors and heavy-handed methods, ultimately leading to its independence as Bangladesh.[68]

The secession led to Zulfikar Ali Bhutto assuming power, as his party won the majority of parliamentary seats in West Pakistan. President Zulfikar Ali Bhutto guided Pakistan towards establishing the 1973 Constitution, which enabled the nation to become an Islamic Republic under Islamic principles on August 14, 1973.[69] In modern times, the revival of ḥisbah oversight systems and other Islamic governance institutions has been largely ceremonial. South Asia continues to lack a complete realization of post-colonial systems.

[66] Minahil Khurshid, "Revisiting the Objectives Resolution 1949: Identity of Pakistan," *Paradigm Shift* (blog), May 7, 2025.

[67] Nasir Islam, "Islam and National Identity: The Case of Pakistan and Bangladesh," *International Journal of Middle East Studies* 13/1 (1981), 55–72.

[68] Jagmohan Meher, "Dynamics of Pakistan's Disintegration: The Case of East Pakistan 1947–1971," *India Quarterly* 71/4 (2015), 300–317; Stanley Maron, "The Problem of East Pakistan," *Pacific Affairs* 28/2 (June 1955), 132.

[69] Ronald J. Herring, "Zulfikar Ali Bhutto and the 'Eradication of Feudalism' in Pakistan," *Comparative Studies in Society and History* 21/4 (October 1979), 519–557.

The marginalization of ḥisbah under colonial and post-colonial governance reflects a broader epistemic dislocation—where Islamic ethical institutions were either absorbed into secular bureaucracies or symbolically retained without operational function. Contemporary Islamic finance in South Asia still grapples with this legacy, often lacking enforceable Sharīʿah auditing frameworks rooted in local jurisprudential traditions. Understanding this decline is critical for reform efforts that aim to recontextualize ethical oversight not as nostalgic restoration, but as adaptive reconstruction anchored in fiqh and local governance realities.

3.2.8 Comparative View: Ḥisbah versus Western Regulatory Models

This section compares the Islamic ḥisbah system with modern Western regulatory frameworks to illuminate core tensions between moral-spiritual oversight and secular legal control. While the former grounds its authority in divine ethics and community norms, the latter emphasizes procedural legitimacy and market efficiency. Understanding this divergence is essential for rethinking Islamic ethical governance in contemporary finance, especially as Sharīʿah-compliant institutions increasingly operate within global regulatory regimes.

The ḥisbah institution, established by Islamic governance, supervised public actions encompassing social conduct, commercial matters, and ethical behavior. The regulatory system of ḥisbah operated as an ethical-religious institution after the Quranic directive "enjoin what is right and forbid what is wrong" (Qur'an 3:104), unlike contemporary Western systems, which originated from secular law-based and utilitarian concepts.[70] Through this regulatory framework, Islamic society received public oversight and moral guidance to maintain Sharīʿah compliance in every aspect of behavior.[71] Today, the principle of *al-amr bi-l-maʿrūf wa-n-nahy ʿani-l-munkar* is conceptually echoed in ethical investment filters, Environmental-Social-Governance (ESG) frameworks, and Sharīʿah-compliant screening tools that aim to align economic action with public morality.

The ḥisbah institution oversaw every economic activity undertaken by members of the public.[72] The authority of market inspectors, who acted as

[70] Michael Cook, *Commanding Right and Forbidding Wrong in Islamic Thought* (Cambridge: Cambridge University Press, 2010), 3–5.

[71] Cook, *Commanding Right and Forbidding Wrong in Islamic Thought*, 76–77.

[72] Maya Shatzmiller, *Labour in the Medieval Islamic World* (Leiden The Netherlands; New York: Brill Academic Pub, 1994), 101–112.

muḥtasibs, extended to regulating marketplace behavior, enforcing ethical standards, and ensuring justice and fairness. All traders used measurements to maintain precise instruments, and vigorous enforcement of the no-speculation prohibition (ihtikār) along with permission for no-usury (ribā), no-price-hiking rules, and non-fraudulent deal protections was common practice.[73] The Islamic theological basis made these legal prohibitions also function as moral requirements.

Market officials could review public utilities, confirm product standards, and Sharīʿah conformity throughout economic spheres, and implement health and hygiene inspections.[74] In addition to its specific commercial duties, the ḥisbah agency directed its activities toward inspecting mosque cleanliness, preventing public immoral conduct, and safeguarding the needs of orphaned and impoverished population groups.

The laws related to ḥisbah officials provided them with notable enforcement capabilities.[75] When non-compliance persisted, ḥisbah officials had the authority to issue penalties and confiscate goods, while also taking additional legal action against persistent violators. The dual-purpose system functioned as both an administrative enforcement tool and a means to keep citizens spiritually accountable, thereby making ḥisbah serve as a legal and moral oversight.

The muḥtasib is appointed by the ruler and charged with maintaining public order by addressing societal maladies, as detailed by al-Māwardī in *al-Aḥkām al-Sulṭāniyyah*. He outlines the inspector's responsibilities, commercial supervision, moral enforcement, and distributive justice as essential elements of public welfare. These principles inform contemporary models of Sharīʿah auditing, where supervisory boards are expected to balance procedural checks with ethical intent. Similarly, Ibn Taymiyyah (d. 1328), in *al-Ḥisbah fī al-Islām*, emphasized the institution's role in preserving the moral equilibrium of Islamic society. His framework has contemporary relevance for public interest screening in Islamic finance—particularly where social harm must be prevented alongside legal compliance.[76] Contemporary scholars of Islamic finance view Ibn Taymiyyah's emphasis on market justice and moral guardianship as foundational for

[73] Islahi, *History of Islamic Economic Thought*, 17–25.

[74] Ibn al-Ukhuwwah, *Maʿālim Al-Qurbah Fī Aḥkām al-Ḥisbah*, 166–170.

[75] Cook, *Commanding Right and Forbidding Wrong in Islamic Thought*, 326–328.

[76] Ibn Taymiyyah, *Al-ḤisbahFī al-Islām*, 16–18.

building Sharīʿah auditing systems that go beyond mere legal compliance to uphold maqāṣid al-sharīʿah (the higher objectives of Islamic law).

On the contrary, Western regulatory systems—such as the US Federal Trade Commission (FTC), European Competition Authorities, or Food and Drug Agencies—derive their legitimacy from secular statutory frameworks. Their primary objectives revolve around consumer protection, market efficiency, and compliance with technical standards, rather than moral or religious mandates. These systems emphasize procedural neutrality, institutional specialization, and rule-of-law governance.[77]

In contrast, Western regulators typically distribute responsibilities across multiple agencies (e.g., separate agencies for food safety, financial regulation, and antitrust enforcement), whereas ḥisbah included an overall unified structure. The muḥtasib oversaw weights and measures, price control, product quality, standards of public morality, and even the modesty of attire and the standard of living.

The ethical sphere of ḥisbah is even more pronounced in Andalusian manuals, such as Ibn ʿAbdūn's *Risāla fī al-ḥisbah*, which states that artisans must demonstrate their professional expertise and that unqualified practitioners have no excuse for practicing (especially in medicine), as it is an obligation to save a life.[78] Similarly, in Ottoman Istanbul, muḥtasibs inspected bakers to maintain standard bread weights and punished corrupt pricing practices, as noted in the local court records (sijillāt).[79] Mustafa Kashif Kurd's administration of market measurement practices in Egypt represented consistency with principles made possible through previous scholarship, such as that of Ibn al-Rifʿa.[80] This comparison may be summarized as follows (Table 3.1).

These differences highlight the challenges faced by contemporary Muslim-majority countries attempting to harmonize faith-based ethics with internationally mandated compliance regimes. Future models may

[77] Anthony I. Ogus, *Regulation: Legal Form and Economic Theory* (London: Hart Publishing, 2004), 1–3, 45–47, 120–122; Giandomenico Majone (ed.), *Regulating Europe* (London: Routledge, 2005), 20–22, 100–102; David Vogel, *The Politics of Precaution: Regulating Health, Safety, and Environmental Risks in Europe and the United States* (Princeton N.J.: Princeton University Press, 2012), 3.

[78] al-Tujībī, *Risālah Fī Al-Qaḍā' Wa al-Ḥisbah*, 27; Ibn ʿAbdūn, 1969, 27.

[79] Faroqhi, *Subjects of the Sultan: Culture and Daily Life in the Ottoman Empire*, 79–81.

[80] André Raymond, *Cairo: City of History* (American University in Cairo Press, 2001), 246–248.

Table 3.1 Comparative framework of classical Ḥisbah and contemporary Western regulatory systems

Feature	*Ḥisbah system*	*Western regulatory models*
Source of authority	Sharīʻah (Divine Law) + Ruler Delegation	Statutory Law (Legislature/ Government)
Primary objective	Ethical conduct, public welfare, justice	Consumer protection, market efficiency, and legal compliance
Inspector role	Muḥtasib: Moral and legal agent	Regulator: Legal-technical bureaucrat
Scope of oversight	Markets, morals, public health, worship, and conduct	Economic and legal sectors only
Sanctions	Legal penalties + moral correction	Legal penalties, fines, license revocations
Accountability	To God, the ruler, and society	To state institutions, courts, and audit bodies
Operational ethos	Moral reform and religious duty	Procedural neutrality and institutional specialization

Source Author's own

need to blend the institutional rigor of Western systems with the moral depth of Islamic governance.

The ḥisbah, therefore, is not a proto-bureaucratic set-up so much as one that forms part of a comprehensive ethical, social, and economic regulating mechanism. It had both moral values and technical administration.[81] In Kashf al-Ẓunūn, it is mentioned that ḥisbah involved knowledge of urban interactions, conduct in the market, and work for the community's needs, all of which are far different from utility-based statecraft.[82]

Although today's Western regulatory schemes are based on legal positivism, specialization, and secular rationalism, the ḥisbah regime represented the idealism of religion, moral duty, and community involvement.[83] Each system expresses one's civilizational ethos, secular proceduralism against Islamic ethical stewardship.

[81] al-Shayzarī, *Nihāyat Al-Rutbah Fī Ṭalab al-Ḥisbah*, 3–5.

[82] Kâtip Çelebi, *Kashf al-ẓunūn 'an asāmī al-kutub wa-al-funūn* (Beirut: Dār al-Kutub al-'Ilmīyah, 1992), 2/1123.

[83] Çelebi, *Kashf al-ẓunūn 'an asāmī al-kutub wa-al-funūn*, 2/5.

Thinkers like Muḥammad ʿAbduh struggled to reconcile the spiritual depth of Islamic law with modern secular philosophies of governance. His ambivalence reflects the broader challenge of constructing hybrid systems that integrate tradition without capitulating to Western legalism.[84] Muhammad Khalid Masud (2009) also notes that Islamic governance models, such as ḥisbah, are deeply embedded in a tradition of jurisprudence that rejects, in strict terms, the compartmentalization that underlies modern, secular legal systems. He stresses that the aspect of flexibility in Shariʿah can best be understood as the possibility of moral reasoning being adapted to the challenges of the present modus vivendi without losing its normative roots.[85]

In light of these contrasts, future Islamic finance systems may benefit from hybrid regulatory models that integrate the moral intentionality of ḥisbah with the procedural clarity of modern institutions. For instance, Malaysia's dual compliance frameworks—combining Sharīʿah supervisory boards with statutory regulation—illustrate a possible synthesis. Such models point to a viable future where Islamic ethics and global standards co-evolve without compromising religious integrity or technical rigor.

3.2.9 Sharīʿah-Based Oversight and Qawāʿid al-Fiqhiyyah in South Asia

This section highlights how South Asian regulators and advisory bodies utilize fiqh-based legal maxims to bridge classical Sharīʿah norms with ethical oversight in modern finance. The actual enforcement and supervision of ethical standards in South Asian Islamic finance derive their framework from both regulatory bodies while following established Sharīʿah rules that appear as Qawāʿid al-Fiqhiyyah.[86] These maxims serve as ethical anchors, offering interpretive flexibility while reinforcing the core purposes of Sharīʿah in financial practice.

[84] Professor Albert Hourani, *Arabic Thought in the Liberal Age 1798–1939* (Cambridge: Cambridge University Press, 1983), 131–135.

[85] Muhammad Khalid Masud et al., *Islam and Modernity Key Issues and Debates* (UK: Edinburgh University Press, 2009), 244–246.

[86] Buerhan Saiti—Adam Abdullah, "The Legal Maxims of Islamic Law (Excluding Five Leading Legal Maxims) and Their Applications in Islamic Finance القواعد الفقهية—عدا القواعد الخمس الكبرى—وتطبيقاتها في التمويل الإسلامي," *Journal of King Abdulaziz University: Islamic Economics* 29/2 (2016), 139–151.

The legal maxims offer three practical benefits, which enable regulators, financial actors, and scholars to address contemporary challenges while preserving Sharīʿah fidelity and operational flexibility. In Pakistan and Bangladesh, the implementation of Sharīʿah boards relies on maxims, including *al-ʿādah muḥakkamah* ("custom is authoritative") and *al-ḍarar yuzāl* ("harm must be eliminated"),[87] as they bridge classical legal principles with contemporary financial operations. The established principles enable the creation of ethical standards while offering guidance toward correcting consumer protection, insurance, and risk-sharing approaches.

Local fatwa councils and community-based advisory groups have taken center stage in South Asian countries like Sri Lanka and India since state-backed Islamic finance regulation exists only minimally or not at all. The actors utilize *maṣlaḥah mursalah* (unrestricted public interest) as their jurisprudential tool to determine whether to authorize or prohibit practices based on current circumstances.[88] In the absence of centralized regulators, such councils perform a hybrid *ḥisbah* function, combining legal opinion with ethical advisory mechanisms in decentralized contexts. Some cooperative finance models and *zakāt*-based microfinance operations receive approval because they contribute to public benefit alongside poverty alleviation and economic justice, rather than through textual evidence. For instance, *zakāt*-linked housing initiatives have been endorsed despite lacking classical analogues, due to their alignment with *maqāṣid*-based outcomes.[89]

The use of unrestricted public interest *maṣlaḥah mursalah* harmonizes with the sacred principles of Sharīʿah (*maqāṣid al-sharīʿah*),[90] which protect religion, life, intellect, progeny, and wealth. Historical records support this reasoning, as the Qur'an received its final form as a single manuscript, and community-taught punishments for murder became established when no direct revelation was apparent.

[87] Fawzy Shaban Elgariani, *Al-Qawa'id al-Fiqhiyyah (Islamic Legal Maxims): Concept, Functions, History, Classifications and Application to Contemporary Medical Issues* (England: University of Exeter, Ph.D., 2012), 45–47.

[88] Sarah Nursaadah Mohd Zameri et al., "Maslahah and Its Application in Islamic Finance," *International Journal of Islamic Business* 9/1 (June 30, 2024), 82–94.

[89] Uddın, "Through Islamic Banks' Zakat House (IBZH)," 4; Uddın-Okur, "Empowering Communities."

[90] Muhammad Iqmal Hisham Kamaruddin et al., "Maqasid Shariah Disclosure: A Case of a Malaysian Shariah-Compliant Company," *Journal of Islamic Accounting and Business Research* ahead-of-print/ahead-of-print (2025).

The practical use of *maṣlaḥah* requires careful attention when applied to modern financial contexts. Public welfare justifications behind deposit insurance and government bailouts may inadvertently create a situation referred to as a moral hazard, in which actors may be incentivized to undertake excessive risks under the expectation that public entities or other parties will bear responsibility for potential losses. Islamic law rejects the application of reward-risk asymmetry because it fails to meet the requirements of justice, thereby depriving parties of equal decision-making power. In practice, this has informed recent *fatwā* revisions in South Asia discouraging *murābaḥah*-based credit excess and promoting equity-based models such as *muḍārabah* and *mushārakah*. To overcome this problem, scholars apply the principle *darʾ al-mafāsid muqaddam ʿalā jalb al-maṣāliḥ*, which means that prevention of harm precedes benefit acquisition.[91]

In Islamic jurisprudence, a doctrine known as *sadd al-dharāʾiʿ* exists to prevent the means that could cause harm.[92] According to this principle, even legal actions become forbidden because they tend to produce prohibited results. The South Asian academic community is leading the implementation of this doctrine to regulate matters involving excessive credit expansion, derivative instruments, and speculative trading. The uncontrolled generation of credit and intricate financial products led to the 2008 global economic crisis, suggesting unauthorized activity under this principle because these approaches endanger the system's stability.

The classical *ḥisbah* tradition provides historical evidence that supports this particular position. In his regulations book, al-Māwardī instructed *muḥtasibs* to prevent ship owners from overloading vessels beyond their capacity or forcing navigation during heavy storms, as business interests must be balanced with safety precautions.[93] From classical Islam to the present day, this historical continuity of ethical oversight in finance instills

[91] Mohamad Akram Laldin—Hafas Furqani, "Developing Islamic Finance in the Framework of Maqasid Al-Shari'ah," *International Journal of Islamic and Middle Eastern Finance and Management* 6/4 (2013), 278–289; A. Syathir Sofyan et al., "Financing Risk Measurement with Maqashid Al-Sharia Qualitative Risk 1," *Share: Jurnal Ekonomi Dan Keuangan Islam* 8/1 (2019), 1–30.

[92] Ahmad Dahlan Salleh et al., "Theory and Application of Sadd Al-Dhara'i' (Blocking the Means) in Shafi'iyya School," *International Journal of Academic Research in Business and Social Sciences* 9/1 (2019), 724–737.

[93] Tengku Nurul Saadah Tengku Zawawi et al., "The Roles of Muhtasib in Islamic Medieval Urban Management," *Environment-Behaviour Proceedings Journal* 6/SI5 (2021), 181–186.

a sense of normative coherence, reminding contemporary scholars and practitioners that financial regulation is not merely a technical exercise but a manifestation of moral responsibility. As South Asian Islamic finance continues to evolve, the integration of Qawāʿid al-Fiqhiyyah into institutional oversight structures—grounded in community needs, fiqh reasoning, and maqāṣid al-sharīʿah—offers a dynamic pathway for sustainable and ethical financial governance. These principles collectively ensure that the ethical spirit of *ḥisbah* is not confined to history but actively shapes emerging systems of accountability, justice, and public welfare in the modern South Asian financial landscape.

The legal framework of Islamic finance remains in development in the emerging Islamic financial sectors of Afghanistan and the Maldives.[94] These foundational jurisprudential principles provide an ethical basis for institutional growth and community validation. The four maxims of *maṣlaḥah, sadd al-dharāʾiʿ, amānah*, and *ʿadl* form a conceptual unity that guides ḥisbahin its emphasis on proactive governance rather than event-based response, ensuring a robust and forward-thinking system.

South Asian Islamic finance will better adhere to the ḥisbah spirit by integrating institutional systems and reasoning based on maxims that focus on upholding justice, maintaining market integrity, and protecting collective welfare.

3.3 Axis II: Institutional Transformation Into Modern Financial Oversight

The guidelines on financial issues in Islamic law evolved into a global economic system that necessitated significant regulatory adjustments. However, technocratic structures, such as Sharīʿah Supervisory Boards (SSBs), local internal compliance departments, and audit committees, have replaced the classical ḥisbah system in Islamic cities.[95] The required structural changes in financial globalization create ambiguities in the relationship between Islamic financial compliance systems and their ethical norms. Critic argues that current Sharīʿah governance frameworks fail to

[94] "Maldives: Country Operations Business Plan (2021–2023)" (Asian Development Bank, November 18, 2020) (Maldives); "Annual Financial Report | Da Afghanistan Bank" (Accessed June 5, 2025).

[95] *The Edinburgh Companion to Shari'ah Governance in Islamic Finance*, critical ed. Syed Nazim Ali et al. (Edinburgh: Edinburgh University Press, 2020), 41–44.

incorporate the community-oriented and pro-ethical elements of ḥisbah.[96] The axis explores the institutional developments and mechanics of Islamic finance's operation while assessing its ethical effect on the system.

3.3.1 Evolution from Ḥisbahto Sharīʿah Governance

Institutionalized ownership of the Sharīʿah of ḥisbah, in turn, facilitates historical and conceptual progression. The ḥisbah was more than a market inspection office; it was an institution of moral economy, regulating maʿrūf (good) and munkar (wrong), whereas the muḥtasib ensured justice outside the confines of narrow financial and technicalities.

The current levels of AAOIFI, IFSB, SBP, BNM, and other national regulatory bodies have significantly enhanced the development of this framework. Such value-driven community oversight is likely to evolve into standardized procedures in contemporary systems.[97] Research suggests conflicting views on the effect of institutional Sharīʿah governance on Islamic economics, with some arguing that it preserves the moral framework while others contend that it constrains it.[98]

Today's financial markets achieve legal lucidity and accountability by employing Sharīʿah Advisory techniques and legal frameworks, such as AAOIFI and BNM, but these act in the spirit of ḥisbah.[99] El-Gamal and Kamali agree with various critics who emphasize that Sharīʿah governance establishes a modern administrative system in place of ethical principles, which are codified. The authors say that ethical instrumentalization undermines Islamic finance's social justice and moral growth agenda.[100]

[96] Zulkifli Bin Hasan, "From Legalism to Value-Oriented Islamic Finance Practices," *Humanomics* 32/4 (November 14, 2016), 437–458.

[97] Dewi Fatmawati et al., "Shariah Governance in Islamic Banks: Practices, Practitioners and Praxis," *Global Finance Journal* 51 (2022), 100555.

[98] Mariah Darus Mat Junus et al., "Ethical Governance through Maqasid Shariah Perspective: A Conceptual Framework," *International Journal of Academic Research in Business and Social Sciences* 14/10 (October 7, 2024), Pages 920–932.

[99] Muhammad Hanif, "Sharīʿah-Compliance Ratings of the Islamic Financial Services Industry: A Quantitative Approach" 10/2 (2018), 162–184.

[100] El-Gamal, *Islamic Finance*, 2006, 169–170; Mohammad Hashim Kamali, *Shari'ah Law: An Introduction* (Oxford: Oneworld Publications, 2010), 68–70.

3.3.2 *Rise of Sharīʿah Supervisory Boards (SSBs) and Audit Committees*

What are Sharīʿah Supervisory Boards (SSBs)?
SSBs are panels of Islamic scholars of the law legally mandated to oversee the behavior of financial products and activities that comply with Sharīʿah principles.[101] Their role is not limited to a legal review; they also consult on ethical consistency, contract structure control, and auditing product mechanisms. Theoretically, they function as the moral police of institutions, much like muḥtasibs do today.

El-Gamal, Kamali, and other scholars have argued that modern Sharīʿah governance adopts a modern bureaucratic system, whose foundation is documentation rather than ethics.[102] As they see it, the instrumentalization of ethics has introduced a gap between Islamic finance and its key role in promoting social justice and moral change.

The coexistence of the regulator and corporate member has advantages and possible challenges. Nowadays, SSBs are modern equivalents of traditional jurists called fuqahāʾ. However, their role was transformed from that of moral advisers to communities and from that of overseeing bodies of financial institutions.[103] Corporate scholars involved in SSBs have a financially authority-controlled hierarchical setup in which their oversight entities will remunerate them.[104]

Being in a supervisory and advisory role enriches the organization with positive opportunities and potential difficulties. SSBs' activities have helped create a formal Islamic financial system, making them more credible. The standardized Sharīʿah compliance system validates the product, building investors' confidence and facilitating the development of the financial markets. The institutions facilitate the Sharīʿah standardization of principles across various locations by integrating activities with

[101] Sara Ashrafkashani, *The Role and Responsibilities of Shari'ah Boards in the Context of Islamic Finance and Their Position in Law, Institute of Advanced Legal Studies* (London: University of London, Doctoral, 2015), 45–49.

[102] El-Gamal, *Islamic Finance*, 2006, 1–4, 46–50; Kamali, *Shari'ah Law*, 68–69.

[103] Rafiullah Sheikh—Khalid Hussain, "Role of Shariah Supervisory Boards (SSBs) in Islamic Financial Engineering: A Critical Review:," *Islamic Banking and Finance Review* 9/2 (December 29, 2022), 42–62.

[104] Azam Abdelhakeem Khalid et al., "The Role of Shariah Supervisory Board on Internal Shariah Audit Effectiveness: Evidence From Bahrain," *Academy of Accounting and Financial Studies Journal* 22/5 (September 17, 2018), 0–286.

Table 3.2 Comparative overview of SSB structures and governance

Country	*SSB structure*	*Audit committees*	*Standardization*
Malaysia	Central SAC + institutional SSBs	Required by SGF	High (regulated by BNM)
Pakistan	Institutional SSBs, SBP oversight	Mandatory audit	Medium (AAOIFI + SBP)
GCC (Bahrain)	Independent SSBs (bank-appointed)	Advised by AAOIFI	Fragmented across banks
Bangladesh	Institutional SSBs only	Inconsistent	Weak (lack of centralized control)

Source From different banks' websites

international organizations, such as the Accounting and Auditing Organization for Islamic Financial Institutions (AAOIFI).[105] Islamic financial products ensure regulatory compliance and operational consistency, a feat previously unattainable through institutionalization.

These new developments have some fundamental problems that cannot be overlooked, despite their progress. Such financial incentives from institutional sponsors pose a significant challenge to scholars, as potential conflicts of interest may taint the supervisory role.[106] The diversity of scholarly viewpoints at SSBs is inevitably limited, as they typically recruit most members from academics affiliated with specific legal frameworks or economic perspectives. Due to the dependent relationship between academic supervisors and their institutions, they tend to participate in less focused talks that shield only safe ideas from being expressed and breakthrough innovations from happening. When manifesting in different institutions, academic board members, as they serve, repeatedly undermine the principles of oversight independence because it allows companies to choose the most favorable regulation for each decision. The underlying frailties of SSBs raise questions about whether they can operate as autonomous bodies that safeguard the moral purity and legal plurality of Islamic laws (Table 3.2).

[105] Sherif Elhalaby et al., "The Adoption of AAOIFI Standards by Islamic Banks: Understanding the Microeconomic Consequences," *Economies* 11/2 (February 2023), 2.

[106] Saleh Abdulrahman Al Amer, *Sharia Supervisory Board in Islamic Banks: A Critical Analysis of the Current Framework* (Leeds: University of Leeds, Phd, 2018), 20–22.

This table gives a comparative overview of Sharīʿah Supervisory Board (SSB) structures, audit practices, and standardization levels in the major Islamic finance jurisdictions: Malaysia, Pakistan, Bahrain (GCC), and Bangladesh. It reveals the disparity of governance quality and regulatory integration, with Malaysia presenting the most concentrated and normalized model, while Bangladesh suffers from weak coordination and uneven auditing.

3.3.3 *Internal Controls, Fatwa Committees, and Compliance Mechanisms*

Today's Islamic financial institutions have comprehensive internal arrangements that enable them to monitor Sharīʿah compliance across their entire operating networks. These arrangements are grounded in internal control frameworks that integrate Sharīʿah auditing mechanisms into the broader compliance environment of the institution. Typically, there is a combination of fatwa bodies, often part of the broader Sharīʿah Supervisory Board (SSB), and internal Sharīʿah review units, where peers review the institution's operations on an ongoing basis.[107] Financial institutions have two internal Sharīʿah review components for daily monitoring of institutional activities. In contrast, they have assigned officers who interconnect the SSB functions with the management teams and regulatory bodies. SSB ethical rulings and rulings can act synergistically through multi-established operational mechanisms. Financial institutions increase the risk of rubber-stamping by informing the fatwa committees of potential interventions by commercial entities. These committees only give a go-ahead after scant independent legal consideration of decisions.[108]

Although initially, the mission of their establishment aimed at establishing internal control structures, they are criticized excessively for their ability to achieve ethical results. The fatwa committees of Islamic financial institutions are becoming passive organizations that merely approve the decisions made by businesses, rather than forming impartial legal

[107] Nur Laili Ab Ghani—Siti Saffa' Shaharuddin, "Internal Control System and Effective Internal Shariah Audit Function: A Conceptual Framework," *International Journal of Islamic Economics and Finance Research* 6/2 December (2023), 121–137.

[108] Alam—Uddın, "Legal and Regulatory Frameworks for Sharīʾa Governance Practices in the Islamic Banking Industry of Bangladesh," 671.

judgments. NUS research confirms that some fatwa-issuing bodies operate as gatekeepers, engaging in fatwa-shopping to favor institutional goals.[109] In instances of ethical deviations and executive decisions, institutions often do not grant authority to internal review units to raise objections to such choices.[110] Although they adopt a technical perspective, compliance departments focus on reducing legal risk rather than upholding the ethical standards of Islamic finance, such as fairness, social justice, and transparency. Bibliometric analysis reveals a notable emphasis on compliance and audit procedures over broader social justice objectives.[111]

Scholars and officials working in the area of regulatory environments continue to engage in endless debates. In their opinion, employees who support codified internal controls will allow greater accountability and transparency while modernizing Sharīʿah implementation through procedural systems. The critics contend these controls insulate management from moral responsibility, and thus, a phony "Shari'ah" control is merely a formality. The regulatory system of Bank Negara in Malaysia has specific Sharīʿah risk assessments. Several experts wonder how these approaches provide quantitative and technical solutions that limit the liberal ethical discourse that would involve maqāṣid al-sharīʿah principles.[112] Efficiencies in operations often conflict with core moral values, which is a significant concern for modern Islamic financial institutions.

3.3.4 Ethical Authenticity versus Procedural Conformity

It should be noted that the discussion in this section draws from ongoing scholarly debates on the tension between procedural Sharīʿah compliance and ethical authenticity in Islamic finance. The critiques are not directed at

[109] Ilyas Salim, "Uncovering the Gatekeepers of Islamic Finance—," National University of Singapore, *NUS–Middle East Institute* (September 15, 2021).

[110] See, Alam—Uddın, "Legal and Regulatory Frameworks For Sharī'a Governance Practices in the Islamic Banking Industry of Bangladesh," 671–677.

[111] Fatimah Tuzzahroh—Sugiyarti Fatma Laela, "Sharia Audit and Shariah Compliance of Islamic Financial Institutions: A Bibliometric Analysis," *Jurnal Ekonomi Syariah Teori Dan Terapan* 9/6 (November 30, 2022), 815–833.

[112] Fatihu Shehu Isa et al., "Shariah Audit Practices in Malaysia: Moving Forward," *Journal of Islamic Finance* 9/2 (2020), 2.

particular institutions but reflect concerns raised in the academic literature regarding the over-formalization of Islamic financial products and the need for maqāṣid-oriented reform[113]

As established in Chap. 1, the ethical dilemma at the heart of Islamic finance stems from the gap between formal Sharīʿah compliance and substantive ethical integrity. The overuse of instruments like murābaḥah, ijārah, and tawarruq, while technically valid, is widely criticized for mimicking conventional finance and bypassing the objectives of social justice.[114] This form-over-substance tendency, often referred to as Shariʿah washing, reveals an organizational bias toward legality over moral legitimacy, where ethical intentions are sacrificed for procedural compliance.[115] Building on that foundation, this section offers a comparative framework to better understand the tension between procedural adherence and ethical authenticity in practice. The chart below summarizes this contrast (Table 3.3).

This table outlines recurring structural limitations, including inadequate legal harmonization, a shortage of trained Sharīʿah professionals, institutional fragmentation, and the dominance of conventional financial logic in dual-banking systems.

Ethical concerns deepen when the use of murābaḥah, ijārah, and tawarruq mimics conventional finance, as Farooq describes it, a drift toward legalism that sacrifices substance for appearance.[116] Scholars like Hasan argue that this

[113] Asutay, "A Political Economy Approach to Islamic Economics," 5–13; Khaliq Ahmad—Datuk AbdelAziz Berghout, *Islamic Finance and Sustainable Development: Balancing Spirituality, Values and Profit* (London: Routledge, 2025); Mehmet Asutay—Isa Yilmaz, "Financialisation of Islamic Finance: A Polanyian Approach on the Hegemony of Market Logic over Islamic Logic," *New Political Economy* 30/2 (2025), 267–286.

[114] İlkay Kaya, "Islamic Finance: Fit for Purpose or Mere Replication?," *İslam Ekonomisi Dergisi* 3/2 (2023), 1–18; Muhammad Abdullah Dewaya, "Innovation in Islamic Finance: Review of Organized Banking Tawarruq," *Review of Islamic Social Finance and Entrepreneurship* 3/2 (2024), 199–211; Mahvish Nawaz Mokal et al., "Murabaha & Tawarruq: An Examination of Issues and Challenges from an Accounting Perspective," *Journal of Islamic Finance* 13/1 (2024), 42–56.

[115] Alex Malyshev, "Is Islamic Banking Truly Shariah-Compliant? Debunking Myths and Clarifying Key Concepts," Financial Market Analyst, *SDK Finance* (blog), December 12, 2024.

[116] Mohammad Omar Farooq, "Islam-Compliance, beyond Shariah-Compliance: Toward a Broader Socioeconomic Transformation," *Arab Law Quarterly*, (July 1, 2022), 1.

Table 3.3 Key regulatory challenges in South Asian Islamic financial institutions

Dimension	*Procedural compliance*	*Ethical authenticity*
Legal orientation	Based on permissibility (*ḥilliyyah*)	Based on ethical obligation (*wujūb akhlāqī*)
Primary objective	Avoidance of *ribā*, *gharar*, *maysir*	Realization of *maqāṣid al-sharīʿah*
Product focus	Murābaḥah, tawarruq, ijārah	Mushārakah, muḍārabah, waqf, qard ḥasan
Governance style	Rubber-stamped Sharīʿah Board approvals	Critical fatwā review with community accountability
Market outcome	Replication of conventional finance	Promotion of social justice, redistribution, and transparency

Source Author's own

formalistic compliance actually "undermines public confidence" and facilitates exploitative practices.[117] Even broader critiques call for a shift from Sharīʿah-compliant to genuinely Sharīʿah-based products.[118]

Ethical authenticity remains a pressing challenge for Islamic finance in South Asia. While legalistic Sharīʿah compliance frameworks have gained institutional ground, they often operate within environments marked by resource asymmetries, plural legal traditions, and weak enforcement. These structural vulnerabilities, when left unaddressed, compromise the transformative and justice-oriented aims of Islamic economic ethics. For South Asia, where resource gaps, regulatory pluralism, and legal fragility are pronounced, ethical authenticity must be reclaimed not only through better-designed financial products but also through structural reforms, including unified fatwa boards, maqāṣid-based Shari'ah audit metrics, and grassroots-level consumer engagement mechanisms. Such reforms are necessary not just for operational efficiency, but for rebuilding trust in Islamic finance as a distinctively moral system responsive to the socio-economic realities of Muslim-majority societies.

[117] Bin Hasan, "From Legalism to Value-Oriented Islamic Finance Practices," 440.

[118] Ryan Calder, "Sharia-Compliant or Sharia-Based? The Changing Ethical Discourse of Islamic Finance," *Arab Law Quarterly* 35/1/2 (2021), 5.

3.3.5 *Structural Problems: Conflict of Interest, Independence, Standardization*

Multiple Sharīʿah governance frameworks have developed substantially, but structural issues that harm Islamic financial oversight consistency, ethical credibility, and oversight integrity have not been completely resolved. The primary problem with existing Sharīʿah Supervisory Boards stems from their members receiving direct payments from the financial institutions they oversee. The conflict of interest created by paid scholars has been extensively documented, with Oseni et al. (2016) demonstrating how fatwā shopping undermines dissent and objectivity.[119] The structural independence of SSBs is similarly compromised, as noted by Al Amer's study, due to the influence of appointment and remuneration under institutional control.[120] Although organizations like AAOIFI and IFSB advocate for standardized governance frameworks, their efforts encounter real-world implementation challenges across various regions.[121] Governance guidelines (AAOIFI, IFSB, BNM) also stipulate independent remuneration and term limits.[122] Empirical evidence further supports the notion that independent SSB members reduce conflict risks and improve oversight quality (Table 3.4).[123]

Considering the above, Table 3.5 summarizes the main structural challenges facing Islamic finance governance, including conflicts of interest, the absence of term limits for Sharīʿah board members, inconsistent fatwa rulings, and pressure from external political or corporate

[119] Umar A. Oseni et al., "The Legal Implications of 'Fatwā Shopping' in the Islamic Finance Industry: Problems, Perceptions and Prospects," *Arab Law Quarterly* 30/2 (February 24, 2016), 111–112.

[120] Al Amer, *Sharia Supervisory Board in Islamic Banks*, 2.

[121] Ahmet Faruk Aysan et al., "Standardization Efforts in Islamic Finance," Unpublished, DOI.org (Datacite), 24–26.

[122] Nawal binti Kasim et al., "Comparative Analysis on AAOIFI, IFSB and BNM Shari'ah Governance Guidelines," *International Journal of Business and Social Science* 4/15 (2013), 223.

[123] Mohamed Sharif Bashir et al., "Does Shari'ah Supervisory Board Characteristics Affect Islamic Banks' Financial Performance? Evidence from Saudi Arabia," *Corporate Board Role Duties and Composition* 19/2 (2023), 15–25.

Table 3.4 Structural challenges in Islamic finance governance

Issue	*Manifestation*	*Example*
Conflict of interest	Scholars paid by banks they supervise	Pakistan, GCC
Lack of term limits	No regular rotation of board members	Bangladesh, Indonesia
Fatwa inconsistency	Divergent rulings for similar products	Sukuk across GCC vs. Malaysia
External pressures	Political or corporate pressure on rulings	South Asia, Gulf States

Source Author's own

Table 3.5 Policy toolkit: Reforming Sharīʿah governance in South Asian Islamic banks

Policy action	*Lead institutions*	*Timeline*
Mandate rotation and term limits for SSB members	Central Banks + Islamic Banks	Within 2 years
Create a unified regional code of ethics for SSBs	OIC Fiqh Academy + AAOIFI	Drafting phase
Require disclosure of fatwā rationale and maqāṣid alignment	Bank regulators + Internal Audit Units	Immediate
Integrate external Shari'ah audits by independent ḥisbah-inspired agencies	National Shari'ah Councils	Medium-term
Publish annual "Ethics in Practice" reports for public transparency	All licensed Islamic banks	Ongoing

Source Author's own

entities. It provides specific country examples to illustrate how these challenges compromise oversight integrity and erode stakeholder confidence (Table 3.5).

While institutional structures such as Shari'ah boards and audit committees ensure procedural Sharīʿah compliance, the underlying methodology by which fatwas are issued within these bodies remains a pivotal, yet often underexplored, jurisprudential concern. To better understand the ethical and legal depth of these institutions, the following section examines the fatwa methodologies employed by fiqh supervisory boards across South Asian Islamic banks.

3.3.6 *The Fiqh Supervisory Boards of the Islamic Banks of South Asian Countries*

The ethical legitimacy of Islamic financial institutions in South Asia hinges on their structural compliance mechanisms and the jurisprudential methodologies employed by their fiqh supervisory boards. These boards, often referred to as Shari'ah Supervisory Boards (SSBs), are responsible for issuing binding fatwas on the permissibility of financial products and practices. This subsection critically explores the operational logic, methodological paradigms, and jurisprudential sources employed by such boards in Pakistan, Bangladesh, Afghanistan, Sri Lanka, the Maldives, and India. This section applies the fatwa lifecycle, source layering, and jurisprudential flexibility to the governance of Islamic finance in South Asia.

3.3.6.1 Jurisprudential Framework and the Role of Fatwa

Several steps are involved in issuing a fatwa in Islamic banking, including identifying the problem, conducting legal analysis, and establishing ethical standards. According to Aksoy's technique, South Asian boards exhibit a similar pattern, even after having diverse backgrounds. This cycle begins with (1) submission of written documentation, continues onto (2) internal scholarly review by experts, which is followed by (3) the official release of a fatwa, then relevant to (4) execution by banking management and ends with (5) periodic reassessment or audit for compliance. It shows that this pattern mirrors universal fatwa practices, including South Asian boards. Although the level of transparency in these stages varies from country to country, this lifecycle can also constitute an excellent metric by which to measure the degree of institutional development and ethical oversight. Several steps are involved in issuing a fatwa in Islamic banking. This cycle mirrors the established classical fatwa model (problem analysis → issuance → implementation → periodic review), as outlined by Usmani (2011).[124] South Asian boards also follow this pattern, as documented in Al-Amer's study.[125] The decisions made by these boards are grounded in the four roots of Sharīʿah and incorporate maqāṣid principles, maṣlaḥah, ḍarūrah, and ʿurf, used in jurisprudential reasoning.[126]

[124] Muhammad Taqi Usmani, *Usul al-ifta wa adabuhu* (Beirut: Daru'l-kalem, 2014), 50–51.

[125] Al Amer, *Sharia Supervisory Board in Islamic Banks*, 22.

[126] Usmani, *Usul al-ifta wa adabuhu*, 112–113.

3.3.6.2 Fatwa Methodologies in Practice

Supervised by the State Bank of Pakistan (SBP), Pakistan's Islamic banks maintain a clearly defined system of Sharīʿah audit culture, which is hierarchical. It entails the internal and external Sharīʿah audits, Sharīʿah compliance reviews, and regulatory inspections. Empirical evidence suggests that the quality of Sharīʿah audits in Pakistan can be predicted by a three-dimensional risk model, which encompasses inherent, control, and detection factors contingent upon the sophistication of products, organizational structure, and the qualifications of auditors.[127] Resident Sharīʿah Board Members' participation, continual internal audits, and official reporting systems maintain effective compliance. Still, significant problems remain unresolved, such as the inadequate number of auditors trained in Islamic jurisprudence and auditing, a lack of absolute standards for audit quality, and suspicions regarding methodological uniformity. The audit infrastructure in Pakistan does not need to be young. Still, it must continually improve to address institutional issues and provide better education, ensuring high ethical and technical performance levels for Sharīʿah audits.[128] Fatwas are developed through structured procedures involving internal review and compliance with both national law and AAOIFI guidelines. Boards frequently cite classical sources and modern standards, and recent efforts aim at greater transparency and public access to rulings.

Although a great deal has been achieved concerning Islamic banking, the architecture of Sharīʿah audit and compliance in Bangladesh is structurally deficient and functionally disjointed. Each Islamic bank has its own internal Sharīʿah Supervisory Committee (SSC). Still, these committees allocate most of their resources to compliance during the pre-execution phase, vetting contracts and documents before any transaction.[129] However, audit functions intended to promote ex-post Sharīʿah compliance are lacking in the system. It's Sharīʿah review mechanisms by SSCs often exclude important aspects of accountability within Islamic finance,

[127] Abdul Rashid—Muhammad Saarim Ghazi, "Factors Affecting Sharīʿah Audit Quality in Islamic Banking Institutions of Pakistan: A Theoretical Framework," *Islamic Economic Studies* 28/2 (2021), 124–140.

[128] Rashid—Ghazi, "Factors Affecting Sharīʿah Audit Quality in Islamic Banking Institutions of Pakistan," 130–132.

[129] Md Kausar Alama et al., "The Reasons Behind the Absence of a Comprehensive Shariah Governance Framework of Islamic Banks in Bangladesh," *International Journal of Economics & Business Administration (IJEBA)* VIII/1 (2020), 134–145.

such as failure to verify whether Sharīʿah shares profit and loss, whether financial gains are from prohibited sources, whether earnings are set aside for charity as prescribed, or whether zakāt is ascertained and addressed correctly.

Moreover, the review involves reviewing papers, and in many cases, between 10 and 20% of contracts and transactions may be audited, which means inadequate coverage for thorough monitoring. Implementing such reviews typically falls to a small cadre of officers known as muraqibs, who often act outside standard audit procedures. Neither the Bangladesh Bank nor the Central Sharīʿah Board for Islamic Banks of Bangladesh (CSBIB) has created a guide for Sharīʿah audits or comprehensive fatwa instructions. Sharīʿah Non-Compliance (SNC) is rarely disclosed to the public, and non-compliant earnings are transferred to the CSR funds, thereby eroding public transparency and confidence.[130]

Another important issue arises from the fact that the practice of Islamic banks in Bangladesh is subject to audit by conventional accounting firms, which apply principles and assumptions based on Western financial philosophy that often contradict the moral basis of Islamic jurisprudence. The historical cost principle, for instance, is paradigmatic of those that frequently distort the real value of assets due to this principle's incompatibility with Islamic moral principles. The matching principle has no relevance for a zakāt-based accountability model, and the going concern assumption, which tacitly assumes corporate perpetuity, violates the religious concept of finite time.[131] The audit process limitations (still applicable to existing methodologies) make it increasingly difficult to guarantee Sharīʿah concordance, as real Sharīʿah audits are impossible to execute by qualified auditors unfamiliar with Islamic law.

Such persistent problems create a critical need for scholars and practitioners to make comprehensive changes. Essential recommendations include the introduction of a one-stop Sharīʿah audit manual under the administration of the CSBIB, expanding the audit to at least 80% of banking deals and protocols, the creation of independent Sharīʿah audit functions in each Islamic bank, and the adoption of digital auditing platforms for continuous, interactive control. In addition, it is recommended

[130] Alam—Uddın, "Legal and Regulatory Frameworks For Sharī'a Governance Practices in the Islamic Banking Industry of Bangladesh," 681–685.

[131] Alama et al., "The Reasons Behind the Absence of a Comprehensive Shariah Governance Framework of Islamic Banks in Bangladesh," 142–143.

that independent audits by qualified Sharīʿah audit agencies or the Bangladesh Bank supervise the external Sharīʿah audits, and any breach of Sharīʿah requirements be published to stakeholders. In the absence of such measures, the assurance, openness, and ethical credibility of Islamic banking in Bangladesh will continue to be undermined, which, in turn, questions its core desirability, thereby undermining its Islamic authenticity.[132]

These countries rely heavily on external authorities, including the Accounting and Auditing Organization for Islamic Financial Institutions (AAOIFI), international Shari'ah boards, and the resolutions of the Islamic Fiqh Academy. In Afghanistan, the fatwa structure under the central bank is weak in terms of a formal Fatwa board; however, it has scholars of Islamic jurisprudence based on Ḥanafī fiqh.[133] Sri Lanka and the Maldives are experimenting with a hybrid model, in which national scholars consult international fatwa bodies, but implementation remains at an early stage.[134] Although India has no official Islamic banks, a vibrant landscape of non-institutional fatwa-based Islamic finance exists through cooperatives and community-led ventures. Entities such as Al-Khair Cooperative Credit Society draw on fatwas issued by institutions like *Dār al-ʿUlūm Deoband* and *Nadwat al-ʿUlamāʾ*. These rulings emphasize textual fidelity and community benefit, often lacking formalized implementation mechanisms but grounded in firm ethical intention.[135] However, core methodological themes of South Asia are;

[132] Uddin, *Bangladeş'teki İslam Bankacılık Uygulamasının Fıkhî Açıdan*.

[133] Zaif Ullah Athari et al., "History of the Afghan Central Bank, Its Sharīʿah Supervision System and Its Effect on Unifying the Sharīʿah Reference: تاريخ البنك المركزي الأفغاني ونظام الرقابة الشرعية فيه وأثره في توحيد المرجعية الشرعية," *International Journal of Fiqh and Usul Al-Fiqh Studies* 8/2 (July 31, 2024), 38–54.

[134] Hayathu Mohamed Ahamed Hilmy—Rusni Hassan, "Shariah Governance Structure of Islamic Financial Institutions in Sri Lanka," *International Journal of Management and Applied Research* 6/4 (November 1, 2019), 245–258; Rabsha Waheed—Baharom Abdul Hamid, "Overcoming Implementation Challenges for Shariah Governance in the Maldives," *International Journal of Islamic Economics and Finance Research* 1 (2023), 63–77.

[135] Wasiullah Shaik Mohammed—Khalid Waheed, "Interest-Free Microfinance in India: A Case Study of the Al-Khair Cooperative Credit Society," *Journal of King Abdulaziz University: Islamic Economics* 31/1 (2018), 1–20.

- *Taḥlīlī (analytical):* Applied particularly in Pakistan and Bangladesh, where complex instruments are broken down and aligned with fiqh categories.
- *Taʿlīlī (causal):* Used in India and Afghanistan, where fatwas are linked to core principles (*ʿillah*) drawn from Ḥanafī jurisprudence.
- *Gāʾī (teleological):* Increasingly adopted in Sri Lanka and the Maldives, where *maqāṣid al-sharīʿah* is invoked to frame compliance within public interest and developmental goals.

This typology, tahlīlī (analytical), taʿlīlī (causal), and gāʾī (teleological), is proposed by the author as an original academic interpretation based on comparative analysis of Shari'ah Supervisory Board (SSB) practices in South Asian Islamic finance institutions.

Boards across these countries demonstrate varying degrees of methodological formality, but all exhibit an orientation toward capital preservation, institutional stability, and community trust. However, challenges and reflections in South Asia are no exception: the limited documentation and lack of published fatwa manuals hinder transparency,[136] and an external dependency on Gulf-based standards may reduce contextual sensitivity.[137] Community trust versus regulatory integration remains a persistent tension, particularly in India and Bangladesh. Despite these challenges, South Asian Islamic finance benefits from a rich heritage in Islamic jurisprudence (fiqh) and a diverse range of institutional models.

3.4 Axis III: Institutional Footprint of AAOIFI Standards in South Asia

3.4.1 Overview of Country-Specific AAOIFI Standard Adoption

This section facilitates a comparative analysis of the actual implementation of AAOIFI (Accounting and Auditing Organization for Islamic Financial Institutions) Shari'ah standards in some selected South Asian jurisdictions, i.e., Afghanistan, the Maldives, Bangladesh, and Pakistan. These countries vary in design, implementation, and the involvement of institutions in

[136] Zulkifli Hasan, *Shari'ah Governance in Islamic Banks* (Edinburgh: Edinburgh University Press, 2012), 87–89.

[137] Aysan et al., "Standardization Efforts in Islamic Finance," 30–33.

meeting AAOIFI's holistic standardization footprint. This is achieved through a well-structured analysis of the regulatory framework and membership status, translation availability, and dual reporting structures to determine how each country formally or informally complies with AAOIFI's harmonization objectives, upholding the highest ethical integrity level in Islamic finance.

AAOIFI Shari'ah standards have been formally adopted by Afghanistan and Pakistan, with the Maldives recognized under secondary reporting. Pakistan and Bangladesh have also adopted accounting and governance standards.[138] The State Bank of Pakistan (SBP) recently made AAOIFI Shari'ah Standard No. 20 on the sale of debt instruments compulsory, exemplifying formal regulatory integration.[139] Bangladeshi banks follow AAOIFI accounting standards voluntarily, while the Maldives allows secondary reporting compliance. Empirical evidence suggests that AAOIFI adoption enhances institutional transparency, as evidenced by improved financial performance and reduced earnings management among institutions across 22 countries.[140]

Additionally, the section refers to well-recognized but underrepresented India and Sri Lanka, which suggests either structural or voluntary disengagement from consultations on adopting international Shari'ah standards. The comparative review presents the adoption status of Shari'ah, as well as accounting, governance, and auditing standards. It illuminates what constitutes the maturity of perspectives, the political will, and the infrastructural constraints governing these national approaches. By studying formal policy implementation and the market realities it affects, this analysis contributes to a deeper understanding of the ethical oversight landscape in South Asia. It highlights the broader impacts of standardization, investor confidence, and transnational conformity in Islamic financial governance.

[138] "Footprint Report: Status of Adoption of AAOIFI Standards," *Accounting and Auditing Organization for Islamic Financial Institutions* (2022).

[139] "IFN—SBP Adopts AAOIFI Standard 20," *Islamic Finance News* (blog), March 24, 2025.

[140] Sherif Elhalaby et al., "The Adoption of AAOIFI Standards by Islamic Banks: Understanding the Microeconomic Consequences," *Economies* 11/2 (January 30, 2023), 1–22; Sherif El-Halaby et al., "Influence of Adoption AAOIFI Accounting Standards on Earning Management: Evidence from Islamic Banks," *Journal of Islamic Accounting and Business Research* 11/10 (2020), 1847–1870.

3.4.2 Country-wise Assessment of AAOIFI Adoption

This section begins with a discussion organized in alphabetical order by country, following the approach adopted by AAOIFI in its report.

Afghanistan has formally adopted AAOIFI standards across several dimensions, with Da Afghanistan Bank (DAB) serving as the central regulator for the country's financial sector. As of August 2022, AAOIFI standards are officially incorporated into national law and regulatory frameworks, and the jurisdiction has made a public commitment to apply them. The implementation spans Sharīʿah, financial accounting, governance, and auditing standards, with all four being officially adopted. Although DAB is not an institutional member of AAOIFI, it actively aligns its Islamic finance framework with AAOIFI's guidance and has developed an extensive documentation infrastructure to enforce compliance.[141] Afghanistan has a central Sharīʿah board in place and allows dual reporting. However, the standards have not yet been translated into the local languages (Pashto or Dari), and the regulatory ecosystem still faces implementation challenges.

The scope of AAOIFI Shari'ah standards adoption in Afghanistan is notably comprehensive. According to source document extracts and product guidelines issued by DAB, the following Sharīʿah Standards are either adopted or referenced in official use: No. 6 (Conversion of Conventional Bank to Islamic Bank), No. 8 (Murābaḥah to the Purchase Orderer), No. 9 (Ijārah and Ijārah Muntahiyah Bittamlīk), No. 10 (Muḍārabah), No. 12 (Sharīkah and Modern Corporations), No. 14 (Documentary Credit), No. 17 (Investment Sukūk), No. 18 (Possession), No. 24 (Syndicated Financing), No. 30 (Tawarruq), No. 38 (Online Financial Dealings), No. 49 (Unilateral and Bilateral Promises), No. 2 (Credit/Debit Cards), and No. 5 (Guarantees). In addition to product-level compliance, Afghanistan has adopted AAOIFI Governance Standard No. 2 on Sharīʿah Review and follows the AAOIFI Code of Ethics for Professional Accountants. The adoption date for these standards across the board is recorded as 2018, in line with the issuance of various DAB regulatory documents such as the *Guidelines on Appointment of External Sharīʿah Auditors*, *Shari'ah Compliance Manual*, and *Conversion of Conventional Bank into Islamic Bank Regulation*.[142]

[141] "Footprint Report: Status of Adoption of AAOIFI Standards" (2022), 74–77.

[142] "Footprint Report: Status of Adoption of AAOIFI Standards" (2022), 74–77.

Significantly, Afghanistan has introduced contextual modifications to certain AAOIFI standards, particularly regarding Late Payment Charges. While AAOIFI's standard practice is retained in principle, the country applies a modified use of Item 6/5 to provide flexibility for customers under default, ensuring compliance with Sharīʿah while addressing practical constraints. Similarly, AAOIFI's standard on Ibraʾ (rebates) is applied in consideration of international Sharīʿah practices, particularly in non-contractual settings, as outlined in the *Qard Product Guide*. Other official documents include the *Murābaḥah Product Guide*, *Verification Process Manual*, and *On-Site Examination Manual*, all of which consistently reference AAOIFI standards and articulate the country's intent to align product structuring and Sharīʿah compliance with global Islamic finance norms.[143]

Although Afghanistan is not a full AAOIFI member and lacks full local language translations, its Islamic finance regulatory landscape exhibits a high level of normative alignment with AAOIFI standards. The regulatory strategy is top-down, with strong central guidance and codified institutional procedures, but actual sectoral maturity and implementation capacity still require strengthening. Nevertheless, Afghanistan stands out in the region for its extensive formal adoption and regulatory backing of AAOIFI standards in both substance and structure.

In the Maldives, a significant development occurred in 2022 with the Maldives Inland Revenue Authority (MIRA), the national tax authority, which formally committed to applying AAOIFI standards in its regulatory practice. MIRA adopted AAOIFI Financial Accounting Standards alongside the International Financial Reporting Standards (IFRS) and IFRS for Small and Medium-sized Entities (IFRS for SMEs), as explicitly stated under Section 8(c) of a tax ruling issued by the authority. Additionally, MIRA recognized the AAOIFI Auditing Standards for tax purposes, applying them in conjunction with the International Standards on Auditing (ISA) and auditing standards issued by the International Federation of Accountants (IFAC). However, like CMDA and MMA, MIRA did not adopt Shariah or governance standards. Across all three institutions, no legal incorporation of AAOIFI standards into national law exists, and no translations or modifications have been made. Nevertheless, the regulatory environment permits dual reporting and recognizes

143 "Footprint Report: Status of Adoption of AAOIFI Standards" (2022), 74–77.

AAOIFI standards within certain operational scopes, particularly in taxation.[144]

While MIRA's 2022 adoption of AAOIFI financial accounting and auditing standards marks a noteworthy advancement, the overall regulatory landscape in the Maldives remains fragmented and partially aligned with AAOIFI. The absence of a unified national policy, the non-adoption of Shariah and governance standards, and the lack of legal codification or localization underscore the incomplete nature of implementation. The Maldives serves as a case of selective and sectoral engagement, reflecting both the opportunities and challenges faced by small developing economies in harmonizing with international Islamic finance standards.

Coming to the Bangladesh chapter, as of the latest AAOIFI Footprint update dated 31 August 2020, Bangladesh demonstrates a partial and fragmented approach to the adoption of AAOIFI standards. The primary regulatory authority involved is the Bangladesh Securities and Exchange Commission (BSEC), which has publicly committed to the application of certain AAOIFI standards, particularly in the context of capital market instruments such as Investment Sukūk. According to the Investment Sukuk Rules 2019, the BSEC makes explicit reference to AAOIFI Shari'ah Standard No. 17, which governs permissible Sukūk structures, including Ijārah, Mushārakah, Murābaḥah, Muḍārabah, and Istisnāʿ contracts.[145]

Regarding financial accounting standards, there is partial adoption, especially for special purpose vehicles (SPVs) associated with Sukūk. According to clause 17(4)(1) of the Sukuk Rules, financial reports must consider AAOIFI Financial Accounting Standards (FAS) in conjunction with IFRS, establishing a dual accounting reference model [3rd image, reference.[146] Furthermore, documents from the Bangladesh Bank (Islamic Banking Guidelines, 2009) and its Guidelines on Specimen Reports and Financial Statements reaffirm the indirect application of AAOIFI standards alongside IFRS and local laws such as the Banking Companies Act 1991.[147]

[144] "Footprint Report: Status of Adoption of AAOIFI Standards" (2022), 144–147.

[145] https://sec.gov.bd/slaws/Investment_Sukuk_Rules,_2019.pdf.

[146] https://sec.gov.bd/crequest/Draft_Rules_on_Sukuk_28.04.19_2019.docx.

[147] https://www.bb.org.bd/aboutus/regulationguideline/islamicbanking/guideislamicbnk.pdf.

However, governance and auditing standards have not been adopted, and no jurisdictional modifications have been made to suit local requirements. Instead, institutions are expected to refer to AAOIFI and Shari'ah Supervisory Committees on a discretionary basis. The Central Shari'ah Board for Islamic Banks of Bangladesh (CSBIB), while influential, is a non-governmental advisory body without binding enforcement power.[148]

Dual reporting is permitted, and individual Islamic banks and Islamic windows are allowed to apply AAOIFI standards where appropriate. Clause 8.1 and 8.8 of the Internal Control and Compliance (ICC) guidelines of 2016 further mention that institutions must conduct Shari'ah audits separately, often guided by SSC or Sharīʿah councils, though implementation varies across the sector.[149]

Bangladesh has partially adopted or referred to the following AAOIFI standards:

Shari'ah Standards

- Standard No. 17—Investment Sukūk
- Indirect reference to other Shari'ah concepts such as Ijārah, Mushārakah, Murābaḥah, Muḍārabah, and Istisnāʿ through the Investment Sukūk guideline.

Accounting Standards

- General reference to AAOIFI accounting standards, influenced by: FAS-1—Murābaḥah, FAS-2—Ijārah, FAS-3—Profit and Loss Sharing.

Bangladesh stands as one of the most active Islamic financial markets in South Asia, but it demonstrates a fragmented and partially voluntary approach to adopting AAOIFI standards. While not formally integrated into national legislation, specific AAOIFI Sharīʿah standards, such as Standard No. 17 on Investment Sukūk, are referenced by regulatory bodies, including the

[148] http://csbib.com/ https://greenwatchbd.com/39th-general-meeting-of-centralshariah-board-held/.

[149] Bangladesh Bank—Guidelines on Internal Control & Compliance in Banks, February 2016, https://www.bb.org.bd/mediaroom/circulars/brpd/mar082016brpd03.pdf.

Securities and Exchange Commission (SEC) and various Islamic banks.[150] Additionally, core contracts such as Ijārah, Mushārakah, Murābaḥah, Muḍārabah, and Istisnāʿ are acknowledged through these indirect references.[151] In terms of accounting, Bangladesh's Islamic financial institutions demonstrate familiarity with select AAOIFI Financial Accounting Standards, particularly FAS-1 (Murābaḥah), FAS-2 (Ijārah), and FAS-3 (Profit and Loss Sharing). However, no official regulatory mandate requires their use.[152]

However, the lack of legal incorporation and the non-binding nature of Sharīʿah governance guidelines have created a system dependent on the discretion of individual institutions. Although the Central Sharīʿah Board for Islamic Banks of Bangladesh (CSBIB) exists to provide centralized guidance, its lack of enforcement authority leads to inconsistent application of standards and varied interpretations across the sector.[153] Despite Bangladesh's large and expanding Islamic finance sector, this hybrid and informal adoption model raises serious concerns regarding transparency, auditability, and public trust.[154]

While Bangladesh has taken concrete steps toward adopting select AAOIFI standards, especially in the capital market and financial reporting domains, the absence of national legal incorporation, lack of governance and auditing adoption, and the non-binding role of CSBIB result in a hybrid model of voluntary and partial compliance. Despite this, the framework allows space for further development through localization, legal integration, and standard enforcement, which would help align Bangladesh's growing Islamic finance industry with international best practices.

[150] "Footprint Report: Status of Adoption of AAOIFI Standards" (2022), 54.

[151] *Guideline for Investment Sukuk* (Dhaka: entral Shariah Board for Islamic Banks of Bangladesh (CSBIB), 2020); Alam—Uddın, "Legal and Regulatory Frameworks For Sharī'a Governance Practices in the Islamic Banking Industry of Bangladesh," 669–683; Uddin, *Bangladeş'teki İslam Bankacılık Uygulamasının Fıkhî Açıdan.*

[152] "Footprint Report: Status of Adoption of AAOIFI Standards" (2022), 83–86.

[153] Riazuddin Ahmed—Mohamad Saifullah Bin Mohamad, "The Practice of Shariah Governance in Islamic Banking and Finance: A Study of Islamic Banks in Bangladesh," *International Journal of Management and Applied Research* 6/4 (November 1, 2019), 271–284.

[154] Mohammad Nazim Uddin et al., "Guidelines for Developing the Shari'ah-Compliant Products and Shari'ah Governance for Sustainable Banks in Bangladesh," *Business Strategy & Development* 7/1 (2024), e309.

Pakistan exhibits the most structured and extensive engagement with AAOIFI standards among South Asian jurisdictions. Both the State Bank of Pakistan (SBP) and the Securities and Exchange Commission of Pakistan (SECP) have demonstrated regulatory and institutional commitment through a partial but formal adoption of AAOIFI Sharīʿah, accounting, governance, and auditing standards.[155] The SBP publicly committed to adopting AAOIFI standards through its Islamic Banking Strategic Plan (2014–2018), with implementation beginning as early as January 12, 2010, when Circular No. 01 adopted Sharīʿah Standards No. 3, 8, 9, and 13 (covering Default in Payment, Murābaḥah, Ijārah, and Istisnāʿ, respectively). This was followed by Circulars No. 01 and 03 of 2013 and Circular No. 01 of 2019, which expanded adoption to include Sharīʿah Standards No. 2, 5, 12, 14, 17, 18, 24, 28, 38, and 49. On January 3, 2020, SBP adopted additional standards, namely, AAOIFI Standards No. 19 and 23, through Circular No. 01 of 2020, further solidifying the institutional reach of AAOIFI compliance.[156]

These standards are adopted on a partial and interpretive basis, meaning they are either incorporated into local regulations or used as guiding principles, with necessary amendments and clarifications tailored to the Pakistani Sharīʿah compliance environment. Importantly, translations of AAOIFI standards into Urdu have been made available to increase accessibility and uniformity in application.

From an accounting standpoint, SECP has issued Financial Accounting Standards (FAS) 1–3 in line with AAOIFI's framework, covering Murābaḥah (FAS-1), Ijārah (FAS-2), and Profit and Loss Sharing on Deposits (FAS-3), across the years 2005, 2007, and 2013, respectively. Meanwhile, governance regulations were updated in 2018 to reflect both AAOIFI and IFSB guidelines, granting regulated institutions discretionary scope to align based on context. While auditing standards are yet to be comprehensively adopted, the SBP and SECP have developed localized Sharīʿah auditing frameworks, many of which refer to AAOIFI's criteria.

[155] Muhammad Bilal Zafar, "Islamic Financial Accounting Standards in Pakistan: A Comparison with AAOIFI," *Journal of Islamic Accounting and Business Research* ahead-of-print/ahead-of-print (June 18, 2024); Asia Rani et al., "Impact of Shari'ah and Corporate Governance on Islamic Banks Performance: Evidence from Pakistan," *Sustainable Business and Society in Emerging Economies* 6/3 (September 30, 2024), 457–468.

[156] "Footprint Report: Status of Adoption of AAOIFI Standards" (2022), 164–166.

Dual reporting is permitted, and certain local modifications have been made to adapt to national banking structures.

As of the 2018 press release by SECP, the Commission has formally adopted Sharīʿah Standards No. 17 (Investment Sukūk), 18 (Qabd), and 23 (Fodooli) and declared its intent to gradually adopt more standards. Collectively, these efforts have made Pakistan the leading South Asian country in terms of AAOIFI alignment, both in regulatory declaration and institutional execution.[157] Despite the absence of a unified national fatwa body or cross-bank Sharīʿah board system, the presence of well-defined Sharīʿah Governance Frameworks, mandatory minimum scholar requirements, and standardized capacity-building protocols reflects a maturing Islamic finance environment with high fidelity to international standards.

Despite this strong regulatory engagement, certain structural limitations remain. The application of AAOIFI standards still varies across financial products and institutions, and Pakistan has yet to establish a unified national fatwa archive or a centralized Sharīʿah Supervisory Board framework. Inconsistencies in institutional interpretation and Sharīʿah auditing further constrain uniform application. Nevertheless, Pakistan represents the most developed case of AAOIFI alignment in South Asia, with substantial implications for ethical compliance, investor confidence, and market transparency. Its consistent issuance of sovereign and corporate sukūk, alongside an expanding portfolio of Shariah-compliant banking products, reflects a maturing system backed by policy-driven centralization and active private sector participation.[158] These features collectively position Pakistan as the region's leading candidate for an Islamic finance hub.

3.4.3 *Contextual Exceptions*

India and Sri Lanka are subject to regulatory and constitutional constraints based on their secular financial framework, so they have not adopted AAOIFI standards. The Reserve Bank of India does not legally recognize Shari'ah-based financial standards under the aegis of Islamic banking. As a result, there is no adoption, institutional membership, or dual reporting.

[157] "Footprint Report: Status of Adoption of AAOIFI Standards" (2022), 164–168.

[158] Kehkashan Nizam, "Perception of Shariah Scholars toward Islamic Banking in Pakistan," *Journal of Islamic Marketing* 16/4 (2024), 1118–1144.

Although Islamic finance is permitted on an institutional level, similar to that in Sri Lanka, the latter still lacks national implementation of the AAOIFI standards. Institutions can choose to follow specific guidelines, but the lack of regulatory oversight and a single regulation to duty bearers makes it difficult for firms to exhibit sector cohesion, especially in the long term.

3.4.4 *Comparative Reflections on Market Size versus Standard Adoption in the South Asian Countries*

An interesting comparison emerges between the size of Islamic finance markets and their adherence to AAOIFI standards. Bangladesh, for instance, hosts one of the largest Islamic finance sectors in the region, accounting for approximately 30% of total banking assets.[159] However, it only partially references AAOIFI standards without formal regulatory incorporation or translation. The reliance on hybrid frameworks and the absence of legal governance and auditing standards create a disjunction between market volume and ethical standardization.

In contrast, Afghanistan, despite its nascent Islamic finance sector with assets estimated in the low billions of USD, has formally adopted multiple AAOIFI Sharīʿah and governance standards.[160] While these standards remain untranslated and lack formal legal enforcement, their adoption illustrates a top-down regulatory ambition that partially offsets infrastructural limitations.

The Maldives, with a significantly smaller Islamic finance footprint, exhibits fragmented and regulator-specific adoption of AAOIFI standards across MIRA, MMA, and CMDA, yet lacks a national Shari'ah compliance strategy. This piecemeal approach underscores institutional capacity but also regulatory inconsistency.

By contrast, Pakistan has developed the region's most mature and integrated Islamic finance ecosystem, with assets exceeding USD 60 billion,

[159] Md Saifullah Azad, "Role of Leadership, Values, and Ethics in Driving Islamic Finance Excellence," *The Business Standard* (2024).

[160] Abdul Samad Keramat—Monzer Kahf, "Sharia Governance Framework of Islamic Financial Institutions in Afghanistan Compare to Pakistan and Nigeria," *İslam Ekonomisi ve Finansı Dergisi (İEFD)* 8/1 (2022), 135–158; Mohammad Walid Hemat, "The Determinants of Trade Deficit in Afghanistan: The Role of Foreign Aid, Exchange Rate and Price Level," *SN Business & Economics* 4/11 (2024), 131.

Urdu-translated AAOIFI standards, and a structured alignment with IFSB guidelines. Through efforts by the State Bank of Pakistan (SBP) and the Securities and Exchange Commission (SECP), Pakistan has localized many Shari'ah, accounting, and governance standards. Its commitment places it at the highest level in AAOIFI standard adoption among South Asian countries, strengthening ethical oversight and investor confidence.[161]

South Asia exhibits a full spectrum of AAOIFI engagement, ranging from Afghanistan's broad adoption, albeit untranslated, to Pakistan's localized and integrated model. Key challenges across the region include the absence of national translations (except in Pakistan), the non-adoption of governance and audit standards, and fragmented regulatory jurisdictions. These challenges undermine transparency, ethical integrity, and regional uniformity. Nevertheless, Pakistan offers a viable model for harmonization, striking a balance between national autonomy and global Shari'ah standardization goals.

A summary table has been prepared to present the technical aspects of AAOIFI adoption in these jurisdictions, completing the narrative described above (Table 3.6).

This table compares AAOIFI membership status, the extent and scope of standard adoption, availability of translations, centralized Sharīʿah boards, and dual-reporting options across South Asian countries. It highlights critical disparities, from Afghanistan's full adoption without translation to India's outright prohibition, illustrating the fragmented institutional landscape of Islamic finance in the region (Table 3.7).

The above table provides an in-depth overview of the adoption levels of AAOIFI standards, including Shari'ah, Accounting, Auditing, and Governance, in the selected key South Asian countries. It raises Pakistan's organized and comprehensive adoption, with specific standard numbers involved, in line with AAOIFI guidelines. Afghanistan and the Maldives have also made significant progress, with Afghanistan fully adopting all AAOIFI standards and the Maldives adopting several standards, most notably in accounting and auditing. On the other hand, Bangladesh exhibits low adoption, with partial implementation of some standards, indicating a potential area where India could expand its standardization efforts in the Islamic finance sector.

[161] Dr Asma Shaheen—Muhammad Kashif Amin, "Bridging the Gap: Aligning Legal Frameworks with the Growth of Islamic Banking and Finance in Pakistan," *Journal of Business Insight and Innovation* 2/1 (2023), 37–45.

Table 3.6 Comparative adoption of AAOIFI standards and institutional structures in South Asian countries

Country	*AAOIFI member*	*Adoption of Shari'ah standards*	*Translation available?*	*Central Shari'ah board*	*Dual reporting allowed*	*Extent of adoption*
Afghanistan	No	Full adoption	No	Yes (DAB)	Yes	Shari'ah, Accounting, Governance, and Auditing standards have been fully adopted
Maldives (CMDA)	Yes (MMA)	Voluntary/Guidance only	No	Yes (MMA and CMDA)	Yes	Shari'ah: optional governance and auditing: not adopted
Maldives (MIRA)	No	Not adopted (Shari'ah), Partial (others)	No	Yes (MIRA)	Yes	Financial accounting and auditing adopted, Shari'ah not adopted
Bangladesh	Yes	Partial adoption	No	Yes (CSBIB)	Yes	Shari'ah and accounting: partial governance and auditing: not adopted
Pakistan (SBP)	Associate member	Partial adoption + Local standards	Yes (Urdu)	Yes (SBP)	Yes	Wide range of Shari'ah standards + tailored governance/auditing
Pakistan (SECP)	Associate member	Partial adoption	Yes	Yes (SECP)	Yes	Sukuk & selective standards adopted; governance open
India	No	Not permitted	No	No	No	Islamic finance is prohibited by the RBI
Sri Lanka	No	Allowed (Institutional only)	No	Institutional level only	No clear data	No formal adoption; voluntary practice is possible

Source AAOIFI Footprint 2022

Table 3.7 AAOIFI standards adopted by country (number-wise summary)

Country	*Shari'ah standards*	*Accounting standards*	*Auditing standards*	*Governance standards*
Pakistan	SS-2, SS-3, SS-5, SS-8, SS-9, SS-10, SS-12, SS-13, SS-14, SS-17, SS-18, SS-19, SS-23, SS-24, SS-28, SS-38, SS-49	FAS-1 (Murābaḥah), FAS-2 (Ijārah), FAS-3 (PLS)	Local standards are aligned with AAOIFI	Local standards aligned with AAOIFI and IFSB
Afghanistan	Not individually numbered, but the report confirms: Full adoption of all Shari'ah, Accounting, Auditing, and Governance standards	Fully adopted	Fully adopted	Fully adopted
Bangladesh	Partial adoption (no standard numbers listed); used in Sukuk: SS-17	Partial adoption; influenced by FAS-1 to FAS-3	Not adopted	Not adopted
Maldives	No numbered standards have been officially adopted; some are used voluntarily in certain institutions	IFRS for SMEs + AAOIFI accounting accepted by MIRA (standard numbers not listed)	MIRA adopts AAOIFI auditing (number not given)	Not adopted

Source AAOIFI Footprint, 2022

3.4.5 *The Role of IFSB Standards in South Asian Islamic Finance*

While AAOIFI standards have received considerable attention in shaping the Sharīʿah compliance frameworks of South Asian Islamic financial institutions, the role of the Islamic Financial Services Board (IFSB) is equally critical, especially in regulating prudential matters such as capital adequacy, risk management, market discipline, and governance structures. The IFSB, established in 2002 and headquartered in Kuala Lumpur, serves as a standard-setting body that issues guidelines aligned with Basel

Committee standards but adapted to the specificities of Sharīʿah-compliant financial institutions.[162] In South Asia, the integration of IFSB standards has been uneven but steadily growing, with countries like Pakistan and Bangladesh emerging as the leading adopters.[163]

3.4.5.1 Overview of IFSB Standards and Their Scope

The IFSB's prudential framework includes core standards such as:

- IFSB-1: Guiding Principles of Risk Management
- IFSB-3: Capital Adequacy for Sharīʿah-compliant Instruments
- IFSB-9: Business Conduct
- IFSB-10: Sharīʿah Governance Framework
- IFSB-12: Liquidity Risk Management
- IFSB-15: Revised Capital Adequacy
- IFSB-16: Revised Liquidity Risk Management
- IFSB-17: Disclosure Requirements

As of 2024, the IFSB has issued a total of 31 standards and guiding principles across various sectors, including banking, takāful, and Islamic capital markets. These range from foundational documents such as *IFSB-1: Risk Management* and *IFSB-3: Capital Adequacy* to the most recent *IFSB-31: Guiding Principles for Effective Supervision of Sharīʿah Governance* (IFSB, 2024). The full suite of standards reflects a matured architecture encompassing capital adequacy, disclosure, governance, and sector-specific solvency. A complete and updated list of these standards is accessible via the official IFSB website.[164]

While AAOIFI focuses primarily on contractual and accounting compliance at the transactional level, the IFSB emphasizes institutional soundness, market discipline, and risk containment.[165] Together, their complementary frameworks provide a dual-layered architecture for Islamic financial regulation. However, South Asian jurisdictions have often adopted one without

[162] Islamic Financial Services Board (IFSB). *IFSB Annual Report 2023.* Kuala Lumpur: IFSB, 2023.

[163] *Strategic Plan for Islamic Banking Industry 2021–25*, SBP (Karachi: State Bank of Pakistan, 2021).

[164] "STANDARDS," *Islamic Financial Services Board* (Accessed August 5, 2025).

[165] IFSB. *Standard IFSB-1: Risk Management for Institutions Offering Islamic Financial Services.* Kuala Lumpur: IFSB, 2005.

fully integrating the other, resulting in regulatory asymmetry and partial Sharīʿah adherence.[166]

These standards supplement Sharīʿah compliance guidelines by addressing systemic risk, capital buffers, stress testing, and the unique risk profiles associated with profit-and-loss sharing (PLS) instruments such as *muḍārabah* and *mushārakah*. In contrast to AAOIFI's focus on product-level Sharīʿah conformity, the IFSB promotes institutional resilience and macroprudential regulation. Aligned conceptually with Basel Core Principles—especially Basel II and III—the IFSB's guidance is tailored to accommodate the operational distinctiveness of Islamic financial instruments.[167] For instance, *IFSB-15* and *IFSB-16* provide capital and liquidity requirements specifically suited for PLS contracts, which carry non-guaranteed capital structures and higher displaced commercial risks compared to fixed-income instruments. These adaptations are essential to ensure macroprudential oversight without compromising Sharīʿah integrity.[168]

Furthermore, *IFSB-10* and *IFSB-17* address the institutional dimensions of governance and transparency. *IFSB-10* delineates the responsibilities of Sharīʿah supervisory boards, internal Sharīʿah controls, and conflict-of-interest mitigation. *IFSB-17* promotes public disclosure of Sharīʿah rulings, compliance mechanisms, and risk exposures—critical elements for building stakeholder trust and aligning with maqāṣid-based ethical principles of transparency (*iẓhār al-ḥaqq*) and accountability (*mas'ūliyyah*) in Islamic finance.[169] Together, these standards reflect a harmonized yet adaptive

[166] Çiğdem Bal—Muharrem Umut, "Uluslararası Standartlar (AAOIFI ve IFSB) Çerçevesinde Kurumsal Yönetim," *Bankacılık ve Finansal Araştırmalar Dergisi* 10/2 (2023), 84–99: Md. Hafij Ullah et al., "Comparative Compliance Status of AAOIFI and IFSB Standards," *Journal of Islamic Accounting and Business Research* 9/4 (2018), 607–628.

[167] Necmeddin Güney, "İslami Finansta Şer'i Yönetim Uygulamalari ve Konuyla İlgili Tartişmalara Genel Bir Bakiş," *Turkish Journal of Islamic Economics* 2/2 (2015), 45–69.

[168] IFSB. *Standard IFSB-15: Revised Capital Adequacy Standard*. Kuala Lumpur: IFSB, 2013.

[169] Hakan Safa Yılmaz—Harun Şencal, "İslam Politik Ekonomisi Açısından Merkezi Fetva Kurullarının Yapısına Dair Bir Değerlendirme," *Journal of Islamic Economics* 2/1 (January 15, 2022), 92–105.

approach to systemic oversight, rooted in both global prudential logic and Islamic legal methodology.[170]

3.4.5.2 Institutional Gaps and the Need for Harmonization Between AAOIFI and IFSB

Despite the complementary mandates of AAOIFI and IFSB, institutional coordination remains limited. In October 2018, the two bodies signed a Memorandum of Understanding to collaborate on developing and revising prudential, Sharīʿah, accounting, and governance standards, plus joint workshops and technical missions for regulators and industry stakeholders.[171] However, practical follow-up has been uneven, resulting in regulatory fragmentation and overlapping compliance requirements.

Empirical data underscores this imbalance. For instance, Islami Bank Bangladesh Limited (IBBL)—the only South Asian institution subject to both frameworks—achieved compliance rates of approximately 46.3% with AAOIFI standards versus 52.5% with IFSB standards during 2008–2012.[172] This disparity reflects real-world challenges in dual compliance, especially within institutional contexts characterized by evolving Sharīʿah governance expectations.

Scholars and regulators have proposed deeper structural alignment, such as a strengthened MoU or a formal consultation platform between AAOIFI and IFSB, to enhance joint standard-setting, reduce duplication, and promote harmonized Sharīʿah oversight frameworks.[173] This is especially relevant for South Asian markets, where Islamic finance regulation is still consolidating; a coordinated approach would likely reduce burden on

[170] syraf Wajdi Dusuki—Abdulazeem Abozaid, "A Critical Appraisal on the Challenges of Realizing Maqasid Al-Shariaah in Islamic Banking and Finance," *International Journal of Economics, Management and Accounting* 15/2 (2007).

[171] "Islamic Finance Standard-Setting Bodies IFSB and AAOIFI Join Forces to Strengthen the Development and Resilience of the Islamic Financial Services Industry," *Islamic Financial Services Board* (2018); "Islamic Finance Standard-Setting Bodies AAOIFI and IFSB Join Forces to Strengthen the Development and Resilience of the Islamic Financial Services Industry," *Accounting and Auditing Organization for Islamic Financial Institutions* (2018).

[172] Ullah et al., "Comparative Compliance Status of AAOIFI and IFSB Standards," 608–615.

[173] "Islamic Finance Standard-Setting Bodies IFSB and AAOIFI Join Forces to Strengthen the Development and Resilience of the Islamic Financial Services Industry" (2018).

IFIs, strengthen governance coherence, and align regulatory architecture with maqāṣid al-sharīʿah principles.

3.4.5.3 Asymmetry in Adoption: Why South Asia Prefers AAOIFI Over IFSB

Despite the complementary aims of the AAOIFI and IFSB, South Asian countries, particularly Pakistan and Bangladesh, have shown a marked preference for adopting AAOIFI standards over those of the IFSB. This regulatory asymmetry stems from multiple structural and institutional factors. Firstly, AAOIFI's focus on product-level Sharīʿah standards (e.g., murābaḥah, ijārah, mushārakah) directly caters to the operational needs of Islamic financial institutions.[174] These standards enable faster product development, documentation, and Sharīʿah board compliance, which makes them more accessible and attractive for banks in competitive dual-banking environments.

In contrast, IFSB standards emphasize macroprudential regulation, including capital adequacy (IFSB-15), liquidity risk (IFSB-16), and Sharīʿah governance frameworks (IFSB-10), which require higher-level integration at the central bank or financial regulator level. This poses a challenge for South Asian jurisdictions, where regulatory fragmentation, limited technical capacity, and a lack of political will may delay systemic reforms. Furthermore, AAOIFI standards can be voluntarily adopted by individual institutions, whereas IFSB guidelines typically require top-down implementation through formal legal mandates or supervisory circulars, which are often absent or weak in developing economies. For example, the State Bank of Pakistan (SBP) has selectively adopted AAOIFI standards in areas such as Islamic accounting, Sharīʿah governance, and auditing. While the SBP has issued guidelines aligned with IFSB-1 and IFSB-10, the absence of a legally binding adoption mechanism means that IFSB's broader prudential standards remain underutilized. Similarly, in Bangladesh, AAOIFI-based products and accounting practices are more common, partly due to the influence of individual Sharīʿah boards and training institutes, whereas IFSB standards lack regulatory enforcement.[175]

[174] Bal—Umut, "Uluslararası Standartlar (AAOIFI ve IFSB) Çerçevesinde Kurumsal Yönetim," 86–89.

[175] Kabir Hassan—Michael Mahlknecht, *Islamic Capital Markets: Products and Strategies* (John Wiley & Sons, 2011).

While Pakistan and Bangladesh illustrate a preference for AAOIFI's bottom-up product-level implementation, countries like Afghanistan have formally mandated AAOIFI standards at the national level through Da Afghanistan Bank, making them legally binding for all Islamic financial institutions. Similarly, the Maldives Monetary Authority (MMA) has integrated AAOIFI accounting and governance standards into its regulatory framework. Even Sri Lanka, though in an early stage, has shown interest in aligning product-level Sharīʿah practices with AAOIFI, with some institutions adopting AAOIFI-based templates voluntarily. These cases highlight that AAOIFI's appeal extends beyond market convenience; it also provides legal and institutional clarity in jurisdictions where the regulatory ecosystem is still maturing (Table 3.8).

This table reflects the adoption status of AAOIFI and IFSB standards in South Asia, highlighting the asymmetrical preference for AAOIFI's product-level clarity over IFSB's macroprudential guidance. Data compiled from regulatory circulars, policy papers, and institutional reports.

However, the adoption of IFSB standards in these same countries remains fragmented or aspirational, largely due to the lack of supervisory capacity or formal legal mechanisms. While Afghanistan and the Maldives have referenced IFSB guidance in policy statements and strategic roadmaps, full operationalization of macroprudential tools—such as IFSB-15 or IFSB-16—remains limited. This divergence reinforces the broader theme that product-level compliance is prioritized over systemic regulation in many South Asian jurisdictions.

This asymmetry not only fragments regulatory coherence but also weakens the ethical oversight mechanisms needed to uphold maqāṣid-based integrity, transparency, and accountability in South Asian Islamic finance. This imbalance in adoption undermines the maqāṣid-based pursuit of justice (ʿadl) and transparency in financial regulation across the region, signaling the urgency for a harmonized ethical framework.

This fragmented regulatory architecture highlights the need for harmonization, not only between AAOIFI and IFSB but also within domestic regulatory agencies. Scholars have suggested formal memoranda of understanding (MoUs) between these two bodies, along with regional standard-setting support to help central banks localize and implement IFSB standards without compromising Sharīʿah integrity or institutional autonomy.

Table 3.8 Comparative adoption of AAOIFI and IFSB standards in South Asia (as of 2024)

Country	*Adopted standard body*	*Standards*	*Adoption status*	*Year/ Period*	*Legal mandate*
Pakistan	AAOIFI	Accounting, Auditing, Governance, Products	Selectively adopted	Since~2015	Partially mandatory (via SBP circulars)
	IFSB	IFSB-1, IFSB-10, IFSB-9	Referenced/ Recommended	Since~2018	No legal enforcement
Bangladesh	AAOIFI	Product-level and Accounting templates	Informally Adopted	Since~2012	Institution-specific
	IFSB	Limited reference (e.g., IFSB-10, IFSB-15)	Not formally adopted	N/A	No
Afghanistan	AAOIFI	Full standard suite	Fully adopted	2020	Mandatory via Da Afghanistan Bank
	IFSB	Referenced in strategic plans	Aspirational	Since~2021	Not yet operational
Maldives	AAOIFI	Accounting, Governance	Adopted	Since~2017	Integrated via MMA
	IFSB	General guidance only	Referenced	2021	Not binding
Sri Lanka	AAOIFI	Some product templates (institution-level)	Voluntary adoption	Since~2016	No
	IFSB	Not yet adopted	Not applicable	N/A	No

Sources AAOIFI Footprint, 2022; IFSB, 2019. 2021, 2023

3.5 Proposing a New Ethical Governance Model

There is a need for a new Islamic finance governance structure in South Asia that incorporates traditional Muslim ethical principles to address current financial requirements.[176] The region actualizes ambition through its implementation framework. To address the complex regulatory challenges faced by South Asian Islamic banks, there is an urgent need to adopt a governance model that effectively combines traditional Islamic forms of oversight with modern accountability mechanisms. The proposed Ethical Governance Model for Islamic Finance in South Asia, centered around the South Asian Ethical Finance Council (SAEFC), serves this purpose by merging classical Sharīʿah principles with modern technologies. This hybrid framework opens a new avenue for bridging national and global standards,[177] making SAEFC responsible for drafting a harmonized version of Sharīʿah guidelines to foster regional cohesiveness among South Asian Muslim countries.

This Fig. 3.1 illustrates the Proposed Ethical Governance Model for South Asian Islamic finance, based on the South Asian Ethical Finance Council (SAEFC). SAEFC serves as a central hub, combining ethical, technological, and regulatory elements. It relates to Knowledge Exchange (fatāwā, forums) to facilitate all-inclusive legal discourse. Digital Platforms for audits and certifications to enhance transparency. National Sharīʿah Boards and Global Standards (e.g., AAOIFI, IFSB) are utilized to ensure a level of multilevel standardization. Modern Tools (ESG metrics, blockchain) enable innovation, while ḤisbahValues (justice, taqwā, accountability) ground operations in classical ethics. Integrated Ethical Governance is the outcome, at the system level, of coordinated engagement. The model seeks to correlate tradition and modernity with increased ethical credibility and cross-border homogenization in Islamic finance among South Asian states. As recent empirical studies confirm, ESG frameworks are increasingly integrated into Islamic finance

[176] Asyraf Wajdi Dusuki-Nurdianawati Irwani Abdullah, "Maqasid Al-Shari'ah, Maslahah, and Corporate Social Responsibility," *American Journal of Islam and Society* 24/1 (January 1, 2007), 25–45.

[177] M. Kabir Hassan—Mervyn K. Lewis, *Handbook of Islamic Banking* (Edward Elgar Publishing, 2007), 128–130; Simon Archer—Rifaat Ahmed Abdel Karim, *Islamic Finance: The New Regulatory Challenge* (New York: Wiley, 2013), 9–13.

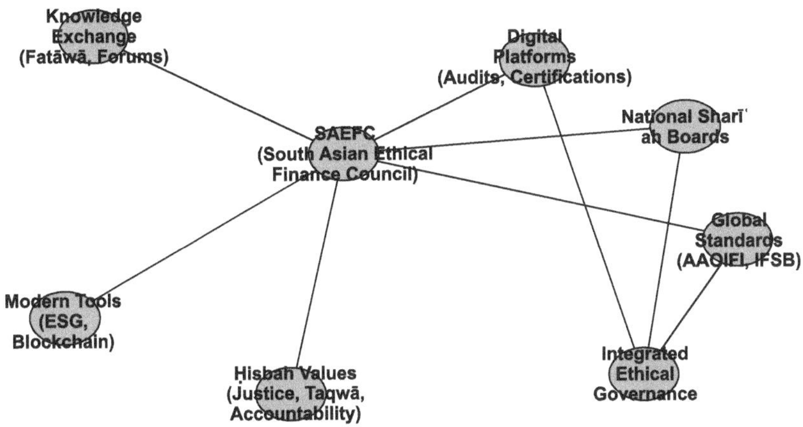

Fig. 3.1 Proposed ethical governance model for South Asian Islamic finance

ecosystems, affirming the compatibility between Shari'ah-driven ethics and modern sustainability metrics.[178]

3.5.1 *SAEFC (South Asian Ethical Finance Council): The Central Node*

Such a proposal creates a South Asia Ethical Finance Council (SAEFC) to promote ethical governance in Pakistan, Bangladesh, India, and Sri Lanka. The autonomous council would exist outside the control of the national regulatory bodies, financial institutions, and Sharīʿah boards but would work closely with them in its region. The main functions will include the development of regional Sharīʿah-compliant ESG guidelines, concurrently with cross-institutional audits via blockchain platforms, and the training of Sharīʿah auditors and ethics officers in dispute resolution through a ḥisbah-style tribunal. Dusuki and Abdullah emphasize that integrating maqāṣid and maṣlaḥah considerations enhances moral accountability in Islamic finance institutions and prevents rule-based ethical minimalism.[179] International

[178] Abdillah Arif Nasution et al., "Environmental, Social, Governance (ESG) and Islamic Finance: A Review," *Management and Sustainability* 1/1 (2023), 1–12.

[179] Dusuki—Abdullah, "Maqasid Al-Shari'ah, Maslahah, and Corporate Social Responsibility," 28–30.

regulation of moral governance via SAEFC would help bridge the ethical gaps in Islamic banking governance across national jurisdictional boundaries.

3.5.2 Knowledge Exchange (Fatāwā, Forums)

Knowledge Exchange is, therefore, structured to respect South Asia's jurisprudential diversity and maintain a dialogical and inclusive model. Facilitated by a synthesis of fatwā repositories, regional conferences, academic seminars, and public forums, the council enables scholars, practitioners, and stakeholders to engage in open dialogue, negate interpretive nodi, and contend with emerging financial innovations. These platforms promote collective ijtihād, diminish interpretive isolation, and help establish a dynamic and ethical response ecosystem, a collaborative publication platform that reconciles disparate legal opinions through comparative analysis. Kamali discusses the critical role of juristic diversity and pluralism in contemporary Islamic law, noting that "plurality in fiqh is not a defect, but a feature of the Sharīʿah"[180] and explores how independent reasoning (ijtihād) enables dynamic fatāwā across contexts.[181] He further emphasizes the alignment of legal objectives (maqāṣid) with broader principles of justice.[182] As Dusuki and Bouheraoua (2011) argue, maqāṣid-based ethics, including justice, public interest, and reasoned disagreement, provide a more principled framework for financial decision-making and jurisprudential harmonization.[183]

This enables regulatory coherence to be promoted and reduces ethical arbitrage across jurisdictions. Despite the availability of global standards, including those of AAOIFI and IFSB, for a wide range of moral considerations, their direct implementation in South Asia is hindered by legal pluralism and institutional disruption. Thus, a proposal is put forward for the establishment of the Regional Fatwā and Sharīʿah Oversight Board for Pakistan, Bangladesh, India, Sri Lanka, and the Maldives, with equal representation from both the Muslim and non-Muslim regions. Instead

[180] Kamali, *Shari'ah Law*, 68–70.

[181] Kamali, *Shari'ah Law*, 175–176.

[182] Kamali, *Shari'ah Law*, 95–96.

[183] Ayraf Wajdi Dusuki—Said Bouheraoua, "The Framework of Maqasid Al-Shari'ah and Its Implication for Islamic Finance ICR Journal," (2020), 320–324.

of copying AAOIFI, this board would function as a harmonizing body that recognizes and adapts interpretive guidance to the region's socio-economic and legal settings. Its mandate would promote moral consistency, enable region-specific ijtihād, and cultivate institutional trust in cross-border Islamic financial governance.

3.5.3 *Coordination Between Knowledge Exchange and National Shariʿah Boards*

A central novelty of this model is the functional integration between Knowledge Exchange mechanisms and national shariʿah boards. Although the Knowledge Exchange is an open system of scholarly discourse, the boards operate as formally authorized juristic bodies; their interaction, under the supervision of SAEFC, guarantees integrated, inclusive, and holder-based ethical oversight.

- *Feedback Loop:* Boards continually discuss insights from fatwā forums and community debates, enabling evidence-based ethical enhancements.
- *Jurisprudential Cross-Fertilization:* Periodic SAEFC-sponsored symposia enable the South Asia board members to harmonize rulings and consult diverse scholarly views.
- *Transparency and Trust*: Accountability and legitimacy are achieved through public-facing fatwa platforms in Shari'ah decision-making.
- *Capacity Building*: The scarcity of regionally based scholarly knowledge and precedents in emerging markets prompts boards to adopt a jurisprudential approach to establishing conflict resolution across borders.
- *Crisis Response:* Forums provide instant scholarly discussion on new topics (e.g., digital currencies), and boards transform them into active data in the form of timely judicial deliberations.

This collaborative mechanism ensures ethical governance, striking a balance between tradition and the ability to respond to financial innovation.

3.5.4 *Incorporating Digital Platforms*

The most up–to-date digital infrastructures, including systems based on blockchain certification and automated audit tools, are crucial for ensuring the transparent implementation of ethical principles.[184] Such tools help curtail the discretionary power of individual actors and enable the SAEFC to conduct standardized compliance checks, which are particularly important in a region with informal economies and regulatory gaps. The model also adheres to internationally recognized ethical standards established by institutions such as the Accounting and Auditing Organization for Islamic Financial Institutions (AAOIFI) or the Basel Institute for Financial Services (BIFSB).[185] SAEFC is responsible for interpreting and adapting these standards to the realities of South Asia, aiming to maintain the standards' applicability while upholding the principles of Shariʿah. This way, we are ensured to be credible worldwide while respecting the particularities of the local environment. Encapsulating environmental, social, and governance (ESG) operational frameworks through blockchain technologies can transform Muslim financial governance.[186] Measurable tools of ESG indicators align well with *fiqh al-muʿāmalāt* because they are concerned with averting damages (dafʿ al-ḍarar). The benefits stakeholders get from blockchain technology include immutable auditing trails, enforced smart contracts, and a highly enhanced communication channel that is transparent. The modern conception, based on classical Islamic propositions, embeds the mechanism of divine accountability within the machinery of market transparency.

3.5.5 Ḥisbahvalues (Justice, Taqwā, Accountability)

This approach rebuilds ḥisbahprinciples on the foundation of justice (ʿadālah), piety (taqwā), and accountability (mas'ūliyyah). Since ancient times, the ethical principles that governed markets and public behavior have remained relevant today, as critical in modern financial ethics as they were in the past.[187] Sharīʿah boards in Modern regulators and South Asia

[184] Mohamed Ariff—Shamsher Mohamad (eds.), *Islamic Wealth Management: Theory and Practice* (Northampton: Edward Elgar Publishing, 2017), 212–215.

[185] Maria Teresa Medeiros Garcia—Frederico Cavaleiro de Mendonça, "Compliance with the Basel Core Principles and Supervisory Structure: A Cross-Country Analysis," *Central Bank Review* 23/2 (2023), 100117.

[186] Sylva Alif Rusmita et al., "Fundamental and Role ESG in Islamic Finance and Business: A Literature Review and Content Analysis," *International Journal of Religion* 5/11 (2024), 8519–8534.

[187] Nurul Aina Johari, "The Relevancy of Hisbah (Accountability) in The Modern Era: A Brief Analysis," *Jurnal Islam Dan Masyarakat Kontemporari* 22/2 (2021), 30–35.

should emulate the impartial nature and approach of Muḥtasibs to enhance the public trust in their work. The application of these principles necessitates the development of real legal instruments that cover the most critical maqāṣid al-sharīʿah features, namely equitable finance terms, a transparent operational process, and social benefits.[188] This node illustrates the integration of National Shariʿah Boards, Global Standards, and Digital Platforms into a unified accountability engine.[189] This integration fosters institutional synergy, ensuring the avoidance of fragmentation, consistency in compliance, and a unified approach to ethical implementation across jurisdictions.

3.5.6 Why This Model Is Important for South Asian Countries

Operating within a highly heterogeneous and frequently unregulated environment, Islamic finance in South Asia operates. The differences include the legal system (common law for India, an Islamic-civil hybrid for Pakistan and Bangladesh, etc.), sectarian diversity, which has included schools such as Ḥanafī, Jaʿfarī, and Ahl-i Ḥadīth, among others, and varying levels of government support, each of which has fostered asymmetric growth in the Islamic finance sector.

The following are ways in which the proposed model addresses these challenges:

- *Regional harmonization*: Devising a common ethical reference point for all the South Asian nations.
- *Decentralized legitimacy*: Exercising national boards while at the same time respecting local jurisprudence.
- *Technological integration*: Using digital platforms to maintain enforceability and real-time surveillance.
- *Maqāṣid-oriented governance*: Simplifying the system from a maximizing, competitive, and profit-oriented entity toward a more justice, inclusivity, and social welfare-oriented entity.

188 M. Rizky Oktaviandi—Yogi Yogi, "Economic Justice Through Al-Hisbah: Reviewing The Role and Performance of Market Supervisory Institutions," *Al-Kharaj: Journal of Islamic Economic and Business* 6/1 (2024).

189 Fawad Khaleel—Alija Avdukic, "Islamic Classical Literature (A.D. 950–1450) on Institutionalisation of Ethics for Regulating Markets and Society," *Religions* 15/12 (2024), 1496.

- *Reducing ethical arbitrage*: Preventing cross-border inconsistencies that erode consumer and investor confidence.

This model is particularly timely, as the world discusses cross-border sukuk, Islamic fintech, and microfinance initiatives for the large Muslim populations in South Asia. Without a strong ethical coordination force, as SAEFC suggests, such developments risk remaining divided, underutilized, or ethically compromised.

3.5.7 *Ethical Oversight Through* **Maṣāliḥ al-Mursalah** *and* **Sadd al-Dharā'i'**

While the parts above have focused on institutional proposals—such as the South Asian Ethical Finance Council (SAEFC), ESG integration, and cross-border standardization—this section shifts towards the juristic roots that underpin and deepen these proposals, such as the concepts of maṣāliḥ al-mursalah (public interest beyond its legal boundaries) and sadd al-dharā'i' (blocking the means to evil). These two rules have traditionally allowed jurists to manage flexibly with new socio-economic situations, and both protect the Muslim legal standards. At the same time, applied to the ethical regulation of financial entities, they offer encouragement and caution for reinventing ḥisbah and murāqabah for our modern era. A review of ḥisbah and Murāqabah needs to move past traditional ritualized practices.[190]

Contemporary Sharī'ah governance frameworks have correctly been seen as descending into compliance checklists (a topic we covered in earlier Sects. (3.3.1, 3.3.2, 3.3.3, and 3.3.4). However, classical ḥisbahwas neither bureaucratic nor detached. It was an ethical mechanism-based living characterized by justice ('adālah), piety (tqwā), and accountability in the community sphere. To prevent the ossification of ethical oversight in formalism, there is a compelling requirement to reapply institutional mechanisms to foundational jurisprudential reasoning, specifically *maṣlaḥah* and *sadd al-dharā'i'*.

[190] Akhtarzaite Binti Abdulaziz, "Al-Dharā'i' and Maqāṣid al-Sharī'ah: A Case Study of Islamic Insurance," *Intellectual Discourse* 18/2 (2010), 266–268; Burhanudin Harahap et al., "Islamic Law, Islamic Finance, and Sustainable Development Goals: A Systematic Literature Review," *Sustainability* 15/8 (2023), 6626.

3.5.7.1 Maṣāliḥ al-Mursalah: Enabling Institutional Innovation

Maṣlaḥah, as a means of legal reasoning, enables the promulgation of legal judgments and regulatory axioms that serve the public interest, notwithstanding their disparity from definitive scriptural sources.[191] Islamic finance draws legitimacy for modern financial institutions through the concept of maṣlaḥah, which supports elements including:

- Shari'ah governance frameworks, which, though not textually prescribed, fulfill the communal interest by ensuring uniformity of ethical mode.[192]
- Laws to protect consumer finance and digital banking, and cybersecurity rules to maintain public confidence and trust.
- Unified zakāt management to avoid losses and wastages in charitable disbursements. For example, the implementation of real-time auditing systems that utilize AI and blockchain technology for digital payment platforms has no direct text.[193]

This perspective enables ethical oversight to evolve dynamically with financial innovation—something increasingly necessary in fintech-heavy contexts, such as Malaysia, and emerging digital economies like India and Bangladesh.

3.5.7.2 Sadd al-Dharāʿiʿ*: Blocking Institutional and Systemic Harm*

Maṣlaḥah functions as a construction process, but *Sadd al-dharāʿiʿ* acts as a locking mechanism. The principle stops activities that cannot be shown to be illegal but create harmful results.[194] The ethical regulation of financial institutions allows this doctrine to justify certain activities. The

[191] Prof Mohammad Hashim Kamali, *Principles of Islamic Jurisprudence* (Cambridge, UK: Islamic Texts Society, 2003), 349–355.

[192] Dusuki—Abdullah, "Maqasid Al-Shari'ah, Maslahah, and Corporate Social Responsibility," 28–30.

[193] Amelia Nur Natasha Nazeri et al., "Exploration of a New Zakat Management System Empowered by Blockchain Technology in Malaysia," *ISRA International Journal of Islamic Finance* 15/4 (2023), 127–147.

[194] Salleh et al., "Theory and Application of Sadd Al-Dhara'i' (Blocking the Means) in Shafi'iyya School," 725–726; Mustafa Mat Jubri Shamsuddin, "Statistical Evaluation of Conduciveness in Sadd Al-Dharāʾiʿ: An Analytical Study," *Journal of Contemporary Islamic Law* 9/2 (2024), 41–42.

application of prohibitions against speculative instruments that resemble gambling strategies includes derivative-linked activities and short-selling. The practice of sadd al-dharāʾiʿ blocks specific corporate and contract models that enable predatory lending, alongside deliberate contractual ambiguities known as gharar. Several financial products have Islamic branding, but regulatory institutions should limit the use of genuine ethical content.[195] Multi-level marketing schemes that produce unpredictable financial results but create foreseeable exploitation among investors become subject to prohibition using sadd al-dharāʾiʿ.

Sharīʿah boards and regulators gain the power to protect Islam through precautionary measures, including banning specific textual breaches and probable economic and moral threats.

3.5.7.3 Integrating Both Principles into a Modern Ethical Framework

The proposed SAEFC as a hybrid governance model needs to develop from the simultaneous implementation of *maṣlaḥah*-oriented facilitation and *sadd al-dharāʾiʿ*-based restriction. Operational efficiency and legal formalism represent only two aspects of the framework it aims to achieve, while its ultimate objective involves creating systems that meet both goals. The system should focus on achieving just outcomes and sustaining stakeholder welfare in the

Table 3.9 Ethical governance applications of Maṣlaḥah and Sadd al-Dharāʾiʿ in South Asian Islamic finance

Principle	*Constructive role (Maṣlaḥah)*	*Restrictive role (Sadd al-Dharāʾiʿ)*
Zakat governance	Centralized digital zakat platforms to increase efficiency and transparency	Criminal penalties for misappropriation or delay of distribution
Fintech regulation	AI-enabled auditing for efficiency and fraud detection	Ban on high-risk crypto-assets prone to speculation
Sharīʿah auditing	Community-based ethical rating systems for transparency	Disqualification of scholars with commercial conflicts of interest

Source Author's own

[195] Wadeema Aldhaheri, "Islamic Green Finance: Shariah-Compliant Pathways towards Sustainable Development Goals (SDGs)," *Open Journal of Applied Sciences* 15/5 (2025), 1294–1309.

long term. The system protects organizations from ethical corruption and the destruction of their reputation. This model must adapt to various financial and environmental elements while defending core principles (Table 3.9).

The following table is a dual-role ethical framework for Islamic financial governance and synchronizes two fundamental legal principles: Maṣlaḥah (public benefit) and Sadd al-Dharāʾiʿ (blocking harm). It demonstrates how each principle can enable either positive or repressive behavior in major issues, including zakat governance, fintech regulation, and Sharīʿah auditing. The objective is to reconcile innovation with integrity by encouraging good tools while avoiding ethical compromise.

3.5.7.4 A Critical Challenge: Avoiding Selective Application

There is a significant concern about the practical application of this principle because *maṣlaḥah* is being used to justify new practices that threaten to undermine the institutional authority of the sadd al-dharāʾiʿ.[196] Critics argue that Many Sharīʿah boards employ maṣlaḥah to justify profit-based objectives, thereby violating the fundamental principles of Islamic law. Regulatory agencies are being asked the question of how ethical their independence is today, since Sadd al-dharāʾiʿ is being dismissed in favor of 'market liberalization.'[197] Technical expertise alone is insufficient; it has to restore the concept of juristic integrity and the classical muḥtasib tradition. An impartial judge eliminates harmful acts or promotes positive behavior.

The governance structure of ḥisbah, the role of murāqabah by maṣlaḥah, and sadd al-dharāʾiʿ affords Islamic finance regulators an ethical discourse that can be used to fulfill their duties today. Modern institutional development and these essential tools may coexist peacefully because their validation does not mean rejecting modernization. Modern financial innovation should link a prophetically planned goal to moral and economic awareness.[198] Islamic finance must no longer be merely a branding exercise, but must become a genuine, transformational system of justice, equity, and trust before it makes its claim.

[196] Hegazy Walid, *Fatwas and the Fate of Islamic Finance: A Critique of the Practice of Fatwa in Contemporary Islamic Financial Markets* (Cambridge, Mass.: Islamic Finance Project, Islamic Studies Program, Harvard Law School, 2005), 134–135.

[197] Dusuki—Bouheraoua, "The Framework of Maqasid Al-Shari'ah and Its Implication for Islamic Finance," 320–324.

[198] See, Faleel Jamaldeen, *Islamic Finance for Dummies* (Hoboken, N.J: Wiley, 2012).

3.6 Islamic Contractual Auditing in Islamic Financial Institutions

In Islamic financial institutions, compliance with the fundamental principles of Islamic law (fiqh) ensures the validity of financial transactions. The basis of Shari'ah governance is Islamic contractual auditing, which involves a comprehensive analytical investigation of economic processes to establish whether these contractual agreements are consistent with the basic principles and preconditions of Islamic jurisprudence. In this section, we examine the underlying provisions and practical relevance of auditing in Islamic banking, while considering some fundamental prerequisites that must be fulfilled and the effectiveness it entails regarding the central contracts used in Islamic finance.

3.6.1 The Significance of Auditing Fundamental Contractual Elements

Within the scope of Islamic finance, the validity and enforceability of agreements are based on fulfilling fundamental contractual prerequisites. The cardinal elements are offer and acceptance (ijab and qabul), consent on the part of both parties, capacity to enter into a binding agreement, a clear definition of the subject matter, and the complete absence of coercive conduct or deception.[199] A contract would be vitiated if the basic criteria are not achieved according to Islamic law standards.[200] Therefore, verifying these elements is crucial and is a key part of adhering to Shari'ah standards.

Additionally, all parties participating must be legally authorized to do so. Shari'ah auditors are responsible for ensuring that both parties willingly consent without harassment (ikrah) or coercion (*taghrir*).[201] Contracts made under duress or fraudulent misrepresentation may be declared void or voidable, depending on the nature of the defect.[202]

[199] 'Alī ibn Abī BakrBurhān al-Dīn Abū al-Ḥasan al-Marginānу, *Al-Hidāyah Sharḥ Bidāyat al-Mubtadī* (Pakistan: Idārat al-Qur'ān wa-al-'Ulūm al-Islāmīyah, 1994), 2/30.

[200] Hayreddin Karaman, *Mukayeseli İslam Hukuku* (İstanbul: İZ YAYINCILIK, 2006), 2/90.

[201] Ali Bardakoğlu, "Gabn", Türkiye Diyanet Vakfi İslam Ansiklopedisi (Erişim 22 Şubat 2024).

[202] Mustafa Ahmad al-Zarqa, *Al-Madkhal al-Fiqhī al-'Āmm* (Syria: Dar al-Kalam Publication, 2004), 1/279–280.

Such watchfulness is essential for maintaining the highest standards in financial transactions and ensuring fair dealing.

In addition, the contractual participants must be legally entitled to understand, of mature age, and freedom from limitations such as bankruptcy or guardianship. If a party's capacity is inadequate, the whole agreement may not be binding.[203] It is also the responsibility of an auditor to determine whether the reason behind the contract aligns with Islamic law. By way of illustration, a transaction crafted to seem interest-like (*ḥiyal*) may be technically valid in appearance but would probably appear ethically questionable.

Auditors should also review how seriously the contract was carried out, ensuring it was genuinely and purposefully implemented. According to classical scholars, a contract entered into for amusement (*hazl*) is unenforceable in law.[204] Although this principle is intellectual, it ensures that genuine intent is upheld and that legal theatrics, which attempt to conceal false intent, are not condoned. Shari'ah auditors, as a result, will have to examine the formal documentation,[205] but they will also evaluate adherence to the ethical principles underlying Islamic contract law.

3.6.2 *Auditing the Legitimacy of the Subject Matter*

One of the defining principles in Islamic contract law is the requirement that the subject matter of the contract must be legitimate, available, and known to both parties.[206] Legitimacy refers to the item's physical existence and conformity to Islamic norms. Items prohibited in Shari'ah, such as alcohol, pork, or illicit services, cannot constitute valid contractual subject matter. As such, auditors have to ensure that the goods or services being exchanged are Shari'ah-compliant.

Further, the party concerned should not raise unnecessary doubt (gharar) or confusion over the subject matter. Auditors must ensure that the details on how the item (description, quantity, quality) is defined are as detailed as possible to rule out any confusion or differences in interpretation. A contract replete with excessive ambiguity is struck down, as it can

[203] al-Zarqa, *Al-Madkhal al-Fiqhī al-'Āmm*, 1/320.

[204] Alī al-Khafīf, *Aḥkām Al-Mu'āmalāt al-Shar'īyah* (Damascus: Dār al-Fikr al-'Arabī, 2008), 347.

[205] 'Alā' al-Dīn al-Samarqandī, *Tuḥfat Al-Fuqahā'* (Beirut: Dār al-Kutub al-'Ilmīyah, 1994), 2/48.

[206] al-Marginany, *Al-Hidāyah Sharḥ Bidāyat al-Mubtadī*, 2/57.

create an exploitative situation, which is forbidden in Shari'ah.[207] It is also essential that the goods or services can be supplied,[208] because contracts are typically found to be unenforceable when the goods and services transacted are naturally undeliverable or suffer from obstacles caused by external elements.[209] Auditors must, therefore, evaluate whether the good or service can be realistically transferred in the agreed timeframe.

3.6.3 *Evaluation of the Price and Consideration (Thaman and 'Iwad)*

The price or consideration (thaman for sales, ujrah for leases) must be well-defined, licensable, and agreed upon by both parties.[210] A vague price can make a transaction vulnerable to disagreements and even invalidation. The Islamic auditors should verify that the cost has been accurately established, including its amount and currency. All arrangements for deferred payments must be rigorously reviewed to prevent the possibility of receiving unjust enrichment (riba al-nasi'ah).

Moreover, the act of considering must be Shari'ah-compliant. Payment with usurious interest or assets not in accordance with Shari'ah rules renders the contract voidable.[211] Furthermore, numerous Islamic financial institutions practice sales on deferred payment with profit margins, such as Murabaha arrangements. The specific profit in such cases should be clearly described, and the financial institution must obtain ownership before the sale to ensure that the contract does not result in an interest-in-lieu-of-debt arrangement.

Auditors are seeking evidence of fraud or intentionally false statements. Minor distortions regarding pricing may not render a contract void, but direct intent to defraud and serious price manipulation accompanied by some misinformation could potentially render a contract void.[212]

[207] c, *Badā'i' Al-Ṣanā'i' Fī Tartīb al-Sharā'i'*, 6/497.

[208] Kāsānī, *Badā'i' Al-Ṣanā'i' Fī Tartīb al-Sharā'i'*, 6/481.

[209] Abdullāh ibn Maḥmūd al-Mawṣilī, *Al-Ikhtiyār Li-Ta'līl al-Mukhtār* (Beirut: Dār al-Kutub al-'Ilmīyah, 1998), 1/253.

[210] al-Dīn al-Samarqandī, *Tuḥfat Al-Fuqahā'*, 2/45.

[211] Nūr al-Dīn Abū al-Ḥasan al-Qārī, *Fatḥ Bāb Al-'ināyah Bi-Sharḥ* (Beirut: Dār al-Arqam, 1997), 2/439.

[212] al-Qārī, *Fatḥ Bāb Al-'ināyah Bi-Sharḥ*, 2/438.

Therefore, auditors should assess whether the price to be paid is, in fact, reasonable and whether all the disclosures are clear and accurate.

3.6.4 *Third-Party Rights, Conditions, and Legal Representations*

A proper audit tests whether the contract influences the legal powers of third parties. Frequent problems arise from ownership disputes, pledges or mortgages, and shuf'ah or pre-emptive rights issues. Discussing these points is basic to verifying the contract's enforceability and compliance with ethical norms.[213]

Contracts must also be free from illegal provisions. Agreements that undermine the essence or objectives of the contract, such as including provisions for post-sale services that would compromise the transfer of ownership, could be considered invalid.[214] Auditors should also confirm whether the agreement was signed by duly authorized agents or by unauthorized persons and whether the latter were then confirmed.[215] In this regard, auditors should verify whether there were any third-party claims on the asset, examine whether the contract contained unlawful or illogical conditions, and confirm whether the agreement was entered into by a duly authorized agent or, if not, whether the actions of an unauthorized individual were later ratified. Each of these issues can influence the contract's legitimacy and, by extension, the permissibility of the resulting financial gains.

3.6.5 *Contract-Based Fiqh Audit Checklist*

The following sections revisit the primary Islamic contract types discussed in Chap. 1, now through the lens of contractual auditing and ethical evaluation. Each contract is reviewed not for its classical definition, but for its Sharīʿah auditing criteria, procedural risks, and practical compliance measures.[216]

[213] al-Dīn al-Samarqandī, *Tuḥfat Al-Fuqahā'*, 2/47.

[214] Kāsānī, *Badā'iʿ Al-Ṣanā'iʿ Fī Tartīb al-Sharā'iʿ*, 511.

[215] al-Khafīf, *Aḥkām Al-Muʿāmalāt al-Sharʿīyah*, 315.

[216] The fiqh-based auditing mechanisms applied here are built upon the classical definitions of these contracts, which are well established in prior literature and briefly introduced in Chap. 1.

In Islamic financial institutions, successful ḥisbah should be accompanied by an audit tailored to each contract, which conforms to the official legal standards and the institution's ethical and theological wholeness. This part examines the core Islamic financial tools through the classical fiqh al-muʿāmalāt prism, highlighting ethical contradictions and their application in modern business affairs. Analysis of each contract focuses on a concise reflection, a feasible example demonstrating possible ḥisbah failings, and a set of questions intended to assist auditors in assessing the appearance and reality of Sharīʿah compliance.

3.6.5.1 Auditing Murābaḥah (Cost-plus Sale) Contracts for Sharīʿah Compliance

Although murābaḥah is a home hub of financing in Islamic law, it presents major fiqh issues: Is the asset in the service of the seller before being resold to the buyer? Is the markup evident, and does the buyer assume all the associated risks? Presenting an asset transfer as a sale without having authentic possession of the underlying asset can be a ḥisbah offense, as issued financing by banks can be disguised as murābahah financing, as banks may represent the asset transfer as a sale. In contrast, for example, banks may close a murābaḥah deal and fail to acquire the goods in question, leaving the buyer to return an item for which the bank had no legal rights. Although marketed as a sale, this deal falls short of what Sharīʿah requires to be accepted as an Islamic loan, as it blends the two types of financing.[217]

Auditor's Caution

- Did the institution thoroughly acquire ownership and possession, either actual or constructive, of the asset before executing the sale, and were any advance payments from the buyer made only after this transfer?
- Was the cost price and profit margin transparently disclosed, documented in writing, and accepted by the buyer before contract execution?
- Is the overall sale structure free from buy-back arrangements or disguised loan features, and does it involve genuine commercial risk distinct from an interest-bearing loan?

[217] "AAOIFI Shariah Standard," 205, 663,675; İsnail Cebeci, *Modern İslam Iktisadı Literatüründe Murabaha Tartışmaları* (Istanbul: Marmara University, PhD, 2010).

3.6.5.2 Auditing Muḍārabah (Profit-sharing Partnership) and Risk Evaluation

The ethical strength of the Muḍārabah system, based on trusting and collaborative risk, is tested in contemporary banking. Are the returns on investment pre-determined, and are the losses that are suffered only accruable to the capital provider (rabb al-māl)? Is the muḍārib independent, or more of an employee of the bank by implicit guarantees? The need for a ḥisbahframework is undermined when institutions subtly insert profit guarantees or limitations over the muḍārib, contrary to the contract's original terms. A common trend of misbehavior is the muḍārabah products that banks sell to savers, where any losses are absorbed through their reserves, rendering the mutual loss-sharing mechanism meaningless.

The ethical strength of muḍārabah, a partnership premised on genuine risk-sharing, is compromised when banks pre-allocate profit ratios and absorb losses through internal reserves, thereby sidestepping the principle of mutual loss. The depositors bear all losses unless caused by negligence, highlighting the problematic shift from trust-driven risk-sharing to bank-dominated control. Observers note that in practice, muḍārabah contracts often emulate fixed-return instruments, effectively undermining their intended form and function, and mirroring the dynamics of conventional loans.[218]

Auditor's Caution

- Are profit ratios clearly pre-agreed as percentages of actual profit, and is there any implicit or explicit guarantee of capital or fixed return by the muḍārib or institution?
- Financial records demonstrate that actual losses, if any, were borne exclusively by the capital provider (rabb al-māl), unless proven negligence or misconduct by the muḍārib is documented.
- Is the operational independence of the muḍārib maintained, and are muḍārabah-based funds and their reporting segregated from conventional interest-based instruments and other deposit accounts?

[218] "AAOIFI Shariah Standard," 390; Irawan Febianto, "Risk Management in Mudharabah and Musharakah Financing of Islamic Banks," *SSRN Electronic Journal*, (2009); Mohamad Handi Khalifah et al., "Challenges in the Implementation of Mudharabah Financing in the Islamic Banking Industry," *Equinox Journal of Economics Business and Political Studies* 11/1 (2024), 1–23.

3.6.5.3 Evaluating Ijārah (Leasing Contract) Contracts in Shari'ah Audit Processes

The structure of ijārah contracts is based on asset ownership, the right to use the asset, and the outright prohibition of sale-lease combinations. The contract involves breaking the rules if there is a firm agreement to sell using the lease, which would then be treated as an installment sale. Institutions often find themselves in trouble when there are no clearly defined boundaries between lease agreements and deferred sales, most especially where title and risk transfer are not concurrent. According to AAOIFI (2022), valid ijārah requires the lessor to hold title and assume maintenance liability, stipulating that rent must exclusively represent the usufruct's value, not ownership transfer.[219]

Auditor's Caution

- Was the lessor the complete legal owner of the asset at the time of signing, and were all maintenance obligations properly assigned and fulfilled by the lessor throughout the lease term?
- Does the lease contract include any binding clause, such as *ijārah wa'l-iqtinā'*, that combines leasing with a sale in a manner that compromises the independence of each contract, and has the asset's residual value been accurately disclosed and appropriately transferred after the lease?
- Is the rental structure genuinely reflective of the asset's usage value, or does it functionally mimic a loan repayment scheme in terms of fixed installments or disguised profit rates?

3.6.5.4 Qarḍ Ḥasan (Benevolent Loan) Ethical Assessment and Oversight Tools

The spiritual foundation of *Qarḍ Ḥasan* lies in its altruistic nature: a loan provided without expecting any return beyond the principal, grounded in sincerity (*ikhlāṣ*) and mutual goodwill. Islamic law emphasizes that such contracts must be free from any implicit or explicit expectation of compensation. However, in practice, this principle is often compromised.

[219] "AAOIFI Shariah Standard," 241, 246, 264; Ismail Mohamed—An Junyuan et al., "The Application of Service Ijarah in Islamic Finance," *International Journal of Management and Applied Research* 11/1 (2024), 80–106.

A frequent concern in contemporary Islamic banking is the imposition of indirect costs disguised as "processing fees" or administrative charges. These costs, though nominal, can undermine the core intent of the contract by introducing quasi-commercial elements.[220] Some institutions even link Qarḍ Ḥasan with additional products or benefits, effectively converting it into a veiled profit-making instrument. Such practices dilute the moral character of the loan and risk transforming it into a form of ribā in spirit, if not in legal form.[221]

Moreover, clients are sometimes subtly led to believe that "voluntary gifts" (*hibah*) are expected in return, especially when these are routinely offered and recorded, raising further questions about the sincerity of the transaction.[222] Auditors must, therefore, verify that Qarḍ Ḥasan arrangements remain free from any conditionality, indirect benefit, or disguised return, ensuring that the contract's implementation truly reflects its benevolent purpose.

Auditor's Caution

- Is there any direct or implied expectation of return beyond the principal, whether through linked services (such as consultancy or credit card offerings), administrative fees not strictly cost-based, or marketing language that encourages gift-return practices?
- Are all fees transparently documented, genuinely limited to cost recovery without embedded profit margins, and free from mechanisms that indirectly compensate the lender?
- Are the loan's repayment terms fully documented, unconditional, and free from any clauses or expectations that could ethically compromise the altruistic nature of the Qarḍ Ḥasan agreement?

[220] "AAOIFI Shariah Standard," 522.

[221] Mohammad Omar Farooq—Nedal El Ghattis, "Qard Hasan, Credit Cards and Islamic Financial Product Structuring: Some Qurranic and Practical Considerations," *Journal of Islamic Financial Studies* 1/1 (2015), 1–17.

[222] Moilim El Azhar Mdawhoma, "Qard—The Good, The Fair, & The Ugly: From an Islamic Finance Perspective," *Journal of Research in Social Science and Humanities* 5/1 (2025), 12–13; "AAOIFI Shariah Standard," 522, 538.

3.6.5.5 Ṣarf (Currency Exchange) Contract Review: Currency Exchange Audit Criteria

Ṣarf contracts in Islamic jurisprudence involve the exchange of currency for currency. They are governed by strict rules to prevent *ribā al-faḍl* (usury due to inequality) *and ribā al-nasīʾah* (usury due to delay). Both parties must take possession of the exchanged currencies in the same sitting (*taqābuḍ*), and no deferral in delivery is permitted, whether physically or electronically.[223] In modern fintech-driven markets, where high-frequency trades and digital platforms dominate, ensuring immediate delivery and mutual possession remains a Shari'ah requirement.[224] Auditors must scrutinize interfaces for delays, algorithmic manipulation, or speculative instruments that mimic forward contracts or derivatives. Ṣarf must remain a spot transaction, not a tool for deferred or margin-based speculation.

Auditor's Caution

- Was the exchange executed immediately for both parties, either physically or electronically, and what mechanisms are in place to verify instant settlement and prevent time-delayed transactions?
- The currencies exchanged of equal value where Sharīʿah requires (e.g., gold for gold), and was the platform free from speculative instruments such as forward or margin trading under the guise of ṣarf?
- How is the delivery timing monitored, and are there system protections in place to make sure the Sharīʿah rule of taqābuḍ (simultaneous possession) is followed to avoid any delayed exchanges?

3.6.5.6 Auditing Salam (Advance Purchase): Ensuring Fair Advance Sales

Salam is a forward sale contract where the buyer pays the price in full at the time of contract formation, while delivery is deferred. This structure

[223] "AAOIFI Shariah Standard," 60–64; Cemil Liv, "İnternet Bankacılığı Aracılığıyla Gerçekleştirilen Sarf Akdinin İslam Hukuku Açısından Değerlendirilmesi," *Gaziosmanpaşa Üniversitesi İlahiyat Fakültesi Dergisi* 7/2 (2019), 41–60.

[224] Şevket Topal—Önder Arık, "Elektronik Transfer Sistemleri Aracılığıyla Yapılan Altın Alım Satım İşlemleri," *Recep Tayyip Erdoğan Üniversitesi İlahiyat Fakültesi Dergisi* 20 (2021), 15–36.

facilitates market liquidity and supports producers with early capital. However, it is highly susceptible to exploitation when product specifications are vague or delivery is delayed beyond agreed timelines, leading to gharar (excessive uncertainty), which is strictly prohibited in Islamic law.

According to classical jurists, for a *Salam* contract to be valid, the subject matter must be clearly specified in terms of type, quantity, quality, and delivery date, and full price must be paid upfront.[225] Failure to meet these conditions renders the contract null and void. Moreover, modern Sharīʿah standards emphasize strict documentation and risk controls to avoid misuse in speculative environments.[226]

Auditors should verify whether the *Salam* price was paid in full at the time of contract, whether the goods are sufficiently defined, and whether delivery dates are fixed and realistic. Any ambiguity or delay not justified by force majeure can render the transaction non-compliant and ethically problematic.

Auditor's Caution

- Was the full price paid at the time of the contract execution, and is the seller operationally capable of delivering the goods as agreed?
- Are the goods clearly and comprehensively specified in terms of type, quantity, quality, and delivery schedule, with no ambiguity or open-ended conditions?
- Is the delivery date fixed and realistic, especially for volatile goods, and has the institution employed adequate risk management to prevent gharar and non-compliance?

3.6.5.7 Istisnāʿ (Manufacturing/Construction Contract) Sharīʿah-Compliant Audit Checklist

Istisnāʿ permits the sale of an item that has not yet been produced, allowing flexibility in manufacturing and construction. However, it carries a risk of ethical failure, mainly when institutions collect upfront payments without initiating production, which is common in speculative real estate. To comply with Sharīʿah, the object must be clearly defined, and timelines

[225] Kāsānī, *Badāʾiʿ Al-Ṣanāʾiʿ Fī Tartīb al-Sharāʾiʿ*, 201–209; Ibn Qudāmah, *Al-Mughnī*, 4/185–190.

[226] "AAOIFI Shariah Standard," 278–283.

agreed upon.[227] Auditors must verify that work begins promptly, that specifications are fixed, and that risk remains with the seller until delivery is complete. This distinction from *salam*, where prepayment is mandatory, is noted by classical jurists such as Ibn ʻĀbidīn.[228]

Auditor's Caution

- Are the product or construction specifications, such as dimensions, materials, and production phases, clearly defined, and does the contract include a right to cancel before work begins if agreed upon?
- Is the production start date documented, with penalties for delays, and are progress payments contractually tied to verifiable milestones in the manufacturing or construction process?
- If a parallel istisnāʿ is employed, has it been structured in a way that maintains clear separation of liability and ensures that each party's delivery obligations remain independent?

3.6.5.8 Key Audit Points in Mushārakah (Partnership) Contracts

Mushārakah, or equity partnership, involves two or more parties contributing capital to a joint venture, sharing profits and losses. Auditors must first examine whether any partner guarantees the capital or profit, which is impermissible in Islamic law unless loss results from negligence or misconduct.[229] Similarly, fixed profit allocations to a partner are prohibited unless clearly defined as indicative percentages agreed upon by all partners.[230] Profit-sharing ratios must be pre-determined in the contract, and any ambiguity deferred until after profits are realized is invalid.[231] Auditors should also confirm whether the contributed capital is clearly defined and whether the currency denomination is agreed upon, especially in multi-currency contributions.[232] However, non-liquid assets (e.g., goods) can only be accepted

[227] "AAOIFI Shariah Standard," 300–309.

[228] Ibn ʻĀbidīn, *Ḥāshiyat Radd Al-Muḥtār, ʻalá al-Durr al-Mukhtār*, 4/221–224.

[229] Kāsānī, *Badāʾiʿ Al-Ṣanāʾiʿ Fī Tartīb al-Sharāʾiʿ*, 6/56–57.

[230] Ibn Qudāmah, *Al-Mughnī*, 4/23–25.

[231] Wahbah Muṣṭafā Zuḥaylī, *Al-Fiqh al-Islāmī Waʾadllatuh* (Damascus: Dār alfkr, 1418), 5/387.

[232] "AAOIFI Shariah Standard," 326–328.

after their value is precisely determined.[233] Additionally, receivables are not permissible as standalone capital contributions. Costs and expenses should not be assigned to a single partner, and the partnership contract must not stipulate that one party alone bears all the losses.[234] The distribution of losses must align with each partner's capital contribution, and any deviation from this rule undermines the legitimacy of the Mushārakah.[235]

Lacking effective auditing, these product designs may appear compliant with external standards, but cannot be said to have undergone a substantive ethical review. The ḥisbah system requires more than the mere fulfillment of legal forms: auditors will have to take responsibility for the ethical oversight, examining not only the legal pacts but also the ethical pacts that guide these pacts. Including these questions in governance systems serves as a guardrail, allowing Islamic finance to remain consistent with its inherent values of justice, trustworthiness, and integrity in all transactional activities.

Auditor's Caution

- Are any capital or profit guarantees provided to any partner, and if so, are they contractually stipulated in a way that contradicts the principle of shared risk?
- Has a fixed profit share been assigned to any partner regardless of actual outcomes, or is the profit distribution linked to the profit ratio agreed upon at inception?
- Is the capital contribution clearly defined, quantified, and in a valid form (e.g., cash or appraised assets), and are the exchange rates or valuations documented correctly in the case of foreign currencies or non-cash inputs?

3.6.5.9 Toward a Structured Methodology for Fiqh-Based Auditing

This classification system allows Islamic financial institutions to apply proportionate responses and integrate Sharīʿah risk assessment into their institutional audit workflows (Table 3.10).

[233] Muḥammad Amīn Ibn ʿĀbidīn, *Radd Al-Muḥtār ʿalá al-Durr al-Mukhtār* (Beirut: Dār al-Kutub al-ʿIlmiyyah, 1994), 4/330–333.

[234] Kāsānī, *Badāʾiʿ Al-Ṣanāʾiʿ Fī Tartīb al-Sharāʾiʿ*, 6/77–78.

[235] "AAOIFI Shariah Standard," 329.

Table 3.10 Fiqh-based classification of audit findings

Level	*Category*	*Definition*
Level 1	(*Fundamental defects*)	Major non-compliance issues that render a contract invalid in Sharīʿah
Level 2	(*Correctable flaws*)	Medium-level issues that require revision but do not invalidate the contract
Level 3	(*Minor irregularities*)	Technical or clerical errors that do not affect Sharīʿah validity

Source Author's own

Before building a comprehensive auditing framework, it is essential to classify potential violations based on their severity under Shari'ah law. A widely accepted structure involves a three-level classification of audit findings:

Considering the above, a comprehensive auditing framework in Islamic finance should incorporate ex-ante (pre-contractual) and ex-post (post-transactional) evaluations. Such a framework must address three dimensions:

1. Substantive Validity: Does the contract comply with all the legal and ethical requirements of Islamic law?
2. Procedural Integrity: Was the contract appropriately executed, with transparency and fairness?
3. Outcome Legitimacy: Are the financial returns derived from the contract Halal justifiable?

A model auditing procedure might include:

- Contract classification and identification
- Validation of all contract elements and preconditions
- Verification of delivery, transfer, and payment mechanisms
- Scrutiny of disclosures, documentation, and pricing
- Confirmation of agent roles and third-party claims
- Final Shari'ah approval based on cumulative findings

To highlight the distinction between conventional auditing and Sharīʿah-based auditing, the following table offers a comparative perspective (Table 3.11).

Table 3.11 Analytical comparison: Traditional audit versus Sharīʿah-based audit

Feature	*Traditional financial audit*	*Sharīʿah-based Fiqhī audit*
Objective	Ensure compliance with legal and accounting standards (e.g., IFRS, GAAP)	Ensure compliance with Islamic legal rulings (aḥkām) and ethical maqāṣid
Framework	Secular legal-financial systems	Fiqh al-muʿāmalāt and maqāṣid al-sharīʿah principles
Authority	External auditors or audit firms	Muḥtasib, Sharīʿah boards, internal or external Sharīʿah auditors
Focus	Accuracy, material misstatement, and financial transparency	Ethical legitimacy, legal validity, avoidance of ribā, gharar, etc.
Oversight body	Audit committees, financial regulators	Sharīʿah supervisory boards, national Sharīʿah councils
Timing	Primarily post-transactional	Both ex-ante (before contract) and ex-post (after execution)
Documentation concern	Financial reporting and audit trails	Contract wording, intent (niyyah), Islamic conditions

Source AAOIFI (2022), IFSIB (2020), CSIBIB (2020), etc

3.6.6 *Juristic Grounds for Contractual Invalidity*

Islamic financial contracts formalized to conform to Sharīʿah standards can be annulled if they contain minor legal flaws or violate explicit religious prohibitions. Where fundamental rulings are violated in classical jurisprudence, a contract can be terminated as void (bāṭil) or defective (fāsid). For instance, a contract can be arranged as a kind of bayʿ al-kālīʾ bi al-kālī. In the view of many scholars, the practice of imitating short-term loans through immediate resale (Bayʿ al-ʿīnah) or manufactured commodity transactions (tawarruq munazzam) is regarded as a deceptive device that permits ribā to be present.

Furthermore, conditionality or contingency (ʿuqūd muʿallaqah) tends to vitiate a contract, as it involves future events whose outcome is uncertain. Such conditions suggest that legal uncertainty arises after the contract is concluded. Furthermore, ribā al-faḍl and ribā al-nasīʾah are frequently used in contemporary ṣarf, murābaḥah, or ijārah transactions, and primarily when payment schedules vary or are imbalanced. It is even possible that once all formalities are complied with, the basic shurūṭ al-ṣaḥaḥah continue to be infringed such that the transaction fails in a juristic view.

As a result, any audit based on fiqh should start by assessing whether this contract has these fundamental legal deficiencies. Such agreements are null irrespective of documented work, intent, or concurrence with internal boards. The frequent use of immediate resale devices, such as *bay' ināh* and organized *tawarruq*, has been widely criticized as a form of *ḥiyal* that conceals *ribā*.[236] According to AAOIFI (2022), these mechanisms are invalid for constituting contractual rules.[237] Conditional or "suspended" contracts (*'uqūd mu'allaqah*) are likewise considered *fāsid* by eminent scholars, such as Al-Shāṭibī, who notes that speculative attachments undermine contractual certainty.[238]

The Sharī'ah auditing must incorporate the principles of ḥisbah, which include holding accounts, making disclosures transparent, and protecting, while maintaining fairness in the markets. Audit procedures must consider the benefits a contract provides to society and its formal validity. It is possible to implement maqāṣid-alignment matrices, benefit–harm (maṣlaḥah–mafsadah) assessments, and stakeholder equity analysis, thus increasing the overall process. In this paradigm, audit processes extend beyond mere compliance to become instruments of social accountability, ensuring that Islamic finance is ethical and serves the public interest in every aspect.

Key Governance Insights:

- The revival of ḥisbah as a conceptual and institutional tool offers a moral compass for Sharī'ah governance, bridging classical ethics with contemporary oversight.

[236] Alif Cahya Setiyadi—Sakiinah Mohammad Aris, "Analysis of the Permissibility of Bai' Al-'Inah Transactions According to the Shafi'i School of Thought and Its Implementation in Malaysia," *JURISTA: Jurnal Hukum Dan Keadilan* 7/2 (2023), 144–164; Muhammad Hamza Shuaib—Hafiz Abdul Basit Khan, "The Direct & Indirect Form of Bay' al-'Inah: An Analytical Study of the AAOIFI Council's Position: بیع عینہ کی بلا واسطہ و بالواسطہ صورت: مجلس ایوفی کے موقف کا تجزیاتی مطالعہ," *Al-Aijaz Research Journal of Islamic Studies & Humanities* 8/2 (2024), 41–66.

[237] "AAOIFI Shariah Standard," 753.

[238] Ibrāhīm ibn Mūsá Abū Isḥāq al-Shāṭibī, *Al-Muwāfaqāt Fī Uṣūl al-Sharī'ah* (Beirut: Dār al-Ma'rifah, 1996), 3/147–150; Sami Al-Daghistani, *The Making of Islamic Economic Thought: Islamization, Law, and Moral Discourses* (England: Cambridge University Press, 2021), 145–220.

- Islamic financial institutions should adopt fiqh-based auditing protocols, as illustrated in the contract-specific checklists (murābaḥah, qarḍ, ṣarf, muḍārabah).
- Regulators can enhance credibility by formalizing independent Sharīʿah boards and ensuring public disclosure of ethical audit results.
- Establishing standardized regional training for Sharīʿah auditors will improve interpretive consistency and cross-border regulatory compatibility.

CHAPTER 4

Conclusion: Toward a Coherent Ethical Future for Islamic Finance in South Asia

This book explores the ethical and jurisprudential foundations of Islamic finance, critically assessing its institutional development across South Asia. Through a tripartite structure, it sought to fill a scholarly gap by examining Islamic finance not merely as a financial sector but as a value-laden system governed by Sharīʿah principles. The work integrated the classical model of *ḥisbah* with contemporary regulatory needs, offering a legal-ethical framework for future institutional design.

This concluding chapter synthesizes the insights gained from the three preceding chapters, evaluates regional strengths and structural inadequacies, and offers a critical yet hopeful perspective on the emergence of a resilient and value-driven Islamic finance ecosystem in South Asia.

In addition to the ethical standardization efforts driven by AAOIFI, the role of the Islamic Financial Services Board (IFSB) must be acknowledged as essential in shaping a comprehensive regulatory landscape for Islamic finance in South Asia. While AAOIFI primarily focuses on Sharīʿah-compliant structures and ethical contractual integrity, IFSB complements this by developing prudential and supervisory standards critical for financial resilience. Key examples include capital adequacy (IFSB-2, IFSB-15), liquidity risk management (IFSB-12, IFSB-16), corporate governance (IFSB-3), Sharīʿah governance (IFSB-10), risk management (IFSB-6),

© The Author(s), under exclusive license to Springer Nature Switzerland AG 2025

A. H. M. E. Uddin, *The Regulation of Islamic Financial Institutions (IFIs) and Ethical Oversight in South Asia*, Palgrave Studies in Islamic Banking, Finance, and Economics,
https://doi.org/10.1007/978-3-032-09828-3_4

and stress testing (IFSB-13). These standards are not merely technical but serve profound ethical functions: they safeguard depositors, reduce systemic risk, and promote long-term market stability—thus advancing maqāṣid al-sharīʿah such as justice (ʿadl), transparency, and preservation of wealth (ḥifẓ al-māl).

Despite these contributions, the implementation of IFSB standards across South Asia remains inconsistent. Countries like Pakistan and Bangladesh have made modest progress, whereas others demonstrate regulatory inertia. As this study argues, any robust ethical model, such as the proposed South Asian Ethical Finance Compliance (SAEFC) framework, must not only incorporate the normative insights and contractual ethics championed by AAOIFI but also align with the risk-based prudential safeguards offered by IFSB. This convergence is essential to ensure that Islamic finance in South Asia is both ethically authentic and institutionally sound. In the end, ethical finance must go beyond formality—it must build trust, deliver stability, and serve the public good.

4.1 Reflections of the Ethical Center of Islamic Finance

Chapter 1 demonstrated that Islamic finance is more than a financial engineering strategy designed to avoid ribā, which has been traditionally prohibited in Islamic finance as a categorized form of interest; it is a value-laden moral economy founded on the higher objectives of Sharīʿah (maqāṣid al-sharīʿah). It aimed to rediscover the ethical grammar of Islamic commercial law (fiqh al-muʿāmalāt) in showing how justice (ʿadl), welfare (maṣlaḥah), transparency (bayān), and responsibility (amānah), provide normative footprints throughout permissible contracts and prohibited actions.

However, as this chapter suggests, the ethical promise of Islamic finance is often compromised by the formalism that tends to dominate most Islamic finance products. The prevalent debt structures, such as the murābaḥah and ijārah, show a systemic tilt away from the risk-sharing ideals of muḍārabah and mushārakah. An abundant supply of legally compliant but ethically questionable financial instruments has provoked criticism of "Sharīʿah-washing," where an institutional practice prioritizes form over substance. Therefore, an acute ethical dilemma persists between compliance and commitment in South Asia's current Islamic finance marketplace.

The ethical integrity of Islamic finance in South Asia is undermined not by a lack of formal Sharīʿah tools but by insufficient alignment with the spirit of maqāṣid. A revival of purpose, not just procedure, is urgently needed.

4.2 Regional Trajectories: Diversity, Innovation, and Fragmentation

4.2.1 *Pakistan and Bangladesh: Duality and Institutional Depth*

In Chap. 2, Pakistan and Bangladesh reveal South Asia's most mature institutional development. Pakistan's state-driven Islamization in the 1980s, combined with the proactive role of Meezan Bank and the State Bank's Islamic Banking Department, has established a fairly coherent regulatory structure. In contrast, Bangladesh has a pragmatic coexistence of non-Islamic finance and Islamic finance under the dual-banking model, driven by grassroots (or local economy) demand and healthy Sharīʿah boards. Moreover, both countries struggle to demonstrate ethical depth. Regulatory structures do exist, but substantive challenges remain, as illustrated below: conflicts of interest in Sharīʿah boards, a lack of innovation in risk-sharing products, and weaker integration of social finance tools such as zakāt and qard al-ḥasan.

4.2.2 *India: Ethical Innovation from Below*

India offers a contrasting model: Islamic finance in India develops unfettered state support or Islamic banking laws. Here, Muslim cooperatives and ethical investment platforms have been designed as grassroots innovations based on solidarity within the community. The informal sector brings resilience and creativity into the spotlight. However, it is plagued by huge regulatory recognition and capital mobilization barriers. Reflecting the unique capacity to marry tradition and technological modernity, the incorporation of waqf-based finance and digital compliance tools also makes India a candidate to be a modern leader in "moral finance without the bank."

4.2.3 *Afghanistan and the Maldives: Between Symbolism and Structural Constraints*

Post-conflict fragility, symbolic Islamization endeavor, and the informal financial networks, i.e., ḥawāla, frame Afghanistan's Islamic finance. Even as such interest increases, the weak regulatory capacity, compounded by political instability, weakens the sector's credibility. By contrast, Maldives provides a small but promising case model, illustrating how a Muslim-majority state can set Islamic finance in a tourism-rich and isolated-by-geography economy. Islamic finance in the Maldives is growing through Islamic windows in conventional banks, through the growth of takaful, and through legal reform that emphasizes Sharīʿah compliance. However, financial illiteracy, deficiencies in institutional capacity, and the market scale prevent the growth of Islamic finance. Both countries must be brought under institutional consolidation, capacity building, and long-term international technical assistance to unlock their ethical and operational potential.

4.2.4 *Sri Lanka: A Pluralistic Islamic Finance Landscape*

Developing Islamic finance in a multi-religious legal framework is possible, just like in Sri Lanka. With an emerging hybrid regulatory architecture whose stances were consonant with the country's plural legal culture, the economic activities and faith-based projects of the Muslim minority clearly indicate a moral market emerging. However, problems such as poor market penetration, adverse product variety range, and the lack of a central Sharīʿah advisory body constrict the industry's ability to scale up.

4.3 Ethical Oversight and the Revival of Ḥisbah

Chapter 3 revisited the continuing tradition of ḥisbah as an eternal model of prophetic regulatory institutions and classical governance. The muhtasib has traditionally been not only a market police officer but also a moral authority that guaranteed justice and economic transparency. The disappearance of ḥisbah during the colonial regime and its marginalization in contemporary financial systems helped create the present ethical legitimacy crisis.

Rediscovering ḥisbah's values, accountability, transparency, and justice inspired the current Sharīʿah governance model. Unfortunately, Sharīʿah supervisory boards today are not more successful due to conflicts of interest between Sharīʿah members and management, a lack of independence and enforcement authority, a focus on formalized approval at the expense of ethics, and standardization fatigue from AAOIFI, which lacks contextual flexibility. These shortcomings resonate with the demand to reconnect oversight structures with substantive ethical commitments, rather than merely procedural resemblance.

4.4 Proposed Ethical Governance Model: SAEFC

The exciting section of this book is the framework it proposes for the South Asian Ethical Finance Council (SAEFC). This model suggests a transnational platform for the ethical oversight of Islamic finance, rooted in classical jurisprudence, yet with a contemporary emphasis on modern institutional requirements. Through SAEFC, SAEFC aims to achieve the convergence of standards, limit fragmentation, and provide Sharīʿah scholars with a forum for collective ijtihād in the region.

By sharing coordinated knowledge with centralized fatwā depositories and digital enforcement technologies, the council would work to unify moral interpretations while maintaining legal multiplicity. It roots control within the context of maṣāliḥ al-mursalah (public interest) and sadd al-dharāʿiʿ (blocking harm), and both preventative regulation and proactive innovation are thus served. Crucially, SAEFC also delivers a remedy to "Sharīʿah-washing" by rooting ethical inquiry in classical legal principles and regional facts.

SAEFC, therefore, is not just a technical fix but a moral anchor that could restore regional coherence and ethical legitimacy to South Asian Islamic finance.

4.5 Strengths and Weaknesses of South Asian Islamic Finance

South Asia constitutes this special mix of demographic strength, intellectual diversity, and grassroots dynamism. The region contains more than half a billion Muslims and, therefore, presents a vast potential market for Sharīʿah-compliant and ethically based financial services. Those three diverging jurisprudential traditions (Ḥanafī, Shāfiʿī, and Jaʿfarī) have a slight fluidity of ijtihād that contrasts with the pluralistic approach to regulatory governance. Furthermore, countries such as India and Bangladesh abound in examples of dynamic community-based financial innovations without formal Islamic banking systems, and the resilience and creativity from below are tested.

Structural and ethical weaknesses, however, balance these weaknesses. The disincentive of geographical regulatory inconsistency in the area prevents cross-border integration and reduces investor confidence. Institutional fragility in Afghanistan and some parts of Sri Lanka leads to feeble enforcement and is open to politicization. More importantly, the ethical dilution of Islamic finance (in its manifestations of mimicry-based products and marginalization of social finance tools) erodes the distinctiveness and legitimacy of Islamic finance. Public awareness of Islamic financial ethics is lacking, and consumer interaction is haphazard, primarily driven by brand over moral consideration.

4.6 Toward a Future Research Agenda

The implications of this study open the door to a raft of research questions that future scholars can pursue. Empirical observation of the ethical performance of Islamic financial institutions against maqāṣid-aligned indicators is one critical direction. Such metrics would enable stakeholders to evaluate compliance and the ethical impact. Another promising area will be to analyze the role of informal and community-based financial institutions, especially in underserved rural areas, and their impact on financial inclusion and social equity.

There is, of course, a need to research governance dynamics within Sharīʿah boards—in terms of how conflict of interest, institutional capture, and lack of participation from women frame the issue of ethical integrity. Institutionalizing zakāt, waqf, and ṣadaqah as part of financial systems is still underdeveloped and could provide new models of redistributive justice. Greater focus should be given to gendered dimensions in ethical finance, especially women's access to capital and the ethical ramifications of these financial decisions. Finally, comparative studies between South Asia and Guelf or South East Asia can enrich the discourse on regional best practices and develop trans-regional solidarity in building ethical Islamic financial ecosystems.

4.7 Policy Suggestions for the South Asian Stakeholders

For effective development of the ethical potential of Islamic finance, concerted and informed policy interventions are needed. National governments need to legislatively formalize the recognition of Islamic finance and establish enabling legal frameworks, particularly in India and Sri Lanka, where Islamic banking has been under-regulated. Central banks, therefore, have to institutionalize Sharīʿah boards with their clear terms of reference, autonomy, and a responsibility framework to guarantee that the interests of commerce do not override their ethical oversight. Regional cooperation through SAARC or OIC platforms should support the inception and operation of SAEFC to build cross-border collaboration and scholarly communication.

Implementing Islamic legal ethics and financial literacy in academic institutions is crucial so that future regulators, bankers, and consumers understand the moral foundation of Islamic finance. Ultimately, financial institutions should strive to move beyond compliance with Sharīʿah to achieve ethical standards. This can be accomplished through accounting for the ESG–maqāṣid hybrid performance indicators, products that cater to an actual need in society, not just commercial value. Only in a multi-stakeholder, multi-scalar fashion can South Asian Islamic finance live up to its promise as a chemistry between God and society.

4.8 Concluding Reflections: Islamic Finance as an Ethical Frontier

The book postulates that Islamic finance in South Asia is at a critical crossroads. Despite an increased institutional presence, its ethical coherence remains a subject of dispute. Closing the gulf between legal form and moral substance is not merely a technical "operation" but a moral imperative emanating from prophetic teachings and a legal tradition.

The resurgence of ḥisbah, the creation of transregional moral oversight, and stakeholder-driven innovation can collectively transform Islamic finance from a niche sector to an ethical and economic powerhouse. The ethical finance envisioned in this study is not a mere alternative to capitalism. They reflect another worldview: commerce is a form of community service, finance is about ennobling the dispossessed, and contracts are promises of trust, not instruments of exploitation.

In this light, South Asia, with its rich Islamic heritage, dynamic civil societies, and growing financial sector, can lead a global reawakening of Islamic ethical finance. By rooting financial governance in the objectives of Sharīʿah and reconnecting legality with moral substance, the region can offer a powerful alternative model for justice-centered markets. This book aspires not merely to critique existing systems but to illuminate a jurisprudential and ethical path forward for ethical finance in the twenty-first century.

Glossary of Key Arabic Terms

To enhance terminological precision and support interdisciplinary engagement, the following Arabic terms, central to Islamic legal and ethical finance discourse, are briefly defined below.

Grouped by Thematic Category for Accessibility

Foundations of Islamic Law and Ethics

ʿAdl (عدل): Justice. A foundational ethical value in Islamic law represents fairness, equilibrium, and legal equity in dealings.

Iḥsān (إحسان): Benevolence or moral excellence. Going beyond justice to show generosity and inner sincerity in actions.

Ijtihād (اجتهاد): Independent reasoning. The scholarly process of deriving new rulings when no clear text exists.

Uṣūl al-Fiqh (أصول الفقه): Principles of Islamic jurisprudence. The methodological basis for interpreting and deriving Islamic legal rulings.

Maqāṣid al-Sharīʿah (مقاصد الشريعة): The higher objectives of Islamic law: protection of religion, life, intellect, lineage, and wealth.

Bayān (بيان): Clarity or transparency in communication and contracts, ethically required to prevent deception.

© The Editor(s) (if applicable) and The Author(s), under exclusive license to Springer Nature Switzerland AG 2025

A. H. M. E. Uddin, *The Regulation of Islamic Financial Institutions (IFIs) and Ethical Oversight in South Asia*, Palgrave Studies in Islamic Banking, Finance, and Economics,
https://doi.org/10.1007/978-3-032-09828-3

Maṣlaḥah (مصلحة): Public welfare or common good. Used in legal reasoning to promote societal benefit.
Niyyah (النية): Intention. Essential in evaluating the ethical authenticity of actions in Islamic law.
Sadd al-Dharāʿiʿ (سد الذرائع): Blocking the means to harm. A principle used to prohibit actions that may lead to unethical outcomes.
Maṣāliḥ al-Mursalah (المصالح المرسلة): Unrestricted public interests. A principle allowing legal rulings based on social benefit when no text exists.

Contracts and Legal Instruments

Fiqh al-Muʿāmalāt (فقه المعاملات): Jurisprudence governing commercial and civil transactions under Sharīʿah.
Murābaḥah (المرابحة): Cost-plus sale where the seller discloses profit margin. Widely used in Islamic banks for asset purchases.
Muḍārabah (المضاربة): Profit-sharing contract where one party provides capital and the other manages the venture.
Mushārakah (المشاركة): Joint investment or partnership where profit and loss are shared according to agreement.
Ijārah (الإجارة): Leasing contract. One party leases an asset to another for a fixed fee without transferring ownership.
Istisnāʿ (الاستصناع): Commissioned manufacturing contract. Payment may be made in advance, in installments, or at delivery.
Salam (السلم): Advance payment for future delivery. Often used in agricultural financing.
Qard al-Ḥasan (القرض الحسن): Interest-free, benevolent loan given for charitable or socially beneficial purposes.
Mutʿa (المتعة): Temporary marriage recognized in Jaʿfarī jurisprudence, usually with a fixed duration and dower.
Bayʿ (بيع): A sale contract. The foundation of Islamic trade and exchange transactions.
Tawarruq (التورق): Structured personal financing involving the sale of commodities to generate cash flow.
Wakālah (الوكالة): Agency contract allowing one party to act on behalf of another.
Kafālah (الكفالة): Guarantee contract. A third party assumes responsibility for another's debt or obligation.

ʿAqd (عقد): Legal contract in Islamic jurisprudence. A binding agreement outlining mutual obligations.

Prohibited Elements in Contracts

Ribā (الربا): Usury or interest. Any guaranteed excess over the principal in loans is strictly forbidden.

Gharar (غرر): Excessive uncertainty in contract terms or subject matter, rendering a contract invalid.

Maysir (ميسر): Gambling or speculation, prohibited due to its unjust enrichment without productive effort.

Bayʿ al-ʿĪnah (بيع العينة): A buy-back arrangement that mimics interest. Often considered a ḥīlah (legal trick) to bypass ribā.

Ḥiyal (حيل): Legal stratagems or tricks. Sometimes used to circumvent legal prohibitions, debated among scholars.

Institutions and Governance

Sharīʿah (الشريعة): The divine law of Islam encompassing rituals, ethics, social conduct, and transactions.

Ḥisbah (الحسبة): The classical Islamic system of market supervision ensuring fair trade and moral behavior.

Muḥtasib (المحتسب): The officer or inspector responsible for enforcing *ḥisbah*in Islamic governance.

Takāful (التكافل): Islamic cooperative insurance based on mutual assistance. Contributors share profits and losses.

Ṣukūk (صكوك): Islamic financial certificates (bonds) backed by tangible assets or services, not debt.

Waqf (الوقف): Endowment made for religious or public welfare purposes, usually permanent and irrevocable.

Takhayyur (التخيير): Juridical method allowing selective adoption of rulings across schools to meet practical needs.

AAOIFI: Accounting and Auditing Organization for Islamic Financial Institutions. Sets Sharīʿah standards globally.

IFSB-Islamic Financial Services Board: An international standard-setting body to promote and enhance the soundness and stability of the Islamic financial services industry.

Ḥawāla (الحوالة): Informal transfer of money, often across borders, based on trust networks. Common in Afghanistan and South Asia.

Sharīʿah Board (هيئة الشريعة): A supervisory body of scholars ensuring compliance of financial products with Islamic law.

OIC Fiqh Academy (مجمع الفقه الإسلامي): A transnational scholarly body developing collective legal opinions on contemporary issues.

Bibliography

A. B. M. Habibullah. *The Foundation of Muslim Rule in India*. Calcutta: University of Calcutta, 1945. http://archive.org/details/in.ernet.dli.2015.283199

Aassouli, Dalal et al. "Can UGITs Promote Liquidity Management and Sustainable Development?" *ISRA International Journal of Islamic Finance* 10/2 (October 11, 2018), 126–142. https://doi.org/10.1108/IJIF-12-2017-0055

Ab Ghani, Nur Laili - Shaharuddin, Siti Saffa'. "Internal Control System and Effective Internal Shariah Audit Function: A Conceptual Framework." *International Journal of Islamic Economics and Finance Research* 6/2 December (December 18, 2023), 121–137. https://doi.org/10.53840/ijiefer106

Abbas, Hassan. *The Return of the Taliban: Afghanistan after the Americans Left*. Yale University Press, 2023.

Abbasi, Muhammad Zubair. *Sharī'a Under the English Legal System in British India: Awqāf (Endowments) in the Making of Anglo-Muhammadan Law*. University of Oxford, 2013.

Abdelrahman, Abdelrahman Yousri. "Sukuk: A Critique of Experience, and Their Possible Role in Muslim Countries Development." *International Journal of Islamic Economics and Finance Studies*. https://doi.org/10.25272/ijisef.473269

Abdul Latheef, Mariyam Rafaa. "Does Community-Based Tourism Contribute to Halal Tourism from a Maqasid Al-Shariah Perspective? A Case Study of Maldives: Adakah Pelancongan Berasaskan Komuniti Menyumbang Kepada Pelancongan Halal Menurut Perspektif Maqasid Al-Shariah? Kajian Kes Di

© The Editor(s) (if applicable) and The Author(s), under exclusive license to Springer Nature Switzerland AG 2025
A. H. M. E. Uddin, *The Regulation of Islamic Financial Institutions (IFIs) and Ethical Oversight in South Asia*, Palgrave Studies in Islamic Banking, Finance, and Economics,
https://doi.org/10.1007/978-3-032-09828-3

Maldives." *Journal of Muwafaqat* 7/1 (April 30, 2024), 39–66.https://doi.org/10.53840/muwafaqat.v7i1.168

Abdulaziz, Akhtarzaite Binti. "Al-Dharāʾi' and Maqāṣid al-Sharīʿah: A Case Study of Islamic Insurance." *Intellectual Discourse* 18/2 (2010), 261–281.

Abdullah, M. H. M. - Hassan, Rusni. "Evaluation on the Practice of Ijarah for Vehicle Financing and Its Regulation in Islamic Financial Institutions in Sri Lanka." *Islamic Sustainable Finance, Law and Innovation: Opportunities and Challenges*. ed. Nadia Mansour - Lorenzo Mateo Bujosa Vadell. 335–343. Cham: Springer Nature Switzerland, 2023. https://doi.org/10.1007/978-3-031-27860-0_30

Abdullah, Ziarmal et al. "The Influence of Awareness, Knowledge, and Religiosity towards Public Perception of Islamic Banking Usage in Southwestern Afghanistan." *El Barka: Journal of Islamic Economics and Business* 7/1 (June 14, 2024), 1–26. https://doi.org/10.21154/elbarka.v7i1.8287

Abedifar, Pejman. "Formalism versus Purposivism in Islamic Jurisprudence: The Case of Islamic Finance Law." *Religions* 14/4 (April 2023), 465. https://doi.org/10.3390/rel14040465

Abraham, Manu. "Shariah Compliance and Earnings Management in India: Insights on Reporting Transparency and Financial Stability." *Modern Finance* 2/1 (2024), 145–165. https://doi.org/10.61351/mf.v2i1.141

Abū Dāwūd, Sulaymān ibn al-Ashʿath. *Sunan Abī Dāwūd*. Beirut: al-Maktabah al-ʿAṣrīyah, 2001.

Abu Kamar, NF et al. "The Role of Shariah Advisory Council (SAC) of Bank Negara Malaysia on Islamic Finance Disputes: Legal Analysis." Kuala Lumpur: UiTM, 2021.

Abū Yūsuf, Yaʿqūb ibn Ibrāhīm ibn Ḥabīb. *Kitāb Al-Kharāj*. Beirut: Dār al-Maʿrifa, 1979.

Acharya, Viral V. et al. *Macroeconomic and financial policy challenges of China and India*. "The Growth of a Shadow Banking System in Emerging Markets: Evidence from India." *Journal of International Money and Finance* 39 (December 1, 2013), 207–230. https://doi.org/10.1016/j.jimonfin.2013.06.024

Aggarwal, Rajesh K. - Yousef, Tarik. "Islamic Banks and Investment Financing." *Journal of Money, Credit and Banking* 32/1 (2000), 93–120. https://doi.org/10.2307/2601094

Ahmad, Abu U. - Hassan, Kabir. "Regulation and Performance of Islamic Banking in Bangladesh." *Thunderbird International Business Review* 49/2 (2007), 251–277.

Ahmad, Altaf - Zakariyah, Habeebullah. "A Comparative Performance Analysis of Islamic and Conventional Banking: A Case Study of Pakistan." *The Importance of New Technologies and Entrepreneurship in Business Development: In The Context of Economic Diversity in Developing Countries*. ed. Bahaaeddin

Alareeni et al. 194/1772–1809. Lecture Notes in Networks and Systems. Cham: Springer International Publishing, 2021. https://doi.org/10.1007/978-3-030-69221-6_129

Ahmad, Khaliq - Berghout, Datuk AbdelAziz. *Islamic Finance and Sustainable Development: Balancing Spirituality, Values and Profit*. London: Routledge, 1st Ed., 2025. https://doi.org/10.4324/9781003505570

Ahmed, Aishath Imthisal - Nizam, Ismail. "The Determinants of Customer Patronage in the Case of Islamic Finance Products in the Maldives." *International Journal of Accounting & Business Management* 7/1 (2019), 1–32.

Ahmed, Habib. "Islamic Law and Finance: Concepts and Principles." *Product Development in Islamic Banks*. 17–52. Edinburgh University Press, 2011. https://www.degruyterbrill.com/document/doi/10.1515/9780748644889-005/pdf?licenseType=restricted&utm_source=chatgpt.com

Ahmed, Habib - Chapra, Mohammad Umar. *Occasional Papers*. "Corporate Governance in Islamic Financial Institution (Occasional Paper)." *Occasional Papers*. https://ideas.repec.org//p/ris/irtiop/0093.html

Ahmed, Irfan et al. "Practices of Islamic Banking in the Light of Islamic Ethics: A Critical Review." *International Journal of Economics, Management and Accounting* 25/3 (November 30, 2017), 465–490. https://doi.org/10.31436/ijema.v25i3.437

Ahmed, Rafiuddin. *The Bengal Muslims: 1871-1906; a Quest for Identity*. Oxford University Press, 1981.

Ahmed, Riazuddin - Mohamad, Mohamad Saifullah Bin. "The Practice of Shariah Governance in Islamic Banking and Finance: A Study of Islamic Banks in Bangladesh." *International Journal of Management and Applied Research* 6/4 (November 1, 2019), 271–284.

Akgündüz, Ahmet. *Osmanlı kanunnâmeleri ve hukukî tahlilleri*. İstanbul: FEY Vakfı, 1990.

Akhtar, Safir. "The Institution of Ḥisbah and Demand for Its Revival." *Policy Perspectives* 6/1 (2009), 89–104.

Akman, Ahmet. "İslam Borçlar Hukukunda Beklenmeyen Hal." *Sakarya Üniversitesi Hukuk Fakültesi Dergisi* 12/1 (July 23, 2024), 234–252. https://doi.org/10.56701/shd.1424981

Akram, Hassan - Rahman, Khalil Ur. "Credit Risk Management: A Comparative Study of Islamic Banks and Conventional Banks in Pakistan." *ISRA International Journal of Islamic Finance* 10/2 (December 10, 2018), 185–205. https://doi.org/10.1108/IJIF-09-2017-0030

Al Amer, Saleh Abdulrahman. *Sharia Supervisory Board in Islamic Banks: A Critical Analysis of the Current Framework*. Leeds: University of Leeds, Phd, 2018. https://etheses.whiterose.ac.uk/id/eprint/22489/

Alam, M. K. - Uddın, Ahm Ershad. "Legal and Regulatory Frameworks For Sharīʿa Governance Practices in the Islamic Banking Industry of Bangladesh."

Mizanü'l-Hak: İslami İlimler Dergisi 17 (December 30, 2023), 663–688. https://doi.org/10.47502/mizan.1332588

Alam, Md Kausar. "A Proposed Centralized Shariah Governance Framework for Islamic Banks in Bangladesh." *Journal of Islamic Accounting and Business Research* 13/2 (December 17, 2021), 364–389. https://doi.org/10.1108/JIABR-03-2021-0106

Alam, Muzaffar. *The Crisis of Empire in Mughal North India: Awadh and the Punjab 1707-1748*. Delhi: Oxford University Press, 1997.

Alam, Nafis et al. "Islamic Deposits in Practice." *Islamic Finance*. by Nafis Alam et al., 79–130. Cham: Springer International Publishing, 2017. https://doi.org/10.1007/978-3-319-66559-7_5

Alam, Nafis et al. "Prohibition of Riba and Gharar in Islamic Banking." *Islamic Finance: A Practical Perspective*. ed. Nafis Alam et al. 35–53. Cham: Springer International Publishing, 2017. https://doi.org/10.1007/978-3-319-66559-7_3

Alam, S.M. Shamsul. "Language as Political Articulation: East Bengal in 1952." *Journal of Contemporary Asia* 21/4 (January 1, 1991), 469–487. https://doi.org/10.1080/00472339180000311

Alama, Md Kausar et al. "The Reasons Behind the Absence of a Comprehensive Shariah Governance Framework of Islamic Banks in Bangladesh." *International Journal of Economics & Business Administration (IJEBA)* VIII/1 (2020), 134–145. https://doi.org/10.35808/ijeba/414

Al-Daghistani, Sami. *The Making of Islamic Economic Thought: Islamization, Law, and Moral Discourses*. England: Cambridge University Press, 1st Ed., 2021. https://doi.org/10.1017/9781108990813

Aldhaheri, Wadeema. "Islamic Green Finance: Shariah-Compliant Pathways towards Sustainable Development Goals (SDGs)." *Open Journal of Applied Sciences* 15/5 (May 9, 2025), 1294–1309. https://doi.org/10.4236/ojapps.2025.155090

Alex Malyshev. "Is Islamic Banking Truly Shariah-Compliant? Debunking Myths and Clarifying Key Concepts." Financial Market Analyst. *SDK Finance* (blog), April 12, 2024. https://sdk.finance/is-islamic-banking-truly-shariah-compliant-debunking-myths-and-clarifying-key-concepts/

Alfian, Ian et al. "Unraveling Gharar Practices: A Literature Study on Islamic Economic Transactions in the Global." *Proceeding International Conference on Economic and Social Sciences* 2 (December 15, 2024), 707–715.

Alhammadi, Salah et al. "Analysing Islamic Banking Ethical Performance from *Maqāṣid al-Sharīʿah* Perspective: Evidence from Indonesia." *Journal of Sustainable Finance & Investment* 12/4 (October 2, 2022), 1171–1193. https://doi.org/10.1080/20430795.2020.1848179

Alharbi, Ahmad. "Development of the Islamic Banking System." *Journal of Islamic Banking and Finance* 3/1 (2015). https://doi.org/10.15640/jibf.v3n1a2

Ali, Mohsin et al. "Credit Risk in Dual Banking Systems: Does Competition Matter? Empirical Evidence." *International Journal of Emerging Markets* 18/4 (May 24, 2021), 822–844. https://doi.org/10.1108/IJOEM-01-2020-0035

Ali, Syed Nazim. *Edinburgh Companion to Shari'ah Governance in Islamic Finance*. Edinburgh University Press, 2020.

Alkhamees, Ahmad A. *A Critique of Creative Shari'ah Compliance in the Islamic Finance Industry*. Martinus Nijhoff Publishers, 2017.

Allie, Feyaad. "India's New Minority Politics." *Journal of Democracy* 36/2 (April 2025), 78–91. https://doi.org/10.1353/jod.2025.a954565

Al-Nahari, Ameen Ahmed Abdullah Qasem et al. "Common Conceptual Flaws in Realizing Maqāṣid Al-Sharīʿah Vis-à-Vis Islamic Finance." *ISRA International Journal of Islamic Finance* 14/2 (April 22, 2022), 190–205. https://doi.org/10.1108/IJIF-12-2020-0259

al-Nawawī, Abū Zakariyyā' Muḥyī al-Dīn Yaḥyā ibn Sharaf. *Al-Majmū' Sharḥ al-Muhadhdhab*. Cairo: Muṣṭafā al-Bābī al-Ḥalabī, 1347.

Al-Shaiji, A. A. K. M. H. *Critical Study and Edition of Al-Turuq al-Ḥukmiyya Fī al-Siyāsa al-Sharʿiyya*. Wales: University of Wales Trinity Saint David, PhD, 2001.

Alwi, Zulfahmi et al. "An Assessment on Islamic Banking Ethics through Some Salient Points in the Prophetic Tradition." *Heliyon* 7/5 (May 1, 2021). https://doi.org/10.1016/j.heliyon.2021.e07103

Aman, Najeebullah. "Islamic Banking Deposits and Finance Products in Afghanistan." *Nangarhar University Social Science Journal* 1/01 (November 24, 2024), 28–31. https://doi.org/10.70436/nussj.v1i01.8

Andalusī, Yaḥyá ibn 'Umar al-. *Aḥkām Al-Sūq*. Beirut: Dār Ibn Ḥazm, 2011.

Anwer, Zaheer et al. "Sharīʿah-Compliant Central Banking Practices: Lessons from Muslim Countries' Experience." *ISRA International Journal of Islamic Finance* 12/1 (March 18, 2020), 7–26. https://doi.org/10.1108/IJIF-01-2019-0007

Archer, Simon - Abdel Karim, Rifaat Ahmed. *Islamic Finance: The New Regulatory Challenge*. New York: Wiley, 2nd ed., 2013.

Ariff, Mohamed - Shamsher Mohamad (eds.). *Islamic Wealth Management: Theory and Practice*. Northampton: Edward Elgar Publishing, 2017.

Arshad, Shaista et al. "Outsourcing the Islamic Way: A Look into the Challenges Faced by Financial Institutions." *Journal of Islamic Economics Banking and Finance* 11/2 (2015), 51–63. https://doi.org/10.12816/0024914

Asher, Catherine B. - Talbot, Cynthia. *India before Europe*. England: Cambridge University Press, 2006.

Ashraf, S. Husain - Ali, Alizadeh Giashi. "Islamic Banking in Iran-Progress and Challenges." *Arabian Journal of Business and Management Review* 12 (2011), 31–44.

Ashrafkashani, Sara. *The Role and Responsibilities of Shari'ah Boards in the Context of Islamic Finance and Their Position in Law. Institute of Advanced Legal Studies.* London: University of London, Doctoral, 2015. https://sas-space.sas.ac.uk/9512/

Askari, Hossein et al. *Introduction to Islamic Economics: Theory and Application.* John Wiley & Sons, 2015.

Asutay, Mehmet. "A Political Economy Approach to Islamic Economics: Systemic Understanding for an Alternative Economic System." *Kyoto Bulletin of Islamic Area Studies* 1/2 (2007), 3–18.

Asutay, Mehmet. "Islamic Moral Economy as the Foundation of Islamic Finance." *Islamic Finance in Europe.* 55–68. Edward Elgar, 2013. https://www.elgaronline.com/display/edcoll/9781781002506/9781781002506.00014.xml

Asutay, Mehmet - Yilmaz, Isa. "Financialisation of Islamic Finance: A Polanyian Approach on the Hegemony of Market Logic over Islamic Logic." *New Political Economy* 30/2 (2025), 267–286. https://doi.org/10.1080/13563467.2024.2424170

Ateed, Hashmatullah - Rehman, Atiq Ur. "Determinants of Bank Choice in Afghanistan." *Journal of Islamic Finance* 9/1 (June 4, 2020), 061–075. https://doi.org/10.31436/jif.v9i1.390

Ateş, Hamza. "A Pioneering Institution for Ombudsman: Hisbah." *Ombudsman Akademik* 6 (June 30, 2017), 21–48. https://doi.org/10.32002/ombudsmanakademik.440042

Athari, Zaif Ullah et al. "History of the Afghan Central Bank, Its Sharīʿah Supervision System and Its Effect on Unifying the Sharīʿah Reference: تاريخ البنك المركزي الأفغاني ونظام الرقابة الشرعية فيه وأثره في توحيد المرجعية الشرعية." *International Journal of Fiqh and Usul Al-Fiqh Studies* 8/2 (July 31, 2024), 38–54. https://doi.org/10.31436/ijfus.v8i2.348

Athari, Zaif Ullah et al. "History of the Afghan Central Bank, Its Sharīʿah Supervision System and Its Effect on Unifying the Sharīʿah Reference: تاريخ البنك المركزي الأفغاني ونظام الرقابة الشرعية فيه وأثره في توحيد المرجعية الشرعية." *International Journal of Fiqh and Usul Al-Fiqh Studies* 8/2 (July 31, 2024), 38–54. https://doi.org/10.31436/ijfus.v8i2.348

Awan, Nafisa et al. "X-Efficiency Analysis of Islamic Banks in Pakistan." *Contemporary Issues in Social Sciences and Management Practices* 4/4 (December 31, 2023), 340–354. https://doi.org/10.61503/cissmp.v2i4.78

Aysan, Ahmet Faruk et al. "Standardization Efforts in Islamic Finance." Unpublished, 2022. Unpublished, DOI.org (Datacite). Accessed June 11, 2025. https://doi.org/10.13140/RG.2.2.18309.42720

Ayub, Muhammad et al. "Revisiting the Paradigm of Sharīʿah Governance of Islamic Financial Institutions." *Journal of Islamic Accounting and Business Research* 15/8 (2024), 1245–1265. https://doi.org/10.1108/JIABR-04-2022-0110

Azad, Md Saifullah. "Role of Leadership, Values, and Ethics in Driving Islamic Finance Excellence." *The Business Standard* (2024). https://www.tbsnews.net/economy/corporates/role-leadership-values-and-ethics-driving-islamic-finance-excellence-797426

Azham, Nur Izzatul Afrina. "Islamic Finance for Social Good: Exploring the Synergy Between Sukuk and Waqf." *SSRN Electronic Journal*. https://doi.org/10.2139/ssrn.4845573

Baghdādī, Abū Bakr Aḥmad ibn ʿAlī Khaṭīb al-. *Tārīkh Baghdād*. Baghdad, 1966.

Bal, Çiğdem - Umut, Muharrem. "Uluslararası Standartlar (AAOIFI ve IFSB) Çerçevesinde Kurumsal Yönetim." *Bankacılık ve Finansal Araştırmalar Dergisi* 10/2 (2023), 84–99. https://doi.org/10.55026/jobaf.1213083

Banna, Hasanul et al. "Islamic Banking Stability amidst the COVID-19 Pandemic: The Role of Digital Financial Inclusion." *International Journal of Islamic and Middle Eastern Finance and Management* 15/2 (August 18, 2021), 310–330. https://doi.org/10.1108/IMEFM-08-2020-0389

Barfield, Thomas J. "Afghanistan: A Cultural and Political History, Second Edition," 1–456.

Barkey, Karen. *Bandits and Bureaucrats: The Ottoman Route to State Centralization*. Cornell University Press, 1994.

Bashir, Mohamed Sharif et al. "Does Shari'ah Supervisory Board Characteristics Affect Islamic Banks' Financial Performance? Evidence from Saudi Arabia." *Corporate Board Role Duties and Composition* 19/2 (2023), 15–25. https://doi.org/10.22495/cbv19i2art2

Bayındır, Abdulaziz. *Ticaret Ve Faiz*. Istanbul: Süleymaniye Vakfi Yayınları, 2016.

Benchea, Laura-Ramona. "Islamic Economics and Finance – a Revival After the Recent Global Financial Crisis." *Ovidius University Annals* 17/2 (2015), 7–12.

Berriah, Mehdi. "A Lack of Resources in the Bayt Al-Māl: A Sine Qua Non Condition for the Imposition of a Tax?" *Islamic Law Blog* (blog), September 30, 2021. https://islamiclaw.blog/2021/09/30/mehdi-berriah-guest-editor-4/

Bhatnagar, Stuti - Shahab Ahmed, Zahid and. "Geopolitics of Landlocked States in South Asia: A Comparative Analysis of Afghanistan and Nepal." *Australian Journal of International Affairs* 75/1 (January 2, 2021), 60–79. https://doi.org/10.1080/10357718.2020.1793896

Bhatti, Maria et al. "Need for Reform in AAOIFI Standards on Murabaha Financing: Evidence from Islamic Banks in Pakistan." *Quality & Quantity* 59/1 (2025), 59–78. https://doi.org/10.1007/s11135-024-01974-y

Bhaumik, Aaratrika. “What Are the Key Changes Proposed in the New Waqf Bill? | Explained.” *The Hindu* (April 2, 2025), sec. India. https://www.thehindu.com/news/national/what-are-the-key-changes-proposed-in-the-new-waqf-bill-explained/article69402993.ece

Bin Hasan, Zulkifli. “From Legalism to Value-Oriented Islamic Finance Practices.” *Humanomics* 32/4 (November 14, 2016), 437–458. https://doi.org/10.1108/H-07-2016-0051

Bjorvatn, K. *Papers*. “Islamic Economics in Principle and Practice.” *Forum for Development Studies* 2 (1998), 229–243.

Bohra, Murtuza. “Is Indian Banking System Ready to Introduce Globally Acclaimed Concept of Indian Banking System?,” 1–10.

Brewster, David - Pethiyagoda, Kadira. “India and the Gulf States.” *External Powers and the Gulf Monarchies*. Routledge, 2018.

Bukhārī, Abū ʿAbdillāh Muḥammad b. Ismāʿīl. *Ṣaḥīḥ Al-Bukhārī*. Dār Ṭawq al-Najāh, 1422.

Calabria, Michael. “Mughal Munificence: Care and Concern for the Poor in Islamic Hindustan from Tuladan to the Taj.” *Poverty and Wealth in Judaism, Christianity, and Islam*. ed. Nathan R. Kollar - Muhammad Shafiq. 31–53. New York: Palgrave Macmillan US, 2016. https://doi.org/10.1057/978-1-349-94850-5_3

Calder, Ryan. “Sharah-Compliant or Shar??Ah-Based? The Changing Ethical Discourse of Islamic Finance.” *Arab Law Quarterly* 35/1/2 (2021), 50–73.

Calder, Ryan. “Sharīʿah-Compliant or Sharīʿah-Based? The Changing Ethical Discourse of Islamic Finance.” *Arab Law Quarterly* 35/1/2 (2021), 50–73.

Çanakçı, Ömer - Yurttadur, Mustafa. “İslami Finans Perspektifinden Kitle Fonlamasının Araştırılması ve Model Önerileri.” *Erzurum Teknik Üniversitesi Sosyal Bilimler Enstitüsü Dergisi* 21 (January 31, 2025), 34–49. https://doi.org/10.29157/etusbed.1494215

Cebeci, Ismail. “Product Development in Islamic Banks By Habib Ahmed.” *Journal of Islamic Studies* 24/1 (January 1, 2013), 122–124. https://doi.org/10.1093/jis/ets083

Cebeci, İsnail. *Modern İslam Iktisadı Literatüründe Murabaha Tartışmaları*. Istanbul: Marmara University, PhD, 2010. https://tez.yok.gov.tr/UlusalTezMerkezi/tezDetay.jsp?id=ev2Q5-PtU3bWX2KTgFH21g&no=4Y4V8N6C3uJGrHxt1uZmwQ

Çelebi, Kâtip. *Kashf al-ẓunūn ʻan asāmī al-kutub wa-al-funūn*. Beirut: Dār al-Kutub al-ʻIlmīyah, 1992.

Çelik, Zeynep. *The Remaking of Istanbul: Portrait of an Ottoman City in the Nineteenth Century*. Berkeley: University of California Press, 1993.

Chandra, Satish. *Medieval India: From Sultanat to the Mughals Part - II*. New Delhi: Har-Anand Publications, 2005.

Chapra, M. Umer. *The Future of Economics: An Islamic Perspective.* The Islamic Foundation, 2000.

Chapra, M. Umer. *The Future of Economics: An Islamic Perspective.* Kube Publishing Ltd, 2016.

Chary, Manish Telikicherla. *India: Nation on the Move: An Overview of India's People, Culture, History, Economy, IT Industry, & More.* iUniverse, 2009.

Chatterjee, Nandini. "The Mughals and the Sufis: Islam and the Political Imagination in India, 1500–1750 By Muzaffar Alam." *Journal of Islamic Studies* 34/3 (September 1, 2023), 423–426. https://doi.org/10.1093/jis/etad010

Chatterjee, Partha. *Nationalist Thought and the Colonial World: A Derivative Discourse.* Zed Books, 1986.

Chattopadhyay, Dilip Kumar. "The Ferazee and Wahabi Movements of Bengal." *Social Scientist* 6/2 (1977), 42–51. https://doi.org/10.2307/3516683

Chishti. "Sachar Committee Report: A Review - Mainstream Weekly." April 24, 2007. Accessed April 20, 2025. https://www.mainstreamweekly.net/article95.html

Cook, Michael. *Commanding Right and Forbidding Wrong in Islamic Thought.* Cambridge: Cambridge University Press, 2010.

Cristofaro, Julie Di et al. "Afghan Hindu Kush: Where Eurasian Sub-Continent Gene Flows Converge." *PLOS ONE* 8/10 (October 18, 2013), e76748. https://doi.org/10.1371/journal.pone.0076748

Cui, Jiayu - Li, Tao. "Religion, Power, and National Identity: The Dual Role of Islam in the History and Modernization of the Maldives." *Religions* 16/2 (February 2025), 201. https://doi.org/10.3390/rel16020201

Dallh, Minlib. "Accumulate but Distribute: Islamic Emphasis on the Establishment of Waqf (Pious Endowment): Research Article." *Religion and Development* 2/1 (September 20, 2023), 21–40. https://doi.org/10.30965/27507955-20230014

Darling, Linda T. "Revenue-Raising and Legitimacy: Tax Collection and Finance Administration in the Ottoman Empire, 1560–1660." Brill, 1966. https://brill.com/display/title/769

Dashti, Zabihullah. "Afghan External Migration Movements in the Historical Process." *Asya Studies* 6/20 (June 30, 2022), 301–314. https://doi.org/10.31455/asya.1055791

Dewaya, Muhammad Abdullah. "Innovation in Islamic Finance: Review of Organized Banking Tawarruq." *Review of Islamic Social Finance and Entrepreneurship* 3/2 (September 12, 2024), 199–211. https://doi.org/10.20885/RISFE.vol3.iss2.art7

Disli, Mustafa et al. "Faithful Finance: Unlocking Banking Islamization in Afghanistan." *Economies* 11/7 (2023), 189. https://doi.org/10.3390/economies11070189

Domat, Chloe. "Islamic Finance: Just For Muslim-Majority Nations?" *Global Finance Magazine* (August 1, 2024). https://gfmag.com/banking/islamic-finance-just-muslim-majority-nations/

D'Souza, Anitha F. N. - Sai Sundar, H. "Overcoming the Challenges of Establishing Islamic Banks in India: A Case Study of Al-Arafah Islamic Investment Bank." *Current Trends in Economics, Business and Sustainability*. ed. J. Aloysius Edward et al. 192–197. Contributions to Environmental Sciences & Innovative Business Technology. Singapore: Springer Nature Singapore, 2023. https://doi.org/10.1007/978-981-99-3366-2_23

Duncan, Hannah - Clark, Kate. "Afghanistan's looming economic catastrophe: What next for the Taleban and the donors?" *Afghanistan Analysts Network - English*. September 6, 2021. Accessed April 21, 2025. https://www.afghanistan-analysts.org/en/reports/economy-development-environment/afghanistans-looming-economic-catastrophe-what-next-for-the-taleban-and-the-donors/

Dusuki, Asyraf Wajdi - Abdullah, Nurdianawati Irwani. "Maqasid Al-Shari'ah, Maslahah, and Corporate Social Responsibility." *American Journal of Islam and Society* 24/1 (January 1, 2007), 25–45. https://doi.org/10.35632/ajis.v24i1.415

Dusuki, Ayraf Wajdi - Bouheraoua, Said. "The Framework of Maqasid Al-Shari'ah and Its Implication for Islamic Finance." *ICR Journal*. https://icrjournal.org/index.php/icr/article/view/651

Eaton, Richard Maxwell. *The Rise of Islam and the Bengal Frontier, 1204-1760*. University of California Press, 1993.

El-Gamal, Mahmoud A. *Islamic Finance: Law, Economics, and Practice*. Cambridge University Press, 2006.

Elgariani, Fawzy Shaban. *Al-Qawa'id al-Fiqhiyyah (Islamic Legal Maxims): Concept, Functions, History, Classifications and Application to Contemporary Medical Issues*. England: University of Exeter, PhD, 2012. https://ore.exeter.ac.uk/repository/handle/10036/4001

El-Halaby, Sherif et al. "Influence of Adoption AAOIFI Accounting Standards on Earning Management: Evidence from Islamic Banks." *Journal of Islamic Accounting and Business Research* 11/10 (2020), 1847–1870. https://doi.org/10.1108/JIABR-10-2019-0201

Elhalaby, Sherif et al. "The Adoption of AAOIFI Standards by Islamic Banks: Understanding the Microeconomic Consequences." *Economies* 11/2 (January 30, 2023), 39. https://doi.org/10.3390/economies11020039

Elhalaby, Sherif et al. "The Adoption of AAOIFI Standards by Islamic Banks: Understanding the Microeconomic Consequences." *Economies* 11/2 (February 2023), 39. https://doi.org/10.3390/economies11020039

El-Merheb, Mohamad - Mehdi Berriah (eds.). *Professional Mobility in Islamic Societies (700-1750)*. Brill, 2021. https://brill.com/edcollbook/title/60543

El-Sheikh, Salah. "Islamic Economics and Finance, Then and Now: A Fiqhäa-Conomic Perspective on Its Doctrines And Debates." *International Journal of Economics, Management and Accounting* 19/1 (2011). https://doi.org/10.31436/ijema.v19i1.178

Ercanbrack, Jonathan. "The Standardization of Islamic Financial Law: Lawmaking in Modern Financial Markets." *The American Journal of Comparative Law* 67/4 (December 31, 2019), 825–860. https://doi.org/10.1093/ajcl/avz010

Ercanbrack, Jonathan. *The Transformation of Islamic Law in Global Financial Markets*. Cambridge: Cambridge University Press, 2015. https://doi.org/10.1017/CBO9781107447929

Ercanbrack, Jonathan G. "Hawala in Criminal Court: The Role of Law and Commercial Culture in Informal Financial Exchange." *Crime, Law and Social Change* 82/3 (October 1, 2024), 659–683. https://doi.org/10.1007/s10611-024-10162-w

Ergene, Boğaç A. *Local Court, Provincial Society and Justice in the Ottoman Empire*. Brill, 2003.

Ershad Uddın, Ahm. "Bangladeş'teki İslami Bankalarin Vedîa ve Fon Toplama Faaliyetleri: İslam Hukuku Perspektifinden Bir İnceleme." *Akademik Platform İslami Araştırmalar Dergisi* 8/2 (August 30, 2024), 203–227. https://doi.org/10.52115/apjir.1503015

Farhat, Zainab. "Spatial Segregation and Muslims in India: A Review." *Journal of Muslim Minority Affairs* 43/1–2 (January 2, 2023), 60–69. https://doi.org/10.1080/13602004.2023.2241244

Farooq, Mohammad Omar. "Islam-Compliance, beyond Shariah-Compliance: Toward a Broader Socioeconomic Transformation." *Arab Law Quarterly*. https://papers.ssrn.com/abstract=4159917

Farooq, Mohammad Omar - El Ghattis, Nedal. "Qard Hasan, Credit Cards and Islamic Financial Product Structuring: Some Qurranic and Practical Considerations." *Journal of Islamic Financial Studies* 1/1 (2015), 1–17. https://doi.org/10.2139/ssrn.2703393

Faroqhi, Suraiya. *Subjects of the Sultan: Culture and Daily Life in the Ottoman Empire*. London: I.B. Tauris, 2005.

Fasa, Muhammad Iqbal. "Islamizing The System of Economy: Solution Toward An Economical Welfare For The Islamic Landscape." *Yogyakarta State University* 2/1 (2017), 1–23.

Fasih, Faisal. *The International Conference on Emerging Economies - Prospects and Challenges (ICEE-2012), 12-13 January 2012*. "Inclusive Growth in India through Islamic Banking." *Procedia - Social and Behavioral Sciences* 37 (January 1, 2012), 97–110. https://doi.org/10.1016/j.sbspro.2012.03.278

Fatmawati, Dewi et al. "Shariah Governance in Islamic Banks: Practices, Practitioners and Praxis." *Global Finance Journal* 51 (February 1, 2022), 100555. https://doi.org/10.1016/j.gfj.2020.100555

Febianto, Irawan. "Risk Management in Mudharabah and Musharakah Financing of Islamic Banks." *SSRN Electronic Journal.* https://doi.org/10.2139/ssrn.1672180

Findley, Carter Vaughn. *Turkey, Islam, Nationalism, and Modernity: A History, 1789–2007.* New Haven: Yale University Press, 2010.

Firdaus, Achmad - Kamilah, Kamilah. "Sustainable Financing for Green Businesses from the Perspective of Islamic Finance." *Advances in Business and Management.* 1–36. Nova Science Publishers, 24th Ed., 2024. https://www.researchgate.net/publication/384256685_Sustainable_Financing_for_Green_Businesses_from_the_Perspective_of_Islamic_Finance

Fitrat, Abdul Qadeer. *The Tragedy of Kabul Bank.* Page Publishing Inc, 2022.

Fowler, Peter. "Ali Riaz. Bangladesh: A Political History since Independence." *Asian Affairs* 48/1 (January 2, 2017), 159–161. https://doi.org/10.1080/03068374.2017.1269516

Garcia, Maria Teresa Medeiros - Mendonça, Frederico Cavaleiro de. "Compliance with the Basel Core Principles and Supervisory Structure: A Cross-Country Analysis." *Central Bank Review* 23/2 (2023), 100117. https://doi.org/10.1016/j.cbrev.2023.100117

Gateway, Salaam. "India's 'Shariah-Compliant' NBFCs and Cooperative Credit Societies Held Back by Lack of Islamic Capital." *Salaam Gateway - Global Islamic Economy Gateway.* 2017. Accessed April 19, 2025. https://salaamgateway.com/story/indias-shariah-compliant-nbfcs-and-cooperative-credit-societies-held-back-by-lack-of-islamic-capital

Gerber, Haim. *State, Society, and Law in Islam: Ottoman Law in Comparative Perspective.* New York: SUNY Press, 1994.

Gerber, Haim. *The Social Origins of the Modern Middle East.* Routledge, 1987.

Ghabin, Ahmad. *Ḥisba, Arts and Craft in Islam.* Deutschland: Otto Harrassowitz Verlag, 2009.

Ghazali, Abu Hamid Muhammad ibn Muhammad al-. *Ihya Ulum Al-Din.* Cairo: Islamic Publication, 1418.

Ghazālī, Abū Ḥāmid Muḥammad ibn Muḥammad al-. *Iḥyā' 'Ulūm Al-Dīn.* Beirut: Dār al-Maʿrifah, 1998.

Ghouse, Ghulam - Bhatti, M. Ishaq. "Strident Response of Islamic Banking Industry to Political, Financial, and Pandemic Events." *Islamic Finance in the Modern Era.* by Hussain Mohi-ud-Din Qadri - M. Ishaq Bhatti, 254–264. London: Routledge, 1st Ed., 2024. https://doi.org/10.4324/9781003366751-16

Gibb, Hamilton Alexander Rosskeen. *Studies on the Civilization of Islam.* Princeton: Princeton University Press, 1982.

Gleave, Robert. "The Near and Middle East - M. Izzi Dien: The Theory and Practice of Market Law in Medieval Islam: A Study of Kitāb Nisāb al-Iḥtisāb of 'Umar b. Muḥammad al-Sunāmī." *Bulletin of the School of Oriental and*

African Studies 62/1 (January 1999), 128–129. https://doi.org/10.1017/S0041977X00017717

Gruzdev, Vladislav V. "Public Administration of the Sultanate of Delhi in the 13th – 15th Centuries-Historical and Legal Review." *Vestnik of Kostroma State University* 30/1 (June 28, 2024), 201–205. https://doi.org/10.34216/1998-0817-2024-30-1-201-205

Gulzar, Sadia. "The Quranic Concept of Economic Welfare." *ĪQĀN* 4/2 (July 30, 2022), 85–95. https://doi.org/10.36755/iqan.v4i2.368

Güney, Necmeddin. "İslami Finansta Şer'i Yönetim Uygulamalari ve Konuyla İlgili Tartişmalara Genel Bir Bakiş." *Turkish Journal of Islamic Economics* 2/2 (2015), 45–69.

Güney, Necmeddin. "Maqāsid Al-Sharī'a in Islamic Finance: A Critical Analysis of Modern Discourses." *Religions* 15/1 (January 16, 2024), 114. https://doi.org/10.3390/rel15010114

Guney, Necmeddin. "Murābaḥah Financing Revisited: The Contemporary Debate on Its Use in Islamic Banks." *Intellectual Discourse* 23 (December 29, 2015). https://doi.org/10.31436/id.v23i0.698

Gupta, Neeru. "Interest-Free Banking in India Legal Challenges." *International Journal of Law Management & Humanities* 5 Issue 5 (2022), 1315.

Habib, Irfan. *The Agrarian System of Mughal India, 1556-1707.* New York: Oxford University Press, 1999.

Ḥājjī Khalīfah, Muṣṭafá ibn 'Abdullāh. *Kashf Al-Ẓunūn 'an Asāmī al-Kutub Wa-al-Funūn.* Tehran: Dār al-Nashr al-Islāmīyah, 1943.

Hakimi, Musawer et al. "DIGITAL TRANSFORMATION OF AFGHANISTAN BANKING: EXPLORING E-BANKING TRENDS AND IMPACTS." *KEUNIS* 12/1 (January 21, 2024), 90. https://doi.org/10.32497/keunis.v12i1.5286

Hamarneh, Sami. "Origin and Functions of the Ḥisbah System in Islam and Its Impact on the Health Professions." *Sudhoffs Archiv Für Geschichte Der Medizin Und Der Naturwissenschaften* 48/2 (1964), 157–173.

Hamber, Norliana - Haneef, Mohamed. *Waqf-Based Social Micro Venture Fund: A Proposal for the Malay-Muslim Community in Singapore* (SSRN Scholarly Paper, October 23, 2017). Social Science Research Network, papers.ssrn.com. Accessed April 6, 2025. https://papers.ssrn.com/abstract=3057588

Hamoudi, Haider. "You Say You Want a Revolution: Interpretive Communities and the Origins of Islamic Finance." *Virginia Journal of International Law* 48 (January 1, 2008), 249.

Hanif, Muhammad. "Sharī'ah-Compliance Ratings of the Islamic Financial Services Industry: A Quantitative Approach" 10/2 (2018), 162–184. https://doi.org/10.1108/IJIF-10-2017-0038

Harahap, Burhanudin et al. "Islamic Law, Islamic Finance, and Sustainable Development Goals: A Systematic Literature Review." *Sustainability* 15/8 (2023), 6626. https://doi.org/10.3390/su15086626

Hasan, Naji al-. *Al-Ḥisbah Fī al-Islām*. Riyadh: Dār al-Sumayʿī, 2005.

Hasan, Shaima - Mohamed, Shereen. "Navigating Uncertainty: Global Islamic Finance Assets Expected to Exceed 6.7 Trillion by 2027." Financial Market Analyst. *LSEG*. February 26, 2024. Accessed April 6, 2025. https://www.lseg.com/en/insights/data-analytics/navigating-uncertainty-global-islamic-finance-assets-expected-to-exceed-67-trillion-by-2027

Hasan, Shaima - Mohamed, Shereen. "Navigating Uncertainty: Global Islamic Finance Assets Expected to Exceed 6.7 Trillion by 2027." February 26, 2024. Accessed April 19, 2025. https://www.lseg.com/en/insights/data-analytics/navigating-uncertainty-global-islamic-finance-assets-expected-to-exceed-67-trillion-by-2027

Hasan, Zulkifli. *Shari'ah Governance in Islamic Banks*. Edinburgh: Edinburgh University Press, 2012.

Hasanuzzaman, S. M. *Nabil A. Saleh, Unlawful Gain and Legitimate Profit in Islamic Law: Riba, Gharar and Islamic Banking* (SSRN Scholarly Paper, 1991). Social Science Research Network, papers.ssrn.com. Accessed April 5, 2025. https://papers.ssrn.com/abstract=3126111

Hassan, Kabir - Lewis, Mervyn. *Handbook of Islamic Banking*. Edward Elgar Publishing, 2009.

Hassan, Kabir - Mahlknecht, Michael. *Islamic Capital Markets: Products and Strategies*. John Wiley & Sons, 2011.

Hassan, M. Kabir et al. "Case Studies of Shariah Governance Practices in Bangladesh: HBKU-QFC Roundtable on Islamic Finance." *The Edinburgh Companion to Shari'ah Governance in Islamic Finance*. ed. Syed Nazim Ali et al. Edinburgh University Press, 2020. https://edinburghuniversitypress.com/book-the-edinburgh-companion-to-shari-ah-governance-in-islamic-finance.html

Hassan, M. Kabir. *Ethical Principles of Islamic Financial Institutions* (SSRN Scholarly Paper, 2013). Social Science Research Network, papers.ssrn.com. Accessed April 6, 2025. https://papers.ssrn.com/abstract=3263118

Hassan, M. Kabir - Lewis, Mervyn K. *Handbook of Islamic Banking*. Edward Elgar Publishing, 2007. https://EconPapers.repec.org/RePEc:elg:eebook:3621

Hathaway, Jane. *The Arab Lands under Ottoman Rule 1516–1800*. Routledge, 2008.

Hayat, Usman - Malik, Adeel. *Islamic Finance: Ethics, Concepts, Practice*. Place of publication not identified: CFA Institute Research Foundation, 2014.

Hegazy, Walid. "Contemporary Islamic Finance: From Socioeconomic Idealism to Pure Legalism." *Chicago Journal of International Law* 7/2 (January 1, 2007). https://chicagounbound.uchicago.edu/cjil/vol7/iss2/13

Hemat, Mohammad Walid. “The Determinants of Trade Deficit in Afghanistan: The Role of Foreign Aid, Exchange Rate and Price Level.” *SN Business & Economics* 4/11 (2024), 131. https://doi.org/10.1007/s43546-024-00735-1

Herring, Ronald J. “Zulfikar Ali Bhutto and the ‘Eradication of Feudalism’ in Pakistan.” *Comparative Studies in Society and History* 21/4 (October 1979), 519–557. https://doi.org/10.1017/S0010417500013165

Heyd, Uriel. *Studies in Old Ottoman Criminal Law*. Oxford: Clarendon Press, 1973.

Hidayatullah, Muhammad Syarif et al. “Reconceptualization of Ideal Islamic Bankers in The Sharia Framework (An Effort to Create a Sharia Compliance Ecosystem).” *Afkaruna: Indonesian Interdisciplinary Journal of Islamic Studies* 20/1 (June 30, 2024), 107–127. https://doi.org/10.18196/afkaruna.v20i1.21393

Hilmy, Hayathu Mohamed Ahamed et al. “Legal Aspects of Shariah Governance Practices in Sri Lankan Islamic Financial Institutions: A Literature Review.” *Journal of Enterprise and Development (JED)* 4/1 (June 1, 2022), 99–113. https://doi.org/10.20414/jed.v4i1.4920

Hilmy, Hayathu Mohamed Ahamed - Hassan, Rusni. “Shariah Governance Structure of Islamic Financial Institutions in Sri Lanka.” *International Journal of Management and Applied Research* 6/4 (November 1, 2019), 245–258. https://doi.org/10.18646/2056.64.19-018

Hilmy, Hayathu Mohamed Ahamed - Saujan, I. “Customer Satisfaction on Digital Banking Services: Evidence from Islamic Financial Institutions in Sri Lanka.” *Journal of Islamic Economic Law* 8/1 (2025).

Hourani, Professor Albert. *Arabic Thought in the Liberal Age 1798-1939*. Cambridge: Cambridge University Press, 1983.

Hunjra, Ahmed Imran et al. “The Role of Islamic Social Finance in Poverty Eradication.” *Islamic Finance in the Modern Era*. by Hussain Mohi-ud-Din Qadri - M. Ishaq Bhatti, 26–39. London: Routledge, 1st Ed., 2024. https://doi.org/10.4324/9781003366751-3

Ibad, Badruddin. “Implementation of Salam and Istishna’ Contracts in Islamic Financial Institutions.” *Rangkiang: Journal of Islamic Economics and Business* 1/1 (December 28, 2023), 12–24. https://doi.org/10.70072/rangkiang.v1i1.3

Ibn Abī Jarādah, Kamāl al-Dīn Ibn al-ʿAdīm ʿUmar ibn Aḥmad. *Bughyah Aṭ-Ṭalab Fī Tārīkh Ḥalab*. Damascus: Dār al-Fikr, 2000.

Ibn al-Qayyim al-Jawziyya, Muḥammad ibn Abī Bakr. *Al-Ṭuruq al-Ḥukmiyyah Fī al-Siyāsah al-Sharʿiyyah*. Beirut: Dār Ibn Ḥazm, 2003.

Ibn al-Ukhuwwah, Ḍiyāʾ al-Dīn Muḥammad ibn Aḥmad ibn Abī Zayd. *Maʿālim Al-Qurbah Fī Aḥkām al-Ḥisbah*. Cairo: The General Egyptian Book Organization, 1408.

Ibn Bassām, Muḥammad ibn Aḥmad. *Nihāyat Al-Rutbah Fī Ṭalab al-Ḥisbah.* Beirut: Dār al-Kutub al-'Ilmīyah, 2003.

Ibn Farḥūn, Ibrāhīm ibn 'Alī ibn Muḥammad. *Tabṣirat Al-Ḥukkām Fī Uṣūl al-Aqḍiyah Wa-Manāhij al-Aḥkām.* Cairo: Maktabat al-Kullīyāt al-Azharīyah, 1986.

Ibn Ḥajar al-ʿAsqalānī, Aḥmad ibn ʿAlī. *Al-Iṣābah Fī Tamyīz al-Ṣaḥābah.* Beirut: Dār al-Kutub al-ʿIlmiyyah, 1995.

Ibn Humām, Kamāl al-Dīn. *Sharḥ Fatḥ Al-Qadīr.* Egypt: Maktabat al-Bābī al-Ḥalabī, 1389.

Ibn 'Ābidīn, Muḥammad Amīn. *Ḥāshiyat Radd Al-Muḥtār, 'alá al-Durr al-Mukhtār.* Egypt: Muṣṭafá al-Bābī al-Ḥalabī, 1386.

Ibn Khaldūn, 'Abd al-Raḥmān. *Dīwān Al-Mubtada' Wa-al-Khabar Fī Tārīkh al-'Arab Wa-al-Barbar Wa-Man 'āṣarahum.* Beirut: Dār al-Fikr, 1981.

Ibn Khaldūn, 'Abd al-Raḥmān. *Muqaddimah Ibn Khaldūn.* Egypt: Dār Nahḍat, 1377.

Ibn Manẓūr, Muḥammad ibn Mukarram Abū al-Faḍl Jamāl al-Dīn. Beirut: Dār Ṣādir, 1414. https://arabiclexicon.hawramani.com/ibn-manzur-lisan-al-arab/

Ibn Nujaym, Zayn al-Dīn ibn Ibrāhīm. *Al'ashbāhu Wālnnaẓā'ir.* Beirut: Dār al-Kutub al-'Ilmīyah, 1999.

Ibn Qudāmah, Abū Muḥammad 'Abd Allāh. *Al-Mughnī.* Cairo: Maktabat al-Qāhirah, 1403.

Ibn Saʿd, Abū ʿAbd Allāh Muḥammad. *Al-Ṭabaqāt al-Kubrā.* Beirut: Dār Ṣādir, 1998.

Ibn Saʿd, Muḥammad. *Ṭabaqāt Al-Kubrā.* Cairo: Maktabat al-Khānjī, 2001.

Ibn Taymīyah, Aḥmad. *Majmū' Al-Fatāwá.* Riyad: Majma' al-Malik Fahd li-Ṭibā'at al-Muṣḥaf, 2004.

Ibn Taymīyah, Taqī al-Dīn 'Abd al-Salām. *Al-Ḥisbah Fī al-Islām Aw Waẓīfat al-Ḥukūmah al-Islāmīyah al-Mu'allif.* Beirut: Dār al-Kutub al-'Ilmīyah, 1st Ed., no date.

Ibn Taymiyyah, Taqī al-Dīn Aḥmad ibn ʿAbd al-Ḥalīm ibn ʿAbd al-Salām. *Al-Ḥisbah Fī al-Islām.* Cairo: Dār al-Shaʿb, 1976.

İbn ʿAbd al-Barr, Yūsuf b. ʿAbd Allāh. *Al-Istīʿāb Fī Maʿrifat al-Aṣḥāb.* Beirut: Dār al-Jīl, 1992.

Ibn ʿĀbidīn, Muḥammad Amīn. *Radd Al-Muḥtār 'alá al-Durr al-Mukhtār.* Beirut: Dār al-Kutub al-ʿIlmiyyah, 2nd Ed., 1994.

Ibn ʿAsākir, ʿAlī ibn al-Ḥasan al-Dimashqī al-Shāfiʿī. *Tārīkh Madīnat Dimashq.* Beirut: Dār al-Fikr, 1995.

Ibrahim, Mohamed - Buang, Ahmad Hidayat. "Maldivian Legal System: Islamic Influence and Legal Reform." *Jurnal Syariah* 26/1 (May 22, 2018), 71–98. https://doi.org/10.22452/js.vol26no1.4

Ilyas Salim. "Uncovering the Gatekeepers of Islamic Finance –." National University Of Singapore. *NUS–Middle East Institute.* September 15, 2021.

Accessed June 10, 2025. https://mei.nus.edu.sg/event/uncovering-the-gatekeepers-of-islamic-finance/?utm_source=chatgpt.com

Imber, Colin. *Ebu's-Su'ud: The Islamic Legal Tradition*. Edinburgh: Edinburgh University Press, 1997.

Inalcik, Halil - Quataert, Donald. *An Economic and Social History of the Ottoman Empire*. Cambridge: Cambridge University Press, 1997. https://www.cambridge.org/universitypress/subjects/history/regional-and-world-history-general-interest/economic-and-social-history-ottoman-empire-volume-1

İnalcık, Halil. *The Ottoman Empire: The Classical Age 1300-1600*. Phoenix Press, 2000.

Iqbal, M. - Molyneux, P. *Thirty Years of Islamic Banking: History, Performance and Prospects*. Palgrave Macmillan, 2005.

Iqbal, Ubais Parayil et al. "Integrating Trust with Extended UTAUT Model: A Study on Islamic Banking Customers' m-Banking Adoption in the Maldives." *Journal of Islamic Marketing* 14/7 (June 3, 2022), 1836–1858. https://doi.org/10.1108/JIMA-01-2022-0030

Isa, Fatihu Shehu et al. "Shariah Audit Practices in Malaysia: Moving Forward." *Journal of Islamic Finance* 9/2 (December 30, 2020), 42–58. https://doi.org/10.31436/jif.v9i2.483

Islahi, Abdul Azim. "History of Islamic Banking and Finance." *Intellectual Discourse* 26/2 (2018), 403–429.

Islahi, Abdul Azim. *History of Islamic Economic Thought: Contributions of Muslim Scholars to Economic Thought and Analysis*. Cheltenham (GB): Edward Elgar Publishing, 2014.

Islahi, Abdul Azim. "Works on Market Supervision and Shar'iyah Governance (al-Hisbah Wa al-Siyasah al-Shar'iyah) by the Sixteenth Century Scholars." *Quarterly Journal of the Pakistan Historical Cociety* 54/3 (2008), 7–20.

Islam, Nasir. "Islam and National Identity: The Case of Pakistan and Bangladesh." *International Journal of Middle East Studies* 13/1 (1981), 55–72.

ISMAIL, ABDUL GHAFAR - ARSHAD, NORAZIAH CHE. "TRACKING THE PRE-AND POST COLONIAL BANKING: THE QUEST FOR ISLAMIC BANKING." 173–184. Malaysia, 2010.

Issath Nimsith, S. et al. "Study on Marketing Strategy for Islamic Banking Industry in Sri Lanka." 239–253. Sri Lanka: South Eastern University of Sri Lanka, 2019. http://ir.lib.seu.ac.lk/handle/123456789/3990

Izzeldin, Marwan et al. "Efficiency Convergence in Islamic and Conventional Banks." *Journal of International Financial Markets, Institutions and Money* 70 (January 1, 2021), 101279. https://doi.org/10.1016/j.intfin.2020.101279

Jabartī, 'Abd al-Raḥmān ibn Ḥasan al-. *Tārīkh 'Ajā'ib Al-Āthār Fī al-Tarājim Wa-al-Akhbār*. Beirut: Dār al-Jīl, 1997.

Jahan, Rounaq. *Pakistan: Failure in National Integration.* USA: Columbia University Press, 1972. https://cir.nii.ac.jp/crid/1130000794808875776

Jain, Nityanand et al. "Global Population Surpasses Eight Billion: Are We Ready for the next Billion?" *AIMS Public Health* 10/4 (October 25, 2023), 849–866. https://doi.org/10.3934/publichealth.2023056

Jamaldeen, Faleel. *Islamic Finance for Dummies.* Hoboken, N.J: Wiley, 2012.

Jawzīyah, Shams al-Dīn Ibn Qayyim al-. *I'lām Al-Muwaqqi'īn 'an Rabb al-'ālamīn.* Beirut: Dār al-Kutub al-'Ilmīyah, 1991.

Johari, Nurul Aina. "The Relevancy of Hisbah (Accountability) in The Modern Era: A Brief Analysis." *Jurnal Islam Dan Masyarakat Kontemporari* 22/2 (2021), 30–35. https://doi.org/10.37231/JIMK.2021.22.2.574

Junejo, Safiullah et al. "Unravelling the Drivers of Profitability in Pakistani Islamic Banking: An Investigation of Key Factors." *Jurnal Ekonomi Pembangunan: Kajian Masalah Ekonomi Dan Pembangunan*, 161–171. https://doi.org/10.23917/jep.v24i1.21988

Junus et al. "Ethical Governance through Maqasid Shariah Perspective: A Conceptual Framework." *International Journal of Academic Research in Business and Social Sciences* 14/10 (October 7, 2024), Pages 920-932. https://doi.org/10.6007/IJARBSS/v14-i10/23148

Kader, Faris. *Human Wellbeing and the Moral Economy: An Islamic Model.* Qatar: Hamad Bin Khalifa University, PhD, 2018. https://www.proquest.com/docview/2644046257?fromopenview=true&pq-origsite=gscholar&sourcetype=Dissertations%20&%20Theses

Kamal, Ch. Raja - Santhosh, V. "A Perspective on the Existence and Development of Islamic Banking in India." *Islamic Finance: New Trends in Law and Regulation.* ed. Nadia Mansour - Lorenzo Bujosa. 207–214. Cham: Springer Nature Switzerland, 2024. https://doi.org/10.1007/978-3-031-48770-5_17

Kamali, Mohammad Hashim. "Islamic Commercial Law: An Analysis of Futures." *American Journal of Islamic Social Sciences 13:2.* 197–224. 12 2. Washington DC: International Institute of Islamic Thought (IIIT), 1996.

Kamali, Mohammad Hashim. *Shariah and the Halal Industry.* Oxford University Press, 2021.

Kamali, Mohammad Hashim. *Shari'ah Law: An Introduction.* Oxford: Oneworld Publications, 2010.

Kamali, Prof Mohammad Hashim. *Principles of Islamic Jurisprudence.* Cambridge, UK: Islamic Texts Society, 2003.

Kamaruddin, Muhammad Iqmal Hisham et al. "Maqasid Shariah Disclosure: A Case of a Malaysian Shariah-Compliant Company." *Journal of Islamic Accounting and Business Research* ahead-of-print/ahead-of-print (May 7, 2025). https://doi.org/10.1108/JIABR-05-2024-0164

Karagöz, Fatma Gül. *The Evolution of Kânûnnâme Writing in the 16th and 17th Century-Ottoman Empire: A Comparison of Kânûn-i'Osmânî of Bayezid II and of Kânûnnâme-i Cedîd.* Ankara: Bilkent Universitesi, Master's Thesis, 2010. https://search.proquest.com/openview/b6451982ad20a8b938f07fda90179a84/1?pq-origsite=gscholar&cbl=2026366&diss=y

Karaman, Hayreddin. *Mukayeseli İslam Hukuku.* İstanbul: İZ YAYINCILIK, 2006.

karūyu, Ibrāhīm Salmān al- - Sharaf al-Dīn, 'Abd al-Tawwāb. *Al-Marji' Fī al-Ḥaḍārah al-'Arabīyah al-Islāmīyah.* Kuwait: Dhāt al-Salāsil lil-Ṭibā'ah wa-al-Nashr, 1984.

Kāsānī, 'Alā' al-Dīn, Abū Bakr ibn Mas'ūd. *Badā'i' Al-Ṣanā'i' Fī Tartīb al-Sharā'i'.* Beirut: Dār al-Kutub al-'Ilmīyah, 1328.

Kashyap, Amit K. *INDIAN BANKING: Contemporary Issues in Law and Challenges.* Allied Publishers, 2014.

Kasim, Nawal binti et al. "Comparative Analysis on AAOIFI, IFSB and BNM Shari'ah Governance Guidelines." *International Journal of Business and Social Science* 4/15 (2013), 220–227.

Kaya, İlkay. "Islamic Finance: Fit for Purpose or Mere Replication?" *İslam Ekonomisi Dergisi* 3/2 (2023), 1–18. https://doi.org/10.55237/jie.1175883

Keramat, Abdul Samad - Kahf, Monzer. "Sharia Governance Framework of Islamic Financial Institutions in Afghanistan Compare to Pakistan and Nigeria." *İslam Ekonomisi ve Finansı Dergisi (İEFD)* 8/1 (June 30, 2022), 135–158. https://doi.org/10.54863/jief.963241

Khafīf, Alī al-. *Aḥkām Al-Mu'āmalāt al-Shar'īyah.* Damascus: Dār al-Fikr al-ʿArabī, 2008.

Khaleel, Fawad - Avdukic, Alija. "Islamic Classical Literature (A.D. 950–1450) on Institutionalisation of Ethics for Regulating Markets and Society." *Religions* 15/12 (December 2024), 1496. https://doi.org/10.3390/rel15121496

Khalid, Azam Abdelhakeem et al. "The Role of Shariah Supervisory Board on Internal Shariah Audit Effectiveness: Evidence From Bahrain." *Academy of Accounting and Financial Studies Journal* 22/5 (September 17, 2018), 0–286.

Khalidi, Omar. "Hinduising India: Secularism in Practice." *Third World Quarterly* 29/8 (December 2008), 1545–1562. https://doi.org/10.1080/01436590802528614

Khalifah, Mohamad Handi et al. "Challenges in the Implementation of Mudharabah Financing in the Islamic Banking Industry." *Equinox Journal of Economics Business and Political Studies* 11/1 (March 21, 2024), 1–23. https://doi.org/10.48064/equinox.1341793

Khān, Abū al-Ṭayyib Muḥammad Ṣiddīq. *Abjad Al-'Ulūm Alwshy Almrqwm Fī Bayān Aḥwāl al-'Ulūm.* Dār Ibn Ḥazm, 2002.

Khan, Feisal. "How 'Islamic' Is Islamic Banking?" *Journal of Economic Behavior & Organization* 76/3 (December 1, 2010), 805–820. https://doi.org/10.1016/j.jebo.2010.09.015

Khan, Umair Pervez. "Hindutva through Legislation: The Waqf Amendment Act in India | Opinion." *Daily Sabah*. April 15, 2025. Accessed April 19, 2025. https://www.dailysabah.com/opinion/op-ed/hindutva-through-legislation-the-waqf-amendment-act-in-india

Kheladze, Bako - Zahir, Nima. "Corruption Issues in Afghanistan: How Did Corruption Enable the Taliban to Gain Control in Afghanistan?" *Confluences Méditerranée* 129/2 (September 17, 2024), 125–138. https://doi.org/10.3917/come.129.0127

Khurshid Ahmad. "Islamıc Bankıng Can Tap Into New Sources of Fınance." Accessed April 19, 2025. https://icif.org.in/icif-news-event.php?event=ei&id=354

Khurshid, Minahil. "Revisiting the Objectives Resolution 1949: Identity of Pakistan." *Paradigm Shift* (blog), May 7, 2025. https://www.paradigmshift.com.pk/objectives-resolution-1949/

Kisman, Zainul. "Risk Management: Comparative Study Between Islamic Banks and Conventional Banks." *Journal of Economics and Business* 3/1 (2020).

Korson, J. Henry. "Endogamous Marriage in a Traditional Muslim Society: West Pakistan; a Study in Intergenerational Change." *Journal of Comparative Family Studies* 2/2 (October 1, 1971), 145–155. https://doi.org/10.3138/jcfs.2.2.145

Kuran, Timur. *The Long Divergence: How Islamic Law Held Back the Middle East*. New Jersey: Princeton University Press, 2011.

Kurpad, Meenakshi Ramesh. "Making a Case for Islamic Finance in India." *Law and Financial Markets Review* 10/1 (January 2, 2016), 38–45. https://doi.org/10.1080/17521440.2016.1154295

Kurter, Osman - Husseini, İmam Ali. "EVALUATION OF STRATEGIC MANAGEMENT ISSUES RELATED TO THE MİCROFINANCE INDUSTRY AND SMALL AND MEDIUM ENTERPRISES IN AFGHANISTAN." *Uluslararası Finansal Ekonomi ve Bankacılık Uygulamaları Dergisi* 2/2 (December 31, 2021), 34–67.

Kütükoğlu, Mübahat S. *Osmanlılarda narh müessesesi ve 1640 tarihli narh defteri*. İstanbul: Enderun Kitabevi, 1983.

Laldin, Mohamad Akram - Furqani, Hafas. "Developing Islamic Finance in the Framework Ofmaqasid Al-Shari'ah." *International Journal of Islamic and Middle Eastern Finance and Management* 6/4 (2013), 278–289.

Laskar, Sakir Hossain. "Islam and Sufism in South Asia: Dynamics of the Chishtī Sufi Order." *ISLAMIC STUDIES* 61/3 (September 30, 2022), 331–343. https://doi.org/10.52541/isiri.v61i3.2430

Lewis, David. *Bangladesh: Politics, Economy and Civil Society*. Cambridge University Press, 2011.

Liv, Cemil. "İnternet Bankacılığı Aracılığıyla Gerçekleştirilen Sarf Akdinin İslam Hukuku Açısından Değerlendirilmesi." *Gaziosmanpaşa Üniversitesi İlahiyat Fakültesi Dergisi* 7/2 (2019), 41–60. https://doi.org/10.5281/zenodo.3594042

Lubis, Asep Ridwan et al. "Practical Implications Of The Prohibition Of Gambling In Islamic Economic Principles." *MIMBAR PENDIDIKAN* 8/2 (September 1, 2023), 117–128. https://doi.org/10.17509/mimbardik.v8i2.81186

Maḥāsinah, Muḥammad Ḥusayn. *Binā' Al-Dawlah al-'Arabīyah al-Islāmīyah: Al-Nuẓum Wa-al-Ḥaḍārah*. Amman, 1999.

Mahmood, Huma et al. "Prospects of Islamic Microfinance: A Study in India." *Journal of Administrative and Business Studies* 6/5 (October 20, 2020). https://doi.org/10.20474/jabs-6.5.2

Mainata, Dedy et al. "Mapping Global Trends and Future Opportunities in Islamic Banking Windows: A 15-Year Bibliometric Perspective (2008–2023)." *Journal of Islamic Accounting and Business Research* ahead-of-print/ahead-of-print (February 19, 2025). https://doi.org/10.1108/JIABR-03-2024-0074

Mājid, 'Abd al-Mun'im. *Tārīkh Al-Ḥaḍārah al-Islāmīyah Fī al-'uṣūr al-Wusṭá*. Cairo: Maktabat al-Anjlū al-Miṣrīyah, 2010.

Majone, Giandomenico (ed.). *Regulating Europe*. London: Routledge, 2005.

Maliha, Dewi - Alhusna, Mahdalina Nanda. "The Meaning of Al-Maysir from the Perspective of Middle Eastern Mufasirs and Its Contex: English." *An-Nur International Journal of The Quran & Hadith* 2/2 (November 30, 2024), 11–23. https://doi.org/10.62032/aijqh.v2i2.53

Manoori, Muhammad Tahir et al. "Feasibility of Bay Salam Finance: A Survey of the Opinions of Stakeholders." *Global Review of Islamic Economics and Business* 6/1 (December 25, 2018), 001. https://doi.org/10.14421/grieb.2018.061-01

Mansoori, Muhammad Tahir. "Is 'Islamic Banking' Islamic? Analysis of Current Debate on Sharī'ah Legitimacy of Islamic Banking and Finance." *Islamic Studies* 50/3/4 (2011), 383–411.

Mansor, Fadillah. "Developments in Islamic Banking: The Case of Pakistan – By M. Mansoor Khan and M. Ishaq Bhatti." *Asian Politics & Policy* 2/2 (April 2010), 301–303. https://doi.org/10.1111/j.1943-0787.2010.01194.x

Margināny, 'Alī ibn Abī BakrBurhān al-Dīn Abū al-Ḥasan al-. *Al-Hidāyah Sharḥ Bidāyat al-Mubtadī*. Pakistan: Idārat al-Qur'ān wa-al-'Ulūm al-Islāmīyah, 1994.

Maron, Stanley. "The Problem of East Pakistan." *Pacific Affairs* 28/2 (June 1955), 132. https://doi.org/10.2307/3035377

Marsoof, Althaf. "Chapter 7: Challenges in Achieving Public Health Objectives through Product Labelling Regulation: Reflections on Sri Lankan Trademark and Constitutional Law," 2016. https://www.elgaronline.com/edcollchap/edcoll/9781784718787/9781784718787.00015.xml

Mastoor, Sameer Ahmad. *Proceedings of International Academic Conferences*. "Islamic Banking System in Afghanistan." *Proceedings of International Academic Conferences*. https://ideas.repec.org//p/sek/iacpro/0200302.html

Masud, Muhammad Khalid et al. *Islam and Modernity Key Issues and Debates*. UK: Edinburgh University Press, 1st Ed., 2009.

Māwardī, Abū al-Ḥasan 'Alī ibn Muḥammad al-. *Al-Aḥkām al-Sulṭānīyah*. Cairo: Dār al-ḥadīth, 1409.

Māwardī, Abū al-Ḥasan 'Alī ibn Muḥammad ibn Ḥabīb al-. *Al-Rutbah Fī Ṭilib al-Ḥisbah*. Beirut: Dār al-Risālah al-'Ālamīyah, 2002.

Māwardī, Abū al-Ḥasan ʿAlī ibn Muḥammad ibn Ḥabīb al-. *Al-Aḥkām al-Sulṭāniyyah Wa al-Wilāyāt al-Dīniyyah*. Beirut: Dār al-Fikr, 1990.

Mawṣilī, Abdullāh ibn Maḥmūd al-. *Al-Ikhtiyār Li-Ta'līl al-Mukhtār*. Beirut: Dār al-Kutub al-'Ilmīyah, 1998.

Mdawhoma, Moilim El Azhar. "Qard –The Good, The Fair, & The Ugly: From an Islamic Finance Perspective." *Journal of Research in Social Science and Humanities* 5/1 (2025). https://doi.org/10.47679/jrssh.v5i1.133

Meher, Jagmohan. "Dynamics of Pakistan's Disintegration: The Case of East Pakistan 1947-1971." *India Quarterly* 71/4 (2015), 300–317.

Meirison, Meirison et al. "The Role of Islamic Da'wah and the Implementation of Sharia on the Existence of Muslims in the Maldives Islands Past and Present." *Jurnal Ilmiah Islam Futura* 24/1 (February 1, 2024), 85–101. https://doi.org/10.22373/jiif.v24i1.18005

Mergaliyev, Arman et al. "Higher Ethical Objective (Maqasid al-Shari'ah) Augmented Framework for Islamic Banks: Assessing Ethical Performance and Exploring Its Determinants." *Journal of Business Ethics* 170/4 (2021), 797–834. https://doi.org/10.1007/s10551-019-04331-4

Minaz, M. N. M. et al. "The Enhancement of Fintech on Islamic Banking and Financial Sector in Sri Lanka: A Literature Review." South Eastern University of Sri Lanka, 2023. http://ir.lib.seu.ac.lk/handle/123456789/6817

Mitra, Ashmita - Baid, Amulya. "Muta Marriage: A Contractual Form of Live-in Relationship." *LexForti Legal Journal* 1 (2020 2019), 67.

Miura, Toru. "Strategy for Religious Endowment: A Comparative Study of the Waqf." *Endowment Studies* 7/1 (November 17, 2023), 5–21. https://doi.org/10.1163/24685968-20230005

Mohamad, Saadiah - Tabatabaei, Ali. *Islamic Hedging: Gambling or Risk Management?* (SSRN Scholarly Paper, August 27, 2008). Social Science Research Network, papers.ssrn.com. Accessed April 6, 2025. https://doi.org/10.2139/ssrn.1260110

Mohamed Ali, Khalifa. *Working Papers*. "Integrating Zakah, Awqaf and Islamic Microfinance for Poverty Alleviation: Three Models Of Islamic Micro Finance." *Working Papers*. https://ideas.repec.org//p/ris/irtiwp/1435_019.html

Mohamed, Hazik. "Integrating Shariah Principles with ESG for Sustainable Finance: A Comprehensive Framework." *World Scientific Annual Review of*

Islamic Finance 02 (January 2024), 2450002. https://doi.org/10.1142/S2811023424500023

Mohamed, Ismail et al. "The Application of Service Ijarah in Islamic Finance." *International Journal of Management and Applied Research* 11/1 (2024), 80–106.

Mohamed, Ismail et al. "The Application of Service Ijarah in Islamic Finance." *International Journal of Management and Applied Research* 11/1 (2024), 80–106. https://doi.org/10.18646/2056.111.24-004

Mohammed, Wasiullah Shaik - Waheed, Khalid. "Interest-Free Microfinance in India: A Case Study of the Al-Khair Cooperative Credit Society." *Journal of King Abdulaziz University: Islamic Economics* 31/1 (2018), 1–20.

Mohsin, Saleha. "US Freezes Afghan Central Bank's Assets of $9.5bn." *Al Jazeera*. Accessed April 21, 2025. https://www.aljazeera.com/economy/2021/8/18/us-freezes-afghan-central-banks-assets-of-9-5bn

Moin, Bilal. "Taming the Untamable: Rethinking, Regulating, and Revamping Hawala." *Journal of Academics Stand Against Poverty* 5/1 (June 1, 2024), 20–43. https://doi.org/10.5281/zenodo.11411586

Mokal, Mahvish Nawaz et al. "Murabaha & Tawarruq: An Examination of Issues and Challenges from an Accounting Perspective." *Journal of Islamic Finance* 13/1 (July 31, 2024), 42–56.

Moore, R. J. "Jinnah and the Pakistan Demand." *Modern Asian Studies* 17/4 (1983), 529–561.

Muhammad, Marjan. *Islamic Financial System Principles & Operations*. ed. Mezbah Uddin Ahmed. Kuala Lumpur: International Shariah Research Academy for Islamic Finance, 2016.

Muneer, Farah - Khan, Foyasal. "QARD-AL-HASSAN AS A TOOL FOR POVERTY ALLEVIATION: A CASE STUDY OF THE FAEL KHAIR WAQF PROGRAM IN BANGLADESH." *Journal of Islamic Monetary Economics and Finance* 5/4 (December 27, 2019), 829–848. https://doi.org/10.21098/jimf.v5i4.1100

Muneeza, Aishath. "Enhancing Zakat Framework of Maldives: A Hundred Muslim Country." *International Conference of Zakat*. https://doi.org/10.37706/iconz.2018.122

Muneeza, Aishath. "Establishment of Islamic Capital Market in Jurisdictions with Limited Islamic Financial Services: Case Study of Maldives." *International Journal of Law and Management* 60/2 (March 12, 2018), 373–385. https://doi.org/10.1108/IJLMA-12-2016-0146

Muneeza, Aishath et al. "Need to Pioneer Islamic Tourism in Tourist Resorts in Maldives." *Journal of Islamic Marketing* 11/4 (July 25, 2019), 895–916. https://doi.org/10.1108/JIMA-01-2019-0004

Muneeza, Aishath. "Short-Term Sharīʿah-Compliant Islamic Liquidity Management Instruments to Sustain Islamic Banking: The Case of Maldives." *Journal of*

Islamic Accounting and Business Research 11/2 (January 20, 2020), 428–439. https://doi.org/10.1108/JIABR-04-2018-0055
Musa, Muhammad. "Integration between ESG Goals and Value-Based Intermediation Approach within the Paradigm of Islamic Finance." *Islamic Banking and Finance Review* 10/2 (December 28, 2023), 31–54.
Muslim, Abū al-Ḥusayn Muslim ibn al-Ḥajjāj. *Ṣaḥīḥ Muslim*. Cairo: Maṭba'at 'Īsá al-Bābī al-Ḥalabī wa-Shurakāh, 1374.
Muslimin, J. M. "Early Islamic Banking Practices And Current Development: A Survey of Legal History And Service Innovation Nisbah." https://ojs.unida.ac.id/JN/article/view/2181
Mustapha, Zakariya et al. "Legal and Sharī'ah Non-Compliance Risks in Nigerian Islamic Finance Industry: A Review of the Literature." *International Journal of Law and Management* 63/2 (November 12, 2020), 275–299. https://doi.org/10.1108/IJLMA-03-2020-0075
Muzaffar Asad, Dr. et al. "A Crital Review of Islamic and Conventional Banking in Digital Era: A Case of Pakistan." *International Journal of Engineering & Technology* 7/4.7 (September 27, 2018), 57–59. https://doi.org/10.14419/ijet.v7i4.7.20382
Nafees, S. M. - Habeebullah, M. T. *Enhancement of Islamic Banking Industry: A Sri Lankan Perspective*. Sri Lanka: South Eastern University of Sri Lanka, 2016. http://ir.lib.seu.ac.lk/handle/123456789/2578
Nafees, S. M. M. et al. "Problems and Prospects of Islamic Banking: A Case Analysis of Sri Lanka." *Sri Lankan Journal of Arabic & Islamic Studies (SLJAIS)* 1/2 (2018), 57–70.
Nairoos, Mohamed Haniffa Mohamed. "The Contribution of Amana Bank in the Islamic Financial Industry in Sri Lanka." *Cognizance Journal of Multidisciplinary Studies* 3/6 (2023), 231–253. https://doi.org/10.47760/cognizance.2023.v03i06.014
Naqvi, Syed M. Imran Haider et al. "Riba Free Loan in Islamic Finance: Key to Social Development and Welfare." *European Online Journal of Natural and Social Sciences* 5/2 (June 26, 2016), 559–567.
Naseh, Hezbullah - Ghalia, Bouhedda. "The Impact of Legislative Environment on the Development of Islamic Banking: A Comparative Study between Malaysia and Afghanistan." *AL-HIKMAH: INTERNATIONAL JOURNAL OF ISLAMIC STUDIES AND HUMAN SCIENCES* 7/4 (December 12, 2024), 31–54. https://doi.org/10.46722/hikmah.v7i4.533
Naseri, Khatera - Sharofiddin, Ashurov. "Exploring the Challenges of the Historical Development of Islamic Banking System in Afghanistan Using Document Analysis." *Journal of Islamic Finance* 9/2 (December 30, 2020), 13–25. https://doi.org/10.31436/jif.v9i2.481
Nasimi, M. Najim et al. "Climate and Water Resources Variation in Afghanistan and the Need for Urgent Adaptation Measures." *International Journal of Food*

Science and Agriculture 4/1 (March 5, 2020), 49–64. https://doi.org/10.26855/ijfsa.2020.03.009

Nasution, Abdillah Arif et al. "Environmental, Social, Governance (ESG) and Islamic Finance: A Review." *Management and Sustainability* 1/1 (November 9, 2023), 1–12. https://doi.org/10.58968/ms.v1i1.285

Nawawī, Muḥyī al-Dīn Yaḥyá ibn Sharaf. *Rawḍat Al-Ṭālibīn Wa-'umdat al-Muftīn*. Amman: al-Maktab al-Islāmī, 1991.

Nazeri, Amelia Nur Natasha et al. "Exploration of a New Zakat Management System Empowered by Blockchain Technology in Malaysia." *ISRA International Journal of Islamic Finance* 15/4 (December 27, 2023), 127–147. https://doi.org/10.55188/ijif.v15i4.568

Nimsith, Subaideen Issath et al. "Factors Influencing Demand for Islamic Bank Products in Sri Lanka." *Journal of Enterprise and Development (JED)* 6/1 (2024), 160–171.

Nisar, Shariq. "Shrinking Space for Islamic Finance in India." *Economic and Political Weekly* 50/17 (2015), 23–25.

Niẓām al-Mulk, al-Ḥasan ibn 'Alī ibn Isḥāq al-Ṭūsī. *Siyāsat Nāmah*. Qatar: Dār al-Thaqāfah, 1407.

Nizam, Kehkashan. "Perception of Shariah Scholars toward Islamic Banking in Pakistan." *Journal of Islamic Marketing* 16/4 (November 4, 2024), 1118–1144. https://doi.org/10.1108/JIMA-03-2024-0138

Noh, Mohd Shahid Mohd et al. "A Review on Gharar Dimension in Modern Islamic Finance Transactions." *Journal of Islamic Accounting and Business Research* ahead-of-print/ahead-of-print (March 29, 2024). https://doi.org/10.1108/JIABR-01-2023-0006

Nouman, Muhammad et al. "Nexus between Higher Ethical Objectives (Maqasid Al Shari'ah) and Participatory Finance." *Qualitative Research in Financial Markets* 13/2 (2021), 226–251. https://doi.org/10.1108/QRFM-06-2020-0092

Nuwayrī, Shihāb al-Dīn Aḥmad ibn 'Abd al-Wahhāb al-. "Nihāyat Al-Arab Fī Funūn al-Adab." Beirut: Daru'l-Kutubi'l-İlmiyye, 2004.

Ogus, Anthony I. *Regulation: Legal Form and Economic Theory*. London: Hart Publishing, 2004.

Ohlan, Ramphul. "Muslim Women in India: Status of Demographic, Socioeconomic and Health Inequalities." *Journal of Muslim Minority Affairs* 40/3 (July 2, 2020), 429–440. https://doi.org/10.1080/13602004.2020.1813991

Oktaviandi, M. Rizky - Yogi, Yogi. "Economic Justice Through Al-Hisbah: Reviewing The Role And Performance Of Market Supervisory Institutions." *Al-Kharaj: Journal of Islamic Economic and Business* 6/1 (March 30, 2024). https://doi.org/10.24256/kharaj.v6i1.5022

Oseni, Umar A. et al. "The Legal Implications of 'Fatwā Shopping' in the Islamic Finance Industry: Problems, Perceptions and Prospects." *Arab Law Quarterly* 30/2 (February 24, 2016), 107–137. https://doi.org/10.1163/15730255-12341319

Pamuk, Şevket. *A Monetary History of the Ottoman Empire*. Cambridge: Cambridge University Press, 2000.

Philips, C. H. - Mary Doreen Wainwright (eds.). *The Partition of India: Policies and Perspectives 1935–1947*. London: Routledge, 2025. https://doi.org/10.4324/9781003627623

Pison, Gilles. "World population: 8 billion today, how many tomorrow?" *Population & Societies* 604/9 (October 19, 2022), 1–4. https://doi.org/10.3917/popsoc.604.0001

Powell, Emilia Justyna - Paldino, Joshua. "The Taliban, Afghan Constitutionalism and Modern Islamic Law States: Renegotiating the Balance of Religious and Secular Law." *Global Constitutionalism*, 1–28. https://doi.org/10.1017/S2045381725000048

Qalqashandī, Shihāb al-Dīn Abū al-ʿAbbās Aḥmad al-. *Ṣubḥ Al-Aʿshā Fī Ṣināʿat al-Inshāʾ*. Beirut: Daru'l-Kutubi'l-İlmiyye, 1987.

Qalʿajī, Muḥammad Rawwās. *Al-Ḥisbah Fī al-Fiqh al-Islāmī*. Damascus: Dār al-Nafāʾis, 1983.

Qārī, Nūr al-Dīn Abū al-Ḥasan al-. *Fatḥ Bāb Al-ʿināyah Bi-Sharḥ*. Beirut: Dār al-Arqam, 1997.

Quamar, Md. Muddassir. "India and the Gulf: Regional Security and India's Multialignment Policy." *Asian Politics & Policy* 15/2 (2023), 274–294. https://doi.org/10.1111/aspp.12682

Qurashī, Bāqir Sharīf al-. *The Life of Ali Ibn Abi Talib*. Qum: Ansariyan Publications, 1999.

Rafiq, Mansha - Ahmad, Khaliq. "Financial Inclusion of the Deprived in India: Historical Perspectives." *Islamic Finance and Sustainable Development*. Routledge, 2025.

Rahimi, Haroun. "Hawala as Credit: Recognizing How Hawala Supports the Business Climate in Afghanistan." *Journal of Money Laundering Control* 23/1 (January 20, 2020), 224–244. https://doi.org/10.1108/JMLC-07-2019-0053

Rahimi, Haroun. "How to Create Better Hawala Regulations: A Case Study of Hawala Regulations in Afghanistan." *Crime, Law and Social Change* 76/2 (September 1, 2021), 131–148. https://doi.org/10.1007/s10611-021-09959-w

Rana, Shahbaz. "Govt Announces End to Riba in Five Years." *The Express Tribune*. November 9, 2022. Accessed April 21, 2025. https://tribune.com.pk/story/2385489/govt-announces-end-to-riba-in-five-years

Rani, Asia et al. "Impact of Shari'ah and Corporate Governance on Islamic Banks Performance: Evidence from Pakistan." *Sustainable Business and Society in Emerging Economies* 6/3 (September 30, 2024), 457–468. https://doi.org/10.26710/sbsee.v6i3.3140

Rashid, Abdul - Ghazi, Muhammad Saarim. "Factors Affecting Sharī'ah Audit Quality in Islamic Banking Institutions of Pakistan: A Theoretical Framework." *Islamic Economic Studies* 28/2 (2021), 124–140.

Raymond, André. *Cairo: City of History*. American University in Cairo Press, 2001.

Rāzī, Zayn al-Dīn ibn 'Abd al-Qādir al-Ḥanafī al-. *Mukhtār Al-Ṣiḥāḥ*. Beirut: al-Maktabah al-'Aṣrīyah, 1999.

Razick, Ahamed Sarjoon et al. *Buddhist and Muslim Interaction in the Post-War of Sri Lanka*. Malaysia: Universiti Kebangsaan Malaysia Press, 2021. http://ir.lib.seu.ac.lk/handle/123456789/5916

Razzak, Mohamed Arkam Mohamed - Shehu, Fatmir. "Exploring the History of Islamic Revivalism in Modern Sri Lanka." *Journal of Islam in Asia (E-ISSN 2289-8077)* 21/1 (June 28, 2024), 206–229. https://doi.org/10.31436/jia.v21i1.1212

Redín, Dulce M. et al. "Exploring the Ethical Dimension of Hawala." *Journal of Business Ethics* 124/2 (2014), 327–337. https://doi.org/10.1007/s10551-013-1874-0

Reporter, Staff. "Alipay+ Goes Live in Sri Lanka with 14 E-Wallets Enabled for Payment | Asian Banking & Finance." March 26, 2025. Accessed April 30, 2025. https://asianbankingandfinance.net/cards-payments/news/alipay-goes-live-in-sri-lanka-14-e-wallets-enabled-payment

Riaz, Ali. *Lived Islam and Islamism in Bangladesh*: Dhaka: Prothoma Prokashan, 2017. https://www.amazon.com/Lived-Islam-Islamism-Bangladesh-Riaz/dp/9849274395

Richard Eton. *India in the Persianate Age, 1000–1765*, 2020. http://archive.org/details/india-in-the-persianate-age-richard-eaton

Rifas, Abi Huraira et al. "Involvement of Micro, Small and Medium Entrepreneurs (MSMEs) in Takaful in Sri Lanka: An Extension of Theory of Planned Behaviour." *Journal of Islamic Marketing* 14/11 (February 3, 2023), 2715–2740. https://doi.org/10.1108/JIMA-11-2021-0371

Riyath, Mohamed Ismail Mohamed - Hussainey, Khaled. "Co-Movement and Information Transmission between Conventional and Islamic Equities in Sri Lanka." *Review of Accounting and Finance* ahead-of-print/ahead-of-print (March 4, 2025). https://doi.org/10.1108/RAF-10-2023-0357

Riza, Ahmed. "Islamic Banking and Financing Industry of Maldives: Snapshot of Today." *Corporatemaldives.Com* (blog), July 2, 2020. https://corporatemaldives.com/islamic-banking-and-financing-industry-of-maldives-snapshot-of-today/

Rofiqoh Lubis, Nurul et al. "Relevansi Strategi Manajemen Risiko Pembiayaan Dalam Konteks Perbankan Syariah." *El-Mal: Jurnal Kajian Ekonomi & Bisnis Islam* 5/4 (February 9, 2024). https://doi.org/10.47467/elmal.v5i4.1334

Rohman, Pupun Saepul et al. "A Review on Literature of Islamic Microfinance from 2010-2020: Lesson for Practitioners and Future Directions." *Heliyon* 7/12 (December 1, 2021). https://doi.org/10.1016/j.heliyon.2021.e08549

Rusmita, Sylva Alif et al. "Fundamental and Role ESG in Islamic Finance and Business: A Literature Review and Content Analysis." *International Journal of Religion* 5/11 (2024), 8519–8534. https://doi.org/10.61707/92eqh267

Sa'ad, Auwal Adam - Pitchay, Anwar Bin Allah. "Financing SMEs Through the Islamic Qard Al-Hasan: A Proposal of Islamic FinTech Interest-Free Lending for Government Initiatives." *Advances in Finance, Accounting, and Economics*. ed. Nader Naifar. 54–64. IGI Global, 2020. https://doi.org/10.4018/978-1-7998-0039-2.ch004

Sachedina, Abdulaziz. *Islamic Ethics Fundamental Aspects of Human Conduct*. Oxford: Oxford University Press, 2022.

Sadek, Daing Maruak et al. "The Practices of Corporate Governance and Shariah Governance in Islamic Financial Institutions." *Ethics, Governance and Risk Management in Organizations*. ed. Intan Marzita Saidon - Roshima Said. 131–147. Singapore: Springer, 2020. https://doi.org/10.1007/978-981-15-1880-5_9

Safi, Lutfullah. "Review of Afghanistan's Development Pattern from 2001 to 2021: A Relative Lack of Sustainability, Inclusiveness, and Prosperity." *Journal of Social and Economic Development* 26/1 (2024), 333–352. https://doi.org/10.1007/s40847-023-00268-7

Sağlam, Muhlis Selman - Eğri, Taha. "Mudarebe Finansmanının Katılım Bankalarında Uygulanmasının Ahlaki Risk Yönünden Değerlendirilmesi: Türkiye Örneği." *Uluslararası İslam Ekonomisi ve Finansı Araştırmaları Dergisi* 6/2 (July 31, 2020), 197–226. https://doi.org/10.25272/ijisef.689009

Şahin, Ibrahim Erem - Humta, Humayun. "Micro Finance in Afghanistan Banking System: A Case Study of First Micro Finance Bank in Afghanistan:" *Asian Journal of Management, Entrepreneurship and Social Science* 3/01 (2023), 92–135. https://doi.org/10.98765/ajmesc.v3i01.187

Şahin, Nurten Zeliha. "İslâmî Finans İlkeleri Çerçevesinde Akıllı Sözleşmeler -İcâre Temelli Azalan Müşâreke Sözleşmesi Özelinde-." *BEÜ İlahiyat Fakültesi Dergisi* 11/2 (December 16, 2024), 371–401. https://doi.org/10.33460/beuifd.1540388

Sairally, Beebee Salma. "Editorial." *ISRA International Journal of Islamic Finance* 16/S1 (May 6, 2024), 1–3. https://doi.org/10.55188/ijif.v16iS1.778

Sairally, Beebee Salma. "Integrating Environmental, Social and Governance (ESG) Factors in Islamic Finance: Towards the Realisation of Maqāṣid al-Sharīʿah."

ISRA International Journal of Islamic Finance 7/2 (December 15, 2015), 145–154.

Saiti, Buerhan et al. "Financing Agricultural Activities in Afghanistan: A Proposed Salam-Based Crowdfunding Structure." *ISRA International Journal of Islamic Finance* 10/1 (June 19, 2018), 52–61. https://doi.org/10.1108/IJIF-09-2017-0029

Saiti, Buerhan - Abdullah, Adam. "The Legal Maxims of Islamic Law (Excluding Five Leading Legal Maxims) and Their Applications in Islamic Finance القواعد الفقهية - عدا القواعد الخمس الكبرى - وتطبيقاتها في التمويل الإسلامي." *Journal of King Abdulaziz University: Islamic Economics* 29/2 (2016), 139–151.

Sajid Puthenpeedikayil. "Notions of Free Market and Social Welfare in Islamic Economics." *Journal of Modern Accounting and Auditing* 11/9 (September 28, 2015). https://doi.org/10.17265/1548-6583/2015.09.005

Salim, Mohammad Salim. "Establishment of Islamic Banking System in Afghanistan: Factors Have Led to the Late Establishment of Islamic Banking." *HIKMATUNA: Journal for Integrative Islamic Studies* 6/2 (January 25, 2021), 90–102. https://doi.org/10.28918/hikmatuna.v6i2.2892

Ṣallābī, ʿAlī Muḥammad. *Al-Dawlah al-Umawiyyah (The Umayyad State)*. Beirut: Dār al-Maʿrifah, 2000.

Salleh, Ahmad Dahlan et al. "Theory and Application of Sadd Al-Dhara'i' (Blocking the Means) in Shafi'iyya School." *International Journal of Academic Research in Business and Social Sciences* 9/1 (February 14, 2019), 724–737. https://doi.org/10.6007/IJARBSS/v9-i1/5475

Samararatne, Dinesha. "Judicial Borrowing and Creeping Influences: Indian Jurisprudence in Sri Lankan Public Law." *Indian Law Review* 2/3 (September 2, 2018), 205–223. https://doi.org/10.1080/24730580.2018.1564961

Samarqandī, 'Alā' al-Dīn al-. *Tuḥfat Al-Fuqahā'*. Beirut: Dār al-Kutub al-'Ilmīyah, 1994.

Saqṭī, Abū ʿAbd Allāh Muḥammad ibn Muḥammad al-. *Fi Ādāb Al-Ḥisbah*. Beirut: Mu'assasat Dār al-Fikr al-Ḥadīth, 1991.

Sarakhsī, Muḥammad ibn Aḥmad. *Al-Mabsūṭ*. Cairo: Maṭba'at al-Sa'ādah, no date.

Sardar, Sadia - Iqbal, Muhammad Farooq. "Risk Management in Islamic Banking System: An Overview of Current Modules." *Journal of Religious and Social Studies* 3/1 Jan-Jun (June 30, 2023), 11–26. https://doi.org/10.53583/jrss05.02.2023

Sen, Sucharita. *Theorizing a Bengali Nation: Abul Hashim and the United Bengal Movement, 1937–1947*. London: Routledge India, 1st Ed., 2024. https://doi.org/10.4324/9781003451242

Setiyadi, Alif Cahya - Mohammad Aris, Sakiinah. "Analysis of the Permissibility of Bai' Al-'Inah Transactions According to the Shafi'i School of Thought and Its

Implementation in Malaysia." *JURISTA: Jurnal Hukum Dan Keadilan* 7/2 (2023), 144–164. https://doi.org/10.22373/jurista.v7i2.73

Shaban, M. A. *Islamic History: A New Interpretation*. Cambridge: Cambridge University Press, 1971.

Shafruddin, Aisyah Syahidah - Shahimi, Shahida. "Strategy and Challenges of Value-Based Intermediation Implementation: The Case of BIMB." *Qualitative Research in Financial Markets* 17/1 (May 16, 2024), 153–168. https://doi.org/10.1108/QRFM-04-2023-0101

Shaheen, Dr Asma - Amin, Muhammad Kashif. "Bridging the Gap: Aligning Legal Frameworks with the Growth of Islamic Banking and Finance in Pakistan." *Journal of Business Insight and Innovation* 2/1 (June 30, 2023), 37–45.

Shahid, Abdullah Ibneyy. *Emergence of Islamic Finance Organizations, 1948 – 2016*. USA: Cornell University, M.A, 2022. https://hdl.handle.net/1813/112050

Shahrani, Nazif M. "War, Factionalism, and the State in Afghanistan." *American Anthropologist* 104/3 (2002), 715–722. https://doi.org/10.1525/aa.2002.104.3.715

Shahrom, Zuraida Rastam - Kunhibava, Sherin. "Malaysia's Sustainable Banking Regulatory Framework: Value-Based Intermediation and Climate Change Principle-Based Taxonomy." *Green Finance Instruments, FinTech, and Investment Strategies: Sustainable Portfolio Management in the Post-COVID Era*. ed. Nader Naifar - Ahmed Elsayed. 125–166. Cham: Springer International Publishing, 2023. https://doi.org/10.1007/978-3-031-29031-2_6

Shakeela, Aishath - Weaver, David. "'Managed Evils' of Hedonistic Tourism in the Maldives: Islamic Social Representations and Their Mediation of Local Social Exchange." *Annals of Tourism Research* 71 (July 1, 2018), 13–24. https://doi.org/10.1016/j.annals.2018.04.003

Shamsuddin, Mustafa Mat Jubri. "Statistical Evaluation of Conduciveness in Sadd Al-Dharāʾiʿ: An Analytical Study." *Journal of Contemporary Islamic Law* 9/2 (2024), 39–46.

Sharif, Khurram et al. "Analyzing Informal Value Transfer Networks through the Lens of Social Exchanges." *Society and Business Review* 17/3 (December 23, 2021), 394–420. https://doi.org/10.1108/SBR-05-2021-0059

Shāṭibī, Ibrāhīm ibn Mūsá Abū Isḥāq al-. *Al-Muwāfaqāt Fī Uṣūl al-Sharī'ah*. Beirut: Dār al-Maʿrifah, 1996.

Shatzmiller, Maya. *Labour in the Medieval Islamic World*. Leiden The Netherlands; New York: Brill Academic Pub, 1994.

Shayzarī, 'Abd al-Raḥmān ibn Naṣr. *Nihāyat Al-Rutba Fī Ṭalab al-Ḥisba*. Cairo: Lajnat al-Ta'līf wa-al-Tarjamah wa-al-Nashr, 1946.

Shayzarī, ʿAbd al-Raḥmān ibn Naṣr ibn ʿAbd Allāh al-. *Nihāyat Al-Rutbah Fī Ṭalab al-Ḥisbah*. Cairo: Maṭbaʿat Lajnat al-Taʾlīf wa al-Tarjamah wa al-Nashr, 1946.

Sheikh, Rafiullah et al. "Federal Shariat Court's Judgment on Ribā-Free Economy of Pakistan: Challenges in Implementation and the Way Forward." *Islamic Banking and Finance Review* 11/1 (September 25, 2024), 47–79. https://doi.org/10.32350/ibfr.111.03

Sheikh, Rafiullah - Hussain, Khalid. "Role of Shariah Supervisory Boards (SSBs) in Islamic Financial Engineering: A Critical Review:" *Islamic Banking and Finance Review* 9/2 (December 29, 2022), 42–62. https://doi.org/10.32350/ibfr.92.03

Shrivastava, Ashwini. "Indian Banks Should Exploit Untapped Potential in Islamic Banking: Experts." 2024. Accessed April 19, 2025. https://icif.org.in/icif-news-event.php?event=ei&id=358

Shuaib, Muhammad Hamza - Khan, Hafiz Abdul Basit. "The Direct & Indirect Form of Bay' al-'Inah: An Analytical Study of the AAOIFI Council's Position: بیع عینہ کی بلا واسطہ و بالواسطہ صورت: مجلس ایوفی کے موقف کا تجزیاتی مطالعہ." *Al-Aijaz Research Journal of Islamic Studies & Humanities* 8/2 (2024), 41–66.

Shujau, Mohamed et al. "Islamic Capital Market in Maldives: A Reform-Oriented Analysis." *IIUM Law Journal* 30/S2 (November 12, 2022), 359–384. https://doi.org/10.31436/iiumlj.v30iS2.772

Siddiqi, Muhammad. "Islamic Economics: Where From, Where To?" *Journal of King Abdulaziz University-Islamic Economics* 27/2 (2014), 59–68. https://doi.org/10.4197/Islec.27-2.3

Siddiqi, Muhammad N. *Muslim Economic Thinking: A Survey of Contemporary Literature (Islamic Economic)*. Islamic Foundation, 2007.

Siddique, Muhammad Zahid - Siddique, Muhammad Abubakar. "Reconciling the Irreconcilable (Talfeeq): The Case of Currency Salam." *International Journal of Finance & Economics* 28/1 (2023), 562–574. https://doi.org/10.1002/ijfe.2436

Siddiqui, Anjum. "Financial Contracts, Risk and Performance of Islamic Banking." ed. M. Mansoor Khan - M. Ishaq Bhatti. *Managerial Finance* 34/10 (January 1, 2008), 680–694. https://doi.org/10.1108/03074350810891001

Siddiqui, Taufeeque Ahmad et al. "A Study on Islamic Finance as an Approach for Financial Inclusion in India." *Accounting*, 487–496. https://doi.org/10.5267/j.ac.2020.11.001

Singh, Harshit. "List of Top Halal Stocks in India: Shariah-Compliant Shares on NSE (2025) - Blog by Tickertape," September 29, 2022. https://www.tickertape.in/blog/halal-stocks-in-india/

Smolo, Edib - Kabir Hassan, M. "The Potentials of Mushārakah Mutanāqisah for Islamic Housing Finance." *International Journal of Islamic and Middle Eastern Finance and Management* 4/3 (January 1, 2011), 237–258. https://doi.org/10.1108/17538391111166476

Sofyan, A. Syathir et al. "Financing Risk Measurement with Maqashid Al-Sharia Qualitative Risk 1." *Share: Jurnal Ekonomi Dan Keuangan Islam* 8/1 (July 15, 2019), 1–30. https://doi.org/10.22373/share.v8i1.4355

Stanikzai, Amin. "Impacts of the Afghan Frozen Assets on the Trade and Banking of Afghanistan." *International Journal of Humanities and Social Science* 8/2 (April 18, 2023), 8–15. https://doi.org/10.53555/eijhss.v8i2.127

Susewind, Raphael. "Muslims in Indian Cities: Degrees of Segregation and the Elusive Ghetto." *Environment and Planning A* 49/6 (June 1, 2017), 1286–1307. https://doi.org/10.1177/0308518X17696071

Suyūṭī, Jalāl al-Dīn al-. *Tārīkh Al-Khulafāʾ*. Beirut: Dār al-Kutub al-ʿIlmiyyah, 2004.

Tajmazinani, Ali Akbar - Mahdavi Mazinani, Zahra. "Foundations of Social Policy and Welfare in Islam." *Social Policy in the Islamic World*. ed. Ali Akbar Tajmazinani. 15–35. International Series on Public Policy. Cham: Springer International Publishing, 2021. https://doi.org/10.1007/978-3-030-57753-7_2

Tengku Zawawi, Tengku Nurul Saadah et al. "The Roles of Muhtasib in Islamic Medieval Urban Management." *Environment-Behaviour Proceedings Journal* 6/SI5 (September 1, 2021), 181–186. https://doi.org/10.21834/ebpj.v6iSI5.2947

Ṭībī, Amīn Tawfīq al-. *Dirāsāt Fī Tārīkh Ṣiqillīyah Al-Islāmīyah*. Iqra' lil-Ṭibāʿah wa-al-Tarjamah, 1990.

Tirmidhī, Abū ʿĪsā Muḥammad ibn ʿĪsā as-Sulamī aḍ-Ḍarīr. *Sunan Al-Tirmidhī*. Beirut: Dār al-Gharb al-Islāmī, 1996.

Tk Jayaraman, Keshmeer Makun. "Tourism and Economic Growth Nexus in Maldives: Asymmetric Analysis and Role of ICT." *International Journal of Business and Society* 23/2 (August 8, 2022), 1086–1105. https://doi.org/10.33736/ijbs.4859.2022

Topal, Şevket - Arık, Önder. "Elektronik Transfer Sistemleri Aracılığıyla Yapılan Altın Alım Satım İşlemleri." *Recep Tayyip Erdoğan Üniversitesi İlahiyat Fakültesi Dergisi* 20 (2021), 15–36. https://doi.org/10.32950/rteuifd.1010331

Tujībī, Muḥammad ibn Aḥmad ibn ʿAbdūn al-. *Risālah Fī Al-Qaḍāʾ Wa al-Ḥisbah*. Beirut: Dār Ibn Ḥazm, 2009.

Ṭūsī, Abī Jaʿfar Muḥammad ibn al-Ḥasan al-. *Al-Nihāyah Fī Mujarrad al-Fiqh Wa-al-Fatāwá*. Beirut: Dār al-Kitāb al-ʿArabī, 1980.

Tuzzahroh, Fatimah - Laela, Sugiyarti Fatma. "Sharia Audit and Shariah Compliance of Islamic Financial Institutions: A Bibliometric Analysis." *Jurnal Ekonomi Syariah Teori Dan Terapan* 9/6 (November 30, 2022), 815–833. https://doi.org/10.20473/vol9iss20226pp815-833

Uddin, A. H. M. Ershad. "Development of Islamic Insurance (Takaful) in Bangladesh: Legal Barriers and Challenges." *Trabzon İlahiyat Dergisi* 10/2 (2023), 7–30.

Uddin, Ahm Ershad. *Bangladeş'teki İslam Bankacılık Uygulamasının Fıkhî Açıdan*. Istanbul: Marmara University, PhD, 2020.

Uddin, Mohammad Nazim et al. "Guidelines for Developing the Shari'ah-Compliant Products and Shari'ah Governance for Sustainable Banks in Bangladesh." *Business Strategy & Development* 7/1 (2024), e309. https://doi.org/10.1002/bsd2.309

Uddin, Sami et al. "Legal Foundations for Shariah-Compliant Islamic Banking in Pakistan: Challenges and the Way Forward (پاکستان میں اسلامی بینکاری کی قانونی بنیادیں: درپیش چیلنجز اور لائحہ عمل)." *Majallah-Yi Talim o Tahqiq* 6/4 (2024), 1–18. https://doi.org/10.2139/ssrn.5076171

Uddin, Sami et al. "Legal Foundations For SHARĪʿAH-COMPLIANT ISLAMIC BANKING IN PAKISTAN: CHALLENGES AND WAY FORWARD." *Majallah-e-Talim o Tahqiq* 6/4 (December 31, 2024). https://ojs.cer.edu.pk/index.php/mtt/article/view/324

Uddin, A. H. M. Ershad.. "Bangladeş'teki İslami Bankalarin Vedîa ve Fon Toplama Faaliyetleri: İslam Hukuku Perspektifinden Bir İnceleme." *Akademik Platform İslami Araştırmalar Dergisi* 8/2 (August 30, 2024), 203–227. https://doi.org/10.52115/apjir.1503015

Uddin, A. H. M. Ershad. "Development of Islamic Insurance (Takaful) in Bangladesh: Legal Barriers and Challenges." *Trabzon İlahiyat Dergisi* 10/2 (2023), 7–30.

Uddin, Ahm Ershad. *Bangladeş'teki İslam Bankacılık Uygulamasının Fıkhî Açıdan*. Istanbul: Marmara University, PhD, 2020.

UUddın, Ahm Ershad - Hira, Ayhan. "Bangladeş'te Kira Sertifikası (Sukuk) Uygulamasının İslam Hukuku Açısından Analizi." *Kafkas Üniversitesi İlahiyat Fakültesi Dergisi* 10/20 (July 28, 2023), 577–601. https://doi.org/10.17050/kafkasilahiyat.1250424

Uddın, Ahm Ershad - Okur, Hüseyin. "Empowering Communities: Redefining Zakat Distribution in Bangladesh Post-Covid-19." *Kocatepe İslami İlimler Dergisi* 6/2 (December 15, 2023), 419–438. https://doi.org/10.52637/kiid.1353946

Ülker, İbrahim. "Ebüssuûd Efendi ve Şânizâde'nin Sakk Kayıtları Işığında İslam ve Osmanlı Hukukunda İcâre (Kira)." *Necmettin Erbakan Üniversitesi Hukuk Fakültesi Dergisi* 6/2 (December 29, 2023), 730–755.

Ullah, Md. Hafij et al. "Comparative Compliance Status of AAOIFI and IFSB Standards." *Journal of Islamic Accounting and Business Research* 9/4 (2018), 607–628. https://doi.org/10.1108/JIABR-11-2014-0040

Usmani, Mufti Muhammad Taqi. *An Introduction to Islamic Finance*. Pakistan: Maktaba ma'ariful qur'an, 2002.

Usmani, Muhammad Taqi. *Usul al-ifta wa adabuhu*. Beirut: Daru'l-kalem, 2014.

Uzunçarşılı, İsmail Hakkı. *Osmanlı Devleti Teşkilâtından Kapukulu Ocakları*. Ankara: Türk Tarih Kurumu, 1988.

Verkoren, Willemijn - Kamphuis, Bertine. "State Building in a Rentier State: How Development Policies Fail to Promote Democracy in Afghanistan." *Development and Change* 44/3 (2013), 501–526. https://doi.org/10.1111/dech.12029

Visser, Hans. *Islamic Finance: Principles and Practice, Third Edition*. Edward Elgar Publishing, 2019.

Vogel, David. *The Politics of Precaution: Regulating Health, Safety, and Environmental Risks in Europe and the United States*. Princeton N.J.: Princeton University Press, 2012.

Vogel, Frank - Hayes, Samuel. *Islamic Law and Finance: Religion, Risk and Return*. Kluwer Law International, 1998.

Waemustafa, Waeibrorheem - Suriani, Sukri. "Theory of Gharar and Its Interpretation of Risk and Uncertainty from the Perspectives of Authentic Hadith and the Holy Quran: Review of Literatures." *International Journal of Economic Perspectives* 10/1 (June 30, 2016), 1–27.

Waheed, Rabsha - Hamid, Baharom Abdul. "Overcoming Implementation Challenges for Shariah Governance in the Maldives." *International Journal of Islamic Economics and Finance Research* 1 (October 11, 2023), 63–77. https://doi.org/10.53840/ijiefer113

Waldman, Matt. "System Failure: The Underlying Causes of US Policy-Making Errors in Afghanistan." *International Affairs* 89/4 (July 2013), 825–843. https://doi.org/10.1111/1468-2346.12047

Walid, Hegazy. *Fatwas and the Fate of Islamic Finance: A Critique of the Practice of Fatwa in Contemporary Islamic Financial Markets*. Cambridge, Mass.: Islamic Finance Project, Islamic Studies Program, Harvard Law School, 2005.

Wan Omar, Wan Ahmad - Abdul Rahim, Hafizah. "Perception of Non-Muslims towards Islamic Banking Revisited: SEM Approach." *Mediterranean Journal of Social Sciences*. https://doi.org/10.5901/mjss.2016.v7n1p139

Warde, Ibrahim. *Islamic Finance in the Global Economy*. Edinburgh: Edinburgh University Press, 2000. https://doi.org/10.3366/edinburgh/9780748612161.001.0001

Wasim Jan, Sahibzada Muhammad. "Shari'ah Governance of Islamic Banking Institutions in Pakistan: An Analytical Overview." *International Journal of Business and Administrative Studies* 6/6 (December 22, 2020), 286–299. https://doi.org/10.20469/ijbas.6.10001-6

Wasim, Mustanir Hussain - Zafar, Muhammad Bilal. "Shariah Governance Framework for Islamic Banking in Pakistan: A Critical Review and Comparison with AAOIFI." *Journal of Islamic Accounting and Business Research*. https://doi.org/10.1108/JIABR-03-2023-0101

Wasiullah Shaik Mohammed, Wasiullah Shaik Mohammed. "Interest-Free Microfinance in India:A Case Study of the Al-Khair Cooperative Credit Society." *Journal of King Abdulaziz University Islamic Economics* 31/1 (January 3, 2018), 47–66. https://doi.org/10.4197/islec.31-1.3

White, Jenny. *Muslim Nationalism and the New Turks*. New Jersey: Princeton University Press, 2013. https://www.jstor.org/stable/j.ctt1r2f65

Whyte, Shaheen. "Are Fatwas Dispensable? Examining the Contemporary Relevance and Authority of Fatwas in Australia." *Oxford Journal of Law and Religion* 11/2–3 (October 1, 2022), 314–342. https://doi.org/10.1093/ojlr/rwac015

Wille, Boris. "The Appropriation of Islam in the Maldives." *Oxford Research Encyclopedia of Asian History*, 2022. https://doi.org/10.1093/acrefore/9780190277727.013.680

Wilson, Rodney. "Islamic Finance: Principles and PracticeBy Hans Visser." *Journal of Islamic Studies* 22/1 (January 1, 2011), 143–146. https://doi.org/10.1093/jis/etq035

Wink, André. "11 Religion and Politics in the Mughal Empire of India." *Volume 1 Empires and Gods: The Role of Religions in Imperial History*. ed. Jörg Rüpke et al. 321–350. De Gruyter, 2024. https://www.degruyterbrill.com/document/doi/10.1515/9783111342009-014/html?lang=en&srsltid=AfmBOoqNnsBvJzz_HWH3o5dur42SpCssmUIeimCpnOwBc9bL1e1h1A4K

Wohab, Abdul. *Secularism and Islam in Bangladesh: 50 Years After Independence*. London: Routledge, 1st Ed., 2023. https://doi.org/10.4324/9781003411222

Yaqub, Aamer. "Amana Bank Sri Lanka Named Best Islamic Bank in South Asia." *The Halal Times* (blog), August 29, 2024. https://www.halaltimes.com/amana-bank-sri-lanka-named-best-islamic-bank-in-south-asia/

Yaqub, Aamer. "Sri Lanka to See First Listed Sukuk Issuance by Local Firm." *The Halal Times* (blog), April 2, 2025. https://www.halaltimes.com/sri-lanka-to-see-first-listed-sukuk-issuance-by-local-firm/

Yar, Fayaz Gul Mazloum. "The Necessity and Importance of Research and Its Role in Afghan Society." *COMPETITIVE: Journal of Education* 3/4 (2024), 257–270. https://doi.org/10.58355/competitive.v3i4.142

Yavuz, M. Hakan. *Islamic Political Identity in Turkey*. Oxford: Oxford University Press, 2005.

YILMAZ, ISA. *Essays in Islamic Moral Economy: Developmentalist Promises, the Delusion of Financialisation and Methodological Dilemma*. Durham University, Doctoral, 2018. https://doi.org/10/1/COMPLETE_THESIS_20181210.pdf

Yılmaz, Hakan Safa - Şencal, Harun. "İslam Politik Ekonomisi Açısından Merkezi Fetva Kurullarının Yapısına Dair Bir Değerlendirme." *Journal of Islamic Economics* 2/1 (January 15, 2022), 92–105.

Yongbao, Wang. "THE IMPACT OF COLONIALISM AND NATIONALISM ON THE MARGINALIZATION OF ISLAMIC LAW IN THE MUSLIM WORLD." *Malaysian Journal of Syariah and Law* 12/2 (August 21, 2024), 375–387. https://doi.org/10.33102/mjsl.vol12no2.653

Yunita, Patria. "Developing A Modern Zakat Management Model Digital Technology 4.0 Version." *AZKA International Journal of Zakat & Social Finance*, 139–156. https://doi.org/10.51377/azjaf.vol2no1.47

Zafar, Muhammad Bilal. "Islamic Financial Accounting Standards in Pakistan: A Comparison with AAOIFI." *Journal of Islamic Accounting and Business Research* ahead-of-print/ahead-of-print (June 18, 2024). https://doi.org/10.1108/JIABR-10-2023-0335

Zafar, Muhammad Bilal - Sulaiman, Ahmad Azam. "Islamic Banking in Pakistan: Emergence, Growth, and Prospects." *Advances in Finance, Accounting, and Economics.* ed. Abdul Rafay. 61–77. IGI Global, 2020. https://doi.org/10.4018/978-1-7998-1611-9.ch004

Zakaria, Mohamad Sabri B. et al. "Evaluating Murābaḥah Financing in Sri Lanka: Practitioner Perception." *Sprin Journal of Arts, Humanities and Social Sciences* 2/05 (May 20, 2023), 72–86. https://doi.org/10.55559/sjahss.v2i05.113

Zakariyah, Luqman. "Harmonising Legality with Morality in Islamic Banking and Finance: A Quest for Maqāṣid al-Sharī'ah Paradigm." *Intellectual Discourse* 23 (December 29, 2015). https://doi.org/10.31436/id.v23i0.700

Zameri, Sarah Nursaadah Mohd et al. "Maslahah and Its Application in Islamic Finance." *International Journal of Islamic Business* 9/1 (June 30, 2024), 82–94. https://doi.org/10.32890/ijib2024.9.1.5

Zarinebaf, Fariba. *Crime and Punishment in Istanbul: 1700-1800.* California: University of California Press, 2010. https://www.jstor.org/stable/10.1525/j.ctt1ppknx

Zarqa, Mustafa Ahmad al-. *Al-Madkhal al-Fiqhī al-ʿĀmm.* Syria: Dar al-Kalam Publication, 2004.

Zubair, Hasan. *Islamic Banking and Finance: Second Edition.* London: Routledge India, 2nd Ed., 2022. https://doi.org/10.4324/9781003366973

Zuḥaylī, Wahbah Muṣṭafā. *Al-Fiqh al-Islāmī Wa'adllatuh.* Damascus: Dār alfkr, 1418.

Zulfiqar, Adnan. *Collective Duties (Farḍ Kifāya) In Islamic Law: The Moral Community, State Authority And Ethical Speculation In The Premodern Period.* Pennsylvania: University of Pennsylvania, Doctorate, 2018.

"AAOIFI Shariah Standard." Manama: Accounting and Auditing Organization For Islamic Institutions, 2022. https://aaoifi.com/e-standards/?lang=en

"Accounting and Auditing Organization for Islamic Financial Institutions." Accessed April 6, 2025. https://aaoifi.com/ss-29-stipulations-and-ethics-of-fatwa-in-the-institutional-framework/?lang=en

Afghanistan Development Update: Uncertainty After Fleeting Stability. The World Bank, 2023.

"Afghanistan: People Suffer as Spending Capacity Shrinks, Prices Rise." July 13, 2022. Accessed April 21, 2025. https://www.icrc.org/en/document/afghanistan-people-suffer-spending-capacity-shrinks-prices-rise

"Annual Financial Report | Da Afghanistan Bank." Accessed June 5, 2025. https://dab.gov.af/Annual-Financial-Report

"DAB and Chamber of Commerce Unite to Stabilize Afghan Currency – Bakhtar News Agency." Accessed April 21, 2025. https://www.bakhtarnews.af/en/dab-and-chamber-of-commerce-unite-to-stabilize-afghan-currency/

"Developing Regional Healthcare Facilities in Maldives through Mudharabah Perpetual Sukuk." *International Journal of Management and Applied Research* 6/2 (2019), 81–96.

"Faculty of Islamic Studies and Arabic Language (FIA) | SEUSL." Accessed April 30, 2025. https://www.seu.ac.lk/fia/program_of_study.php

Accounting and Auditing Organization for Islamic Financial Institutions. "Footprint Report: Status of Adoption of AAOIFI Standards." 2022. Accessed June 11, 2025. https://aaoifi.com/aaoifi-footprint-report/?lang=en

Guideline for Investment Sukuk. Dhaka: entral Shariah Board for Islamic Banks of Bangladesh (CSBIB), 2020.

"Guideline for Islamic Banking." Accessed July 30, 2025. https://www.bb.org.bd/aboutus/regulationguideline/islamicbanking/islamicguide.php

"Guidelines on Shariah Governance Framework for Islamic Financial Institutions," 2010. https://www.bnm.gov.my/-/newly-updated-guidelines-on-shariah-governance-framework-for-islamic-financial-institutions

"Halal Stocks Finder and Screener | Shariah Advisor for Your Halal Investments-Islamicly." Accessed April 20, 2025. https://www.islamicly.com/?utm_source=chatgpt.com

"Home | Maldives Islamic Bank." Accessed May 1, 2025. https://www.mib.com.mv/

"Humanitarian Crisis in Afghanistan: Changing Global Dynamics and Pakistan's Policy Choices - Muhammad Fahim Khan, Asad Hassan, Aamer Raza, 2023." Accessed April 21, 2025. https://journals.sagepub.com/doi/full/10.1177/20578911221148520?casa_token=MAJJj666zTUAAAAA%3AuBxox3y2DrAOfxFd0XMjp1vaIedx8SHnMnbCVRjVupf53T8FtKbEDmHbIp4VfLRva3NMpn3Zd61dig

Islamic Finance News. "IFN - SBP Adopts AAOIFI Standard 20," March 24, 2025. https://www.islamicfinancenews.com/sbp-adopts-aaoifi-standard-20.html

Islamic Finance News. "IFN - The Association of Alternate Financial Institutions of Sri Lanka." October 3, 2024. Accessed April 30, 2025. https://www.islamicfinancenews.com/the-association-of-alternate-financial-institutions-of-sri-lanka.html

Islamic Finance News. "IFN - Vidullanka Pioneers Sri Lanka's First Listed Sukuk Issuance." April 22, 2025. Accessed April 30, 2025. https://www.islamicfinancenews.com/vidullanka-pioneers-sri-lankas-first-listed-sukuk-issuance.html

"IsDB Just Transition Conceptual Framework & Action Plan 2023-2025," no date.

State Bank of Pakistan. "Islamic Banking." Accessed April 21, 2025. https://www.sbp.org.pk/IB/abt-his.asp

"Islamic Banking, American Regulation | Richmond Fed." Accessed April 6, 2025. https://www.richmondfed.org/publications/research/econ_focus/2014/q2/feature1?utm_source=chatgpt.com

"Islamic Finance in South Asian Association for Regional Cooperation (SAARC) Countries." *Islamic Finance in Eurasia*. 45–79. Edward Elgar Publishing, 2024. https://doi.org/10.4337/9781035308705.00011

Accounting and Auditing Organization for Islamic Financial Institutions. "Islamic Finance Standard-Setting Bodies AAOIFI and IFSB Join Forces to Strengthen the Development and Resilience of the Islamic Financial Services Industry." 2018. Accessed August 5, 2025. https://aaoifi.com/announcement/islamic-finance-standard-setting-bodies-aaoifi-and-ifsb-join-forces-to-strengthen-the-development-and-resilience-of-the-islamic-financial-services-industry/?lang=en

Islamic Financial Services Board. "Islamic Finance Standard-Setting Bodies IFSB and AAOIFI Join Forces to Strengthen the Development and Resilience of the Islamic Financial Services Industry." 2018. Accessed August 5, 2025. https://www.ifsb.org/press-releases/islamic-finance-standard-setting-bodies-ifsb-and-aaoifi-join-forces-to-strengthen-the-development-and-resilience-of-the-islamic-financial-services-industry/

Islamic Financial Services Industry Stability Report 2024. Malaysia: Islamic Financial Services Board, 2024. https://www.ifsb.org/publication-document/islamic-financial-services-industry-stability-report-2024/

"Maldives: Country Operations Business Plan (2021-2023)." Asian Development Bank, November 18, 2020. Maldives. https://www.adb.org/documents/maldives-country-operations-business-plan-2021-2023

"Maldives Monetary Authority." Accessed May 1, 2025. http://www.mma.gov.mv

"Maldives Monetary Authority." Accessed July 30, 2025. http://www.mma.gov.mv

"Our Model - Amãna Bank PLC, Sri Lanka." Accessed April 30, 2025. https://www.amanabank.lk/knowledge-center/our-model.html

"Pakistan's Islamic Finance Prospects Positive on Government Push." Accessed April 21, 2025. https://www.fitchratings.com/research/non-bank-financial-institutions/pakistans-islamic-finance-prospects-positive-on-government-push-30-01-2024

https://imamsadiq.ac/Imam Sadiq Academy. "Practical Islamic Laws." Accessed July 30, 2025. https://imamsadiq.ac/en/course/islamic-laws-intro

"Resolution No. 179 (19/5): On Organized Tawarruq." Jeddah: OIC, 2009.

"Search Indian Ethical, Halal & Shariah Compliant Share IPO & Mutual Fund." Accessed April 20, 2025. https://halalstock.in/?utm_source=chatgpt.com

The Economic Times. "Sharia Banking: RBI Proposes Islamic Window in Banks" (November 20, 2016). https://economictimes.indiatimes.com/industry/banking/finance/banking/sharia-banking-rbi-proposes-islamic-window-in-banks/articleshow/55524538.cms?utm_source=chatgpt.com

"Shariah Governance Structure of Islamic Financial Institutions in Sri Lanka." *International Journal of Management and Applied Research* 6/4 (2019), 245–258.

"Shariah Resolutions in Islamic Finance." Accessed April 6, 2025. https://www.bnm.gov.my/-/shariah-resolutions-in-islamic-finance-second-edition-

Islamic Financial Services Board. "STANDARDS." Accessed April 6, 2025. https://www.ifsb.org/standards-page/

Islamic Financial Services Board. "STANDARDS." Accessed August 5, 2025. https://www.ifsb.org/standards-page/

"State Bank of Pakistan." Accessed July 30, 2025. https://www.sbp.org.pk/ibd/bulletin/bulletin.asp

Strategic Plan for Islamic Banking Industry 2021-25. SBP. Karachi: State Bank of Pakistan, 2021.

The Edinburgh Companion to Shari'ah Governance in Islamic Finance. critical ed. Syed Nazim Ali et al. Edinburgh: Edinburgh University Press, 2020. https://www.jstor.org/stable/10.3366/j.ctv2f4vqnp

World Bank. "Turkey's SMEs Prosper Through Islamic Financing." 2016. Accessed April 6, 2025. https://www.worldbank.org/en/news/feature/2016/09/12/turkeys-smes-prosper-through-islamic-financing

UNDP. "UNDP Core Funding: Powering Sustainable Development Where It Matters Most." Accessed April 21, 2025. https://www.undp.org/blog/undp-core-funding-powering-sustainable-development-where-it-matters-most

"US Senator Claims Cash Shipments Still Flowing into Afghanistan despite Foreign Aid Freeze | Ariana News," February 9, 2025. https://www.ariananews.af/us-senator-claims-cash-shipments-still-flowing-into-afghanistan-despite-foreign-aid-freeze/

Zoya Blog. "Zoya Blog." April 2, 2025. Accessed April 20, 2025. https://blog.zoya.finance/

Index

© The Editor(s) (if applicable) and The Author(s), under exclusive license to Springer Nature Switzerland AG 2025

A. H. M. E. Uddin, *The Regulation of Islamic Financial Institutions (IFIs) and Ethical Oversight in South Asia*, Palgrave Studies in Islamic Banking, Finance, and Economics,
https://doi.org/10.1007/978-3-032-09828-3

FSC
www.fsc.org
MIX
Papier | Fördert
gute Waldnutzung
FSC® C083411

Kolibri 360 GmbH
Ferdinand-Jühlke-Straße 7
99095 Erfurt, Deutschland
produktsicherheit@kolibri360.de